THE BLACK FAMILY

Essays and Studies

OTHER TITLES OF RELATED INTEREST IN SOCIOLOGY

Research Methods and Statistics

Earl Babbie, *Observing Ourselves: Essays in Social Research*

Earl Babbie, *The Practice of Social Research*, Fourth Edition

Earl Babbie, *Survey Research Methods*

Joseph Healey, *Statistics: A Tool for the Social Sciences*

John Hedderson, *SPSS-X Made Simple* (forthcoming)

Margaret Jendrek, *Through the Maze: Statistics with Computer Applications*

John Lofland/Lyn Lofland, *Analyzing Social Settings: A Guide to Qualitative Observation and Analysis*, Second Edition

June True, *Finding Out: Conducting and Evaluating Social Research*

Marriage and the Family

Leonard Cargan, *Marriage and Family: Coping with Change*

Mary Ann Lamanna/Agnes Riedmann, *Marriages and Families*, Second Edition

Marcia Lasswell/Thomas Lasswell, *Marriage and the Family,* Second Edition (forthcoming)

Bud McClure/Robert Milardo, *The Marriage and Family Workbook*

Lloyd Saxton, *The Individual, Marriage, and the Family,* Sixth Edition

Specialized Texts

Robert Atchley, *Aging: Continuity and Change,* Second Edition (forthcoming)

Robert Atchley, *Social Forces in Aging,* Fourth Edition

Donald Cowgill, *Aging around the World*

Martin Marger, *Elites and Masses,* Second Edition (forthcoming)

Martin Marger, *Race and Ethnic Relations: American and Global Perspectives*

David Miller, *Introduction to Collective Behavior*

Judith Perrolle, *Computers and Social Change: Information, Property, and Power* (forthcoming)

Arnold Sherman/Aliza Kolker, *The Social Bases of Politics* (forthcoming)

James Spates/John Macionis, *Sociology of Cities,* Second Edition (forthcoming)

John Weeks, *Population,* Third Edition

James Wood/Maurice Jackson, *Social Movements: Development, Participation, and Dynamics*

Computer Software for the Social Sciences

William Bainbridge, *Experiments in Sociology* (in the *Study Guide to Accompany Sociology,* by Rodney Stark)

William Bainbridge, *Sociology Laboratory: Computer Simulations for Principles of Sociology*

Cognitive Development Company, *Showcase: Demonstrating Sociology Live in the Classroom,* with demonstration scripts by Rodney Stark

THE BLACK FAMILY

Essays and Studies

THIRD EDITION

Robert Staples
University of California, San Francisco

Wadsworth Publishing Company, Inc. Belmont, California
A Division of Wadsworth, Inc.

Sociology Editor   *Sheryl Fullerton*
Assistant Sociology Editor   *Liz Clayton*
Production Editor   *Jerilyn Emori*
Designer   *Merle Sanderson*
Print Buyer   *Ruth Cole*
Copy Editor   *Judith Hibbard*
Technical Illustrator   *Reese Thornton*
Cover   *Merle Sanderson*
Cover Illustrator   *Regan Dunnick*

Printed in the United States of America

2 3 4 5 6 7 8 9 10—90 89 88 87   **49**

ISBN 0-534-07218-6

Library of Congress Cataloging-in-Publication Data

Staples, Robert.
     The Black family.

     1. Afro-American families.   I. Title.

E185.86.S7   1986   306.8'96073   86-13293

ISBN 0-534-07218-6

DEDICATION

To my aunts—

Geraldine Anthony

Arnisha Anthony

Harris Radcliffe

Virginia Self

Reva Staples

CONTENTS

PREFACE

Since 1960 the conceptualization and study of Black families has gone through three distinct stages. During the 1960s the Moynihan Report and its predecessors theorized that the Black family was a dysfunctional unit that was impeding the progress of all Black Americans. The report singled out the high rate of out-of-wedlock births and female-headed households, matriarchy, and Black male emasculation as pathological elements in Black family patterns. The second stage was characterized by the negative response to the Moynihan Report and a singular focus on positive elements in Black family life. During the 1970s researchers and theorists stressed the strengths of Black families in the form of extended family supports, role adaptability, healthy sexual patterns, and so on. The third—and current—stage can be seen as a problems approach to the study of Black families. Emerging in the 1980s, it diverged from the Moynihan perspective by singling out socioeconomic forces that had an impact on Black family patterns. The imbalanced sex ratio, unemployment among Black males, and misguided public policies often were cited as causes for the increases in out-of-wedlock births, marital disruptions, and female-headed households.

The previous two editions of *The Black Family: Essays and Studies* reflected the first two stages. A third edition was needed to mirror current trends in Black family theory and research. Certainly the Black family has become the subject of immense public concern in the eighties. From the president of the United States to the *New York Times*, the major civil rights organizations to grass roots groups,

the Black family has been a much-discussed topic. The third edition addresses many of the major issues concerning contemporary Black family life. It remains the most comprehensive book available on the subject, with a collection of articles that are accessible to undergraduate students.

In this new edition considerable space is devoted to the three major problems facing the Black family today. They are not new problems nor are they problems unique to Black families, but their incidence is more pronounced and devastating to the Black population. These problems are the tensions in the Black male/female relationships, which cause large numbers of Blacks to remain single and which dissolve a huge number of marriages each year; teenage pregnancy, which creates new families in which all members are at risk; and nonemployment and unemployment, which are the most serious of all the problems faced by Black families because they are the primary reasons for their poverty.

This new edition addresses, in a balanced way, the causes and nature of these problems. All of the articles are empirically based or are theoretical formulations that avoid blaming the victim for the problems of Black families. Many of them have not been published elsewhere or were published in diverse venues not accessible either to teachers or to students; more than two-thirds of the articles are new to this edition. Among the subjects that are new in this edition are the feminization of poverty thesis, teenage pregnancy, child abuse, working wives, and polygamy. Most of these new articles contain current statistical data. It is a much improved, stream-lined edition with enhanced value as a text in un-dergraduate classrooms.

For their help in putting together this book I am indebted to a number of people. Steve Rutter originally suggested the third edition and facilitated its publication. Sheryl Fullerton, the sociology edi-tor, made invaluable suggestions and managed to put out the book we all are proud of. Attention to rudimentary details, a cheerful disposition, and the coordination of a hundred tasks made Liz Clayton a most valuable member of the production team, along with Robert Kauser, who handled permis-sions. Jerilyn Emori, Helga Newman, Karen Rovens, and Merle Sanderson also contributed much to the book's final shape. I am appreciative of the technical assistance provided by David Barrows and Sally Maeth, who abstracted articles and typed the au-thors' introductions. For their help in reviewing the table of contents and new articles, I wish to thank Talmadge Anderson, Washington State University; David Fulton, California State University, North-ridge; Dean Knudsen, Purdue University; and Patri-cia Bell Scott, University of Connecticut.

PART ONE

The Setting

Many changes have occurred in this country since 1954, covering a wide array of personalities, values, and institutions and bringing about a marked change in the functioning of society as a whole. These changes have been most dramatic within the institution of the family where they have had a most telling effect on our personal lives. We are all, to some degree, affected by increasing sexual permissiveness, changes in sex role expectations, a declining fertility rate, altered attitudes toward childbearing and childrearing, a continuing increase in the divorce rate, and the like.

One would not expect Black families to be immune to the forces modifying our family forms. There is ample evidence that they are not. At the same time, their special status as a racial minority with a singular history continues to give the Black marital and family patterns a unique character. Despite what many allege to be the positive gains of the sixties and seventies, the problems of poverty and racial oppression continue to plague large numbers of Afro-Americans. Black Americans are still spatially segregated from the majority of the more affluent white citizenry, and certain cultural values distinguish their family life in form and content from that of the middle-class, white, Anglo-Saxon model.

Nevertheless, the commonality of the two may be greater than the differences. We lose nothing by admitting this. Moreover, the variations within the Black population may be greater than the differences between the two racial groups. Therefore, it becomes even more important to view the Black family from the widest possible perspective, from its peculiar history to the alternate family life-styles now emerging.

The Changing Black Family

It is generally accepted that the precursor of contemporary sociological research and theories on the Black family is the work of the late Black sociologist E. Franklin Frazier. Although Frazier's investigations of the Black family began in the twenties, his works are still considered the definitive findings on Black family life in the United States (Frazier, 1939). As a sociologist, Frazier was primarily interested in race relations as a social process, and he sought to explain that process through the study of the Black family. Through his training in the University of Chicago's social ecology school under the tutelage of Park, Wirth, Burgess, and others, Frazier came to believe that race relations proceeded through different stages of development to the final stage of assimilation.

Since it is through the family that the culture of a group is transmitted, Frazier chose this group as the object of his sociological study. Using the natural history approach, he explained the present condition of the Black family as the culmination of an evolutionary process, its structure strongly affected by the vestiges of slavery, racism, and economic exploitation. The institution of enslavement and slavery virtually destroyed the cultural moorings of Blacks and prevented any perpetuation of African kinship and family relations. Consequently, the Black family developed various forms according to the different situations it encountered (Frazier, 1939).

Variations in sex and marital practices, according to Frazier, grew out of the social heritage of slavery; and what slavery began—the pattern of racism and economic deprivation—continued to impinge on the family life of Afro-Americans. The variations Frazier spoke of are: (1) the matriarchal character of the Black family whereby Black males are marginal, ineffective figures in the family constellation; (2) the instability of marital life resulting from the lack of a legal basis for marriage during the period of slavery, which meant that marriage never acquired the position of a strong institution in Black life and casual sex relations were the prevailing norm; and (3) the dissolution—caused by the process of urbanization—of the stability of family life that had existed among Black peasants in an agrarian society (Frazier, 1939).

Most of Frazier's studies were limited to pre–World War II Black family life. His research method was the use of case studies and documents whose content he analyzed and from which he attempted to deduce a pattern of Black family life. The next large-scale theory of the Black family was developed by Daniel Moynihan (1965); it was based largely on census data and pertained to Black family life as it existed in the sixties. In a sense, Moynihan attempted to confirm statistically Frazier's theory that the Black family was disorganized as a result of slavery, urbanization, and economic deprivation. But he added a new dimension to Frazier's theory: "At the heart of the deterioration of the fabric of Negro society is the deterioration of the Negro family" (Moynihan, 1965:5). Moynihan attempted to document his major hypothesis by citing statistics on the dissolution of Black marriages, the high rate of Black illegitimate births, the prevalence of female-headed households in the Black community, and how the deterioration of the Black family had led to a shocking increase in welfare dependency (Moynihan, 1965).

This study of the Black family, commonly referred to as the Moynihan Report, generated a largely critical response from members of the Black community. It drew a mixed response from members of the white academic community, some critically supporting most of Moynihan's contentions, others imputing no validity to his assertions (Rainwater and Yancy, 1967; Staples and Mirande, 1980). The reasons for the negative reaction to Moynihan's study are manifest. In effect, he made a generalized indictment of all Black families. And, although he cited the antecedents of slavery and high unemployment as historically important variables, he shifted the burden of Black deprivation onto the Black family rather than the social structure of the United States.

The Moynihan Report assumed a greater importance than other studies on the Black family for several reasons. As an official government publication, it implied a shift in the government's position in dealing with the effects of racism and economic deprivation on the Black community. However, the Moynihan Report did not spell out a plan for action. The conclusion drawn by most people was that whatever his solution, it would focus on strengthening the Black family rather than dealing with the more relevant problems of segregation and discrimination.

In the years since the publication of the Moynihan Report, the indices of Black family pathology have more than doubled, leading some students of the Black family to claim that Moynihan was right. One of them is Blanche Bernstein, whose article "Since the Moynihan Report . . ." updates Moynihan's statistics and reaffirms his conclusion that it is the Black family structure that has impeded the group's progress in the United States. Robert Staples, on the other hand, declares that structural conditions are what have torn the Black family asunder. In particular, it is the inability of Black men to secure employment that is largely responsible for the proliferation of Black female-headed households. He contends that only by enhancing Black males' employment opportunities can the family be made whole again.

Historical Background

The most ground-breaking research on Black families has been conducted by historians. For years the work of Frazier (1939), together with that of Stanley

Elkins, had been accepted as the definitive history of Black families and posited as a causal explanation of their contemporary condition. Using traditional historical methods based on plantation records and slave owner testimony, both historians reached the conclusion that slavery destroyed the Black family and decimated Black culture. The first historian to challenge this thesis was Blassingame (1972), whose use of slave narratives indicated that in the slave quarters Black families did exist as functioning institutions and role models for others. Moreover, strong family ties persisted in face of the frequent breakups deriving from the slave trade. To further counteract the Frazier–Elkins thesis, Fogel and Engerman (1974) used elaborate quantitative methods to document that slave owners did not separate a majority of the slave families. Their contention, also controversial, was that capitalistic efficiency of the slave system meant it was more practical to keep slave families intact.

Continuing in the vein of revisionist historical research, Genovese used a mix of slave holders' papers and slave testimony. Still, he concluded that Black culture, through compromise and negotiation between slaves and slave owners, did flourish during the era of slavery. Within that cultural vortex there was a variety of socially approved and sanctioned relationships between slave men and women. The alleged female matriarchy extant during that era was described by Genovese as a closer approximation to a healthy sexual equality than was possible for whites. Finally, the landmark study by Gutman (1976) put to rest one of the most common and enduring myths about Black families. Using census data for a number of cities between 1880 and 1925, Gutman found that the majority of Blacks of all social classes were lodged in nuclear families. Through the use of plantation birth records and marriage applications, he concluded that the biparental household was the dominant form during slavery. More important than Gutman's compelling evidence that slavery did not destroy the Black family was his contention that their family form in the past era had evolved from family and kinship patterns that had originated under slavery. This contention gives credence to the Africanity model, which assumes African origins for Afro-American family values, traits, and behavior.

Using a classical theory of slave family life, Stanley Elkins made a comparative analysis of the effect of slavery on the bondsman's family life in North and South America. His thesis was that the principal differences between the two regions was the manumission process and the legal basis of marriage between slaves. That is, slaves could become free citizens more easily in South America and those who remained in bondage were permitted to have legal marriage ceremonies. The sanctity of the family was sanctioned in both law and the canons of the Catholic church. The reverse was true, he asserted, in the slave system of the United States. One should view the Elkins research critically since other historians contend that the slave code of which he speaks was not only unenforced but never promulgated in any of the South American countries. In fact, it is claimed, some of the measures encouraging marriage among slaves were designed to bind the slaves to the estates via family ties (Hall, 1970).

However, these historical studies demonstrate that the Black family was a stable unit during slavery and in the immediate postslavery years. The rise in out-of-wedlock births and female-headed households are concomitants of twentieth-century urban ghettos. A doubling of those phenomena is a function of the economic contingencies of industrial America. Unlike the European immigrants before them, U.S. Blacks were disadvantaged by the hard lines of Northern segregation along racial lines. Moreover, families in cities were more vulnerable to disruptions due to the traumatizing experiences of urbanization, the reduction of family functions, and the loss of extended family supports. In order to understand the modern Black family, it is necessary to look at how its structure is affected by socioeconomic forces.

References

Blassingame, J.
1972   *The Slave Community.* New York: Oxford University Press.

Fogel, W., and S. Engerman
1974   *Time on the Cross.* Boston: Little, Brown.

Frazier, E. F.
1939   *The Negro Family in the United States.* Chicago: University of Chicago Press.

Gutman, H.
1976   *The Black Family in Slavery and Freedom, 1750–1925.* New York: Pantheon.

Hall, G. Midlo
1970   "The Myth of Benevolent Spanish Slave Law." *Negro Digest* 19:31–39.

Moynihan, Daniel P.
1965   *The Negro Family: The Case for National Action.* Washington, D.C.: U.S. Government Printing Office.

Rainwater, L., and W. Yancy
1967   *The Moynihan Report and the Politics of Controversy.* Cambridge, Mass.: M.I.T. Press.

Staples, R., and A. Mirande
1980   "Racial and Cultural Variations among American Families: A Decennial Review of the Literature on Minority Families." *Journal of Marriage and the Family* 42:887–903.

1 / The Changing Black Family

THE TANGLE OF PATHOLOGY

Daniel P. Moynihan

In this controversial and much-debated report on the Black family, the author claims that weaknesses in family structure account for many of the problems Afro-Americans encounter in American society. The reason for welfare dependency, out-of-wedlock children, educational failure, crime and delinquency, and so on, is the unnatural dominance of women in the family structure. Without tongue in cheek the author recommends, as remedy, increased involvement of Black men in the military.

That the Negro American has survived at all is extraordinary—a lesser people might simply have died out, as indeed others have. That the Negro community has not only survived, but in this political generation has entered national affairs as a moderate, humane, and constructive national force is the highest testament to the healing powers of the democratic ideal and the creative vitality of the Negro people.

But it may not be supposed that the Negro American community has not paid a fearful price for the incredible mistreatment to which it has been subjected over the past three centuries.

In essence, the Negro community has been forced into a matriarchal structure which, because it is so out of line with the rest of the American society, seriously retards the progress of the group as a whole, and imposes a crushing burden on the Negro male and, in consequence, on a great many Negro women as well.

There is, presumably, no special reason why a society in which males are dominant in family relationships is to be preferred to a matriarchal arrangement. However, it is clearly a disadvantage for a minority group to be operating on one principle, while the great majority of the population, and the one with the most advantages to begin with, is operating on another. This is the present situation of the Negro. Ours is a society which presumes male leadership in private and public affairs. The arrangements of society facilitate such leadership and

Condensed from *The Negro Family: The Case for National Action*, by the Office of Policy Planning and Research, United States Department of Labor (U.S. Government Printing Office, March 1965), pp. 29–44. Tables have been deleted and footnotes renumbered.

reward it. A subculture, such as that of the Negro American, in which this is not the pattern, is placed at a distinct disadvantage.

Here an earlier word of caution should be repeated. There is much evidence that a considerable number of Negro families have managed to break out of the tangle of pathology and to establish themselves as stable, effective units, living according to patterns of American society in general. E. Franklin Frazier has suggested that the middle-class Negro American family is, if anything, more patriarchal and protective of its children than the general run of such families.[1] Given equal opportunities, the children of these families will perform as well or better than their white peers. They need no help from anyone, and ask none.

While this phenomenon is not easily measured, one index is that middle-class Negroes have even fewer children than middle-class whites, indicating a desire to conserve the advances they have made and to insure that their children do as well or better. Negro women who marry early to uneducated laborers have more children than white women in the same situation; Negro women who marry at the common age for the middle class to educated men doing technical or professional work have only four-fifths as many children as their white counterparts.

It might be estimated that as much as half of the Negro community falls into the middle class. However, the remaining half is in desperate and deteriorating circumstances. Moreover, because of housing segregation it is immensely difficult for the stable half to escape from the cultural influences of the unstable one. The children of middle-class Negroes often as not must grow up in or next to the slums, an experience almost unknown to white middle-class children. They are therefore constantly exposed to the pathology of the disturbed group and constantly in danger of being drawn into it. It is for this reason that the propositions put forth in this study may be thought of as having a more or less general application.

In a word, most Negro youth are in *danger* of being caught up in the tangle of pathology that affects their world, and probably a majority are so entrapped. Many of those who escape do so for one generation only: as things now are, their children may have to run the gauntlet all over again. That is not the least vicious aspect of the world that white America has made for the Negro.

Obviously, not every instance of social pathology afflicting the Negro community can be traced to the weakness of family structure. If, for example, organized crime in the Negro community were not largely controlled by whites, there would be more capital accumulation among Negroes, and therefore probably more Negro business enterprises. If it were not for the hostility and fear many whites exhibit towards Negroes, they in turn would be less afflicted by hostility and fear and so on. There is no one Negro community. There is no one Negro problem. There is no one solution. Nonetheless, at the center of the tangle of pathology is the weakness of the family structure. Once or twice removed, it will be found to be the principal source of most of the aberrant, inadequate, or antisocial behavior that did not establish, but now serves to perpetuate the cycle of poverty and deprivation.

It was by destroying the Negro family under slavery that white America broke the will of the Negro people. Although that will has reasserted itself in our time, it is a resurgence doomed to frustration unless the viability of the Negro family is restored.

Matriarchy

A fundamental fact of Negro American family life is the often reversed roles of husband and wife.

Robert O. Blood, Jr., and Donald M. Wolfe, in a study of Detroit families, note that "Negro husbands have unusually low power,"[2] and while this is characteristic of all low income families, the pattern pervades the Negro social structure: "the cumulative result of discrimination in jobs . . . , the segregated housing, and the poor schooling of Negro men."[3] In 44 percent of the Negro families studied, the wife was dominant, as against 20 percent of white wives. "Whereas the majority of white families are equalitarian, the largest percentage of Negro families are dominated by the wife."[4]

The matriarchal pattern of so many Negro families reinforces itself over the generations. This process begins with education. Although the gap appears to be closing at the moment, for a long while, Negro females were better educated than Negro males, and this remains true today for the Negro population as a whole.

The difference in educational attainment between nonwhite men and women in the labor force is even greater; men lag 1.1 years behind women.

The disparity in educational attainment of male and female youth age 16 to 21 who were out of school in February 1963 is striking. Among the nonwhite males, 66.3 percent were not high school graduates, compared with 55.0 percent of the females. A similar difference existed at the college level, with 4.5 percent of the males having completed 1 to 3 years of college compared with 7.3 percent of the females.

The poorer performance of the male in school exists from the very beginning, and the magnitude of the difference was documented by the 1960 Census in statistics on the number of children who have fallen one or more grades below the typical grade for children of the same age. The boys have more frequently fallen behind at every age level. (White boys also lag behind white girls, but at a differential of 1 to 6 percentage points.)

In 1960, 39 percent of all white persons 25 years of age and over who had completed 4 or more years of college were women. Fifty-three percent of the nonwhites who had attained this level were women.

However, the gap is closing. By October 1963, there were slightly more Negro men in college than women. Among whites there were almost twice as many men as women enrolled.

There is much evidence that Negro females are better students than their male counterparts.

Daniel Thompson of Dillard University, in a private communication on January 9, 1965, writes:

As low as is the aspirational level among lower class Negro girls, it is considerably higher than among the boys. For example, I have examined the honor rolls in Negro high schools for about 10 years. As a rule, from 75 to 90 percent of all Negro honor students are girls.

In 1 out of 4 Negro families where the husband is present, is an earner, and some one else in the family works, the husband is not the principal earner. The comparable figure for whites is 18 percent.

More important, it is clear that Negro females have established a strong position for themselves in white collar and professional employment, precisely the areas of the economy which are growing most rapidly, and to which the highest prestige is accorded.

The President's Committee on Equal Employment Opportunity, making a preliminary report on employment in 1964 of over 16,000 companies with nearly 5 million employees, revealed this pattern with dramatic emphasis.

In this work force, Negro males outnumber Negro females by a ratio of 4 to 1. Yet Negro males represent only 1.2 percent of the males in white collar occupations, while Negro females represent 3.1 percent of the total female white collar work force. Negro males represent 1.1 percent of all male professionals, whereas Negro females represent roughly 6 percent of all female professionals. Again, in technician occupations, Negro males represent 2.1 percent of all male technicians while Negro females represent roughly 10 percent of all female technicians. It would appear therefore that there are proportionately 4 times as many Negro females in significant white collar jobs than Negro males.

Although it is evident that office and clerical jobs account for approximately 50 percent of all Negro female white collar workers, it is significant that 6 out of every 100 Negro females are in professional jobs. This is substantially similar to the rate of all females in such jobs. Approximately 7 out of every 100 Negro females are in technician jobs. This exceeds the proportion of all females in technician jobs—approximately 5 out of every 100.

Negro females in skilled jobs are almost the same as that of all females in such jobs. Nine out of every 100 Negro males are in skilled occupations while 21 out of 100 of all males are in such jobs.[5]

This pattern is to be seen in the Federal government, where special efforts have been made recently to insure equal employment opportunity for Negroes. These efforts have been notably successful in Departments such as Labor, where some 19 percent of employees are now Negro. (A not disproportionate percentage, given the composition of the work force in the areas where the main Department offices are located.) However, it may well be that these efforts have redounded mostly to the benefit of Negro women, and may even have accentuated the comparative disadvantage of Negro men. Seventy percent of the Negro employees of the Department of Labor are women, as contrasted with only 42 percent of the white employees.

Among nonprofessional Labor Department employees—where the most employment opportunities exist for all groups—Negro women outnumber Negro men 4 to 1, and average almost one grade higher in classification.

The testimony to the effects of these patterns in Negro family structure is widespread, and hardly to be doubted. . . .

Duncan M. MacIntyre

The Negro illegitimacy rate always has been high—about eight times the white rate in 1940 and somewhat higher today even though the white illegitimacy rate also is climbing. The Negro statistics are symptomatic of some old socioeconomic problems, not the least of which are underemployment among Negro men and compensating higher labor force propensity among Negro women. Both operate to enlarge the mother's role, undercutting the status of the male and making many Negro families essentially matriarchal. The Negro man's uncertain employment prospects, matriarchy, and high cost of divorces combine to encourage desertion (the poor man's divorce), increase the number of couples not married, and thereby also increase the Negro illegitimacy rate. In

the meantime, higher Negro birth rates are increasing the nonwhite population, while migration into cities like Detroit, New York, Philadelphia, and Washington, D.C., is making the public assistance rolls in such cities heavily, even predominantly, Negro.[6]

Robin M. Williams, Jr., in a Study of Elmira, New York

Only 57 percent of Negro adults reported themselves as married—spouse present, as compared with 78 percent of native white American gentiles, 91 percent of Italian-American, and 96 percent of Jewish informants. Of the 93 unmarried Negro youths interviewed, 22 percent did not have their mother living in the home with them, and 42 percent reported that their father was not living in their home. One-third of the youths did not know their father's present occupation, and two-thirds of a sample of 150 Negro adults did not know what the occupation of their father's father had been. Forty percent of the youths said that they had brothers and sisters living in other communities; another 40 percent reported relatives living in their home who were not parents, siblings, or grandparents.[7]

The Failure of Youth

Williams' account of Negro youth growing up with little knowledge of their fathers, less of their fathers' occupations, still less of family occupational traditions, is in sharp contrast to the experience of the white child. The white family, despite many variants, remains a powerful agency not only for transmitting property from one generation to the next, but also for transmitting no less valuable contacts with the world of education and work. In an earlier age, the Carpenters, Wainwrights, Weavers, Mercers, Farmers, Smiths acquired their names as well as their trades from their fathers and grandfathers. Children today still learn the patterns of work from their fathers even though they may no longer go into the same jobs.

White children without fathers at least perceive all about them the pattern of men working.

Negro children without fathers flounder—and fail.

Not always, to be sure. The Negro community produces its share, very possibly more than its share, of young people who have the something extra that carries them over the worst obstacles. But such persons are always a minority. The common run of young people in a group facing serious obstacles to success do not succeed.

A prime index of the disadvantage of Negro youth in the United States is their consistently poor performance on the mental tests that are a standard means of measuring ability and performance in the present generation.

There is absolutely no question of any genetic differential: Intelligence potential is distributed among Negro infants in the same proportion and pattern as among Icelanders or Chinese or any other group. American society, however, impairs the Negro potential. The statement of the HARYOU report that "there is no basic disagreement over the fact that central Harlem students are performing poorly in school"[8] may be taken as true of Negro slum children throughout the United States.

Eighth grade children in central Harlem have a median IQ of 87.7, which means that perhaps a third of the children are scoring at levels perilously near to those of retardation. IQ *declines* in the first decade of life, rising only slightly thereafter.

The effect of broken families on the performance of Negro youth has not been extensively measured, but studies that have been made show an unmistakable influence.

Martin Deutch and Bert Brown, investigating intelligence test differences between Negro and white 1st and 5th graders of different social classes, found that there is a direct relationship between social class and IQ. As the one rises so does the other: but more for whites than Negroes. This is surely a result of housing segregation, referred to earlier, which makes it difficult for middle-class Negro families to escape the slums.

The authors explain that "it is much more difficult for the Negro to attain identical middle- or upper-middle-class status with whites, and the social class gradations are less marked for Negroes

because Negro life in a caste society is considerably more homogeneous than is life for the majority group."[9]

Therefore, the authors look for background variables other than social class which might explain the difference: "One of the most striking differences beween the Negro and white groups is the consistently higher frequency of broken homes and resulting family disorganization in the Negro group."[10]

Further, they found that children from homes where fathers are present have significantly higher scores than children in homes without fathers.

The influence of the father's presence was then tested *within* the social classes and school grades for Negroes alone. They found that "a consistent trend within both grades at the lower SES [social class] level appears, and in no case is there a reversal of this trend: for males, females, and the combined group, the IQ's of children with fathers in the home are always higher than those who have no father in the home."[11]

The authors say that broken homes "may also account for some of the differences between Negro and white intelligence scores."[12]

The scores of 5th graders with fathers absent were lower than the scores of 1st graders with fathers absent, and while the authors point out that it is cross sectional data and does not reveal the duration of the fathers' absence, "What we might be tapping is the cumulative effect of fatherless years."[13]

This difference in ability to perform has its counterpart in statistics on actual school performance. Nonwhite boys from families with both parents present are more likely to be going to school than boys with only one parent present, and enrollment rates are even lower when neither parent is present.

When the boys from broken homes are in school, they do not do as well as the boys from whole families. Grade retardation is higher when only one parent is present, and highest when neither parent is present.

The loneliness of the Negro youth in making fundamental decisions about education is shown in a 1959 study of Negro and white dropouts in Connecticut high schools.

Only 29 percent of the Negro male dropouts

discussed their decision to drop out of school with their fathers, compared with 65 percent of the white males (38 percent of the Negro males were from broken homes). In fact, 26 percent of the Negro males did not discuss this major decision in their lives with anyone at all, compared with only 8 percent of white males.

A study of Negro apprenticeship by the New York State Commission Against Discrimination in 1960 concluded:

> *Negro youth are seldom exposed to influences which can lead to apprenticeship. Negroes are not apt to have relatives, friends, or neighbors in skilled occupations. Nor are they likely to be in secondary schools where they receive encouragement and direction from alternate role models. Within the minority community, skilled Negro "models" after whom the Negro youth might pattern himself are rare, while substitute sources which could provide the direction, encouragement, resources, and information needed to achieve skilled craft standing are nonexistent.*[14]

Delinquency and Crime

The combined impact of poverty, failure, and isolation among Negro youth has had the predictable outcome in a disastrous delinquency and crime rate.

In a typical pattern of discrimination, Negro children in all public and private orphanages are a smaller proportion of all children than their proportion of the population although their needs are clearly greater.

On the other hand Negroes represent a third of all youth in training schools for juvenile delinquents.

It is probable that at present, a majority of the crimes against the person, such as rape, murder, and aggravated assault, are committed by Negroes. There is, of course, no absolute evidence; inference can only be made from arrest and prison population statistics. The data that follow unquestionably are biased against Negroes, who are arraigned much more casually than are whites, but it may be doubted that the bias is great enough to affect the general proportions.

Again on the urban frontier the ratio is worse: 3 out of every 5 arrests for these crimes were of Negroes.

In Chicago in 1963, three-quarters of the persons arrested for such crimes were Negro; in Detroit, the same proportions held.

In 1960, 37 percent of all persons in Federal and State prisons were Negro. In that year, 56 percent of the homicide and 57 percent of the assault offenders committed to State institutions were Negro.

The overwhelming number of offenses committed by Negroes are directed toward other Negroes: the cost of crime to the Negro community is a combination of that to the criminal and to the victim.

Some of the research on the effects of broken homes on delinquent behavior recently surveyed by Thomas F. Pettigrew in *A Profile of the Negro American* is summarized below, along with several other studies of the question.

Mary Diggs found that three-fourths—twice the expected ratio—of Philadelphia's Negro delinquents who came before the law during 1948 did not live with both their natural parents.[15]

In predicting juvenile crime, Eleanor and Sheldon Glueck also found that a higher proportion of delinquent than nondelinquent boys came from broken homes. They identified five critical factors in the home environment that made a difference in whether boys would become delinquents: discipline of boy by father, supervision of boy by mother, affection of father for boy, affection of mother for boy, and cohesiveness of family.

In 1952, when the New York City Youth Board set out to test the validity of these five factors as predictors of delinquency, a problem quickly emerged. The Glueck sample consisted of white boys of mainly Irish, Italian, Lithuanian, and English descent. However, the Youth Board group was 44 percent Negro and 14 percent Puerto Rican, and the frequency of broken homes within these groups was out of proportion to the total number of delinquents in the population.[16]

In the majority of these cases, the father was usually never in the home at all, absent for the major proportion of the boy's life, or was present only on occasion.

(The final prediction table was reduced to three factors: supervision of boy by mother, discipline of boy by mother, and family cohesiveness within what family, in fact, existed; it was, nonetheless, 85 percent accurate in predicting delinquents and 96 percent accurate in predicting nondelinquents.)

Researchers who have focussed upon the "good" boys in high delinquency neighborhoods noted that they typically come from exceptionally stable, intact families.[17]

Recent psychological research demonstrates the personality effects of being reared in a disorganized home without a father. One study showed that children from fatherless homes seek immediate gratification of their desires far more than children with fathers present.[18] Others revealed that children who hunger for immediate gratification are more prone to delinquency, along with other less social behavior.[19] Two psychologists, Pettigrew says, maintain that inability to delay gratification is a critical factor in immature, criminal, and neurotic behavior.[20]

Finally, Pettigrew discussed the evidence that a stable home is a crucial factor in counteracting the effects of racism upon Negro personality.

A warm, supportive home can effectively compensate for many of the restrictions the Negro child faces outside of the ghetto; consequently, the type of home life a Negro enjoys as a child may be far more crucial for governing the influence of segregation upon his personality than the form the segregation takes—legal or informal, Southern or Northern.[21]

A Yale University study of youth in the lowest socioeconomic class in New Haven in 1950 whose behavior was followed through their 18th year revealed that among the delinquents in the group, 38 percent came from broken homes, compared with 24 percent of nondelinquents.[22]

The President's Task Force on Manpower Conservation in 1963 found that of young men rejected for the draft for failure to pass the mental tests, 42 percent of those with a court record came from broken homes, compared with 30 percent of those without a court record. Half of all the nonwhite rejectees in the study with a court record came from broken homes.

An examination of the family background of 44,448 delinquency cases in Philadelphia between 1949 and 1954 documents the frequency of broken homes among delinquents. Sixty-two percent of the Negro delinquents and 36 percent of white delinquents were not living with both parents. In 1950, 33 percent of nonwhite children and 7 percent of white children in Philadelphia were living in homes without both parents. Repeaters were even more likely to be from broken homes than first offenders.[23]

The Armed Forces

The ultimate mark of inadequate preparation for life is the failure rate on the Armed Forces mental test. The Armed Forces Qualification Test is not quite a mental test, nor yet an education test. It is a test of ability to perform at an acceptable level of competence. It roughly measures ability that ought to be found in an average 7th or 8th grade student. A grown young man who cannot pass this test is in trouble.

Fifty-six percent of Negroes fail it.

This is a rate almost four times that of the whites.

The Army, Navy, Air Force, and Marines conduct by far the largest and most important education and training activities of the Federal Government, as well as provide the largest single source of employment in the nation.

Military service is disruptive in some respects. For those comparatively few who are killed or wounded in combat, or otherwise, the personal sacrifice is inestimable. But on balance service in the Armed Forces over the past quarter-century has worked greatly to the advantage of those involved. The training and experience of military duty itself is unique; the advantages that have generally followed in the form of the G.I. Bill, mortgage guarantees, Federal life insurance, Civil Service preference, veterans' hospitals, and veterans' pensions are singular, to say the least. . . .

In 1963 the Civil Rights Commission commented on the occupational aspect of military service for Negroes. "Negro enlisted men enjoy relatively better opportunities in the Armed Forces than in the civilian economy in every clerical, technical, and skilled field for which the data permit comparison."[24]

There is, however, an even more important issue involved in military service for Negroes. Service in the United States Armed Forces is the *only* experience open to the Negro American in which he is truly treated as an equal: not as a Negro equal to a white, but as one man equal to any other man in a world where the categories "Negro" and "white" do not exist. If this is a statement of the ideal rather than reality, it is an ideal that is close to realization. In food, dress, housing, pay, work—the Negro in the Armed Forces *is* equal and is treated that way.

There is another special quality about military service for Negro men: it is an utterly masculine world. Given the strains of the disorganized and matrifocal family life in which so many Negro youth come of age, the Armed Forces are a dramatic and desperately needed change: a world away from women, a world run by strong men of unquestioned authority, where discipline, if harsh, is nonetheless orderly and predictable, and where rewards, if limited, are granted on the basis of performance.

The theme of a current Army recruiting message states it as clearly as can be: "In the U.S. Army you get to know what it means to feel like a man."

At the recent Civil Rights Commission hearings in Mississippi a witness testified that his Army service was in fact "the only time I ever felt like a man."

Yet a majority of Negro youth (and probably three-quarters of Mississippi Negroes) fail the Selective Service education test and are rejected. Negro participation in the Armed Forces would be less than it is, were it not for a proportionally larger share of voluntary enlistments and reenlistments. (Thus 16.3 percent of Army sergeants are Negro.)

Alienation

The term alienation may by now have been used in too many ways to retain a clear meaning, but it will serve to sum up the equally numerous ways in which large numbers of Negro youth appear to be withdrawing from American society.

One startling way in which this occurs is that the men are just not there when the Census enumerator comes around.

According to Bureau of Census population estimates for 1963, there are only 87 nonwhite males for every 100 females in the 30-to-34-year age group. The ratio does not exceed 90 to 100 throughout the 25-to-44-year age bracket. In the urban Northeast, there are only 76 males per 100 females 20 to 24 years of age, and males as a percent of females are below 90 percent throughout all ages after 14.

There are not really fewer men than women in the 20-to-40 age bracket. What obviously is involved is an error in counting: the surveyors simply do not find the Negro man. Donald J. Bogue and his associates, who have studied the Federal count of the Negro man, place the error as high as 19.8 percent at age 28; a typical error of around 15 percent is estimated from age 19 through 43.[25] Preliminary research in the Bureau of the Census on the 1960 enumeration has resulted in similar conclusions, although not necessarily the same estimates of the extent of the error. The Negro male *can* be found at age 17 and 18. On the basis of birth records and mortality records, the conclusion must be that he is there at age 19 as well.

When the enumerators do find him, his answers to the standard questions asked in the monthly unemployment survey often result in counting him as "not in the labor force." In other words, Negro male unemployment may in truth be somewhat greater than reported.

The labor force participation rates of nonwhite men have been falling since the beginning of the century and for the past decade have been lower than the rates for white men. In 1964, the participation rates were 78.0 percent for white men and 75.8 percent for nonwhite men. Almost one percentage point of this difference was due to a higher proportion of nonwhite men unable to work because of long-term physical or mental illness; it seems reasonable to assume that the rest of the difference is due to discouragement about finding a job.

If nonwhite male labor force participation rates were as high as the white rates, there would have been 140,000 more nonwhite males in the labor force in 1964. If we further assume that the 140,000 would have been unemployed, the unemployment rate for nonwhite men would have been 11.5 percent instead of the recorded rate of 9 percent, and the ratio between the nonwhite rate and the white rate would have jumped from 2:1 to 2.4:1.

Understated or not, the official unemployment rates for Negroes are almost unbelievable.

The unemployment statistics for Negro teenagers—29 percent in January 1964—reflect lack of training and opportunity in the greatest measure, but it may not be doubted that they also reflect a certain failure of nerve.

"Are you looking for a job?" Secretary of Labor Wirtz asked a young man on a Harlem street corner. "Why?" was the reply.

Richard A. Cloward and Robert Ontell have commented on this withdrawal in a discussion of the Mobilization for Youth project on the lower East Side of New York.

What contemporary slum and minority youth probably lack that similar children in earlier periods possessed is not motivation but some minimal sense of competence.

We are plagued in work with these youth, by what appears to be a low tolerance for frustration. They are not able to absorb setbacks. Minor irritants and rebuffs are magnified out of all proportion to reality. Perhaps they react as they do because they are not equal to the world that confronts them, and they know it. And it is the knowing that is devastating. Had the occupational structure remained intact, or had the education provided to them kept pace with occupa-

tional changes, the situation would be a different one. But it is not, and that is what we and they have to contend with.[26]

Narcotic addiction is a characteristic form of withdrawal. In 1963, Negroes made up 54 percent of the addict population of the United States. Although the Federal Bureau of Narcotics reports a decline in the Negro proportion of new addicts, HARYOU reports the addiction rate in central Harlem rose from 22.1 per 10,000 in 1955 to 40.4 in 1961.[27]

There is a larger fact about the alienation of Negro youth than the tangle of pathology described by these statistics. It is a fact particularly difficult to grasp by white persons who have in recent years shown increasing awareness of Negro problems.

The present generation of Negro youth growing up in the urban ghettos has probably less personal contact with the white world than any generation in the history of the Negro American.[28]

Until World War II it could be said that in general the Negro and white worlds lived, if not together, at least side by side. Certainly they did, and do, in the South.

Since World War II, however, the two worlds have drawn physically apart. The symbol of this development was the construction in the 1940's and 1950's of the vast white middle- and lower-middle-class suburbs around all of the Nation's cities. Increasingly, the inner cities have been left to Negroes—who now share almost no community life with whites.

In turn, because of this new housing pattern—most of which has been financially assisted by the Federal government—it is probable that the American school system has become *more*, rather than less segregated in the past two decades.

School integration has not occurred in the South, where a decade after *Brown* v. *Board of Education* only 1 Negro in 9 is attending school with white children.

And in the North, despite strenuous official efforts, neighborhoods and therefore schools are becoming more and more of one class and one color.

In New York City, in the school year 1957–58

there were 64 schools that were 90 percent or more Negro or Puerto Rican. Six years later there were 134 such schools.

Along with the diminution of white middle-class contacts for a large percentage of Negroes, observers report that the Negro churches have all but lost contact with men in the Northern cities as well. This may be a normal condition of urban life, but it is probably a changed condition for the Negro American and cannot be a socially desirable development.

The only religious movement that appears to have enlisted a considerable number of lower-class Negro males in Northern cities of late is that of the Black Muslims: a movement based on total rejection of white society, even though it emulates white mores.

In a word: the tangle of pathology is tightening.

[1]*E. Franklin Frazier,* Black Bourgeoisie *(New York, Collier Books, 1962).*

[2]*Robert O. Blood, Jr., and Donald M. Wolfe,* Husbands and Wives: The Dynamics of Married Living *(New York, The Free Press, 1960), p. 34.*

[3]Ibid., *p. 35.*

[4]Ibid.

[5]*Based on preliminary draft of a report by the President's Committee on Equal Employment Opportunity.*

[6]*Duncan M. MacIntyre,* Public Assistance: Too Much or Too Little? *(New York, New York State School of Industrial Relations, Cornell University, Bulletin 53-1, December 1964), pp. 73–74.*

[7]*Robin M. Williams, Jr.,* Strangers Next Door *(Englewood Cliffs, N.J., Prentice-Hall, Inc., 1964), p. 240.*

[8]Youth in the Ghetto *(New York: Harlem Youth Opportunities Unlimited), p. 195.*

[9]*Martin Deutch and Bert Brown, "Social Influences in Negro–White Intelligence Differences,"* Social Issues, *April 1964, p. 27.*

[10]Ibid., *p. 29.*

[11]Ibid.

[12]Ibid., *p. 31.*

[13]Ibid.

[14]*"Negroes in Apprenticeship, New York State,"* Monthly Labor Review, *September 1960, p. 955.*

[15]*Mary H. Diggs, "Some Problems and Needs of Negro Children as Revealed by Comparative Delinquency and Crime Statistics,"* Journal of Negro Education, *19, 1950, pp. 290–297.*

[16]*Maude M. Craig and Thelma J. Glick, "Ten Years Experience with the Glueck Social Prediction Table,"* Journal of Crime and Delinquency, *July 1963, p. 256.*

[17]*F. R. Scarpitti, Ellen Murray, S. Dinitz, and W. C. Reckless, "The 'Good' Boy in a High Delinquency Area: Four Years Later,"* American Sociological Review, *25, 1960, pp. 555–558.*

[18]*W. Mischel, "Father-Absence and Delay of Gratification: Cross-Cultural Comparisons,"* Journal of Abnormal and Social Psychology, *63, 1961, pp. 116–124.*

[19]*W. Mischel, "Preference for Delayed Reinforcement and Social Responsibility,"* Journal of Social and Abnormal Psychology, *62, 1961, pp. 1–7; "Delay of Gratification, Need for Achievement, and Acquiescence in Another Culture,"* Journal of Abnormal and Social Psychology, *62, 1961, pp. 543–552.*

[20]*O. H. Mowrer and A. D. Ullman, "Time as a Determinant in Integrative Learning,"* Psychological Review, *52, 1945, pp. 61–90.*

[21]*Thomas F. Pettigrew,* Profile of the Negro American *(New York: Van Nostrand, 1964), p. 22.*

[22]*Erdman Palmore, "Factors Associated with School Dropouts on Juvenile Delinquency Among Lower Class Children,"* Social Security Bulletin, *October 1963, p. 6.*

[23]*Thomas P. Monahan, "Family Status and the Delinquent Child,"* Social Forces, *March 1957, p. 254.*

[24]Ibid., *p. 174.*

[25]*Donald J. Bogue, Bhaskar D. Misra, and D. P. Dandekar, "A New Estimate of the Negro Population and Negro Vital Rates in the United States, 1930–1960,"* Demography, *Vol. 1, No. 1, 1964, p. 350.*

[26]*Richard A. Cloward and Robert Ontell, "Our Illusions about Training,"* American Child, *January 1965, p. 7.*

[27]Youth in the Ghetto, op. cit., *p. 144.*

[28]*Nathan Glazer and Daniel Patrick Moynihan,* Beyond the Melting Pot *(Cambridge, Mass.: M.I.T. Press, 1965).*

SINCE THE MOYNIHAN REPORT...

Blanche Bernstein

The Moynihan Report, issued in 1965, called for national action to increase the stability of the family structure of lower-class blacks. Since the report was written the instability of black families has increased: 40 percent of black families are now headed by women and an increasing number of teenagers give birth to children and become trapped in a life of poverty. The author discusses recent efforts to combat increases in teenage pregnancy.

In March 1965, Daniel Patrick Moynihan, then head of the Office of Planning and Research in the U.S. Department of Labor, authored a report entitled *The Negro Family: The Case for National Action.*[1] It is fascinating to reread it almost 20 years later; it is also instructive to review its major thesis, the reaction to it, developments since its publication, and consider again the case for national action.

Moynihan warmly welcomed the establishment of the President's Committee on Equal Opportunity, the Manpower Development and Training Act of 1962, the Economic Opportunity Act of 1964, and the Civil Rights Act of 1964, all efforts to improve the economic position of blacks, abolish poverty, and eliminate legal and formal discrimination against blacks. The report also eloquently and sympathetically describes in the chapter on the "Roots of the Problem" the ill effects of the period of slavery, the frequently high levels of unemployment and low wages, and inferior education on the structure and well-being of the black family.

But as Moynihan studied the economic and demographic trends evident in available data for 1940–1963, he foresaw a serious clash between the newly enunciated black goals of achieving not just equal opportunity but equal results—in the sense of a comparable distribution of income, education etc., as between whites and nonwhites—and what he referred to as the crumbling of the black family. He noted that the white family "has achieved a high degree of stability" and is maintaining it, but in contrast, "the family structure of lower class Negroes is highly unstable, and in many urban centers is approaching complete breakdown." He added that "so long as this situation persists, the cycle of poverty and disadvantage will continue to repeat itself" and he called for national action "directed to a new kind of national goal: the establishment of a stable Negro family structure."

Did the report bring about a widespread public recognition of the role of family stability in improving the economic and social situation of blacks and a plan for national action? Quite the contrary: it elicited a sustained, vociferous attack from black leaders and many liberal white opinion makers. Moynihan was labeled racist and reactionary, as was anyone else who argued similarly in the ensuing years. And this despite the fact that some outstanding blacks had already written, or were to write in a similar vein: among others, E. Franklin Frazier in 1939 and Andrew Brimmer, then a member of the Federal Reserve Board, who in 1970, while noting the significant economic progress made by blacks during the 1960s, pointed out the deepening schism

From *New Perspectives* 16 (2, Fall 1984):3–7. Figures have been deleted.

in the black community evident "above all in the dramatic deterioration in the position of Negro families headed by a female." Despite those and some other voices raised in defense of the Moynihan thesis, the overwhelming reaction in terms of its influence on public policy was one of rejection. Some defended early child bearing on the grounds that black girls were more mature than whites and even plans to expand family planning services to blacks were labeled genocide.

As in the period prior to the passage of equal opportunity and civil rights legislation, the focus of attention of black leaders and others remained on denial of civil rights, discrimination, unemployment, and low wages. At the 1980 White House Conference on Families and Children, though President Carter began with the notion of strengthening the intact family, an HEW task force urged a more "neutral" model as the liberal goal; the task force won. As a result, the White House Conference degenerated into a conference on ways of aiding any and all types of families rather than focussing on the intact family. Indeed, the intact family got short shrift in the proceedings, and little consideration, if any, was given to possible programs for the prevention of family break-up or the nonformation of families.

During the almost 20 years since the publication of the Moynihan Report, has the economic and social situation of blacks improved and what do the data which became available in this period tell us about the current situation of the black family and its impact on their well-being?

Between 1940 and 1960–64 (the period examined in the Report), Moynihan found that the rate of black births out-of-wedlock had risen from 17 to 24 percent of all live births; the comparable figures for whites was from two to three percent. Between 1950 and 1960 the ratio of female-headed black families rose from 18 to 21 percent; among whites the figure was unchanged at about nine percent. The big increase in the indices of the deterioration of the black family were yet to come. At the beginning of the 1980s, the proportion of black families headed by women had reached 41 percent, almost a doubling of the ratio in two decades. It should be noted that the increase in families headed by a woman as a result of divorce, desertion, or nonfor-

mation of a family is evident among all income and ethnic groups, but among whites it reached 12 percent and among Hispanics, 20 percent, as compared to 41 percent among blacks.

Does family structure make a difference in terms of the family's standard of living? Indeed it does. In general, it takes about 1.3 wage earners per four-person family to achieve the Bureau of Labor Statistics lower-level standard of living ($15,323 in 1981 prices—later figures have not yet been published), 1.7 for the moderate level ($24,407) and two wage earners for the higher level ($38,060). The female-headed family is clearly at a serious disadvantage with limited opportunities for moving up the economic ladder. The data on the family characteristics of those in poverty are even more compelling. In 1982, only eight percent of two-parent families were poor compared to 36 percent of female-headed families. Among intact families with two wage earners, only five percent of white families, nine percent of black families, and 12 percent of Hispanic families were poor.

During the 1960s, the black/white income ratio improved—from 54 percent in 1959 to 63 percent in 1968—though the differential remained substantial. But the differential widened again in the 1970s. According to an analysis published in 1981, "a fundamental reason for the deterioration of the black/white income ratio between 1970 and 1976 is the substantially faster rate of growth of female-headed families among blacks than among whites. In fact, if the patterns of family composition that existed in 1970 had been present in 1978, the black/white income gap would have been narrowed in that period by five percentage points. If one went back to 1960, the gain would have been greater" (Sandell, 1981). And it was Dr. Robert Hill of the National Urban League who pointed out that the number of poor black families rose by 19 percent between 1969 and 1975 due to the sharp rise of black families headed by women. While the number of poor black families headed by men fell by 34 percent—the number of poor black families headed by women soared by 64 percent, accounting for all the increase in the number of poor black families.

Perhaps the most vulnerable of the female-headed families are those headed by a teenager or a mother who was a teenager when she had her first child. A study published by the Urban Institute found that women who were teenagers at the birth of their first child account for more than half of total AFDC expenditures in the country and comprise an astounding 71 percent of all AFDC mothers under 30 years of age (Moore and Burt, 1981).

Teenage mothers under 16 incur the most long-term disadvantages. They exhibit a high drop-out rate from school, have larger families, less opportunity for employment, and lower earnings when they do work. Further, they are more likely to find themselves and their children trapped in long-term poverty with its harmful consequences for health, housing, learning, and social development.

Reviewing trends from 1940 to 1960, Moynihan already expressed concern about the fact that black women were having babies at younger ages, but the problem then was still of modest dimension. It was not until the '60s and '70s that teenage pregnancy grew to enormous proportions and became the single most important cause of long-term poverty.

A few figures are necessary to delineate the growth and size of the problem, as well as its impact on the well-being of the major ethnic communities. The number of teenage out-of-wedlock births rose from 91,700 in 1960 to 262,500 in 1979; if one counts only those under 17, the increase is from 48,300 to 129,500. While out-of-wedlock teenage births have increased more rapidly among whites than among blacks, the rate of 15 births to unmarried teenagers per 1,000 white births is still far below the rate of 87 for blacks. In 1971, of all females 15–19 years old, eight percent conceived a child; by 1979 the figure had risen to 12 percent, or one out of nine teenagers. Births have also increased among children 13–15 years old. Some 1.3 million children in this country live with teenage mothers; an additional 1.6 million children under five years of age live with mothers who were teenagers when they gave birth.

Perhaps even more revealing than the data on births to teenagers are the trends in teenage sexual activity and its outcome. Between 1971 and 1979, while the number of teenagers 15 to 19 rose by six percent, the number who were sexually active almost doubled; from 2.5 to 4.7 million. Among whites the figure went from 41 percent to 65 percent; among blacks, from 78 percent to 89 percent. Further, the number of teenagers who conceived a child was about double the number who gave birth out-of-wedlock. In other words, about half the conceptions terminated in an abortion or miscarriage, mainly the former.

The acceleration of family breakup and teenage pregnancy was reflected not only in a tripling of the welfare caseload during the 1960s and further substantial increases until the mid-1970s, but in the increase in crime, juvenile delinquency, and drug use, with the youngsters on welfare disproportionately represented in all those areas as well as among school dropouts. The "tangle of pathology" has become ever more tangled.

One cannot put all the blame for this dismaying picture on unemployment, or even on discrimination, though racial discrimination has not yet been eliminated from our society. Moynihan traced a positive correlation between black unemployment rates and family instability for the two decades he studied, but he noted that this connection appeared to have been broken in 1962–3; at that time he could only wonder whether it was the beginning of a trend. It was. From the early '60s to the early '70s unemployment declined from an overall rate of about six percent to three to four percent, and though unemployment for blacks remained higher than that for whites, it too declined. We were in fact in a tight labor market.

And yet, these were the very years of the explosion in the welfare caseload and the increasing evidence of social pathology. What was overlooked during this period of turbulence—when there was concern about the continued existence of poverty within the country; evidence of continuing though diminishing discrimination against blacks and other minorities; and violent reaction, as reflected in riots in many cities, to what was perceived as past and current injustices—was the enormous growth in female-headed families because of family breakup mainly as a result of teenage child-bearing. For more than two decades, the problem was largely ignored by the black community. In *A Statistical*

Overview of Black America published by the National Urban League in December, 1982, the family structure explanation of the economic disorder which had befallen blacks was discounted with the statement that "People are not poor because they are female and household heads; they are poor because they do not have jobs or adequate income." And the subject of black family structure was taboo among a significant section of the white community as well. Only recently has this changed.

At first only individual black voices were heard—William Raspberry in the *Washington Post*, Robert Curvin in the *New York Times*, William Haskins of the National Urban League, among others. They were saying publicly that in effect the blacks needed to concern themselves about the structure of the black family and particularly with teenage pregnancy. The major breakthrough came with the publication of a pamphlet in June, 1983, entitled *A Policy Framework for Racial Justice*, issued by 30 liberal black leaders (known as The Tarrytown Group) and members of the Black Leadership Forum. These leaders list the following as the most urgent problems to be tackled to bring poor blacks into the mainstream: progress in the economy, *the condition of the black family* (my emphasis), and educational opportunity. They add that unless major efforts are made quickly "The condition of a large portion of the black population will deteriorate beyond the point where any program of action can be effective." On the subject of teenagers they say "Teenagers and young men and women need to be encouraged to pursue training, work, and personal development while they delay pregnancy and family formation" and further that "For young people, there is a special need for sex education and education about the importance of *delaying sex, pregnancy, and marriage* (my emphasis)."

The issuance of *A Policy Framework for Racial Justice* served to galvanize the black community to action on a national scale. It was followed within a year by a Black Family Summit Conference called by the National Association for the Advancement of Colored People and the National Urban League. The news release issued at the end of the conference, May 5, 1984, contains language not heard for many years; for example John Jacobs, President of NUL, warned that "some of our problems may be self-inflicted, that we may have allowed our just anger at what America has done to obscure our own need for self-discipline and strengthened community values."

If one reads through the summary recommendations of each of the ten task forces established at the conference, it is not difficult to be critical of its laundry list aspect or the lack of specificity of many of the recommendations. What is more important, however, is the recognition of the nature of the problem and the beginning effort to outline a strategy for dealing with it, a strategy which clearly must stress the economic and social advantages of family stability and the behavior necessary to achieve it and not rest solely on an appeal to morality.

The public recognition by black leaders of the responsibility of the black community for improvement in the structure of the black family and for persuading teenagers and young people, boys and girls alike, to postpone sexual activity and pregnancy has also made it easier for the white-sponsored foundations and other philanthropic organizations to assist in developing and funding necessary programs, and also to evaluate the effectiveness of different approaches. Hitherto, the foundations approached these issues very cautiously, concerned that they might be considered racist.

The importance of evaluation of the effectiveness of programs cannot be overemphasized. The belated recognition of the causes of poverty among blacks in the 1960s and onward—not to be confused with the causes of poverty in the 1930s or earlier—have resulted in a problem of enormous size and complexity. No one knows exactly how to promote family stability and persuade teenage boys and girls to postpone sexual activity after two decades of permissiveness and the erosion of earlier held values. Efforts to develop programs of any major scope are no more than two years old and some remain statements of intention rather than programs which can be implemented beginning next month. One of the early ones—Teaching Teens to Say No—begun on a demonstration basis in Cleveland and Atlanta and now being carried out on a large scale in the schools in Atlanta, is being evaluated by the Ford Foundation. Governor Mario Cuomo of New York has initiated a program on adolescent pregnancy which is, however, still largely on the drawing board, and the New York City public school system has within recent months initiated an updated sex education curriculum dealing with teenage pregnancy among other issues. Other efforts are underway in various cities sponsored by various foundations. What is needed is a national central repository of information on what programs are being tried, and which show promise of success under what circumstances, so that scarce resources are not wasted on reinventing the wheel, especially wheels that don't turn.

Government at all levels should join in the effort to strengthen the black family in appropriate ways. The federal government might well fund the national depository of information suggested above. Washington and the states should focus more attention and resources on advancing the educational achievement of the children in welfare families since there is a positive correlation between

progress in schools and delaying sexual activity. The names and addresses of the roughly 8 million children in the nation on welfare are known to local welfare departments. But little is done to provide extra assistance to them in the early years of schooling though it is known that they are disproportionately represented among school dropouts. If the effort is not made in the early grades we will continue to face a costly remediation effort—as we are now—in the high schools and even the colleges, as we seek with only limited success to prepare them for the existing opportunities in the world of work.

It is urgent that the effort to postpone teenage sexual activity succeed if we are to avoid the heavy costs to society of teenage child bearing and the even heavier costs to the teenager, her child, and the black community, as well as the costs of continuing conflict between blacks, whites, and other ethnic groups over the distribution of the nation's product. Moynihan was right.

---

[1]*The report itself does not indicate any individual authorship, only the government agency which issued it, but is well known as the Moynihan Report and he took the brunt of the attack against it. Beginning with the second half of the 1960s the word "Negro" became a term of opprobrium and "black" came into use. In this article, I follow current usage, unless I am quoting.*

References

Moore, Kristin A., and Martha F. Burt

1981 *Private Crisis, Public Cost: Policy Perspective on Teen Age Child Bearing*. Washington, D.C.: Urban Institute.

Sandell, Steven H.

1981 *Family Income in the 1970's; The Demographics of Black/White Differences*, Technical Analysis Paper No. 23, U.S. Dept. of Health and Human Services, December, Office of Planning and Evaluation, Office of Income Security Policy Evaluation.

CHANGES IN BLACK FAMILY STRUCTURE:
The Conflict between Family Ideology and Structural Conditions

Robert Staples

This article compares the family ideology of Black Americans with actual family arrangements and life-styles. Dissonance between the two is explained by the intervention of structural conditions that prevent the fulfillment of normative familial roles by Black males. Exchange theory is presented to explain the conflict between family ideology and structural conditions. In general, the author argues, Black women fail to marry or remain married when the costs of such an arrangement outweigh the benefits.

Historically, family theorists have argued that family structure and achievement interact with one another (Goode, 1963; Parson and Bales, 1955). While that may have some validity for certain ethnic groups in America, none of those groups share the history and current social conditions of the Black population in the United States. The peculiar history of Black Americans, combined with structural conditions inimical to family formation and maintenance, have precipitated a crisis in the Black family.

The basic theoretical perspective that informs the present analysis of Black family life is that of exchange theory. This theory focuses on the reinforcement patterns, the history of rewards and costs, that lead people to do what they do. Essentially it argues that people will continue to do what they have found rewarding in the past. The basic premise here is that certain kinds of family structures exist when there is an exchange of rewards; on the other hand, family arrangements that are costly to one or both parties are much less likely to continue (Blau, 1964; Homans, 1961).

We assume, first, that being married is important to the majority of Blacks, especially women. The fact that a near majority of Black Americans are not married and living in traditional nuclear family units is not a result of any devaluation of marriage qua institution but rather a function of limited choices to find individuals in a restricted and small pool of potential partners who can successfully fulfill the normatively prescribed familial roles. While many blacks fail to marry, the history of Black marriages shows only a minority surviving a lifetime with the same people. Exchange theory suggests that a person will not remain in a relationship where the services provided seem relatively meager compared with what the person knows about other relationships. It appears, then, that Blacks do not marry because the perceived outcome, derived from knowledge of past rewards and costs, is one where alternative sources of goal mediation are preferred risks (Thibaut and Kelley, 1959). This

---

From *Journal of Marriage and the Family* 47 (November 1985):1005–1015. © 1985 by the National Council on Family Relations. Reprinted by permission. The author is grateful to Paul Rosenblatt for his comments on an earlier draft of this paper.

cost-benefit analysis is mediated by structural conditions among the Black male population that give rise to dissonance between Black family ideology and actual family arrangements.

Black Family Ideology

The popular image of Blacks as a group pressing for change in the area of race relations and economic opportunities often is translated into the image of a radical group in the forefront of social change. Other than being opposed to unfair discrimination against any group and favoring liberal social and economic policies, Blacks often hold very traditional, even conservative, attitudes on other social issues—attitudes that place them in the mainstream of American mores and folkways. Some years ago Robert Hill (1972) noted that Blacks have a strong work, achievement, and religious orientation. In particular, they believe strongly in the institution of the family. Gary and his associates (1983) found that the greatest source of life satisfaction among their Black subjects was family life.

Their unconventional family arrangements and lifestyles easily can mislead outsiders to assume the Blacks are strongly in accord with newly emerging alternative family lifestyles. While they are tolerant of people—especially Blacks—who live in other than nuclear families, the family ideology of most Blacks is in the direction of traditional family forms. Several studies, for instance, show that Black women wish to marry and maintain traditional roles in the conjugal relationship (Broderick, 1965; Kulesky and Obordo, 1972). One indication of the Black value of marriage is the fact that in the past more Black women entered into a marital union than their white counterparts. In 1973, among Black women 65 years and over, only 3.5% had never married, compared with 6.9% of white women (U.S. Bureau of the Census, 1978).

Among the most traditional of values is that of motherhood and childrearing. Except for college-educated Black women, almost all Black women bear children unless infertile. The role of mother is regarded as more important than any other role, including that of wife (Bell, 1971). While respectful of a woman's right to control her body, Blacks tend to have a more negative attitude towards abortion. The Zelnik and Kantner (1974) study revealed that 35% of white teenagers terminated their first pregnancy by abortion compared with only 4% of Black teenagers. However, some of this racial variation may reflect differential access to abortion rather than differential inclination. The Black mother's childrearing techniques are also more traditional. She is more likely than the white mother to use physical, rather than verbal, punishment to enforce child discipline. Threatening the child with withdrawal of the mother's love, used by some white mothers, is uncommon among Black women, which is one reason that the Black mother–child bond remains strong throughout adult life (Nolle, 1972; Scanzoni, 1971).

Although there has been a noticeable increase in feminist ideology among women in the last 20 years, Black women are greatly underrepresented in the women's liberation movement. Many Black women continue to perceive racism—not sexism—as the biggest obstacle to their career and family goals. They are relatively uninvolved in such prominent feminist issues as pornography, sexual harassment, abortion, comparable pay, rape, etc. Moreover, they are more traditional in their definition of the roles that men and women should play in society and the family (Hershey, 1978). While their attitudes remain very traditional, the family lifestyles and arrangements of Blacks are definitely unconventional. . . . We explain it as a conflict between family ideology and structural conditions. . . .

Some 20 years since the publication of the Moynihan Report (1965), the figures he cited as evidence that the Black family was deteriorating have doubled, almost tripled in some areas. How is it that a group that regards family life as its most important source of satisfaction finds a majority of its women unmarried? Why does a group with more traditional sexual values than its white peers have a majority of its children born out-of-wedlock? Finally, we must ask how a group that places such importance on the traditional nuclear family finds a near majority of its members living in single-parent households. While a number of reasons have been cited by theorists, we suggest that the dominant force can be found in structural conditions of the Black population.

Family Ideology vs. Structural Conditions

The basis of a stable family rests on the willingness, and ability, of men and women to marry, bear and rear children, and fulfill socially prescribed familial roles. In the case of women, those roles have been defined traditionally as the carrying out of domestic functions such as cooking and cleaning; giving birth to children and socializing them; providing sexual gratification, companionship, and emotional support to their husbands. There is abundant evidence that Black women are willing and able to fulfill those roles (Staples, 1973). Conversely, the roles of men in the family are more narrowly confined to economic provider and family leader, but there are indications that a majority of Black American males cannot implement those roles. When it comes to a choice between remaining single or getting married, individuals often do a cost-benefit analysis. Marriage is frequently a quid pro quo arrangement. The desire to enter and maintain a conjugal relationship is contingent on their perception of the benefits that can be acquired and, conversely, of the anticipated costs (Blau, 1964). . . .

The major problem for Black women, however, is not the quantity of the available supply of potential mates, but the quality. Whereas Black women may select a mate on the basis of a number of attributes, a minimum prerequisite is that he be gainfully and regularly employed. According to a study by Joe and Yu (1984), almost a majority of working-age Black males fail to meet those minimum prerequisites. After an analysis of the economic and census data, they concluded that 46% of the 8.8 million Black men of working age were not in the labor force. Based on 1982 statistics, they found that 1.2 million Black men were unemployed, 1.8 million had dropped out of the labor force, 186,000 were in prison, and 925,000 were classified as "missing" because the Census Bureau said it could not locate them.

Furthermore, their study overstates the number of "desirable" and available Black males in the marriage pool. Even with the census undercount, there are still a half million more Black women over the age of 14 than Black men. Also, we must subtract from the marriage pool Black men with certain characteristics by which they substantially outnumber Black women. Among those characteristics would be Blacks serving in the Armed Forces. Approximately 90% of them will be male. The U.S. Bureau of the Census (1983) reports that there were 415,000 Blacks under arms in 1982, representing 20% of all United States military personnel. It can be stated reliably that a large number of those Black males had poor prospects for employment in the civilian labor force (Stewart and Scott, 1978). While the salaries and other benefits of military personnel have improved in recent years and a number of Black soldiers are currently married, the military does take out of circulation a number of marriage-age Black males by stationing them in foreign posts and isolated military stations. Furthermore, once their period of enlistment ends, Black veterans experience a higher rate of unemployment, even in relation to Black civilian males with no military service (Stewart and Scott, 1978). Hence, military service only postpones the entry of Black males into the ranks of the unemployed, one reason Black males have a higher rate of re-enlistment than their white counterparts. . . .

Another group of Black males regarded as undesirable or unavailable are those confined to mental institutions or who are otherwise mentally unstable. While their exact number is unknown, Black males are more likely to be committed to mental institutions than are Black women, and the strictures of racism are such that Blacks are more likely to suffer from mental distress. In 1970, 240 non-whites per 100,000 population were confined to mental institutions, compared with 162 whites per 100,000 population. Blacks also used community mental health centers at a rate almost twice their proportion in the general population. The rate of drug and alcohol abuse is much greater among the Black population—especially males—based on their overrepresentation among patients receiving treatment services (U.S. Dept. of Health, Education and Welfare, 1979:163–183). It is estimated that as many as one-third of the young Black males in the inner city have serious drug problems (Staples, 1982). Many of the mentally unstable, drug and alcohol abusers will have been included in the figures on Black males who have dropped out of the labor force or are incarcerated in prison. The magnitude of the problem simply reinforces the fact that Black women are seriously disadvantaged in choosing from the eligible and desirable males in the marriage pool.

A large category of Black males who fit into the desirable group must also be considered not available. By all reliable estimates, the Black male homosexual population is considerably larger than the Black female homosexual population (Bell and Weinberg, 1978). Based on the often-quoted Kinsey estimate (Kinsey et al., 1948) that 10% of the adult male population is homosexual, that would mean about 800,000 Black men are not available to heterosexual Black women. Of course, many of these gay males do marry, for a variety of reasons, and serve well in the roles of husband and father; but, due to the increasing public tolerance of overt male homosexuality, it is reasonable to expect that fewer gay males will choose to enter into heterosexual marriages in the future. Finally, it should be noted that Black men marry outside their race at a rate twice as great as that of Black women (Heer, 1974; Staples, 1982).

Although the shortage and desirability of Black males in the marriage pool largely affects the non-college-educated Black woman's marriage chances, the college-educated Black female is not spared the problem if she desires to marry within her race and socioeconomic level. In 1980 there were 133,000 more Black women enrolled in college than Black men—about 57% of all Black college students. Moreover, Black male students have a much higher attrition rate than their female peers. In the University of California system, for instance, only 12 of every 100 Black male students graduate within four years. Thus, in 1981, 36,200 of 60,700 bachelor's degrees awarded to Blacks went to women (60%); and between the years 1976 and 1981, Black women receiving bachelor's degrees increased by 9%, and comparable Black males declined by 9%. These same trends existed for graduate degrees during the years 1976–1981: Black women declined by 12% and Black men by 21% in the receipt of the master's degree; in the receipt of the first professional degree, Black women increased by 71% while Black men declined by 21%; and the doctoral level, Black men declined by 10%,

while Black women increased at a rate of 29% (National Center for Education Statistics, 1983).

College-educated Black women do have the option of marrying men with less education and making a viable choice. In the past as many as 50% of college-educated Black women married men of a lower socioeconomic level (Noble, 1956), but increasingly there is resistance among these women to marrying down. Almost one-third of college-educated Black women remain unmarried past the age of 30 (Bayer, 1972; Staples, 1981). Of course, they face a similar shortage in the marriage pool of male high school graduates and must compete with lesser educated Black women for these same men. Also, such middle-level men tend to marry early and have the most stable marriages in the Black community (Glick and Mills, 1974). The marriage patterns of college-educated Black males tend to put college-educated Black women at a disadvantage. Many of these men marry women of a lower educational level, and the interracial marriage rate is highest in this group of Black men (Heer, 1974; Staples, 1981).

Structural Conditions and the Changing Black Family

There is no great mystery as to what has happened to the Black family in the last 20 years: it is an acceleration of trends set in motion during the 1960s. A highly sexualized culture—via media, clothing, and example—has conveyed to American youth the notion that nonmarital sexual relations are not only acceptable but required for individual fulfillment. Women are reaching puberty earlier and emotional maturity later. Furthermore, the consequences of teenage sexual behavior are counteracted somewhat by easier access to effective contraceptives and abortion; and the number of pregnant teenagers has not really increased—only the proportion of births to that group of women as a result of the rapid decline in births to older married women.

While the nonmarital sexual activity rate of Black and white teenage women is converging, the Black female is more likely to be engaged in unprotected intercourse and less likely to marry or have an abortion if she becomes pregnant. According to Zelnik and Kantner (1974) only 8.5% of their Black sample (15–19 years) entered into marriage as an outcome of premarital pregnancy, compared with 50.8% of comparable white women. In addition, 35.5% of white women had their premarital pregnancies terminated by abortion, in contrast to 4.9% of similar Black women.

While it is reasonable to question the wisdom of young Black women attaining motherhood at such an early age, their decision to bear the children and raise them alone reflects their traditional values and limited options in life. Among Black males their age, the official unemployment rate is 52%, and as many as 75% of young Black men remain outside the work force (Malabre, 1980). While employment may be easier for Black women to obtain, it often will be in dead-end jobs that pay only half the wages earned by white males. Rather than remain childless and husbandless, these women choose to have the children and raise them alone. A good explanation of these life choices is given by Hortense Canady, President of Delta Sigma Theta Sorority (1984:40): "Having a child is probably the best thing that's ever going to happen to them in their whole lifetime and the only thing they can contribute—this is not true in most other countries in the world. But if you belong to a class or a group of people who have no educational opportunities stretching out before them, no other goals, that's probably the single, best thing that's ever going to happen to you in your life."

Having limited educational and career options . . . is not the only reason for the increase in female-headed households. A welfare system that often requires men to be absent from the home is part of the problem; and Black women realize that the meager welfare payments are more reliable than a class of men who may never know gainful employment in their entire lives. In general, unemployed men do not make good husbands and fathers. Since employment and income are the measure of a man's masculinity in this society, men who have neither do not tend to feel good about themselves or act very positively toward their wives and children. In the Hampton (1980) study, for example, husbands who were not satisfied with themselves had a fairly high level of marital disruption.

However, the major reason for the increase in Black female-headed households is the lack of "desirable" men with whom to form monogamous marriages. According to Joe and Yu (1984), between 1976 and 1983 the number of Black families headed by women rose by 700,000, and the ranks of Black men out of the labor force or unemployed increased by the same number. The same trend has existed for the last 25 years: almost 75% of Black men were working in 1960, and Black families headed by women accounted for 21% of all Black families in the same year; but by 1982 only 54% of all Black men were in the labor force, and 42% of all Black families were headed by women (Joe and Yu, 1984).

Having a child out-of-wedlock and failing to marry accounts for 41% of all Black households headed by women. Another 51% are divorced or separated from their spouses (U.S. Bureau of the Census, 1983). These marriage disruptions are generally susceptible to the same structural conditions that plague never-married Black women. Unemployment and underemployment, the public assistance complex, the educational system, and the health care system all produce economic and psychological alienation in the Black male. As Hampton (1980) found, the pressures that push many Black males out of other social institutions within society also work to push them out of marital relationships. For every 1,000 Black married persons with spouses present, the number of divorces increased from 92 in 1971 to 233 in 1981; the comparable increase for whites was from 48 to 100. Black separations increased from 172 to 225 per 1,000 married persons in the same period; white separations rose from 21 to 29 (U.S. Bureau of the Census, 1983).

A number of social characteristics place Blacks at risk for divorce. They have a higher rate of urbanization, greater independence of women, earlier age at marriage, earlier fertility, a higher education and income levels for the wife and lower income status for the husband (Cherlin, 1981). Most Black marriages involve a wife who is more highly educated than her husband (Spanier and Glick, 1980). In one out of five Black marriages, the wife earns a higher income than her husband (U.S. Bureau of the Census, 1983). This incongruity between the socially assigned roles of the male as the primary provider and the wife as a subordinate member of the marital dyad may undermine the husband's self-esteem, frustrate the wife, and create marital dissatisfaction for both partners. In Hampton's (1980) study, the highest percentage of disrupted marriages (27.4%) was observed among wives with incomes accounting for 40% or more of the family's income. His explanation is that, when women have other means of support in the form of welfare or their own earnings, they may be less constrained to remain in a personally unsatisfying relationship. Alternatively, the wife may be satisfied with the husband's role; but her high income may threaten the husband's authority and status, undermining his self-concept so that *he* becomes unhappy.

These problems of the Black family are only variations of the general problems of American families. The direction of change in the family structure is basically the same for all racial groups in the United States and for the same reasons. Guttentag and Secord (1983) demonstrated that unbalanced sex ratios have certain predictable consequences for relationships between men and women. They give rise to higher rates of singlehood, divorce, out-of-wedlock births, and female-headed households in different historical epochs and across different societies. According to Ehrenreich (1983) the breakdown of the family began in the 1950s when men began a flight from commitment to the husband and father role. In the case of the Black family, it stems from the institutional decimation of Black males.

Discussion

The basic thesis here is that the dissonance between Black family ideology and actual family arrangements is caused by the intervention of structural conditions that impede the actualization of Black aspirations for a traditional family life and roles. The central factor in this situation is the inability of Black males to meet the normative responsibilities of husband and father. Questions may be raised as to how the problem has reached its present magnitude and why it is so pronounced among the Black population. The answer appears to involve a combination of cultural and economic forces which have been ascendant in the last 20 years.

A basic cause of Black male unemployment has been the change in the economy and composition of the work force: automation and foreign competition have eliminated large numbers of jobs in manufacturing industries in the United States over the last couple of decades. Because Black males were disproportionately concentrated in these industries, Black males with years of seniority were displaced, and there were no high-paying unionized occupations for younger and newer workers to enter. Even low-paying menial jobs were automated or taken over by new immigrants, both legal and illegal. The expansion of the economy was in the private sector's high technology and service industries, which brought Black males into competition (or noncompetition) with the burgeoning numbers of white women entering and reentering the labor force.

Women, both Black and white, were better prepared to deal with the educational qualifications of an economy based on high technology and service industries. They require basic reading and writing skills precisely at the time when the public school system began to decline in its ability to produce students with those attributes. During this period Black and Hispanic males had the highest rate of functional illiteracy among the 23 million Americans so classified; estimates are that as many as 40% of the Black male population is not able to read and write well enough to function in a technological society (Staples, 1982). Moreover, the Black male's functional illiteracy can be traced to problems in America's urban school system. One explanation is that when a Black male perceives the opportunity structure as not allowing for his upward mobility through education, he is more likely to divert his energy into sports, music, or hustling. On the other hand, Black females—with fewer opportunities—continue to progress in the same educational system, possibly because, as Hale (1983) has noted, traditional classrooms are generally oriented toward feminine values; teachers are disproportionately female, and the behaviors tolerated and most encouraged are those that are more natural for girls.

The same general trends also occur to varying degrees among whites, but they affect their family structure differently. White male teenagers have an unemployment rate half that of the officially re-corded rate for similar Black males. Moreover, the white male teenager ultimately uses his kinship and friend-of-the-family networks more effectively to se-cure employment, while many Black male teenag-ers who lack such networks drop out or never join the work force. The poor employment prospects for young Black males is illustrated by the fact that some employers refused to hire them for jobs that were totally subsidized by federal funds (Malabre, 1980). Lack of steady employment largely accounts for the Black male's high enlistment in the military, drug and alcohol abuse, and participation in criminal ac-tivities, ultimately leaving less than half the Black male population as rational husband and father can-didates (Glasgow, 1979).

One other distinguishing characteristic of the Black population is the early age at which Black women give birth to their first children. More than 40% of Black women have given birth at least once by the time they reach 20 years of age. Estimates are that only one-sixth of the Black males in that age range have jobs (Cummings, 1983). Should they marry before age 20, more than 7 out of 10 such marriages fail (Cherlin, 1981). Exacerbating this sit-uation is the fact that even gainfully employed Black men earn significantly less than white men. In 1982 the median income of Black men was $10,510, com-pared with $15,964 for white men (U.S. Bureau of the Census, 1983).

Under positive conditions there are good in-dications that the Black family is strong. College-educated Black women, for example, have their children later and in smaller numbers than any other socioeconomic or racial group in the United States. While probably as sexually active as lower income Black women, they are more effective in the use of birth control and more likely to resort to abortion if pregnancy occurs (Gebhard et al., 1958). Although college-educated Black males earn less in-come than white male high school dropouts, ap-proximately 90% of them are married and living with their spouses (U.S. Bureau of the Census, 1978). Where negative social conditions are absent, family ideology prevails.

A central question that remains is why Black family ideology has not changed or adjusted to changing conditions. One answer is that it *has*

changed among one stratum of the Black popula-tion: the middle class. Within that segment of the Black community, mainstream values—even chang-ing ones—are stronger because they have a higher level of acculturation into those norms due to their greater participation in the majority group's institu-tions (Staples, 1981). Even among this group, how-ever, traditional values are still strong and exert an influence on their ideological posture toward the family. In part, that is a function of their recent entry into the middle class and the retention of values from their class of origin. Another factor, however, is that their participation in mainstream institutions and embrace of normative ideologies are still mar-ginal, keeping traditional values attractive to many. Gary and his associates (1983) found that their middle-class Black subjects cited their family life as the source of most satisfaction, while the source of least satisfaction was their job. Hence, traditional family life remains the one viable option for Black Americans of all socioeconomic strata because it is less subject to the vagaries of race than any other institution in American life.

Similarly, lower income Blacks sustain tradi-tional beliefs about marriage and the family because the many traumas experienced by this group have cultivated a stronger belief in the value of the family as a resource for their survival in a society not al-ways hospitable to their aspirations. Other than the church, the family has been the only institution to serve as a vehicle for resisting oppression and facil-itating their movement toward social and economic equality. Another factor may be the continued phys-ical and social isolation of Blacks—especially lower income Blacks—from members of the majority group who are in the forefront of social and cultural change. In any context of social change, there is a gap between the ideal statements of a culture and the reality in which people live out their lives—a time lag between the emergence of new cultural forms and their internalization by the individuals who must act upon them. Thus, it would appear that Black family ideologies will change only as their social and economic isolation diminishes.

In many ways this situation is nothing new for the Black population. Social scientists continue to view the deterioration of the family as the problem when, in reality, the raison d'être of Black family structure is the structural conditions that prevent the fulfillment of Black family ideology. Given the present political and economic trends, there is little reason to expect an abatement of these trends in the Black family. In fact, female-headed families are projected to be 59% of all Black families with children by the year 1990 (Joe and Yu, 1984). Almost 75% of Black children will live in such families, and 70% of Blacks with incomes below the poverty level will belong to these families. The problem of the Black family cannot be solved without resolving the economic predicament of Black men. They are one and the same.

References

Bayer, A.

1972 "College Impact on Marriage." *Journal of Marriage and the Family* 34 (November):600–610.

Bell, A., and M. Weinberg

1978 *Homosexualities*. New York: Simon & Schuster.

Bell, R.

1971 "The Related Importance of Mother and Wife Roles among Black Lower Class Women." In *The Black Family: Essays and Studies* (2nd ed.), R. Staples, ed., pp. 248–255. Belmont, Calif.: Wadsworth.

Blau, P.

1964 *Exchange and Power in Social Life*. New York: John Wiley.

Broderick, C.

1965 "Social Heterosexual Development among Urban Negroes and Whites." *Journal of Marriage and the Family* 27 (May):200–203.

Canady, H.

1984 Quoted in "Words of the Week." *Jet Magazine* (March 19):40.

Cherlin, H.

1981 *Marriage, Divorce, Remarriage*. Cambridge, Mass.: Harvard University Press.

Cummings, J.

1983 "Breakup of the Black Family Imperils Gains of Decades." *The New York Times* (November 20):1, 36.

Ehrenreich, B.

1983 *The Hearts of Men: American Dreams and the Flight from Commitment*. Garden City, N.Y.: Doubleday.

Gary, L., L. Beatty, G. Berry, and M. Price

1983 "Stable Black Families." Final Report, Institute for Urban Affairs and Research. Washington, D.C.: Howard University.

Gebhard, P., W. Pomeroy, C. Martin, and C. Christenson

1958 *Pregnancy, Birth and Abortion*. New York: Harper.

Glasgow, D.

1979 *The Black Underclass*. San Francisco: Jossey-Bass.

Glick, P., and K. Mills

1974 "Black Families: Marriage Patterns and Living Arrangements." Paper presented at the W.E.B. DuBois Conference on American Blacks, Atlanta.

Goode, W.

1963 *World Revolution and Changing Family Patterns*. Glencoe, Ill.: The Free Press.

Guttentag, M., and P. Secord

1983 *Too Many Women: The Sex Ratio Question*. Beverly Hills, Calif.: Sage.

Hale, J.

1983 *Black Children*. Provo, Utah: Brigham University Press.

Hampton, R.

1980 "Institutional Decimation, Marital Exchange and Disruption in Black Families." *Western Journal of Black Studies* 4 (Summer):132–139.

Heer, D.

1974 "The Prevalence of Black-White Marriages in the United States 1960 and 1970." *Journal of Marriage and the Family* 35 (February):246–258.

Hershey, M.

1978 "Racial Differences in Sex Role Identities and Sex Stereotyping: Evidence against a Common Assumption." *Social Science Quarterly* 58 (March):583–596.

Hill, R.

1972   *The Strengths of Black Families*. New York: Emerson Hall.

Homans, G.

1961   *Social Behavior: Its Elementary Forms*. New York: Harcourt, Brace and World.

Joe, T., and P. Yu

1984   *The "Flip-Side" of Black Families Headed by Women: The Economic Status of Black Men*. Washington, D.C.: The Center for the Study of Social Policy.

Kinsey, A., W. Pomeroy, and C. Martin

1948   *Sexual Behavior in the Human Male*. Philadelphia: W. B. Saunders.

Kulesky, W., and A. Obordo

1972   "A Racial Comparison of Teenage Girls' Projections for Marriage and Procreation." *Journal of Marriage and the Family* 34 (February):75–84.

Malabre, A., Jr.

1980   "Recession Hits Blacks Harder than Whites." *The Wall Street Journal* (August 21):1.

Moynihan, D. P.

1965   *The Negro Family: The Case for National Action*. Washington, D.C.: U.S. Government Printing Office.

National Center for Education Statistics

1983   *Participation of Black Students in Higher Education: A Statistical Profile from 1970–71 to 1980–81*. Washington, D.C.: U.S. Department of Education.

Noble, J.

1956   *The Negro Woman College Graduate*. New York: Columbia University Press.

Nolle, D.

1972   "Changes in Black Sons and Daughters: A Panel Analysis of Black Adolescents' Orientation toward Their Parents." *Journal of Marriage and the Family* 34 (August):443–447.

Parson, R., and R. Bales

1955   *Family, Socialization and Interaction Process*. Glencoe, Ill.: The Free Press.

Scanzoni, J.

1971   *The Black Family in Modern Society*. Boston: Allyn & Bacon.

Spanier, G., and P. Glick

1980   "Mate Selection Differentials between Blacks and Whites in the United States." *Social Forces* 58 (March):707–725.

Staples, R.

1973   *The Black Woman in America: Sex, Marriage and the Family*. Chicago: Nelson-Hall.

1981   *The World of Black Singles: Changing Patterns of Male-Female Relations*. Westport, Conn.: Greenwood Press.

1982   *Black Masculinity: The Black Male's Role in American Society*. San Francisco: The Black Scholar Press.

Stewart, J., and J. Scott

1978   "The Institutional Decimation of Black Males." Western Journal of Black Studies 2 (Summer):82–92.

Thibaut, J. W., and H. W. Kelley

1959   *The Social Psychology of Groups*. New York: John Wiley.

U.S. Bureau of the Census

1978   Current Population Reports. March 1977, Series P-20, No. 314. Washington, D.C.: U.S. Government Printing Office.

1983   *America's Black Population, 1970 to 1982: A Statistical View*. July 1983, Series P10/POP83. Washington, D.C.: U.S. Government Printing Office.

U.S. Dept. of Health, Education and Welfare

1979   *Health Status of Minorities and Low-Income Groups*. Washington, D.C.: Government Printing Office.

Zelnik, M., and J. F. Kantner

1974   "The Resolution of Teenage First Pregnancies." *Family Planning Perspectives* (Spring):74–80.

2 / Historical Background

THE MYTH OF THE ABSENT FAMILY

Eugene D. Genovese

This article examines some common myths about the Black family during the period of slavery. Genovese finds that despite considerable constraints on their ability to carry out normative family roles and functions, the bondsmen created impressive norms of family life and entered the post-emancipation era with a strong respect for the family and a comparatively stable family base.

The recent controversy over the ill-fated Moynihan Report has brought the question of the black family in general and the slave family in particular into full review. Largely following the pioneering work of E. Franklin Frazier, the report summarized the conventional wisdom according to which slavery had emasculated black men, created a matriarchy, and prevented the emergence of a strong sense of family.[1] Historians and sociologists, black and white, have been led astray in two ways. First, they have read the story of the twentieth-century black ghettos backward in time and have assumed a historical continuity with slavery days. Second, they have looked too closely at slave law and at the externals of family life and not closely enough at the actual temper of the quarters.

During the twentieth century blacks went north in great waves and faced enormous hardship. The women often could find work as domestics; the men found themselves shut out of employment not so much by their lack of skills as by fierce racial discrimination. Some disorientation of the black family apparently followed; evaluation of its extent and social content must be left to others who can get beyond simple statistical reports to an examination of the quality of life.[2] But those inclined to read the presumed present record back into the past have always had a special problem, for by any standard of judgment the southern rural black family, which remained closer to the antebellum experience, always appeared to be much stronger than the northern urban family.[3]

The evidence from the war years and Reconstruction, now emerging in more systematic studies than were previously available, long ago should have given us pause.[4] Every student of the Union occupation and early Reconstruction has known of the rush of the freedmen to legalize their marriages; of the widespread desertion of the plantations by whole families; of the demands by men and women for a division of labor that would send the women out of the fields and into the homes; of the militancy of parents seeking to keep their children from apprenticeship to whites even when it would have been to their economic advantage; and especially of the heart-rending effort of thousands of freedmen to find long-lost loved ones all over the South. These events were prefigured in antebellum times. Almost every study of runaway slaves uncovers the importance of the family motive: thousands of slaves ran away to find children, parents, wives, or husbands from whom they had been separated by sale. Next to resentment over punishment, the attempt to find relatives was the most prevalent cause of flight.[5]

These data demand a reassessment of slave family life as having had much greater power than generally believed. But a word of warning: the pressures on the family, as E. Franklin Frazier, W. E. B. DuBois, Kenneth M. Stampp, Stanley M. Elkins, and other scholars have pointed out, were extraordinary and took a terrible toll. My claims must be read within limits—as a record of the countervailing forces even within the slavocracy but especially within the slave community. I suggest only that the slaves created impressive norms of family life, including as much of a nuclear family norm as conditions permitted, and that they entered the postwar social system with a remarkably stable base. Many families became indifferent or demoralized, but those with a strong desire for family stability were able to set norms for life in freedom that could serve their own interests and function reasonably well within the wider social system of white-dominated America.

The masters understood the strength of the marital and family ties among their slaves well enough to see in them a powerful means of social control. As a Dutch slaveholder wrote from Louisiana in the 1750s: "It is necessary that the Negroes have wives, and you ought to know that nothing attaches them so much to a plantation as children."[6] No threat carried such force as a threat to sell the children, except the threat to separate husband and wife. The consequences for the children loomed large in the actions of their parents. When—to take an extreme example—a group of slaves planned a

mass suicide, concern for their children provided the ground for sober second thoughts.[7]

Evidence of the slaveholders' awareness of the importance of family to the slaves may be found in almost any well-kept set of plantation records. Masters and overseers normally listed their slaves by households and shaped disciplinary procedures to take full account of family relationships. The sale of a recalcitrant slave might be delayed or avoided because it would cause resentment among his family of normally good workers. Conversely, a slave might be sold as the only way to break his influence over valuable relatives.[8] Could whites possibly have missed the content of their slaves' marital relationships when faced with such incidents as the one reported by James W. Melvin, an overseer, to his employer, Audley Clark Britton?

> [Old Bill] breathed his last on Saturday the 31st, Jan. about 8-1/2 o'clock in the morning. He appeared prepared for Death and said he was going to heaven and wanted his wife to meet him there. When he took sick he told all it would be his last sickness—I was very sorry to lose him.[9]

The pretensions of racist propagandists that slaves did not value the marriage relation fell apart in the courts, which in a variety of ways wrestled with the problems caused by the lack of legal sanction for slave marriages. However much they insisted on treating the slaves' marriages as mere concubinage, they rarely if ever denied the moral content of the relationship or the common devotion of the parties to each other. Thus, Georgia and Texas illogically and humanely would not permit slave wives to testify against their husbands while continuing to insist that their relationship had no standing at law. The high courts of South Carolina and other states took a more consistent stand on the question of testimony but repeatedly acknowledged the painful problems caused by the lack of legal sanction for relationships everyone knew to be meaningful and worthy of respect.[10]

Many slaveholders went to impressive lengths to keep families together even at the price of considerable pecuniary loss, although, as Kenneth Stampp forcefully insists, the great majority of slaveholders chose business over sentiment and broke up families when under financial pressure. But the choice did not rest easy on their conscience. The kernel of truth in the notion that the slaveholders felt guilty about owning human beings resides largely in this issue. They did feel guilty about their inability to live up to their own paternalistic justification for slavery in the face of market pressure.[11]

The more paternalistic masters betrayed evidence of considerable emotional strain. In 1858, William Massie of Virginia, forced to decrease his debts, chose to sell a beloved and newly improved homestead rather than his slaves. "To know," he explained, "that my little family, white and *black*, [is] to be fixed permanently together would be as near that thing happiness as I ever expect to get. . . . Elizabeth has raised and taught most of them, and having no children, like every other woman under like circumstances, has tender feelings toward them."[12] An impressive number of slaveholders took losses they could ill afford in an effort to keep families together.[13] For the great families, from colonial times to the fall of the regime, the maintenance of family units was a matter of honor.[14] Foreign travelers not easily taken in by appearances testified to the lengths to which slaveholders went at auctions to compel the callous among them to keep family units together.[15] Finally, many ex-slaves testified about masters who steadfastly refused to separate families; who, if they could not avoid separations, sold the children within visiting distance of their parents; and who took losses to buy wives or husbands in order to prevent permanent separations.[16] Stampp's insistence that such evidence revealed the exception rather than the rule is probably true, although I think that exceptions occurred more frequently than he seems to allow for. But it does demonstrate how well the whites understood the strength of the slaves' family ties and the devastating consequences of their own brutal disregard of the sensibilities of those they were selling.

Masters could not afford to be wholly indifferent to slave sensibilities. "Who buys me must buy my son too," a slave defiantly shouted from an auction block. Better to buy in Virginia than Louisiana, wrote J. W. Metcalfe to St. John R. Liddell, for we stand a better chance of buying whole families, whose attachments will make them better and less

troublesome workers. Enough slaves risked severe punishment in demanding that their families be kept intact to make masters thoughtful of their own self-interest.[17] So far as circumstances permitted, the slaves tried to stay close to brothers and sisters, aunts and uncles.[18] A woman with a husband who struck her too freely might turn to her brother for protection. A widowed or abandoned aunt could expect to live in a cabin with an affectionate niece and her husband. An old slave without spouse or children could expect attention and comfort from nieces, nephews, and cousins when facing illness and death.[19] Brothers looked after their sisters or at least tried to. An overseer killed a slave girl in Kentucky and paid with his own life at the hands of her brother, who then made a successful escape. In Virginia terrible whippings could not prevent a young man from sneaking off to visit a cherished sister on another plantation.[20]

The more humane masters took full account of their slaves' affection for and sense of responsibility toward relatives. Charles West wrote to the Reverend John Jones of Georgia to ask if a certain Clarissa was alive and about, for her sister, Hannah, in Alabama wanted to visit her during the summer. Dr. Bradford, a slaveholder in Florida, hired out three sisters at a lower price than he could have gotten because he would not separate them even for a year.[21] Few slaveholders took such pains to respect the strong ties of brothers and sisters, but fewer still could claim as excuse that they did not have evidence of the slaves' feelings. Three-quarters of a century after slavery, Anne Harris of Virginia, at age ninety-two, told her interviewer that no white person had ever set foot in her house.

> *Don't 'low it. Dey sole my sister Kate. I saw it wid dese here eyes. Sole her in 1860, and I ain't seed nor heard of her since. Folks say white folks is all right dese days. Maybe dey is, maybe dey isn't. But I can't stand to see 'em. Not on my place.*[22]

In the late antebellum period several states moved to forbid the sale of children away from their mother, but only Louisiana's law appears to have been effective. At that, Governor Hammond of South Carolina had the audacity to argue that the slaveholders deserved credit for efforts to hold slave families together and that the slaves themselves cared little.[23]

Masters not only saw the bonds between husbands and wives, parents and children, they saw the bonds between nieces and nephews and aunts and uncles and especially between brothers and sisters. Nowhere did the slaveholders' willful blindness, not to say hypocrisy, concerning the strength of their slaves' family ties appear so baldly as in their reaction to separations attendant upon sales. They told themselves and anyone who would listen that husbands and wives, despite momentary distress, did not mind separations and would quickly adjust to new mates. Not content with this fabrication, some slaveholders went so far as to assert that separation of mothers from children caused only minimal hardship. Most slaveholders knew this claim to be nonsense, but they nevertheless argued that the separation of fathers from their children was of little consequence.

From time to time a slave did prefer to stay with a good master or mistress rather than follow a spouse who was being sold away. In these cases and in many others in which slaves displayed indifference, the marriage had probably already been weakened, and sale provided the most convenient and painless form of divorce. Such incidents reveal nothing about the depth of grief aroused by the sale of cherished wives and husbands. The slaveholders knew that many slave marriages rested on solid foundations of affection. Slaves on all except the most entrenched and stable plantations lived in constant fear of such separations and steeled themselves against them. When the blow came, the slaves often took it with outward calm. A discernible decline in a master's fortune or growing trouble with the overseer or master might have given warning of what was coming. If the slaves suffered quietly and cried alone, their masters had an excuse to declare them indifferent.

No such excuses, frail as they were, could explain the slaveholders' frequent assertions that mothers and children adjusted easily to separations. The slaveholders saw the depth of the anguish constantly, and only the most crass tried to deny it. John A. Quitman said that he had witnessed the separation of a family only once. It was enough: "I never saw such profound grief as the poor creatures manifested." Mary Boykin Chesnut remarked to a visiting Englishwoman as they passed a slave auction, "If you can stand that, no other Southern thing need choke you."[24]

John S. Wise's testimony may stand for many others. An apologist who put the best face he could on the old regime, he described an auction in which a crippled man of limited use was in danger of being separated from his wife and children. Israel, the man, spoke up in his own behalf:

> *"Yes, sir, I kin do as much ez ennybody; and marsters, ef you'll only buy me and de chillum with Martha Ann, Gord knows I'll wuk myself to deth for you." The poor little darkeys, Cephas and Melinda, sat there frightened and silent, their white eyes dancing like monkey-eyes, and gleaming in the shadows. As her husband's voice broke on her ear, Martha Ann, who had been looking sadly out of the window in a pose of quiet dignity, turned her face with an expression of exquisite love and gratitude towards Israel. She gazed for a moment at her husband and at her children, and then looked away once more, her eyes brimming with tears.*[25]

Wise's story—of course—ended happily when a slaveholder accepted a loss he could not easily afford in order to buy the family as a unit. But Wise, a man of the world, had to know, as Brecht later reminded us, "In real life, the ending is not so fine/ Victoria's Messenger does not come riding often."

John Randolph of Roanoke, a slaveholder himself, who had known Patrick Henry, Henry Clay, and all the great political orators of the day and who himself ranked at the top, was asked whom he thought to have pride of place. "The greatest orator I ever heard," he replied, "was a woman. She was a slave and a mother and her rostrum was an auction block."[26]

All except the most dehumanized slaveholders knew of the attachments that the slaves had to their more extended families, to their friends, and to most of those who made up their little communities and called each other "brother" and "sister." Kate Stone wrote in 1862: "Separating the old family

Negroes who have lived and worked together for so many years is a great grief to them and a distress to us."[27] Those who pretended that the separations came easy never explained why so many ruses had to be used to keep men and women occupied while one or another of their children was being whisked off. Robert Applegarth, an Englishman, described a common scene in which slaves suffered threats and punishments at auctions in response to their wailing and pleading to be kept together.[28] So well did the slaveholders understand the strength of these family ties that the more humane among them found it useful to argue against separations on the grounds of economic expediency by pointing out that the slaves worked much better when kept together.[29]

The extent of separation of wives from husbands and children from parents will probably remain in dispute. The impressive econometric work by Robert Fogel and Stanley Engerman suggests that separations occurred less frequently than has generally been believed, but the data do not permit precise measurement.[30] The nostalgic son of an antebellum planter did not fear contradiction when he recalled long after emancipation: "Were families separated by sale, etc.? Yes, quite often."[31] The potential for forced separation—whatever the ultimate measure of its realization—struck fear into the quarters, especially in the slave-exporting states of the Upper South. If the rich and powerful Pierce Butler of the Sea Islands had to sell hundreds of slaves to cover debts in the 1850s, was anyone safe? Even planters willing to take financial losses to keep families intact could not always control events. Once slaves passed out of the hands of their old masters, their fate depended upon the willingness of professional traders to honor commitments to keep families together or upon the attitude of new masters. And many masters did not respect their slaves' family feelings and did not hesitate to sell them as individuals.

Frederick Douglass referred to "that painful uncertainty which in one form or another was ever obtruding itself in the pathway of the slave."[32] Perhaps no single hardship or danger, not even the ever-present whip, struck such terror into the slaves and accounted for so much of that "fatalism" often attributed to them. If the spirit of many did crack and if many did become numb, nothing weighs so heavily among the reasons as the constant fear of losing loved ones. In the weakest slaves it instilled reckless irresponsibility and a fear of risking attachments—of feeling anything—and in the strongest, a heroic stoicism in the face of unbearable pain. A majority of the slaves probably suffered from some effects of these fears, but their vibrant love of life and of each other checked the slide into despair.

But the pain remained, and the slaveholders knew as much. Is it possible that no slaveholder noticed the grief of the woman who told Fredrika Bremer that she had had six children, three of whom had died and three of whom had been sold: "When they took from me the last little girl, oh, I believed I never should have got over it! It almost broke my heart!"[33] Could any white southerner pretend not to know from direct observation the meaning of Sojourner Truth's statement: "I have borne thirteen chillun and seen 'em mos' all sold off into slavery, and when I cried out with a mother's grief, none but Jesus heard. . . ."[34] Whatever the whites admitted to others or even themselves, they knew what they wrought. And the slaves knew that they knew. A black woman, speaking to Lucy Chase, recalled her first husband's being sold away from her: "White folks got a heap to answer for the way they've done to colored folks! So much they won't never pray it away!"[35]

---

[1] *Lee Rainwater and William L. Yancey,* The Moynihan Report and the Politics of Controversy *(Cambridge, Mass., 1967), which includes the text of the report; Frazier,* Negro in the United States *and* Negro Family; *Elkins,* Slavery.

[2] *For a brief general critique of prevailing notions of family disorganization see Charles V. Willie, "The Black Family in America,"* Dissent, *Feb., 1971, pp. 80–83. The specialized literature is growing rapidly. For one of the most careful and responsible of*

the older studies see Drake and Cayton, Black Metropolis, *II, 582–583.*

[3] *See, e.g., Myrdal,* American Dilemma, *p. 935; Jessie Bernard,* Marriage and Family among Negroes *(Englewood Cliffs, N.J., 1966), p. 21; Powdermaker,* After Freedom, *p. 143.*

[4] *See esp. Peter Kolchin,* First Freedom: The Responses of Alabama's Blacks to Emancipation and Reconstruction *(Westport, Conn., 1972), Ch. 3.; Herbert G. Gutman, "Le Phénomène in-*

visible: La Composition de la famille et du foyer noirs après la Guerre de Sécession," Annales: Économies, Sociétés, Civilisations, XXVII (July–Oct., 1972), 1197–1218. Of special interest in these studies are the data from marriage certificates in the Union archives, which show an impressive number of cases in which slaves had lived together for ten years and longer, sometimes much longer.

[5]Mullin, Flight and Rebellion, p. 109; Sydnor, Slavery in Mississippi, p. 103; Bancroft, Slave Trading, p. 206.

[6]Quoted in M. Le Page Du Pratz, History of Louisiana or of the Western Parts of Virginia and Carolina (London, 1924), p. 365.

[7]WPA, Negro in Virginia, p. 74; Fisk University, Unwritten History of Slavery, p. 136.

[8]See, e.g., Agnew Diary, Aug. 19, 1862 (II, 124a–124b); Sitterson, Sugar Country, pp. 103–104; the correspondence of Charles C. Jones, Jr., and C. C. Jones, Oct., 1856, in Myers, ed., Children of Pride.

[9]James W. Melvin to A. C. Britton, Feb. 11, 1863, in the Britton Papers.

[10]Catterall, ed., Judicial Cases, I, passim; III, 89–90, 160; V, 182; also C. P. Patterson, Negro in Tennessee, pp. 57, 154.

[11]Kenneth Stampp, having studied the wills of a large number of slaveholders, concludes that the financial return to the heirs constitutes the overriding consideration; see Peculiar Institution, p. 204. But see also J. B. Sellers, Slavery in Alabama, p. 168, for a somewhat different reading.

[12]Quoted in Phillips, Life and Labor, p. 243.

[13]For some evidence of masters who went to great lengths to keep the families of even recalcitrant slaves together, or who took financial losses to avoid separations, see the Witherspoon–McDowall Correspondence for 1852; Richard Whitaker to A. H. Boykin, Nov. 17, 1843, in the Boykin Papers; J. B. Hawkins to Charles Alston, Nov. 28, 1847, in the Alston Papers; William Otey to Octavia A. Otey, Nov. 20, 1855, in the Wyche–Otey Papers; Ernest Haywood Correspondence, 1856–1857; Lewis Stirling to his son, Jan. 10, 1843; Henry A. Tayloe to B. O. Tayloe, Jan. 5, 1835; Correspondence of Joseph Bryan of Savannah, Ga., a slave trader, in the Slave Papers, Library of Congress; Gavin Diary, July 2, 1857; George W. Clement to Capt. John P. Wright, Oct. 28, 1849, in the Pocket Plantation Record. For evidence and analyses in secondary works see esp. R. H. Taylor, Slaveholding in North Carolina, p. 85; Phillips, Life and Labor, pp. 274–275; McColley, Slavery and Jeffersonian Virginia, pp. 66–68.

[14]See, e.g., Morton, Robert Carter of Nomini Hall, p. 111; Joseph Clay to Edward Telfair, Dec. 6, 1785, in the Telfair Papers; Heyward, Seed from Madagascar, p. 88; W. T. Jordan, Hugh Davis, passim; Myers, ed., Children of Pride, passim; John Lynch to Ralph Smith, Oct. 13, 1826, in Pocket Plantation Record; J. B. Grimball Diary, June 20, 1835, Jan. 11, 1860, July 17, 1863; C. C. Mercer to John and William Mercer, July 28, 1860; wills dated Dec. 12, 1849, July 9, 1857, Feb. 2, 1862, in the Lawton Papers; A.G.G. to Thomas W. Harriss, Oct. 28, 1848, in the Harriss Papers; Gavin Diary, Sept. 9, 1856; William McKean to James Dunlop, April 4, 1812, in the McKean Letterbook; Eaton, Henry

Clay, pp. 120–121; John Kirkland to his son, Sept. 15, 1858, in the Wyche–Otey Papers.

[15]See, e.g., Lyell, Second Visit, I, 209–210; Stirling, Letters from the Slave States, p. 260.

[16]Fisk University, Unwritten History of Slavery, pp. 1, 33: Rawick, ed.,S. C. Narr., II (1), 206; III (3), 2; Texas Narr., IV (2), 110; Indiana Narr., VI (2), 10; George Teamoh Journal, Pts. 1–2, p. 31, in the Woodson Papers.

[17]Schoepf, Travels in the Confederation, II, 148; Metcalfe to Liddell, June 24, 1848, in the Liddell Papers. Also Charles M. Manigault to Louis Manigault, Jan. 8, 1857; John W. Pittman invoice and note, in the Slave Papers, Library of Congress.

[18]In general see Rawick, Sundown to Sunup, p. 90.

[19]For illustrations of each of these cases see Fisk University, Unwritten History of Slavery, pp. 140, 143; Phillips, Life and Labor, p. 270; Henry [the Driver] to William S. Pettigrew, July 1, 1857, in the Pettigrew Papers; Eliza G. Roberts to Mrs. C. C. Jones, May 20, 1861, and Mary Jones to Mary S. Mallard, Nov. 7, 1865, in Myers, ed., Children of Pride.

[20]Rawick, ed., Kansas Narr., XVI, 71; Ohio Narr., XVI, 12.

[21]Charles West to John Jones, July 23, 1855, in the John Jones Papers; Chatham, "Plantation Slavery in Middle Florida," unpubl. M.A. thesis, University of North Carolina, 1938, p. 80. See also Father Henson's Story of His Own Life, pp. 147–148, 157; Fisk University, Unwritten History of Slavery, p. 78.

[22]WPA, Negro in Virginia, p. 34.

[23]DBR, VIII (Feb., 1850), 122. For a discussion of the state laws designed to protect families from separation see Bancroft, Slave Trading, pp. 197–199.

[24]Quitman as quoted in Bancroft, Slave Trading, p. 308; Chesnut, Diary from Dixie, p. 18.

[25]Wise, End of an Era, p. 84; also pp. 85–86.

[26]As quoted by R. E. Park in his introduction to Doyle, Etiquette of Race Relations, p. xxvii.

[27]Kate Stone, Brokenburn, p. 84. Or see the remarks of the court in Nowell v. O'Hara (S.C.), 1833, in Catterall, ed., Judicial Cases, II, 352.

[28]See Applegarth's statement in the Slave Papers, Library of Congress.

[29]See, e.g., Judge DeSaussure of South Carolina in Gayle v. Cunningham, 1846, in Catterall, ed., Judicial Cases, II, 314; or Judge Slidell of Louisiana in Bertrand v. Arcueil, Ibid., III, 599–600.

[30]Fogel and Engerman, Time on the Cross, pp. 126–144. See also the suggestive article by William Calderhead, "How Extensive Was the Border State Slave Trade: A New Look," CWH, XVIII (March, 1972), 42–55.

[31]J. A. McKinstry to H. C. Nixon, Feb. 11, 1913, in Correspondence: Slavery, Tennessee State Library and Archives. In general see Bancroft, Slave Trading, esp. Chs. 2 and 10.

[32]Life and Times of Frederick Douglass, p. 96.

[33]Bremer, Homes of the New World, II, 93.

[34]Quoted in Du Bois, Gift of Black Folk, p. 143.

[35]Swint, ed., Dear Ones at Home, p. 124.

SLAVERY IN CAPITALIST AND NONCAPITALIST CULTURES

Stanley M. Elkins

In this article, Elkins shows that the position of the slave in this society was precarious at best. The position of the slave family in the United States, according to Elkins, was based on the market economy of slavery, in contrast to other societies, notably Brazil.

The four major legal categories which defined the status of the American slave may be roughly classified as "term of servitude," "marriage and the family," "police and disciplinary powers over the slave," and "property and other civil rights." The first of these, from which somehow all the others flowed, had in effect been established during the latter half of the seventeenth century; a slave was a slave for the duration of his life, and slavery was a status which he transmitted by inheritance to his children and his children's children.

It would be fairest, for several reasons, to view the remaining three categories in terms of the jurisprudence of the nineteenth century. By that time the most savage aspects of slavery from the standpoint of Southern practice (and thus, to a certain extent, of law) had become greatly softened. We may accordingly see it in its most humane light and at the same time note the clarity with which its basic outlines remained fixed and embodied in law, much as they had been laid down before the middle of the eighteenth century.

That most ancient and intimate of institutional arrangements, marriage and the family, had long since been destroyed by the law, and the law never showed any inclination to rehabilitate it. Here was

the area in which considerations of humanity might be expected most widely to prevail, and, indeed, there is every reason to suppose that on an informal daily basis they did: the contempt in which respectable society held the slave trader, who separated mother from child and husband from wife, is proverbial in Southern lore. On the face of things, it ought to have been simple enough to translate this strong social sentiment into the appropriate legal enactments, which might systematically have guaranteed the inviolability of the family and the sanctity of the marriage bond, such as governed Christian polity everywhere. Yet the very nature of the plantation economy and the way in which the basic arrangements of Southern life radiated from it made it inconceivable that the law should tolerate any ambiguity, should the painful clash between humanity and property interest ever occur. Any restrictions on the separate sale of slaves would have been reflected immediately in the market; their price would have dropped considerably. Thus the law could permit no aspect of the slave's conjugal state to have an independent legal existence outside the power of the man who owned him: "The relation of master and slave is wholly incompatible with even the qualified relation of husband and wife, as it is supposed to exist among slaves."[1] Marriage, for them, was denied any standing in law. Accordingly, as T. R. R. Cobb of Georgia admitted, "The contract of marriage not being recognized among slaves, none of its consequences follow."[2] "The relation between slaves," wrote a North Carolina judge in 1858, "is essentially different from that of man and

---

From *Slavery: A Problem in American Institutional and Intellectual Life* (Chicago: University of Chicago Press, 1968), pp. 52–55 and 72–74. Copyright © 1968, The University of Chicago. Reprinted by permission. Footnotes have been renumbered.

wife joined in lawful wedlock . . . [for] with slaves it may be dissolved at the pleasure of either party, or by the sale of one or both, depending on the caprice or necessity of the owners."[3]

It would thus go without saying that the offspring of such "contubernial relationships," as they were called, had next to no guarantees against indiscriminate separation from their parents.[4] Of additional interest is the fact that children derived their condition from that of their mother. This was not unique to American slavery, but it should be noted that especially in a system conceived and evolved exclusively on grounds of property there could be little doubt about how such a question would be resolved. Had status been defined according to the father's condition—as was briefly the case in seventeenth-century Maryland, following the ancient common law—there would instantly have arisen the irksome question of what to do with the numerous mulatto children born every year of white planter-fathers and slave mothers. It would have meant the creation of a free mulatto class, automatically relieving the master of so many slaves on the one hand, while burdening him on the other with that many colored children whom he could not own. Such equivocal relationships were never permitted to vex the law. That "the father of a slave is unknown to our law" was the universal understanding of Southern Jurists.[5] It was thus that a father, among slaves, was legally "unknown," a husband without the rights of his bed,[6] the state of marriage defined as "only that concubinage . . . with which alone, perhaps, their condition is compatible,"[7] and motherhood clothed in the scanty dignity of the breeding function. . . .[8]

Neither in Brazil nor in Spanish America did slavery carry with it such precise and irrevocable categories of perpetual servitude, "durante vita" and "for all generations," as in the United States. The presumption in these countries, should the status of a colored person be in doubt, was that he was free rather than a slave.[9] There were in fact innumerable ways whereby a slave's servitude could be brought to an end. The chief of these was the very considerable fact that he might buy his own freedom. The Negro in Cuba or Mexico had the right to have his price declared and could, if he wished, purchase himself in installments. Slaves escaping to Cuba to embrace Catholicism were protected by a special royal order of 1733 which was twice reissued. A slave unduly punished might be set at liberty by the magistrate. In Brazil the slave who was the parent of ten children might legally demand his or her freedom.[10] The medieval Spanish code had made a slave's service terminable under any number of contingencies—if he denounced cases of treason, murder, counterfeiting, or the rape of a virgin, or if he performed various other kinds of meritorious acts. Though all such practices did not find their way into the seventeenth- and eighteenth-century legal arrangements of Latin America, much of their spirit was perpetuated in the values, customs, and social expectations of that later period. It is important to appreciate the high social approval connected with the freeing of slaves. A great variety of happy family events—the birth of a son, the marriage of a daughter, anniversaries, national holidays—provided the occasion, and their ceremonial was frequently marked by the manumission of one or more virtuous servitors. It was considered a pious act to accept the responsibility of becoming godfather to a slave child, implying the moral obligation to arrange eventually for its freedom. Indeed, in Cuba and Brazil such freedom might be purchased for a nominal sum at the baptismal font.[11] All such manumissions had the strong approval of both church and state and were registered gratis by the government.[12]

In extending its moral authority over men of every condition, the church naturally insisted on bringing slave unions under the holy sacraments. Slaves were married in church and the banns published; marriage was a sacred rite and its sanctity protected in law. In the otherwise circumspect United States, the only category which the law could apply to conjugal relations between slaves—or to unions between master and slave—was concubinage. But concubinage, in Latin America, was condemned as licentious, adulterous, and immoral; safeguards against promiscuity were provided in the law,[13] and in Brazil the Jesuits labored mightily to regularize the libertinage of the master class by the sacrament of Christian marriage.[14] Moreover, slaves owned by different masters were not to be hindered from marrying, nor could they be kept separate after marriage. If the estates were distant, the wife was to go with her husband, and a fair price was to be fixed by impartial persons for her sale to the husband's master.[15] A slave might, without legal interference, marry a free person. The children of such a marriage, if the mother were free, were themselves free, inasmuch as children followed the condition of their mother.[16]

---

[1]Howard v. Howard, 6 Jones N.C. 235 (December, 1858), quoted in Helen T. Catterall, Judicial Cases Concerning American Slavery and the Negro (Washington: Carnegie Institution, 1926 ff.), II, 221.

[2]Thomas R. R. Cobb, An Inquiry into the Law of Slavery in the United States of America (Philadelphia: T. & J. W. Johnson, 1858), p. 246.

[3]Quoted in Catterall, Judicial Cases, II, 221.

[4]The few exceptions—none of which meant very much in practice, except perhaps the law of Louisiana—are discussed in Bancroft, Slave-trading, pp. 197–221. "Louisiana, least American of the southern States," writes Mr. Bancroft, "was least inhuman. In becoming Americanized it lost many a liberal feature of the old French code noir, but it forbade sale of mothers from their children less than ten years of age (and vice versa) and bringing into the State any slave child under ten years of age without its mother, if living. The penalty for violating either prohibition was from $1,000 to $2,000 and the forfeiture of the slave. That would have meant much if it had been strictly enforced" (p. 197). Louisiana's Spanish and French background, plus the fact that in both the legal and social senses slavery in Latin America generally was very different from slavery in North America, may furnish significant clues to some of the idiosyncrasies in the Louisiana code. See below.

[5]Frazier v. Spear, 2 Bibb (Ken.), 385 (Fall, 1811), quoted in Catterall, Judicial Cases, I, 287.

[6]"A slave has never maintained an action against the violator of his bed. A slave is not admonished for incontinence, or punished for fornication or adultery; never prosecuted for bigamy, or petty treason for killing a husband being a slave, any more than admitted to an appeal for murder." Opinion of Daniel Dulany, Esq., The American Slave Code in Theory and Practice (New York: American and Foreign Anti-Slavery Society, 1853), pp. 106–107.

[7]State v. Samuel (a slave), 2 Dev. and Bat. (N.C.), 177 (December, 1836), quoted in Catterall, Judicial Cases, II, 77.

[8]The picturesque charge that planters deliberately "bred" their slave women has never been substantiated, and Avery Craven's point that white women bred about as young and as often as their black sisters is a sensible one. But with no law to prevent the separation of parents and children, and with the value of a slave being much in excess of what it cost to rear him, the temptation to think and talk about a prolific Negro woman as a "rattlin' good breeder" was very strong.

[9]"In the Cuban market freedom was the only commodity which could be bought untaxed; every negro against whom no one had proved a claim of servitude was deemed free." William Law Mathieson, British Slavery and Its Abolition (London: Longmans, Green, 1926), pp. 37–38.

[10]Johnston, Negro in the New World, p. 89.

[11]What I have said in this paragraph is virtually a paraphrase of the information which Mr. Tannenbaum has collected and so skillfully summarized on pp. 50, 53–54, 57–58 of Slave and Citizen.

[12]Johnston, Negro in the New World, p. 42.

[13]"The master of slaves must not allow the unlawful intercourse of the two sexes, but must encourage matrimony." Spanish slave code of 1789, quoted in ibid., p. 44. Although slaves were allowed "to divert themselves innocently" on holy days, the males were to be kept apart from the females. Ibid., p. 44.

[14]Freyre, The Masters and the Slaves, p. 85.

[15]Johnston, Negro in the New World, pp. 44–45. A diocesan synod of 1680 in Cuba issued weighty regulations on this subject which were supposed to supplement and have equal force with civil law. "Constitution 5 established that 'marriage should be free' and ordered that 'no master prohibit his slaves from marriage, nor impede those who cohabit therein, because we have found that many masters with little fear of God and in grave danger of their consciences, proscribe their slaves from marrying or impede their cohabitation with their married partners, with feigned pretexts'; and also prohibited 'that they go away to sell them outside the city, without that they take together husband and wife.'" Ortiz, Los Negros Esclavos, p. 349. The church even made some concessions here to African tribal marriage arrangements, to the extent that a slave with multiple wives might—if the first-married wife's identity could not be ascertained—pick out the one he preferred and have his marriage with her solemnized under the sacraments. Ibid., p. 349.

[16]Tannenbaum, Slave and Citizen, p. 56.

PART TWO

The Dyad

Dating and Sexual Patterns

Each unit of the family begins as a dyad, usually two members of the opposite sex who occupy a range of roles based on the stage of their relationship. Historically, the first stage in the process of forming a family has been dating and courtship. Changes in attitudes toward the family have brought about variations in the practice of these behaviors. Among the most marked changes in the dating and courtship system are the differing characteristics of its participants, the changing purpose of dating, and variations in its form. Dating, for instance, now involves not only the very young; the increasing numbers of individuals who remain unmarried until fairly advanced ages means that a dating partner could as easily be 38 as 18. Spiraling divorce and low remarriage rates create another large pool of dating partners. Dating has also become time contained, often existing only for the moment for sexual or recreational purposes, and is no longer automatically presumed to be a prelude to courtship or marriage. Even the concept of dating has been modified as men and women get together without making formal arrangements for an evening out in a public setting.

Much of this description is relevant to the white middle class, which has developed a new ideology about the nature and content of the dating system. There are limitations to the generalizations we can make about Black dating because there is less literature on the subject. The practice of Black dating varies by region, epoch, and social class. In the past, when Blacks formed a small, cohesive community in the rural and urban South, what might be called dating behavior centered on the neighborhood, church, and school. In general it was a casual process where men and women met, formed emotional attachments, and later married. Most of the participants were members of larger social units whose members or reputation were generally known to the community. As Blacks moved into urban areas outside of the South, the anonymity of individuals in these settings modified dating patterns. The school and house party became centers for fraternizing between the sexes, particularly among the lower class. In the middle-class group, dating habits took on the characteristics of mainstream culture as they included more activities like movies, dances, or bowling.

Black sexuality is another area of Black family life neglected in the literature. This is particularly difficult to understand in light of the special role accorded to Blacks—that of a peculiarly desirable or essentially different sexual object. Yet, although we have witnessed a full-blown sexual revolution, at least in the media, a reliable study of Black sexuality is hard to find. Blacks rarely are included in the many studies on white sexual attitudes and behavior. The paucity of past research on Black sexuality makes it difficult to assess what, if any, changes have occurred as a result of the fundamental transformation of sexual attitudes and practices occurring among the general population.

We do know that historically Black sexuality differed from its white counterpart in a number of ways. This difference began with the African and European conceptions of the nature of human sexuality. While Europeans traditionally have viewed sex as inherently sinful, Africans have viewed it as a natural function that should be enjoyed. These contrasting views may suggest a dichotomy of permissiveness versus puritanism. However, within the African continent a wide range of sexual codes and practices coexisted, differing from the European sexual traditions in the secular basis for the code as well as in the belief that sex is a natural function for humans.

Slavery exercised another influence on Afro-American sexuality. Women in bondage, unlike their white counterparts, had no way to protect their sexual purity. This fact has led to the assumption that because Black women could not be accorded any respect for, or defense of, their sexual integrity, it failed to have any strong value for them. Although such an assumption might be logical, it ignores the existence of moral codes related to sex in the Black community that, while different from mainstream norms, do regulate sexual activity for both men and women.

The articles in this section give us some insight into the nature of Black dating and sexuality. In the article by Schulz we see the variety of behaviors exhibited by men who play the boyfriend role, which ranges from that of men who are attempting to exploit women for financial gain to that of others who form liaisons with single mothers and contribute to their economic maintenance. Such a wide spectrum of behavior in the boyfriend role illustrates the problems Black men have in reconciling their exploitative ethic with the impulse to love and take care of a woman. It also demonstrates how informal arrangements take care of the problems faced by women who are ostensibly raising children alone. Also included is a longitudinal study by West-

ney and her colleagues, which assesses the sexual maturation and sociosexual behaviors of a group of middle- and lower-income boys and girls. They found considerable variation in the stages of maturation by chronological age, which was more pronounced for girls. Genital development in boys was significantly related to their sexual behavior. The selection by Staples attempts to debunk some of the sexual stereotypes surrounding Black males. He cites some of the relevant studies of Black male sexual behavior and shows how sexuality is linked to societal definitions of masculinity. His conclusion is that the misuse of sexuality is confined to a small segment of lower-income Black males.

Sex Roles

In recent years the issue of sex roles and their definition has received much attention. The debate has centered on the issue of female subordination and male dominance and privilege, but Blacks have considerably different problems in terms of their sex role identities. They must first overcome certain disabilities based on racial membership, not gender affiliation. However, this does not mean that sex role identities within the Black community do not carry with them advantages and disadvantages. In many ways they do, but instead of fighting over the question of who is the poorest of the poor, Blacks must contend with the plaguing problems of an unemployment rate that is as high as 45 percent among Black men. Correlates of that central problem are the declining life expectancy rate of Black men and rises in drug abuse, suicide, crime, and educational failures. These facts do not warrant much support for a movement to equalize the condition of men and women in the Black community.

Along with the economic conditions that impinge on their role performance, Black men are saddled with a number of stereotypes that label them as irresponsible, criminalistic, hypersexual, and lacking in masculine traits. Some of these stereotypes become self-fulfilling prophecies because the structure of the dominant society prevents many Black men from achieving the goals of manhood. At the same time, the notion of the castrated Black male is largely a myth. While mainstream culture has deprived many Black men of the economic wherewithal for normal masculine functions, most of them function in such a way as to gain the respect of their mates, children, and communities.

Along with all the dynamic changes occurring in U.S. society are slow but perceptible alterations in the role of Black women. The implications of these changes are profound in light of the fact that women are central figures in the family life of Black people. Historically, the Black woman has been a bulwark of strength in the Black community. From the time of slavery onward, she has resisted the destructive forces she has encountered in American society. During the period of slavery she fought and survived the attacks on her dignity by the slave system, relinquished the passive role ascribed to members of her gender to ensure the survival of her people, and tolerated the culturally induced irresponsibility of her man in recognition of this country's relentless attempts to castrate him.

Too often the only result of her sacrifices and suffering has been the invidious and inaccurate labeling of her as a matriarch, a figure deserving respect but not love. The objective reality of the Black woman in America is that she occupies the lowest rung of the socioeconomic ladder of all sex–race groups and has the least prestige. The double burden of gender and race has put her in the category of a super-oppressed entity. Considering the opprobrium to which she is subjected, one would expect her to be well represented in the woman's liberation movement. Yet that movement remains primarily white and middle class. This is due in part to the class-bound character of the women's movement, which is middle class while most Black women are poor or working class. Their low profile in that movement also stems from the fact that many of the objectives of white feminists relate to psychological and cultural factors such as language and sexist behavior, while the Black woman's concerns are economic.

There is a common ground on which Black and women can and do meet: on issues like equal pay for equal work, child care facilities, and female parity in the work force. Instead of joining the predominantly white and middle-class women's movement, many Black women have formed their own organizations such as the Welfare Rights Organization, Black Women Organized for Action, and the Black Feminist Alliance. There is little question that there is a heightened awareness among Black women of the problems they face based on their sex roles alone. Whether the struggle of Black women for equal rights will come in conflict with the movement for Black liberation remains to be seen. It is fairly clear that Black women have to be freed from the disabilities of both race and sex.

The selections in this section examine four dimensions of Black gender roles. Marable explores the historical forces that have shaped Black masculinity and the Black man's image in U.S. society. His interpretation of socioeconomic and political indicators suggests that the Black male is facing an unprecedented crisis today and must overcome his own inherent and deeply ingrained sexism. Franklin and Pillow report that the problems of Black men derive from their socialization into sexist values of male dominance without the societal support to help them approximate the ideal that their white counterparts have. The paper by Collier-Watson and Williams illustrates that while men gain in some areas, they lose in others. Being male may carry with it certain prestige and privileges, but men have lower rates of survival and higher rates of suicide, mental illness, incarceration, and other negative correlates of masculinity. White women have the best survival rates, whereas Black men have the lowest. The paper by Stack illustrates how Black women form an extensive network of friends and kin to overcome some of the problems of poverty and of rearing children alone. Through the use of the network, poor women are able to draw on a number of economic and psychological resources and to adapt to their situation collectively.

Male/Female Relationships

Relationships between Black men and Black women have had a peculiar evolution. Unlike the white family, which was a patriarchy and was sustained by the economic dependence of women, the Black dyad in North America has been characterized by more equalitarian roles and economic parity. The system of slavery did not permit the Black male to assume the superordinate role in the family constellation because the female was not economically dependent on him. Hence relationships between the sexes were based on sociopsychological factors rather than on economic compulsion to marry and remain married. This fact, in part, explains the unique trajectory of Black male/female relationships.

Finding and keeping a mate is complicated by a number of sociopsychological factors as well as structural restraints. Social structure and individual attitudes interface to make male/female relationships ephemeral rather than permanent. The imbalance in the sex ratio will continue to deny large numbers of professional Black women a comparable mate, and there are only a limited number of ways to deal with that irreversible fact of life. At the same time there exists a pool of professional Black males who are available to this group of women, and the tension between them builds barriers to communicating and mating. This is a complex problem and there is no easy solution.

Although there are some Black men who are threatened by the successful Black woman, further investigation reveals other underlying forces. Men are torn between the need for security and the desire for freedom, the quest for a special person to call their own and the temptation of sexual variety. They see marriage as a way of establishing roots but are seduced by the enticement of all the attractive, possibly "better," women in their midst. Given the advantage they have as males in a sexist society, and a high prestige (which is in short supply in the Black community), Black males have little incentive to undertake the actions needed to meet the needs of women. Consequently, women who feel that their emotional needs are not being met begin to recoil and to adopt their own agenda based on a concept of self-interest.

Some recognition must be made of the changing relations between men and women. The old exchange of feminine sexual appeal for male financial support is declining. Women increasingly are able to define their own status and to be economically independent. What they seek now is the satisfaction of emotional needs, not an economic cushion. While men must confront this new reality, women must realize that emotional needs can be

taken care of by men in all social classes. Although similar education and income can mean greater compatibility in values and interests, they are no guarantee of this compatibility nor of personal happiness. Common needs, interests, and values are more a function of gender than of class.

We should not be deluded by the ostensible reluctance of many Black singles to enter the conjugal state. People who have not been able to develop a lasting permanent relationship with a member of the opposite sex must make the best of whatever circumstances they have at the moment. The industrial and urban revolution has made singlehood more viable as a way of life, but it has also made the need for belonging more imperative. The tensions of work and the impersonality of the city have created a need to escape depersonalization by retreating into an intimate sanctum. This is especially imperative for Blacks in the middle class who have their personhood tested daily by a racist society and who often must work and live in isolation. In modern society individuals are required to depend on each other for permanence and stability. That function was previously served by a large familial and social network.

It is the fear that even marriage no longer provides permanence and stability that causes people to enter and exit relationships quickly. It is the fear of failure that comes from failure. Until Black singles develop the tenacity to work at relationships as they did at schooling and jobs, we will continue to see this vicious cycle repeated again and again. Marriage and the family continue to be the most important buffer for Blacks against racism and depersonalization. When we look at the strongest predictors of happiness in the United States, they are inevitably social factors such as marriage, family, friends, and children. Across the board, married people tend to be happier than unmarrieds. The best confirmation of this fact is that most people who divorce eventually remarry. Before people can find happiness in a marriage, they have to form a strong basis for marriage. That task continues to perplex Black singles.

The article by Staples describes the growing trend toward singlehood among Blacks in the United States. A majority of Black women over the age of eighteen are no longer married and living with a spouse. While the institutional decimation of Black males is the primary factor in this unprecedented number of singles, other sociocultural forces have an impact on the relationships between Black men and women. Staples discusses the changes in Black institutions and values as problems for Blacks in finding and keeping a mate. Franklin's paper traces the conflict between Black men and women to incompatible role enactments by the two sexes. The societal prescription that women are to be passive and men dominant is counteracted by Black women who resist Black men's dominance and Black men who wish to be accorded the superior male role but cannot fulfill the economic provider role, which supports the dominance of men in U.S. society.

Husbands and Wives

We are all aware that marriages are very fragile nowadays. Fewer people are getting married and the divorce rate in the United States is at an all-time high. It is estimated that the majority of marriages no longer will last a lifetime. Many forces are responsible for this changing pattern, including changing attitudes and laws on divorce, changing and conflicting definitions of sex roles and their functions in the family, economic problems, and personality conflicts. The increase in divorce cuts across racial and class lines, but divorce is still more pronounced among Blacks. Only one out of every three Black couples will remain married longer than ten years.

It is not easy to pinpoint unique causes of Black marital dissolution because they are similar to those for their white counterparts. In some cases it is the severity of the problems they face. Economic problems are a major factor in marital conflicts and there are three times as many Blacks with incomes below the poverty level as whites. The tensions Blacks experience in coping with the pervasive incidents of racism often have their ramifications in the marital arena. A peculiar problem Blacks face is the imbalanced sex ratio, which places many women in competition for the available males. Too often the males they compete for are not

available, and this places serious pressure on many Black marriages.

At the same time, many Blacks are involved in functional marriages. Many adult Blacks are married and have positive and loving relationships with their spouses. Unfortunately, practically no research exists on marital adjustment and satisfaction among Blacks. What little research we have does indicate that Black wives are generally less satisfied with their marriages than are white wives. But the source of their dissatisfaction is often associated with the problems of poverty and racism.

The 1970s witnessed a significant increase in interracial dating and marriage. Among the reasons for this change in Black/white dating and marriage was the desegregation of the public school system, the work force, and other social settings. In those integrated settings Blacks and whites met as equals, which facilitated heterogeneous matings. There were, of course, other factors such as the liberation of many white youth from parental control and the racist values conveyed to them.

Not only has the incidence of interracial relations increased but their character has also changed. In the 1960s, the most typical interracial pairing was a Black male and a white female, with the male partner generally of a higher status. This pattern was so common that social theorists even developed a theory of racial hypergamy. In essence, it was assumed that the high-status Black male was exchanging his socioeconomic status for the privilege of marrying a woman who belonged to a racial group that was considered superior to all members of the Black race. Contemporary interracial relations are much more likely to involve persons with similar educational backgrounds and occupational statuses.

Although no research studies have yet yielded any data on the subject, there appears to be a change in interracial unions toward a decline in Black male/white female couples and an increase in Black female/white male pairings. Several factors seem to account for this modification of the typical pattern. Many Black women are gravitating toward white men because of the shortage of Black males and their disenchantment with those to whom they have access. Similarly some white men are dissatisfied with white females and their increasingly vociferous demands for sex role parity. At the same time, there is a slight but noticeable decrease in Black male/white female unions. A possible reason is that these are no longer as fashionable as they were a few years ago. Also, much of the attraction of the members of both races to each other was based on the historic lack of access to each other and the stereotypes of Black men as superstuds and white women as forbidden fruit. Once there was extensive interaction the myths were exploded and the attraction consequently diminished.

It should be fairly clear that there are relatively normal reasons for interracial attractions and matings. At the same time it would be naive to assume that special factors are not behind them in a society that is stratified by race. Given the persistence of racism as a very pervasive force, many interracial marriages face rough sledding. In addition to the normal problems of working out a satisfactory marital relationship, interracial couples must cope with social ostracism and isolation. A recent phenomenon has been the increasing hostility toward such unions by the Black community, which has forced some interracial couples into a marginal existence. It is such pressures that cause the interracial marriage rate to remain at a very low level. Less than 5 percent of all marriages involving a Black person are interracial.

Lacking any solid research articles of recent vintage on Black marital dynamics, we have chosen an article by Spanier and Glick that describes the demographic variables involved in Black mate selection. Because of the male shortage, many Black women violate certain norms of mate selection that generally obtain when the sex ratio is equal. The report by the United States Civil Rights Commission cites statistical data revealing that many women in the United States are only a husband away from poverty. Ball's study indicates that formerly married Black women appear to adapt to the loss of their spouse and to enjoy levels of life satisfaction as high as those of married women. Apparently, "going it alone" for many Black women is as conducive to life satisfaction as is marriage.

3 / Dating and Sexual Patterns

THE ROLE OF THE BOYFRIEND IN LOWER-CLASS NEGRO LIFE

David A. Schulz

The author develops a typology of boyfriends based on the longevity of their liaisons and the extent of their economic support of the female partner. He shows that in these relationships the male is either contributing to the economic maintenance of the female partner or he is attempting to exploit her for economic gain.

The importance of the boyfriend's role becomes apparent when one realizes that four of the five women in this group who are now heading households receive support from boyfriends. The amount of support and the type of relationship that exists vary considerably and suggest a typology consisting of four different roles which a boyfriend may play and for which there is some support from segments of this population. These types are: the quasi-father, the supportive biological father, the supportive companion, and the pimp. The image of the pimp has dominated the literature thus far. In this relationship the male is largely exploitive.

However, there is also in the literature some evidence that these nonmarital liaisons between men and women of the Negro lower class are more

stable than is commonly acknowledged. In *Blackways of Kent*, Lewis mentions in passing that "gifts and some degree of support from the male are taken for granted and freely discussed. There is some informal ranking of men on a basis of the regularity and amount of gifts or support."[1] In this section fuller documentation of this support in nonmarital liaisons will be presented. In so doing, we hope to make it apparent that the lower-class Negro man contributes to the welfare of his woman more than is commonly acknowledged, and plays an important role of surrogate father to her children.

The Quasi-Father

The distinguishing marks of the quasi-father are that (1) he supports the family regularly over long periods of time (eleven years is the longest known, though this was interrupted by a short marriage; five years is the longest consecutive time known at present). Often he will go with his woman to the store and buy her week's food. (2) His concern extends directly to her children as well. He will give them allowances or spending money, attempt more or

From David A. Schulz, *Coming Up Black: Patterns of Ghetto Socialization*, pp. 136–144. © 1969. Reprinted by permission of Prentice-Hall, Inc., Englewood Cliffs, New Jersey.

less successfully to discipline them, and will take them out to the park, to the movies, or to other places for entertainment. (3) He frequently visits the family during the week, and may or may not reside with them in the project—usually not. The relationship is not ordinarily conducted clandestinely, but in full knowledge of kin on both sides— particularly the parents, if they reside in the same city with the couple. In return for this he receives (1) his meals (some or all if residing with the family); (2) washing and ironing; (3) sexual satisfaction; and (4) *familial companionship*. In short, he seems to be bargaining for more than just a woman in seeking intimacy in the context of a family. To illustrate let us take the example of Jay and Ethyl.

Ethyl Perry (thirty-three) went with Jay (twenty-four) for over five years. During that time he took her out, bought her the majority of her furniture, and supplied her with fifteen to twenty dollars per week, usually by means of buying her week's food. In addition his family contributed several pieces of furniture and invited Ethyl over for meals on occasion. None of her six children is his. Ethyl describes Jay as a "nice person . . . kind-hearted" and by this she means that ". . . he believes in survival for me and my family, me and my kids. He don't mind sharing with my youngsters. If I ask him for a helping hand, he don't seem to mind that. The only part of it is that I dislike his drinking." It's not the drinking as such that Ethyl dislikes, but the man Jay becomes when he drinks. He becomes angry and quick tempered, but has yet to beat Ethyl when in such a state.

Jay's concern for Ethyl's children is expressed in various ways. As Dovie, Ethyl's fifteen-year-old daughter, sees Jay, he tends to be bossy. "He be all right sometimes but he drinks and that's the reason I don't like him. . . . He tries to boss people. Like if my boyfriends come over here he be saying I can't have no company." But Mary, her eighteen-year-old daughter, revealed that Jay gave her a small washing machine for her baby's diapers. She said, "My mother's *boyfriend* bought it. . . . It was about three days after my baby was born."

Jay's concern is expressed in other ways as well. He took the children to the movies, to the park, gave them a small allowance as spending money each week when he bought the groceries,

and once, when Ethyl was sick, he took care of the youngest two for nearly a month while she was in the hospital. During the years that they were going together Jay visited the family several times a week, most frequently spending the weekend with them. He continually asked Ethyl to marry him, though Ethyl felt he was only half serious. Jay was asked why he bothered to take care of Ethyl and he replied, "That's a personal question. . . . Well, first of all I help her because I love her and we're going to get married sometime, but not just now because we can't afford it."

A second example is that of Tilly (thirty-three) and Sam (thirty-four—looks twenty-five). Tilly has been going with Sam for over eleven years—even while married to her second husband, whom she finally left for Sam. He helps the budget regularly out of his pay as a dock worker in a river barge yard. Tilly says, "Sam gives me thirty dollars a week." He has also bought several small pieces of furniture and takes her out almost every weekend. He lives just around the corner with his cousin, visits the family almost every night, and sometimes spends the night, though he usually sleeps with his cousin.

Tilly feels that Sam "treats her kids better than their daddy do. He buys them certain things [such as] clothes. He spanks them. . . . He takes them different places." She further feels that it is very important that a man treat her kids right. "If they don't care for the kids or anything then that's a bad man. . . . First he's got to love your kids before he loves you."

Her sons Richard (ten) and William (seventeen) confirm the fact that Sam is concerned about the children. Richard says, "He takes up for us when we get a whipping. . . . He tells her not to whip us this time." When asked, "Does he have pretty good control over the kids?" William replied, "They do what he say most of the time. Irvin [eighteen] don't, but the rest of them will."

They are still going together and Sam proposes marriage with some regularity, but Tilly shies away. "I think I'm better off just not having a husband. . . . I wouldn't definitely say I would get a good one. I might get a bad one. I don't want to take a chance." Even though she has known Sam since childhood, she is not certain about him. He drinks a lot but is not to her knowledge the violent type—

at least he is not as a single man. Her fear is that when he "has papers on her" he might change. Her experience with her second husband taught her how quickly a man could change on her.

And so Ethyl broke up with Jay, never having seriously considered marriage while going with him, and Tilly says that *maybe* in three or four years she will be ready for marriage to Sam. Marriage has not yet resulted because in both instances the family is doing better under the combined resources of welfare and the boyfriend's assistance than they could do under his wages alone, and in both instances the woman is afraid of the man's drinking behavior. In both instances the boyfriends are well known by the women's families and visit frequently with them.

Since breaking with Jay, Ethyl has been living with a new boyfriend, Raymond (twenty-nine), and says that she is seriously considering marriage to him—at least to the extent that she has decided to get a divorce. Thus, marriage may or may not be a result of a quasi-father relationship, but it does provide the context in which a woman with children is likely to make up her mind one way or another about a man. It is interesting to remember here that three of the five women [in the study] still living with their husbands began their relationship "common law." Only one of the quasi-fathers at present lives with his woman.

The Supportive Biological Father

A second type of boyfriend is the supportive biological father. Here the concern of the man—and largely that of the woman also—is to support the children that they have brought into the world without seriously considering marriage to one another. In some instances the man or woman may well be married to someone else. The man's support may be voluntary, as in the case of Edward Patterson, or it may be as the result of a voluntarily signed acknowledgment that the children are his.

In the case of Leona Wards (fifty) and Larry (forty-nine), Leona was married once and had four children by her first husband. His "cutting out" and drinking led to a separation and Leona took up with Larry, who gave her three children, in ages now

from eighteen to thirteen, before he married another woman a couple of years ago. He played the role of supportive biological father before he married. They had been going together for nearly *sixteen* years, though only Leona was true to the relationship. She has never remarried and claims that even now she has no boyfriend because they are too much trouble at her age, although she admits that she would enjoy a companion in her declining years.

Larry has taken the children on long trips, such as the one to Arizona in 1963, he has bought them clothes, especially at Christmas time, and has paid regularly the amount of fifteen to twenty dollars a week for their support since 1954. At that time he acknowledged that the children are his and the court fixed the amount for their support.

Leona's being true to Larry is a part of her rearing as she sees it. Her mother died in 1927 and "daddy went haywire," so she went to live with her maternal aunt and her husband, Uncle Paul— "gentle Paul"—who was a Baptist minister. Her aunt was a very strict woman and quite respectable.

Leona's marriage lasted fourteen years, and at the end she left her husband because he was undependable in his support of her and the children. While separated she met Larry, her boyfriend:

> *At the time I met Larry, my first husband and I wasn't together. I met Larry through the [same] church. He asked me [to marry] and I told him not until my husband's children got off my hands and out of the way. I never wanted a stepfather over my children . . . it was something that Lewis and I have always said.*

Her main departure from her rearing was having children out of wedlock, and while she loves the children, she regrets the departure:

> *That's the only thing in life I didn't want— to have children without being married. I just wasn't reared like that. But they are all by one man. They're not by this, that one, nor the other one. They're all by one man.*

Leona is proud to be able to say, "I have been by Larry as if he and I were married." But he was not true to her. She broke off their relationship by cutting him with a knife.

While it is true that Larry is legally obligated to care for his children, it is noteworthy that he claimed them as his in the first place and that he supports them in gifts over and above his legal obligations. His inability to believe that Leona was true to him, plus her reluctance to have a stepfather over her husband's children, at least one of whom has not yet left home, contributed to the factors other than economic that mitigated against their marriage—but did not prevent them from courting for sixteen years.

Most of the care that fathers give to their outside children seems to be much less regular than Larry's, but is, nevertheless, largely voluntary. Edward Patterson, for example, has three by two different women. His outside children live with their mothers, and when he gets tired of his wife he moves out and lives with Leddie B., by whom he has had two children. His legitimate children complain that when he goes to visit one of the outsiders, he gives her and her siblings more money for spending than he gives his legitimate children. His wife protests that he stole their TV set and gave it to the mother of one of these children, and his son claims that when he returned to his home in the country recently, he bought several dresses for his outside child living there. Mr. Patterson will not speak of these outsiders and keeps his money matters to himself. His wife has opened letters from the mothers of these children requesting regular support, but does not know if he is giving only to them. She believes that he spends most of the $406 a month take-home pay he earns from his job on these women and their children.

The Supportive Companion

A less durable relationship exists in the case of the "supportive companion" who "keeps a woman." Here the concern of the male is mainly to have a good time with a clean woman. The concern of the woman is for support and companionship. Such a relationship is not to be confused with prostitution,

for it is not a mere matter of a business transaction but a search for intimacy on both parts, a search conducted in the context of severe economic and emotional handicaps. In this community such a relationship is likely to occur between an older man (late twenties, early thirties) and a younger woman (early twenties, teens) who has had children outside of wedlock.

In such a relationship, the man rarely keeps the woman in her own apartment, as would be the case in more solvent circumstances, where the woman is usually single and without children. Rather, he provides a regular "weekend away" at his apartment or other suitable place where they can be together away from the children. He takes her out, provides her with spending money and a good time. Should she conceive a child, he is least likely of all types to want to assume support of the child. Responsibility is what he is trying to avoid.

The example of Madeline (sixteen) and Jerry (twenty-three) is a case in point. They knew each other about a year during 1959–1960. Madeline had already had two children by two other men. Jerry came by for dinner occasionally, but usually he made the weekend scene at a motel apartment he rented for the occasion. When Friday came round, he would give Madeline money which she often turned into dresses or other items to enhance her appearance. Madeline says, "Jerry's not like a lot of men that you find. A lot of men, if they do something for you they feel they own you." Jerry gave her "fifteen or twenty dollars, sometimes more" each week and had keys to a two-room kitchenette for the weekend. Madeline says "We were always together [on the weekend]. Where I went he usually went, where he went I went. We'd go to the apartment and everything. But lots of times we would go and just watch TV or sit and talk or have a drink or something. Then we would go—especially in the summertime—we'd go there because they had air conditioning."

The Pimp

... The pimp is characteristic of the young man of the street who lives off the labors of prostitutes or off women who are able to earn their own way through wages or welfare. He is kept by his woman and dresses like a dandy. None of the women living in broken homes has had a pimp, but Andrew Buchanan claims he was one as a youth. The pimp relationship may be, for the man at least, quite often a *pre*marital experience. . . .

Speculation on Extensiveness and Relationship in Time

While there is no accurate measure of the prevalence of these four types of boyfriends, the data are suggestive. The pimp is the most talked about male-female nonmarital relationship in the literature. These data, however, suggest that it is not as prevalent in the project as is commonly assumed. It is possible that pimping may be more or less restricted to the younger men and may phase out into less exploitive relationships with females as the men grow older. Therefore, the frequency of the pimping relationship may well be exaggerated, since the younger men tend to be more vocal about their exploits, and the older men who now view such activity with a certain resentment may bewail the fact that "things used to be much better."

A man may play one or more boyfriend roles in his life. We can thus see these types as phases in a developmental sequence. The pimp is an early role of the young man of the street who would rather "live sweet" than work, or who has found that his value on the love market is greater than it is on the labor market. The data suggest that such a relationship is quite likely to terminate when the man reaches his mid-thirties. He may then decide to marry the woman he has pimped off because by then he has had one or more children by her, or

because he is, after having sown his wild oats, seeking now a more intimate and lasting relationship. If he does marry her, then he comes under the norm that it is "unfair" to pimp off a woman you are married to.

No one, however, has gone from a pimping relationship directly to marriage with the same woman. In the case of Edward Patterson, who pimped off several women for several years before marriage, a quasi-father relationship was entered into with another woman for four or five years before he married her as the result of an unwanted pregnancy. This marriage has lasted nineteen years.

The quasi-fathers are in their late twenties or early thirties, and in one of the three instances, marriage is actively sought by the woman. In the other two the males are still being tested. This opportunity to get to know a man under near familial situations is a boon to these women, who have been disappointed in marriage one or more times. He can prove that he is a good provider and a gentle, "good" man. Not all quasi-father relationships terminate in marriage.

The supportive companion is, if the data from these inferences are correct, more likely to be the relationship that exists between an older man (late twenties or early thirties) and a younger woman (late teens, early twenties). It may be an alternative for a rejected quasi-father, who sought but could not obtain marriage, and whose income is stable enough to permit such indulgence. Finally, most men can play, if they so desire, the role of supportive biological father throughout most of their lives, since almost every male has had at least one child outside of wedlock. For some who never marry, this may be the extent to which their craving for familial companionship is expressed—the occasional gift to an illegitimate child.

---

[1]Hylan Lewis, Blackways of Kent *(Chapel Hill: University of North Carolina Press, 1961), p. 84. See also E. Franklin Frazier,* The Negro Family in the United States *(Chicago, University of Chicago Press, 1939), and St. Clair Drake and Horace Cayton,* Black Metropolis *(New York: Harcourt, Brace and Company, 1945).*

SEXUAL DEVELOPMENT AND BEHAVIOR IN BLACK PREADOLESCENTS

Ouida E. Westney · Renee R. Jenkins
June Dobbs Butts · Irving Williams

In this article the authors report results of a study of sexual development in Black preadolescents. They examined both sexual maturation and heterosexual behavior. There was considerable variation in sexual maturation for chronological age. Heterosexual activities were generally at the lower end of the scale. For girls there was no association between heterosexual activities and degree of biological maturation. For boys, genital development was related to sexual behavior.

There is considerable concern in this country regarding the decreasing age of first sexual intercourse and the increasing rate of premarital pregnancy among very young teenagers. In their study of sexual behavior among teenagers, one of the strongest associations reported by Zelnik, Kantner, and Ford (1980) was between the age at menarche and age of first intercourse. This finding is of particular concern given that black teenage girls have reported earlier ages both for menarche and first intercourse as compared to white girls.

Afro-American girls are among the earliest maturing girls in the world. Harlan, Harlan, and Grillo (1980) reported that black girls were ahead of white girls in the development of breasts and pubic hair. Further, although adolescence is commonly considered as beginning at age 12, many black girls have developed early signs of pubertal changes by age 9, with menarche (a late-stage pubertal marker) coming on the average at 12.5 years of age (MacMahon, 1973). The implication of this early sexual development during the preadolescent period (age 9 through 12) and its impact on sexual behavior, in the broadest sense, has not received much attention in the research literature.

With respect to black boys, Harlan, Grillo, Cornoni-Huntley, and Leaverton (1979) reported that they are similar to their 12- to 17-year-old white counterparts in the timing of development of their secondary sex characteristics. However, with regard to sexual behavior at the preadolescent level, black boys have been reported to be ahead of white boys and girls, as well as ahead of black girls in heterosexual behaviors (Broderick, 1965). Research which examines biological sequencing in boys in relation to sexual behaviors has not been reported. This report focuses on relationships between maturational sequencing and sexual behavior in black preadolescent girls and boys.

Background Theory and Research

Classic psychoanalytic theory views preadolescence as a period of psychosexual quiescence (S. Freud, 1938). Neopsychoanalytic investigations, however, suggest that during this period there is renewed

From *Adolescence* 19 (75, Fall 1984):557–568. © Libra Publishers, 1984. Reprinted by permission. This research was supported by the Behavioral Science Branch, National Institute of Child Health and Human Development through Contract No. 1–HD–82840.

psychosexual struggle to avert fixation to pre-oedipal levels (Blos, 1962; Peller, 1958). For boys, this struggle is manifested by "despising" girls while simultaneously experiencing heterosexual curiosity and covert heterosexual strivings. Girls deal with the struggle by manifesting pseudo-mature behaviors including display of feminine charms, subtle "seducing strategies," as well as the imitation of masculine traits and activities (Kohen-Raz, 1971).

Although preadolescent boys and girls are often described as being hostile toward each other, it is possible that this apparent mutual hostility may instead be a mechanism for coping with their psychosexual concerns. Actually, in the Broderick (1965) study, preadolescent boys and girls were reported generally as being friendly toward each other. Some preadolescents reported having boy/girl friends, kissing, dating, and going steady.

In attempting to explain the psychology underlying individual behaviors in adolescents, Petersen and Taylor (1980) utilized a biopsychosocial model. They proposed interacting biological, sociocultural, and self-perception pathways leading to the psychological adaptations of developing adolescents. The biological factors include genetic potentials, endocrine changes, secondary characteristics, and time of pubertal onset. Sociocultural factors encompass attractiveness standards, peer and parental responses, and stereotypes of early and late maturers. Self-perception factors include body-image, self-image, self-esteem, and gender identity. Although the authors were tracing pathways to personal responses during adolescence, it is not unreasonable to apply this model to preadolescence. Our larger study addresses variables in each of the categories outlined by Petersen and Taylor. At this time, however, we are dealing with the biological aspect of the model—specifically the relationships between the development of secondary characteristics and sexual behaviors.

It is known that there is a causal relationship between the elaboration of sex hormones and the development of secondary sex characteristics. There is growing evidence from cross-sectional data correlating increasing levels of sex hormones with the progression in maturational staging. Gupta, Attanasio, and Raaf (1975) in their cross-sectional study demonstrated stage-related (Tanner, 1955) increases in dihydrotestosterone and testosterone for males and in estradiol and estrogen for females. Other cross-sectional studies (Angsusingha, Kenny, Nankin, and Taylor, 1974; Korth-Schultz, Levine, and New, 1976) also report similar increases in hormones which are related to maturational staging. Longitudinal studies to support these findings have not yet been reported.

Since there is growing empirical evidence linking progression in the elaboration of certain sex hormones to stages of biological maturation, two related questions may be asked: (1) What is the relationship between increase in sex hormones and sexual behavior during the process of maturation? and, (2) What is the relationship between biological maturation (staging) and sexual behavior during the maturational process? Regarding the relationship between increasing sex hormone levels and sexual behavior, Katchadourian (1980) indicated that there was a more consistent correlation between testosterone levels and sexual interest levels and behavior in maturing males than between estrogen levels and sexual behavior in maturing females. It is to the substance of the second question, the relationship between maturational staging and heterosexual behavior, that this report addresses itself.

Method

Subjects

The 101 preadolescent participants in this study were 46 boys and 55 girls living in a metropolitan area and its suburbs in the eastern United States. This volunteer sample was obtained through several sources including the Well-Child Clinics of a university hospital which serves a predominantly black clientele, independent schools, churches, and other agencies. The ages of the boys ranged from 8.5 to 11.4 years, with a mean age of 10.0 years. The girls ranged in age from 8.3 to 11.2 years with a mean age of 10.1 years. Sixty-two of the participants were from middle-income families and 37 from low-income families. Socioeconomic status was defined in terms of parental income and education.

Procedure

A medical assessment was completed on all participants by two pediatricians with formal training in adolescent medicine. A standard age-appropriate history was obtained and physical examination conducted. From this assessment, data on sociosexual behaviors and physical maturation characteristics were obtained. Most of the historical information was elicited through an open-ended interview rather than a questionnaire format. Sexual maturation was assessed according to Tanner's (1955) criteria on a scale from I through V, with I representing the prepubertal stage, and progressing through pubescence to V, the adult stage. Except for two boys, each individual was examined by a pediatrician of the same sex as the participant.

Reported heterosexual behaviors as heterosexual physical activities (HPA) ranging from game playing to intercourse were quantified on a weighted scale which utilized the following designations: game playing = 1 point; holding hands, or hugging, or kissing = 2 points; light petting = 3 points; heavy petting = 4 points; and intercourse = 5 points. Thus, an HPA score was obtained by transforming each heterosexual activity into the appropriate code and summing the responses. This score represented the composite sexual behavior variable. For example, if a preadolescent reported participation in game playing, hugging, and kissing, the HPA score was 5.

Frequencies for all data were expressed in the form of percentages. Relationships between the HPA score, biological, and other variables were assessed using Spearman correlations. Significance was established at .05 level.

Findings

Sexual Maturation

Complete Tanner staging data were obtained on 43 boys and 50 girls. Staging data on breast development in girls and genital development in boys can be seen in Table 1. Most of the boys (67%) were prepubertal with respect to genital development. The remainder were at Stages II and III with mean ages of 10.7 and 10.8 years, respectively. Thirty-six percent of the girls showed no signs of breast development. The others were at various stages of development from Stage II through Stage IV. For these stages of breast development, their mean ages were 10.2, 10.6, and 10.9 years, respectively. There were marked overlaps in the age ranges for Stages I through III in the boys, and Stages I through IV in the girls.

Data regarding pubic hair development for both sexes appear in Table 2. Girls were more advanced than boys in pubic hair maturation. Again, the most advanced stage of pubic hair development attained by the boys was Stage III, while some girls had progressed to Stage IV. As with breast and genital development, wide variations in the ages of

---

TABLE 1   Genital Development of Boys and Breast Development of Girls

Tanner stages	BOYS (*n* = 43)			GIRLS (*n* = 50)		
	Mean age	Age range	*n*	Mean age	Age range	*n*
I	10.0	8.5–11.3	29	10.0	8.9–11.2	18
II	10.7	9.6–11.8	12	10.2	8.3–10.9	9
III	10.8	10.4–11.1	2	10.6	10.0–11.3	18
IV	—	—	—	10.9	10.2–11.6	5
V	—	—	—	—	—	—

TABLE 2   Pubic Hair Development of Boys and Girls

Tanner stages	BOYS (*n* = 43)			GIRLS (*n* = 50)		
	Mean age	Age range	*n*	Mean age	Age range	*n*
I	10.0	8.5–11.3	33	10.0	8.3–10.9	16
II	10.7	9.6–11.3	7	10.6	9.3–11.6	17
III	11.1	10.4–11.9	3	10.6	10.2–11.3	14
IV	—	—	—	10.9	10.5–11.4	3
V	—	—	—	—	—	—

Tanner staging were observed in pubic hair growth. Among the sample, 33% of the boys and 76% of the girls had begun pubertal development.

Figure 1 shows the Tanner staging concordance of genital and pubic hair development in boys and breast and pubic hair development in girls at 9, 10, and 11 years. It is evident that at each age level, an increasing percentage of both boys and girls were pubescents. Although there was considerable variability in the progression of development in the pubescent boys and girls with regard to their respective secondary sex characteristics, there was complete Tanner staging concordance in many cases. This was more true for the boys than for the girls (57% and 32%, respectively).

For boys, the correlation between genital development and pubic hair development was significant at the .001 level; and for girls, the correlation between breast development and the development of pubic hair was also significant at the .001 level.

Sociosexual Behavior

When asked whether they had a special boy or girl friend of the opposite sex, 60.9% of the boys and 56.4% of the girls responded affirmatively. The places where heterosexual activity occurred are reported in Table 3. The school was the most common location for interaction. Although the telephone cannot be strictly categorized as a place of heterosexual interaction, so many children (particularly

girls) gave this as an answer that it is included in Table 3. Table 4 presents reported heterosexual physical activities of the participants. For both boys and girls, the number who reported having special opposite-sex friends was greater than those claiming involvement in heterosexual physical activities. Although comparatively more girls were involved in heterosexual activities than boys, these involvements were at the lower end of the HPA scale. The girls reported no behaviors beyond level 2 on the HPA scale (holding hands, kissing, and hugging). In addition to level 1 and level 2 behaviors, a small percentage of the boys reported involvement in

---

TABLE 3   Places of Heterosexual Activity

Places	PERCENTAGES	
	Boys (*n* = 46)	Girls (*n* = 55)
School	23.9	36.4
His home	8.7	9.1
Her home	6.5	12.7
Recreation center	4.3	1.8
Church	0	1.8
Telephone*	2.2	36.4
Other	2.2	3.6

*Technically, the telephone is not a place, but it was included in the table because of the frequency with which it was reported as an interacting medium.

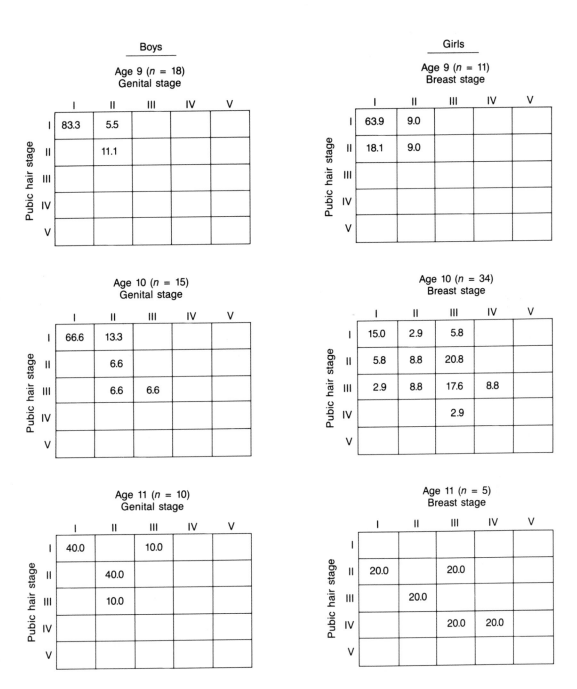

FIGURE 1

TABLE 4   Reported Heterosexual Activities

	PERCENTAGES	
HPA	Boys ($n = 46$)	Girls ($n = 55$)
Any activity	30.4	47.2
Playing games	17.4	29.1
Holding hands	10.9	5.5
Kissing	13.0	16.4
Hugging	8.7	7.3
Light petting	—	—
Heavy petting	4.3	—
Intercourse	2.2	—

TABLE 5   Correlates of Heterosexual Physical Activities

	BOYS ($n = 43$)		GIRLS ($n = 50$)	
	r	p	r	p
Age in months	.091	.274	.166	.122
Having a girl/boy friend	.550	.001*	.311	.020*
Genital stage	.404	.005*	—	—
Breast stage	—	—	.004	.488
Pubic hair stage	.143	.195	.056	.354
Socioeconomic status	.173	.146	.150	.158

*Significant beyond .05 level.

heavy petting, and coitus, levels 4 and 5 behaviors on the HPA scale.

The games in which the boys and girls were involved were chiefly heterosexual chasing and tagging. Behaviors reported as possibilities when, for example, a boy chased a girl and caught her ranged from hitting her, to kissing her, to performing "humping" actions toward her.

Relationships between HPA and Biological Maturation

The occurrence of heterosexual behaviors as represented by the HPA score was correlated with the maturational and other relevant variables; the results appear in Table 5. For both boys and girls, there was no significant relationship between age and involvement in heterosexual activities. The 9-, 10-, and 11-year-old girls who reported heterosexual activities generally participated in level 1 and level 2 activities without respect to age. Regarding the boys, those who reported heavy petting and coitus were exclusively in the 9-year-old age group. In boys there was a significant relationship between the HPA score and genital staging ($r = .404$; $p < .005$), but no clear relationship existed between pubic hair staging and the HPA score. In the case of the girls, both breast and pubic hair development bore no significant relationship to the HPA score.

The relationship between the HPA score and reports of having a girlfriend or boyfriend was significant beyond the .001 level for boys and beyond the .05 level for girls. However, for both boys and girls, there were no significant relationships between having a girl/boy friend and the maturational variables. The small degree of relationship that existed was positive for the boys but inverse for the girls. Socioeconomic status for both boys and girls had no relationship of importance to the HPA score.

Discussion

Our data indicate that chronologically, the girls are ahead of the boys in biological development, a finding which is consistent with earlier research (Tanner, 1978). Staging progressions of genital development among boys and breast development in girls are within the age spans provided by Tanner. However, placed in Tanner's frame of reference, it appears that our sample is weighted toward the younger portion of these age spans. According to Tanner, the average age for acceleration of penis growth is about age 12½, but sometimes as early as 10½, and sometimes as late as 14½ years. In our sample, 16.6%, 33.1%, and 60%, respectively, of the 9-, 10-, and 11-year-old boys were at or beyond the beginning of penile growth. For girls, Tanner's mean age for breast development is 11 years with a range of 9.0 to 13.0 years. Eighteen percent of the 9-year-old girls were at or beyond Stage II of breast development; so were 73.8% of these who were 10, and 80% of those who were 11 years old. Of course, one limitation in comparing this sample with these normative standards is evidenced by the absence of blacks in Tanner's sample.

The National Health Survey data analyzed by Harlan and his associates (1979, 1980) contain staging information on black children, but the exclusion of children younger than 12 from the sample precludes meaningful comparisons. These researchers noted that 80% of the 12-year-old girls (actually, 87% of the black 12-year-old girls) had progressed beyond Stage II of breast development. In our younger sample of girls, 76% and 80% of the 10- and 11-year-old girls, respectively, were at or beyond Stage II of breast development. The absence of large representative preadolescent samples with which to compare the onset of maturation in smaller samples indicates the need for further research to establish norms for pubertal development in black children.

Boys showed greater agreement in the progression of their staging characteristics than girls. The greater concordance between genital and pubic hair development in boys than between breast and pubic hair development in girls may be explained by the hormonal sources which stimulate the growth of these structures. Androgens influence both genital development and pubic hair development in boys, while breast development is controlled by estrogen, and pubic hair by androgen in girls (Root, 1973).

Regarding heterosexual interaction, more than half of the boys and girls (boys more frequently than girls) stated that they had special opposite-sex friends. In this period of emerging sociosexual interaction, it is difficult to ascertain the quality of sexual content of the boyfriend/girlfriend relationship reported by these participants. A larger portion of the heterosexual relationships may be platonic.

The significant relationships between the occurrence of HPA and having a girlfriend and a boyfriend are noteworthy. One researcher (Furstenberg, 1976) reported that young adolescents who had opposite-sex friends and dated, compared with others, were more likely to be involved in advanced levels of sexual behavior as late adolescents.

The representation of the girls in the lower levels of HPA may imply somewhat of a developmental progression in these activities, as compared with the boys during the pubescent period. Even in the case of the boys, however, advanced behaviors were by no means generalized. Actually, taking all reported activities into consideration, girls were more involved in HPA than boys, most of the activity being at the game-playing level. Preadolescent girls characteristically have been identified as demonstrating prominent behavior features including, among others, activeness, zest, and initiative (Deutsch, 1945; Kohen-Raz, 1971). It is possible that preadolescent girls, as well as boys, view game-playing as a benign yet satisfying means of having fun while at the same time associating with persons of the other sex.

More advanced levels of heterosexual interaction among black preadolescent boys, as compared with girls, have been reported by Broderick (1965). From samples of teenagers, Udry (1981) and Sorensen (1973) suggest that black teenagers report less mid-range behaviors preceding intercourse than do white teenagers. These studies also portray females as being less involved in sexual activity than males. In this preadolescent group, patterns of heterosexual activity are just beginning to emerge. However, among the boys in the sample, none reported light petting, but 4.3% reported heavy petting, and 2.2% reported coitus.

With respect to relationships between biological maturation and heterosexual activities, for girls the data revealed no significant association between the prevalence of HPA and maturation in terms of the development of the breasts and the development of pubic hair. It appears that for females at this level of development, involvement in sociosexual behaviors does not vary with staging. However, most of the girls are at Stages II and III of breast development, and none have yet achieved Stage V. The breasts, as easily observable secondary sex characteristics, may show greater relationships to sexual behavior as maturation progresses.

For boys, there was a significant relationship between genital development and the HPA score.

Further research is needed to ascertain whether degree of genital development could emerge as a possible predictor of heterosexual behavior during preadolescence. It appears that this finding regarding the significant correlation of HPA with genital development, but not with breast development, is akin to findings regarding a stronger correlation between male hormone levels and sexual behavior in developing boys than between female hormone levels and sexual behaviors in developing girls (Katchadourian, 1980).

Summary

The findings in this aspect of the study have indicated that biologically, this 9- to 11-year-old sample of black boys and girls is essentially in the pre- and early pubertal stages of development. Although the maturation of the participants is dispersed through Stages I to IV, confirming the considerable variability in sexual maturation as it related to chronological age, the sample is predominantly early maturational. The sociosexual behaviors are distributed most heavily in the less intimate categories, but are more advanced for the boys than the girls. At this stage, no significant association exists between sociosexual behavior and maturational staging for the girls, but in the boys genital staging is positively and significantly related to sexual behavior.

As stated earlier, these are findings from the baseline data of a longitudinal study. Further assessments will chart advancement in sexual maturation and sociosexual behavior among these developing young people. Research on these variables using larger samples of preadolescents would be of great value.

References

Angsusingha, K., F. M. Kenny, H. R. Nankin, and F. H. Taylor
1974 "Unconjugated Estrone, Estradiol, and FSH and LH in Prepubertal and Pubertal Males and Females." *Journal of Clinical Endocrinology and Metabolism* 39:63–68.

Blos, P.
1962 *On Adolescence*. New York: Free Press.

Broderick, C. B.
1965 "Social Heterosexual Development among Urban Negroes and Whites." *Journal of Marriage and the Family* 27:200–203.

Deutsch, H.
1945 *The Psychology of Women*. New York: Grune & Stratton.

Freud, S.
1938 *The Basic Writings of Sigmund Freud* (A. A. Brill, ed.). New York: Random House.

Furstenberg, F. F.
1976 *Unplanned Parenthood: The Social Consequences of Teenage Childbearing*. New York: Free Press.

Gupta, D., A. Attanasio, and S. Raaf
1975 "Plasma Estrogen and Androgen Concentrations in Children during Adolescence." *Journal of Clinical Endocrinology and Metabolism* 40: 636–643.

Harlan, W. R., G. P. Grillo, J. Cornoni-Huntley, and P. E. Leaverton
1979 "Secondary Sex Characteristics of Boys 12 to 17 Years of Age: The U.S. Health Examination Survey." *The Journal of Pediatrics* 95:293–297.

Harlan, W. R., E. A. Harlan, and G. Grillo
1980 "Secondary Sex Characteristics of Girls 12 to 17 Years of Age: The U.S. Health Examination Survey." *The Journal of Pediatrics* 96:1074–1078.

Katchadourian, H.
1980 "Adolescent Sexuality." *Pediatric Clinics of America* 27:17–28.

Kohen-Raz, R.
1971 *The Child from 9 to 13: The Psychology of Preadolescence and Early Puberty*. New York: Atherton.

Korth-Schultz, S., L. S. Levine, and M. I. New
1976 "Serum Androgens in Normal Prepubertal and Pubertal Children with Precocious Andrenarche." *Journal of Clinical Endocrinology and Metabolism* 42:117–124.

MacMahon, B.

1973   *Age at Menarche.* United States Department of Health, Education and Welfare Publication No. (HRA) 74–1615, NHS Series 11, No. 133. Rockville, Md.: National Center for Health Statistics.

Peller, L.

1958   "Reading and Day Dreaming in Latency." *Journal of the American Psychoanalytic Association* 6:57–60.

Petersen, A. C., and B. Taylor

1980   "The Biological Approach to Adolescence: Biological and Psychological Adaptation." In *Handbook of Adolescent Psychology,* J. Adelson, ed. New York: Wiley.

Root, A. W.

1973   "Endocrinology of Puberty." *Medical Progress* (83 [1] July):1–19.

Sorensen, R.

1973   *Adolescent Sexuality in Contemporary Society: Personal Values and Sexual Behavior, 13–19.* New York: World.

Tanner, J. M.

1955   *Growth at Adolescence.* Springfield, Ill.: Thomas.

1978   *Fetus to Man.* Cambridge, Mass.: Harvard University Press.

Udry, J. R.

1981   "A Biosocial Model of Adolescent Sexual Behavior." Paper presented at the National Institute of Child Health and Human Development. Bethesda, Maryland, June.

Zelnick, M., J. F. Kantner, and K. Ford

1980   *Determinants of Fertility Behavior among U.S. Females Aged 15–19, 1971 and 1976.* Final Report, Contract No. 1–HD–28248.

BLACK MASCULINITY, HYPERSEXUALITY, AND SEXUAL AGGRESSION

Robert Staples

Stereotypes of the Black male's sexuality are examined in this essay. The author finds that racial differences in male sexual expression are a function of blocked opportunity structures for Black men. Lacking normal access to the society's values, many lower-income Black men take refuge in hypersexual behavior and sexual aggression. It is concluded that Black male sexuality can only be understood in the context of race and class constraints.

It is difficult to think of a more controversial role in U.S. society than that of the Black male. He is a visible figure on the scene, yet a member of the least understood and studied of all sex–race groups in the United States. His cultural image is typically one of several types: the sexual superstud, the athlete, and the rapacious criminal. That is how he is perceived in the public consciousness, interpreted in the media, and ultimately how he comes to see and internalize his own role. Rarely are we exposed to his more prosaic role as worker, husband, father, and American citizen. Even when he might be applauded for acts of heroism, as in the disproportionate number of Black men who served in the Vietnam War, public approbation eludes him because the war effort was considered both criminal and unsuccessful.

The following discussion focuses on the stereotypical roles of Black male sexuality, not to reinforce them but to penetrate the superficial images of Black men as macho, hypersexual, violent, and exploitative. Obviously, there must be some explanation for the dominance of Black men in the nation's negative statistics on rape, out-of-wedlock births, and premarital sexual activity. Thus, this essay might be seen as an effort to explore the reality behind the image. For pedagogical purposes, the topics can be organized into adolescent male sexuality and fatherhood and sexual violence in the Black community. The perspective or ideology is based on conflict theory. As a starting point, the Black male is seen as being in conflict with the normative definition of masculinity. This is a status that few, if any, Black males have been able to achieve. Masculinity, as defined in this culture, has always implied a certain autonomy and mastery of one's environment. It can be said that not many white U.S. males have attained this ideal either. Yet white males did achieve a dominance in the nuclear family. Even that semblance of control was to be largely denied the Black man. During the era of slavery he could receive the respect and esteem of his wife, children, and kinsmen. But he had no formal legal authority over his wife or filial rights over his children. And there are numerous and documented instances of the slave-owning class's attempts to undermine his respect and esteem in the eyes of his family (Staples, 1978).

Beginning with the equal subjugation of slave men and women to the capricious authority of the slaveholder, the African male saw his masculinity challenged by the rape of his woman, sale of his children, the rations issued in the name of the woman and children bearing her name. While those practices may have presaged the beginning of a healthier sexual egalitarianism than was possible for whites, they also provoked contradictions and dilemmas for Black men in American society. Parity between men and women may be a current societal goal among some segments of the society, but it was hardly the American ideal of the nineteenth century. Instead, it led to the Black male's self-devaluation qua man and set the stage for internecine conflict within the Black community.

Sex role identity is crucial to a person's values, life-style, and personality. Black men have always had to confront the contradiction between the normative expectations attached to being male in this society and the proscriptions on their behavior and achievement of goals. Surely this has psychological ramifications that have yet to be explored or understood. They are subjected to societal opprobrium for failing to live up to the standards of manhood on the one hand and for being "super macho" on the other. It is a classical case of "be damned if you do and damned if you don't." In the past there was the assertion that Black men were effeminate because they were raised in households with only a female parent or with a weak father figure. They are presently being attacked in the literature, in plays, and at conferences as having succumbed to the male chauvinist ideal.

Although the sexual stereotypes apply equally to Black men and women, it is the Black male who has suffered the worst, because of the white notions of his hypersexuality. Between 1884 and 1900 more than 2,500 Black men were lynched, the majority of whom were accused of sexual interest in white women. The Black man, it was said, had a larger penis, a greater sexual capacity, and an insatiable sexual appetite. These stereotypes depicted Black men as primitive sexual beasts without the white male's love for home and family (Staples, 1982). These stereotypes persist in the American consciousness.

In the area of Black male sexuality folk beliefs are abundant but empirical facts are few. Despite the renaissance of research on the Black family, few of those studies have dealt with the sex life of the Black population. Even the increased interest and research on human sexuality has largely ignored Black sexual patterns. The reasons for this are apparently the very controversial nature of the topic. White researchers who attempt to investigate the subject are at a disadvantage in understanding this very intimate aspect of Black interpersonal relations. It is much easier for them to make valid observations of child-rearing patterns or husband–wife interaction than to make authoritative interpretations about the dynamics of Black sexual behavior. Because white beliefs about Black immorality were often used to justify racially segregated institutions, white researchers also run the risk of having their research employed to further the racial polarization extant in American life.

For similar reasons Black social scientists fear the opening up of a Pandora's box if they attempt to deal with the subject of Black sexual behavior. But this reluctance to scientifically investigate the topic has allowed the stereotypes related to Black sexual values and behavior to persist while the empirical evidence to counteract them lay dormant. Public policy, sex education, and therapeutic programs to deal with the sex-related problems of Black people cannot be developed to fit their particular needs until we know the nature and dynamics of Black sexual behavior. Thus, it is incumbent upon the Black researcher to throw some light on an area enmeshed in undocumented myths and stereotypes.

Sexuality of the Male Adolescent

The Kinsey data, cited by Bell, reveals that Black males acquire their knowledge of condoms at a later age than white males. The white male learns about sexual intercourse at a later age than Black males. As a result of poorer nutrition, the Black male reaches puberty at a later age than his white male counterpart. A critical distinction between Black and white males is the tendency of the more sexually repressed white male to use substitutes of masturbation, fellatio, and fantasy for direct sexual intercourse. Masturbation, for instance, is more likely to be the source of the first ejaculation for the white male whereas intercourse is more likely for the Black male. A larger percentage of white males reported being sexually aroused by being bitten during sexual activity, seeing a member of the opposite sex in a social situation, seeing themselves nude in the mirror or looking at another man's erect penis, hearing dirty jokes, reading sadomasochistic literature, and viewing sexy pictures. Conversely, Black males tended to engage in premarital intercourse at earlier ages and to have intercourse and to reach orgasm more frequently. As Bell (1978) noted in his analysis of these data, the Black male's

overabundance of sexuality is a myth. The sexuality of Black and white men just tends to take different forms and neither group has any more self-control or moral heroism than the other.

Among young Black U.S. males, sexual activity begins at an earlier age, is more frequent, and involves more partners. In part, this racial difference is actually a function of social class differences. Although some studies focused on college-level males, the studies among Blacks tend to be of lower-class males who may be beholden to their class of origin's values regarding sexual matters. One racial or cultural factor is the greater involvement of the young Black male with women at a younger age. Apparently white males are more likely to confine their associations in the adolescent years with other men. Larson and his associates (1976) found that Black male adolescents were twice as likely to be romantically involved with women than white males. The kind of rigid gender segregation found in white culture is largely absent from black society. For example, Blacks are less likely to have such an extensive number of all-male clubs, organizations, or colleges.

The sexual code of young Black males is a permissive one. They do not, for example, divide Black women into good (suitable for marriage) and bad (ineligible for marriage) categories. In the lower-income groups, sexual activity is often a measure of masculinity. Thus, there is a greater orientation toward premarital sexual experimentation. Ira Reiss, in his study of premarital sexual standards among Blacks and whites in the 1960s (1968), found that the white male's sexual permissiveness could be affected by a number of social forces, such as religion, but the Black male was influenced by none of them. Leanor Johnson and this author (1978) found that few Black male adolescents were aware of the increased risk of teenage pregnancy, but there was an almost unanimous wish not to impregnate their sexual partner. Another survey of Black male high school students reported their group believed that a male respects his partner when he uses a condom.

The period of adolescence with its social, psychological, and physical changes (particularly sex role identity and sexuality) is deemed the most

problematic of the life cycle stages. The prolonga-
tion of adolescence in a complex technological society and the earlier onset of puberty have served to
compound the problem. While adolescents receive
various messages to abandon childlike behavior,
they are systematically excluded from adult activity
such as family planning. This exclusion is justified
not only by their incomplete social and emotional
maturity, but also by their lack of the marketable
skills necessary to command meaningful, status-
granting jobs. Unskilled adolescents are further disadvantaged if they are members of a minority racial
group in a racially stratified society.

Parenthood

Parenthood at this stage of the life cycle is most
undesirable. Nevertheless, recently there has occurred an upsurge in teenage pregnancy and parenthood, specifically among females younger than
14. Approximately 52 percent of all children born to
Black women in 1982 were conceived out of wedlock. Among Black women under age 20 about 75
percent of all births were out of wedlock, compared
to only 25 percent of births to young white women
(U.S. Bureau of the Census, 1984). Although the rate
of white out-of-wedlock pregnancy is increasing
and the rate for nonwhites is decreasing, Black
unwed parenthood remains higher than that of
whites.

Because life and family support systems of
Black males are severely handicapped by the effects
of poverty and discrimination, the consequences of
combining parenthood with adolescence is compounded for the Black parent. Little is known, however, about the psychosocial development of Black
male youth with respect to their sexuality, the resulting problems that emerge when out-of-wedlock
pregnancy occurs, and their relationship to family
planning agencies. While many agencies operating
in Black communities deliver counseling and family
planning services to the unwed mother, the father
is usually involved only superficially or punitively—
when efforts are made to establish legal paternity
for assessing financial responsibility. This omission,
however, is not unique to Black males. The present
sexist value system robs the term *fatherhood* of the

richness of connotative meaning elicited by that ascribed to *motherhood*. A father is a person who
provides financial security. This narrow definition
obscures his potential contribution to the psychological well-being of mother and child and leads
social agencies to ignore generally the adolescent
father, who is often without financial resources. It
is, perhaps, the single fact of inadequate economic
provision that has resulted in the social agencies'
premature conclusion that unwed fathers are unwilling to contribute to the future of their child and
the support of the mother. This sexist assumption is
extended further by the traditional double standard, which holds that although it was his fault for
getting her pregnant, she failed to exercise the negative control expected by females. Hence, he is not
really responsible. Frequently, the girl's parents forbid the boy from seeing their pregnant daughter.
His absence is interpreted as an uncaring attitude
and, again, he is ignored or treated punitively. This
situation is further compounded when Black males
are involved. Sociological theory purports that slavery broke the Black man's sense of family responsibility. Thus, it is assumed that Black women do
not expect nor demand that their Black men support them.

Recent evidence suggests that the matrifocality of present theory and social services is myopic.
A study conducted at Los Angeles Vista Del Mar
Child-Care Service and another at the juvenile division of the Philadelphia County Court demonstrated that most unwed fathers are willing to face
their feelings and responsibilities (Connolly, 1978).
Although Misra's (1967) study of lower-income
Black males focused on those who were married,
his findings suggest that unmarried males do not
consider family planning a domain of the female,
but rather a joint responsibility to be shared by both
partners. When it is realized that fertility decline in
the Western world has largely resulted from male
methods of family planning and that the leading
forms of contraceptives, especially among teenagers, are methods involving male initiative, the need
to focus attention on males is evident and urgent.
However, when Black males are the target the task
is more difficult.

A reviewing of the literature on fertility patterns throughout the world shows that psycholog-

ical and sociological variables are important predictors in differential birth rates among certain groups. One of the most important of those variables is the male attitude toward family planning and the factors responsible for this attitude. Too often we are accustomed to thinking of reproduction as primarily a female responsibility. Because women are the main bearers and rearers of children it is expected that only they should be concerned with planning the size of their family and developing those techniques of contraception consistent with a family's earning power, their own health and happiness, and the psychological well-being of their children.

However, in a male-dominated world it is women who are given all the burden of having and raising children while it is often men who determine what the magnitude of that burden should be. Unfortunately, the male's wishes in regard to the size of his family is not contingent on the effect of childbearing on the female partner but are shaped by his own psychological and status concerns. The main need met by the male's procreative ability is the affirmation of his masculine identity.

Within many societies, among males there is an inseparable link between their self-image as men and their ability to have sexual relations with women and the subsequent birth of children from those sexual acts. Such a masculine norm is so common that the Spanish-speaking groups have coined a word for this concept: *machismo*. This word means "maleness," the ability to have children, which defines the status of a man in his society. For a strong male-dominated society the other issues involved in reproduction are subordinated to the male's desire to affirm his virility, which in turn confirms his fulfillment of the masculine role.

Because having an unlimited number of children is no longer compatible with the needs of many countries and, most importantly, is not consistent with the trend toward the liberation of women from their biology, the concept of machismo is increasingly an anachronism on the world scene. The research literature tells us that the male virility cult is strongest in countries and among groups where the need for family planning is greatest. Thus we find that in underdeveloped countries and among low-income ethnic groups in industrialized societies, many males are resistant to anything but natural

controls on the number of children they have. Studies show that males who strongly believe that their masculine status is associated with their virility do not communicate very well with their wives on the subject of family planning. As a result the wives are less effective in limiting their families to the number of childen they desire.

Sexual Aggression

Crimes of sexual attacks against women are pervasive and sharply increasing in the United States. The typical rapist is a Black male and his victim is most often a Black female. However, the most severe penalties for rapes are reserved for Black males accused of raping white women. Although 50 percent of those convicted for rape in the South were white males, over 90 percent of those executed for this crime in that region were Black. Most of their alleged victims were white. No white male has ever been executed for raping a Black woman (Bowers, 1974).

As is probably true for rape of white females, the incidence of rape of Black women is underreported. Ladner (1971) reported that an eight-year-old girl has a good chance of being exposed to rape and violence if she is a member of the Black underclass. Widespread incidents of this kind are rooted in the sexist socialization of all men in society, and it is pronounced among Black men who have other symbols of manhood blocked to them. Various explanations have been put forth to explain why Black men adopt these attitudes. Poussaint (1972) attributed it to the tendency of Black men to adopt the attitudes of the majority group toward Black women. Because white men have historically raped Black women with impunity, many Black males believe they can do the same.

Sexual violence is also rooted in the dynamics of the Black dating game. The majority of Black rape victims are familiar with their attacker, who was a friend, relative, or neighbor. Many of the rapes occur after a date and are what Amir (1974) described as misfired attempts at seduction. A typical pattern is for the Black male to seek sexual compliance from his date, encounter resistance that he thinks is feigned, and proceed to extract sexual gratification forcibly from her. Large numbers of Black men believe sexual relations to be their right after a certain amount of dating. A truly reluctant Black woman is often victimized by the tendency of many Black women to play a coquettish role in resisting male sexual demands when they actually are willing to engage in sexual intercourse. Such a pattern of rape is defined as situational and led feminist Germaine Greer (1973) to label seduction as a four-letter word.

Rape, however, is not regarded as the act of a sexually starved male but rather as an aggressive act toward females. Students of the subject suggest that it is a long-delayed reaction against authority and powerlessness. In the case of Black men, it is asserted that they grow up feeling emasculated and powerless before reaching manhood. They often encounter women as authority figures and teachers or as the head of their household. These men consequently act out their feeling of powerlessness against Black women in the form of sexual aggression. While such a characterization of Black rapists may be fairly accurate, rape should be viewed as both a sexual and political act because it is a function of external stress factors, such as racial discrimination, which maintain barriers to normal channels of manhood for Black males.

Manhood in U.S. society is closely tied to the acquisition of wealth. Wealth is power—power to control others. Men of wealth rarely feel it necessary to rape women because they gain sexual access through other means. The secretary or other female employee who submits to sexual demands of a male employer in order to advance her job is as much an unwilling partner in this situation as is the rape victim. The rewards for her sexual compliance are normatively sanctioned, whereas the rapist does not often have the resources to induce such sexual compliance. Moreover, the concept of women as sexual property is at the root of rape as a crime that is ipso facto a male transgression. This concept is peculiar to capitalistic, European societies rather than to African nations, where the incidence of rape is much lower. For Black men, rape is often an act of aggression against women because the kinds of status men can acquire through success in a job are not available to them.

Summary

Black male sexuality can only be understood in the context of race and class constraints on the expression of that sexuality. Because other avenues of mobility have been blocked by the persistent racial barriers, sexual expression has taken on a status beyond mere fulfillment of physical desires. Sexual competence becomes a status-enhancing value, which is often translated into hypersexuality on the part of Black males. However, such perversion of a "normal" or healthy sexual appetite seems largely confined to lower-class Black males and only a minority of men in that class. Only through the elimination of poverty and the provision of adequate employment opportunities can we hope to avoid the use of sexuality as an instrument of domination and control. Once sexual expression is freed from its link to definitions of masculinity, both men and women can develop healthy modalities of sexual communication and interaction.

References

Amir, Menachim
1974 "Sociocultural Factors in Forcible Rape." In *Sexual Behavior,* L. Gross, ed., pp. 1–12, Spectrum Publications.
Bell, Alan P.
1978 "Black Sexuality: Fact and Fancy." In *The Black Family: Essays and Studies* (2nd ed.), R. Staples, ed., pp. 77–80. Belmont, Calif.: Wadsworth.
Bowers, William J.
1974 *Executions in America*. Lexington, Mass.: Lexington Books.

Connolly, Lisa
1978   "Boy Fathers." *Human Behavior* 45 (January):40–43.

Greer, Germaine
1973   "Seduction Is a Four-Letter Word." *Playboy* (January):92–97.

Johnson, Leanor, and Robert Staples
1978   "Minority Youth and Family Planning: A Pilot Project." *The Family Coordinator* 28 (October):534–543.

Ladner, Joyce
1971   *Tomorrow's Tomorrow: The Black Woman.* Garden City, N.Y.: Doubleday.

Larson, David, et al.
1976   "Social Factors in the Frequency of Romantic Involvement among Adolescents." *Adolescence* 11 (Spring):7–12.

Misra, B. D.
1967   "Correlates of Males' Attitudes toward Family Planning." In *Sociological Contributions to Family Planning Research*, D. Bogue, ed., pp. 161–167.

Poussaint, Alvin
1972   *Why Blacks Kill Blacks.* New York: Emerson-Hall.

Reiss, Ira
1968   *The Social Context of Premarital Sexual Permissiveness.* New York: Holt, Rinehart & Winston.

Staples, Robert
1978   *The Black Family: Essays and Studies* (2nd ed.). Belmont, Calif.: Wadsworth.
1982   *Black Masculinity.* San Francisco: The Black Scholar Press.

U.S. Bureau of the Census
1984   *Fertility of American Women.* Washington, D.C.: U.S. Government Printing Office.

4 / Sex Roles

THE BLACK MALE:
Searching beyond Stereotypes

Manning Marable

Every socioeconomic and political indicator illustrates that the Black male in the United States is facing an unprecedented crisis. Despite singular examples of successful males in elected politics, business, labor unions, and the professions, the overwhelming majority of Black men find it difficult to acquire self-confidence and self-esteem in the chaos of modern economic and social life. Stereotypes imposed by white history and by their lack of knowledge of their own past have too often convinced younger Black men that their struggle is overwhelming.

What is a black man? Husband and father. Son and brother. Lover and boyfriend. Uncle and grandfather. Construction worker and sharecropper. Minister and ghetto hustler. Doctor and mineworker. Automechanic and presidential candidate.

What is a black man in an institutionally racist society, in the social system of modern America? The essential tragedy of being black and male is our inability, as men and as people of African descent, to define ourselves without the stereotypes which the larger society imposes upon us, and through various institutional means perpetuates and permeates within our entire culture. Our relations with our sisters, our parents and children, and indeed across the entire spectrum of human relations, are imprisoned by images of the past, false distortions which seldom if ever capture the essence of our being. We cannot come to terms with black women until we understand the half hidden stereotypes which have crippled our development and social consciousness. We cannot challenge racial and sexual inequality, both within the black community and across the larger American society, unless we comprehend the critical difference between the myths about ourselves and the harsh reality of being black men.

Confrontation with White History

The conflicts between black and white men in contemporary American culture can be traced directly through history to the earliest days of chattel slavery.

From *National Scene* 53 (6, 1984):5–6, 26–30. Reprinted by permission of the author. Figures have been deleted.

White males entering the New World were ill adapted to make the difficult transition from Europe to the American frontier. As recent historical research indicates, the development of what was to become the United States was accomplished largely, if not primarily, by African slaves, men and women alike. Africans were the first to cultivate wheat on the continent; they showed their illiterate masters how to grow indigo, rice and cotton; their extensive knowledge of herbs and roots provided colonists with medicines and preservatives for food supplies. It was the black man, wielding his sturdy ax, who cut down most of the virgin forest across the southern colonies. And in times of war, the white man reluctantly looked to his black slave to protect him and his property. As early as 1715, during the Yemassee Indian war, black troops led British regulars in a campaign to exterminate Indian tribes. After another such campaign in 1747, the all-white South Carolina legislature issued a public vote of gratitude to black men, who "in times of war, behaved themselves with great faithfulness and courage, in repelling the attacks of his Majesty's enemies." During the American Revolution, over two thousand black men volunteered to join the beleaguered Continental Army of George Washington, a slaveholder. A generation later, two thousand blacks from New York joined the state militia's segregated units during the War of 1812, and blacks fought bravely under Andrew Jackson at the battle of New Orleans. From Crispus Attucks to the 180,000 blacks who fought in the Union Army during the Civil War, black men gave their lives to preserve the liberties of their white male masters.

The response of white men to the many sacrifices of the sable counterparts was, in a word, contemptuous. Their point of view of black males was conditioned by three basic beliefs. Black men were only a step above the animals—possessing awesome physical powers, but lacking in intellectual ability. As such, their proper role in white society was as laborers, and not as the managers of labor. Second, the black male represented a potential political threat to the entire system of slavery. And third, but by no means last, the black male symbolized a lusty sexual potency which threatened white women. This uneven mixture of political fears and sexual anxieties were reinforced by the white

males' crimes committed against black women, the routine rape and sexual abuse which all slave societies permit between the oppressed and the oppressor. Another dilemma, seldom discussed publicly, was the historical fact that some white women of all social classes were not reluctant to request the sexual favors of their male slaves. These inherent tensions produced a racial mode of conduct and social control, which transcended the colonial period and embraced much of the twentieth century. The white male-dominated system dictated that the *only* acceptable social behavior of any black male was that of subservience—the loyal slave, the proverbial Uncle Tom, the ever-cheerful and infantile Sambo. It was not enough that black men must cringe before their white masters; they must express open devotion to the system of slavery itself. Politically, the black male was unfit to play even a minor role in the development of democracy. Supreme Court Chief Justice Roger B. Tawney spoke for his entire class in 1857: "Negroes [are] beings of an inferior order, and altogether unfit to associate with the white race, either in social or political relations; and so far inferior that they have no rights which the white man was bound to respect." Finally, black males disciplined for various crimes against white supremacy—such as escaping from the plantation, or murdering their masters—were often punished in a *sexual* manner. On this point, the historical record is clear. In the colonial era, castration of black males was required by the legislatures of North and South Carolina, Virginia, Pennsylvania, and New Jersey. Black men were castrated simply for striking a white man, or for attempting to learn to read and write. In the late nineteenth century, hundreds of black male victims of lynching were first sexually mutilated before being executed. The impulse to castrate black males was popularized in white literature and folklore, and even today, instances of such crimes are not entirely unknown in the rural South.

The relations between black males and white women were infinitely more complex. Generally, the vast majority of white females viewed black men through the eyes of their fathers and husbands. The black man was simply a beast of burden, a worker who gave his life to create a more comfortable environment for her and her children. And yet, in truth, he was still a man. Instances of interracial marriage were few, and were prohibited by law even as late as the 1960s. But the fear of sexual union did not prohibit many white females, particularly indentured servants and working class women, to solicit favors from black men. In the 1840s, however, a small group of white middle class women became actively involved in the campaign to abolish slavery. The founders of modern American feminism—Susan B. Anthony, Elizabeth Cady Stanton and Lucretia Mott—championed the cause of emancipation, and defended blacks' civil rights. In gratitude for their devotion of black freedom, the leading black abolitionist of the period, Frederick Douglass, actively promoted the rights of white women against the white male power structure. In 1848, at the Seneca Falls, New York women's rights convention, Douglass was the only man, black or white, to support the extension of voting rights to all women. White women looked to Douglass for leadership in the battle against sexual and racial discrimination. Yet curiously they were frequently hostile to the continued contributions of black women to the cause of freedom. When the brilliant orator Sojourner Truth, second only to Douglass as a leading figure in the abolitionist movement, rose to lecture before an 1851 women's convention in Akron, Ohio, white women cried out, "Don't let her speak!" For these white liberals, the destruction of slavery was simply a means to expand democratic rights to white women: the goal was defined in racist terms. Black men like Douglass were useful allies only so far as they promoted white middle class women's political interests.

The moment of truth came immediately following the Civil War, when Congress passed the Fifteenth Amendment, which gave black males the right to vote. For Douglass and most black leaders, both men and women, suffrage was absolutely essential to preserve their new freedoms. While the Fifteenth Amendment excluded females for the electoral franchise, it nevertheless represented a great democratic victory for all oppressed groups. For most white suffragists, however, it symbolized the political advancement of the black male over white middle class women. Quickly their liberal rhetoric gave way to racist diatribes. "So long as the Negro was lowest in the scale of being, we were

willing to press his claims," wrote Elizabeth Cady Stanton in 1865. "But now, as the celestial gate to civil rights is slowly moving on its hinges, it becomes a serious question whether we had better stand aside and see 'Sambo' walk into the kingdom first." Most white women reformists concluded that "it is better to be the slave of an educated white man, than of a degraded, ignorant black one." They warned whites that giving the vote to the black male would lead to the widespread rape and sexual assaults of white women of the upper classes. Susan B. Anthony vowed that "I will cut off this right arm of mine before I will ever work for or demand the ballot for the Negro and not the (white) woman." In contrast, black women leaders like Sojourner Truth and Frances E. Watkins Harper understood that the enfranchisement of black men was an essential initial step for the democratic rights of all people. The division between white middle class feminists and the civil rights movement of blacks, beginning over a century ago, has continued today in debates over affirmative action and job quotas. White liberal feminists frequently use the rhetoric of racial equality, but often find it difficult to support public policies that will advance black males over their own social group. Even in the 1970s, liberal women writers like Susan Brownmiller continued to resurrect the myth of the "black male-as-rapist," and sought to define the white women, in crudely racist terms. The weight of white history, from white women and men alike, has been an endless series of stereotypes used to frustrate the black man's images of himself, and to blunt his constant quest for freedom.

Confronting the Black Woman

Images of our suffering—as slaves, sharecroppers, industrial workers, and standing in unemployment lines—have been intermingled in our relationship with the black woman. We have seen her straining under the hot Southern sun, chopping cotton row upon row, and nursing our children on the side. We have witnessed her come home, tired and weary after working as a nurse, cook, or a maid in white men's houses. We have seen her love of her children, her commitment to the church, her beauty and dignity in the face of political and economic exploitation. And yet, so much is left unsaid. All too often the black male, in his own silent suffering, fails to communicate his love and deep respect for the mother, sister, grandmother and wife who gave him the courage and commitment to strive for freedom. The veils of oppression and the illusions of racial stereotypes limit our ability to speak the inner truths about ourselves and our relationships to black women.

The black man's image of the past is, in most respects, a distortion of social reality. All of us can feel the anguish of our great-grandfathers as they witnessed their wives and daughters being raped by their white masters, or as they wept when their families were sold apart. But do we feel the double bondage of the black woman, trying desperately to keep her family together, and yet at times distrusted by her own black man? Less then a generation ago, most black male social scientists argued that the black family was effectively destroyed by slavery; that the black man was much less than a husband or father; and that a "black matriarchy" emerged which crippled the economic, social and political development of the black community. Back in 1965, black scholar C. Eric Lincoln declared that the slavery experience had "stripped the Negro male of his masculinity" and had "condemned him to a eunuch-like existence in a culture which venerates masculine primacy." The rigid rules of Jim Crow applied more to black men than to their women, according to Lincoln: "Because she was frequently the white man's mistress, the Negro woman occasionally flouted the rules of segregation.... The Negro [male] did not earn rewards for being manly, courageous, or assertive, but for being accommodating—for fulfilling the stereotype of what he has been forced to be." The social byproduct of black demasculinization, concluded Lincoln, was the rise of black matriarchs, who psychologically castrated their husbands and sons. "The Negro female has had the responsibility of the Negro family for so many generations that she accepts it, or assumes it, as second nature. Many older women have forgotten why the responsibility developed upon the Negro woman in the first place, or why it later became institutionalized," Lincoln argued. "And young Negro women do not think it absurd to reduce the relationship to a matter of money since many of

them probably grew up in families where the only income was earned by the mothers: the fathers may not have been in evidence at all." Other black male sociologists perpetuated these stereotypes, which only served to turn black women and men against each other instead of focusing their energies and talents in the struggle for freedom.

Today's social science research on black female–male relations tells us what our common sense should have indicated long ago—that the essence of black family and community life has been a positive, constructive and even heroic experience. Andrew Billingsley's *Black Families and the Struggle for Survival* illustrates that the black "extended family" is part of our African heritage which was never eradicated by slavery or segregation. The black tradition of racial cooperation, the collectivist rather than individualistic ethos, is an outgrowth of the unique African heritage which we still maintain. It is clear that the black woman was the primary transmitter and repositor of the cultural heritage of our people, and played a central role in the socialization and guidance of black male and female children. But this fact does not by any way justify the myth of a "black matriarchy." Black women suffered from the economic exploitation and racism which black males experienced—but they also were trapped by institutional sexism and all of the various means of violence that have been used to oppress all women, such as rape, "wife beating," and sterilization. The majority of the black poor throughout history have been overwhelmingly female; the lowest paid major group within the labor force in America is black women, not men.

In politics, the sense of the black man's relations with black women are again distorted by stereotypes. Most of us can cite the achievements of the great black men who contributed to the freedom of our people: Frederick Douglass, Dr. W. E. B. DuBois, Marcus Garvey, Martin Luther King, Jr., Malcolm X, Paul Robeson, Medgar Evers, A. Philip Randolph. Why then are we often forgetful of Harriet Tubman, the fearless conductor on the Underground Railroad, who spirited over 350 slaves into the North? What of Ida B. Wells, newspaper editor and anti-lynching activist; Mary Church Terrell, educator, member of the Washington, D.C. Board of Education from 1895–1906, and civil rights leader;

Mary McLeod Bethune, college president and Director of the Division of Negro Affairs for the National Youth Administration; and Fannie Lou Hamer, courageous desegregation leader in the South during the 1960s? In simple truth, the cause of black freedom has been pursued by black women and men equally. In black literature, the eloquent appeals to racial equality penned by Richard Wright, James Baldwin and DuBois are paralleled in the works of Zora Neale Hurston, Alice Walker, and Toni Morrison. Martin Luther King, Jr., may have expressed for all of us our collective vision of equality in his "I Have A Dream" speech at the 1963 March on Washington—but it was the solitary act of defiance by a black woman, Rosa Parks, that initiated the great Montgomery Bus Boycott in 1955, and gave birth to the modern civil rights movement. The struggle of our foremothers and forefathers transcend the barrier of gender, as black women have tried to tell their men for generations. Beyond the stereotypes, we find a common heritage of suffering, and a common will to be free.

The Black Man Confronts Himself

The search for reality begins and ends with an assessment of the actual socioeconomic condition of black males within the general context of the larger society. Beginning in the economic sphere, one finds the illusion of black male achievement in the marketplace is undermined by statistical evidence. Of the thousands of small businesses initiated by black entrepreneurs each year, over ninety percent of them go bankrupt within thirty-six months. The black businessman suffers from redlining policies of banks, which keep capital outside his hands. Only one out of two hundred black businessmen have more than twenty paid employees and over 80 percent of all black men who start their own firms must hold a second job, working sixteen hours and more each day to provide greater opportunities for their families and communities. . . .

Advances in high technology leave black males particularly vulnerable to even higher unemployment rates over the next decades. Millions of black men are located either in the "old line" industries such as steel, automobiles, rubber, and textiles,

or in the public sector—both of which have experienced severe job contractions. In agriculture, to cite one typical instance, the disappearance of black male workers is striking. As late as forty years ago, two out of every five black men were either farmers or farm workers. In 1960, roughly five percent of all black men were still employed in agriculture, and another three percent owned their own farms. By 1983, however, less than 130,000 black men worked in agriculture. From 1959 to 1974, the number of black-operated cotton farms in the South dropped from 87,074 to 1,569. Black tobacco farmers declined in number from 40,670 to barely 7,000 during the same period. About three out of four black men involved in farming today are not self-employed. From both rural and urban environments, the numbers of jobless black adult males have soared since the late 1960s. . . . These statistics fail to convey, however, the human dimensions of the economic chaos of black male joblessness. Thousands of jobless men are driven into petty crime annually, just to feed their families; others find temporary solace in drugs or alcohol. The collapse of thousands of black households and the steady proliferation of female-headed, single parent households is a social consequence of the systemic economic injustice which is inflicted upon black males.

Racism also underscores the plight of black males within the criminal justice system. Every year in this country there are over two million arrests of black males. About 300,000 black men are currently incarcerated in federal and state prisons or other penal institutions. At least half of the black prisoners are less than thirty years of age, and over one thousand are not even old enough to vote. Most black male prisoners were unemployed at the time of their arrests; the others averaged less than $8,000 annual incomes during the year before they were jailed. And about 45 percent of the 1,300 men currently awaiting capital punishment on death row are Afro-Americans. As Lennox S. Hinds, former National Director of the National Conference of Black Lawyers has stated, "someone black and poor tried for stealing a few hundred dollars has a 90 percent likelihood of being convicted of robbery with a sentence averaging between 94 to 138 months. A white business executive who embezzled hundreds of thousands of dollars has only a 20 percent likelihood of conviction with a sentence averaging about 20 to 48 months." Justice is not "color blind" when black males are the accused. . . .

Every socioeconomic and political indicator illustrates that the black male in America is facing an unprecedented crisis. Despite singular examples of successful males in electoral politics, business, labor unions, and the professions, the overwhelming majority of black men find it difficult to acquire self confidence and self esteem within the chaos of modern economic and social life. The stereotypes imposed by white history, by the lack of knowledge of our own past, often convince many younger black males that their struggle is too overwhelming. Black women have a responsibility to comprehend the forces which destroy the lives of thousands of their brothers, sons and husbands. But black men must understand that they, too, must overcome their own inherent and deeply ingrained sexism, recognizing that black women must be equal partners in the battle to uproot inequality at every level of the society. The strongest ally black men have in their battle to achieve black freedom is the black woman. Together, without illusions and false accusations, without racist and sexist stereotypes, they can achieve far more than they can ever accomplish alone.

THE BLACK MALE'S ACCEPTANCE OF THE PRINCE CHARMING IDEAL

Clyde W. Franklin II · Walter Pillow

The Prince Charming ideal is the other half of the Cinderella complex, which encourages women to repress full use of their minds and creativity and to become dependent upon others. The Prince Charming ideal holds that becoming a mature man means assuming a protective, condescending, patriarchal role toward one's female mate and toward women in general. The authors differentiate between internalization of the Prince Charming ideal and acting in accordance with it. They develop a model of these differences and discuss the implications for male–female relationships.

Jeanne Noble's *Beautiful Also Are the Souls of My Black Sisters* and Colette Dowling's *The Cinderella Complex* serve as points of departure in this paper, which is devoted to an exploration of the Black male role and its effect on Black male–female social interaction (Dowling, 1981; Noble, 1978). The above books are provocative in that their theses propose two distinct, though related, empirical statements about male–female relationships in the United States. Of the two, Noble's book admittedly is more specific and more critical of Black men. She suggests that Black males have destructive, sexist attitudes. Dowling's work, which is oriented more toward sex role relationships in the United States

From *Black Caucus* 13 (Spring 1982):3–7. © 1982 by the National Association of Black Social Workers. Reprinted by permission.

generally, characterizes women as being engulfed in a destructive and debilitating fear of independence which is posited as the main reason for female subjugation in our society.

Noble's thesis implicitly blames Black men for negative social interaction between themselves and Black females. Dowling's thesis implies that a complex set of factors may be responsible for the state of Black male–female relationships. It is within the context of the latter thesis that we explore the role of the Black male and its effects on intersex social interaction.

Two important assumptions underlie our efforts. The first is that, despite Dowling's contention, which is based on Horner's studies indicating that Black females appear to be less fearful of independence than are white females *and* Black males, another observation might be more accurate. This is due to the fact that Horner's studies, which were conducted at the University of Michigan during the middle of the late 1960's, might be outdated. We suggest instead that present day Black women only *appear* to be more independent than are white women and Black men due to their historically imposed independent subsistence relative to the former. In actuality, Black females internalize values regarding not only their roles in society, but also those of Black males that are similar to the ones internalized by their white counterparts. The result is that Black females are just as emotionally dependent upon Black men as white women are on white men.

A second assumption is that Black men presently are socialized into the Prince Charming ideal *to the same extent* as are white males with one exception—they do not receive either the means or the societal support by which to approximate the ideal as do their white counterparts. Moreover, Black males oftentimes accede to the idea that Black females are independent, assertive, and so forth. Wallace's observations are instructive here:

> Black men and women were separated, given conflicting roles, and the creation of various myths assured our nation would be disunified. One of the most harmful myths was . . . the idea of the Black matriarchy. The Black woman's role was defined in such an intentional manner as to emasculate our men and give them limited responsibility (Wallace, 1979:122).

Because Black females actually *are* dependent upon Black males and many Black males' role responses are not congruent with Black female dependence, Black male–Black female social interaction suffers. The purpose of this paper, therefore, is *to explore factors within the Black male role which militate against fulfilling dependency needs in Black females*. These factors, we submit, are entrenched in *Black male responses to the "Prince Charming" ideal*—the role model for males to use in their relationships with females in the United States. This ideal, Black male responses to the ideal, and the implications of those responses to Black male–Black female relationships are the subject of this article.

The Prince Charming Ideal

In the fairy tale, not only was there a Cinderella, but there was also a Prince Charming. Dowling's book concentrated on Cinderella; we focus our attention on Prince Charming—at least the "Prince Charming" ideal which is just as pervasive in the fantasies of Black men and Black women as it is in the fantasies of their white counterparts. Dowling defines the "Cinderella complex" as "a network of largely repressed attitudes toward the full use of their minds and creativity. . . . That psychological dependency—the deep wish to be taken care of by others—is the chief force holding women down today (Dowling, 1981:31).

While Dowling's thesis certainly is thought-provoking, we contend that more than the Cinderella complex holds women down today. More specifically, the Prince Charming ideal also contributes to the subordination of women in society. In fact, the authors contend that the Prince Charming ideal negatively affects the Black male in the performance of his role as he interacts with the Black female. The Prince Charming ideal may be defined as the *philosophical belief that being a responsible, mature male means the assumption of a protective, condescending, providing and generally patriarchal role regarding one's female mate and women in general.* Implicit in this definition is a denial of the ability of women to fend for themselves as well as all of the psychological implications of the philosophical stance. Goldberg describes the syndrome in detail in his book, although he does not refer to the "Prince Charming" labels (Goldberg, 1976). Instead, he refers to so-called masculine traits such as competition, internalization of the Protestant work ethic, domination, emphasis on independence, intellect, activity, and the like.

It is interesting to note that, prior to the Black male-led civil rights movement of the late '60's and early '70's, relatively few Black Prince Charmings existed in the Black subculture in America because few Black Cinderellas existed. We contend that this social movement had the latent function of producing Black Cinderellas and Black Charmings without a fairyland. Let us explore this contention further.

Antecedent to the modern day civil rights movement, Black women generally were taught to be much more assertive, competitive, and active than were Black men. Black parents, fearing for the safety of their male offspring, generally taught them to assume the deferential mask . . . to be submissive. In 1968, Grier and Cobbs wrote at length about how Black parents tended to curb aggression, competitiveness, and domination in their male offspring for fear that it was too dangerous for them to exhibit such traits in the United States (Grier and Cobbs, 1968:62). Because Black females were not perceived by white American society to be as threatening as were Black males, Black females generally were allowed greater access to the meager opportunities for social mobility available to Blacks. This resulted in widespread perceptions of the Black females as the more dominant, aggressive, and authoritarian figure in the Black race substructure. This perception was held not only by the larger American society, but also by many Black men at the outset, and during the course, of the Black movement. These "new" Black males who were leaders and supporters of the movement, viewed the Black male as a sexual victim of matriarchal tyranny (Porter, 1979). As a result, Black females were exhorted to assume supportive rather than leadership roles in the movement, to get behind Black men, to become less aggressive and domineering, and to become more submissive in social interaction with Black men. Succinctly stated, many Black men felt that for the first time in American history they were ready to become Black Prince Charmings. Of Black female response to the Black male and Black female sex-role modification, Wallace states, "When she stood by silently as he (the Black male) became a man, she assumed that he would finally glorify and dignify Black womanhood just as the white man had done for white women" (Wallace, 1979:14). Wallace could have stated that Black females transformed themselves from self-reliant, independent, confident, and mature adults into Black Cinderellas waiting for their Black Prince Charmings. The length of the waiting period is what has troubled growing numbers of Black females and is the topic of our next section.

Black Male Responses to the Prince Charming Ideal

Once Black males and Black females accepted the Prince Charming ideal for Black males, Black male role expectations changed appreciably. The responses to these changes are the focus of our attention in this section. In a sense, it is possible to say that Black males respond to the Prince Charming ideal on two levels: an *internalization level* and an *action level.* Let us consider the nature of these responses.

Black male responses on an internalization level. Black males learn the Prince Charming ideal (that is, the "appropriate" male role), both formally and informally. Sources for this instruction are both external and internal to the Black race subculture. Instruction on the appropriate role models for men in our society may result when Black men are exposed to formal socialization from educational institutions, religious institutions, the mass media, and other basic societal institutions. While such instruction historically has occurred, it was not until the civil rights movement that increasing numbers of Black males *adopted*, and numerous Black females submissively *accepted*, the Prince Charming ideal. As a result, the Black subculture as a whole began to accept this role model. This acceptance paved the way for subcultural support of the internalization of the Prince Charming ideal by young Black males who were being instructed in appropriate male sex roles. Morever, it is suggested that many older Black males similarly became resocialized with respect to the appropriate male sex roles which Black men should internalize.

As a result of this change in Black male sex role socialization, we submit that a majority of Black males have internalized the Prince Charming ideal. This position places us diametrically opposite popular beliefs which posit that one reason for disharmony among increasing numbers of Black males and Black females is a failure of Black males to internalize a male sex role which emphasizes the assumption of responsibility, self-reliance, assertiveness, competitiveness, independence, and the like. Indeed, the myth of Black males' noninternalization of the normative male sex role probably persists because of the failure of many persons to distinguish between the two levels of Black male responses to the role ideal—that is, internalization and action. Internalizing the ideal does not automatically result in behavior congruent with the ideal, as will be shown below. Given the inordinate number of societal constraints Black males experience when they attempt to exhibit behavior congruent with their internalized values, it is not surprising that, on the whole, Black male actions are viewed as being divergent from the Prince Charming ideal. Such perceptions seemingly support the notion that a majority of Black males reject the ideal and, therefore, do not act in accordance with the ideal. The authors contend that this is not the case and, instead, offer an alternative explanation of Black male action on the ideal.

Black male response on an action level. For Black males, unlike counterparts in our society, there is not a linear relationship between internalization of the Prince Charming ideal and action congruent with the ideal. On the contrary, for Black males, numerous societal factors militate against their actualization of the Prince Charming ideal. Such factors are well known, and have been explored extensively. The important point to note is that a failure to act upon the ideal may not reflect a rejection of the ideal. Acting upon the ideal is some function of class status for Black males just as it is

for white males. However, for Black males, unlike white males, it is also some function of actual and perceived opportunities for obtaining the means by which to act upon the ideal. This means that Black males continue to be inhibited in their efforts to act upon the Prince Charming ideal. The existence of this inhibition illuminates the need for social science scholars and practitioners to conduct research and respond to clients on the basis of a model of the Black male role as one that involves not only internalizing and acting upon the ideal, but also a failure to do so. The accompanying table shows the proposed model.

At a simple action response level, Black males either act or fail to act in accordance with the Prince Charming ideal. Because two levels of Black male responses are suggested, Black male responses always involve at least two variables *and* one of two subtypes of each variable. Thus, the Black male response to the Prince Charming ideal at the most simple level assumes one of four possible forms. First, some Black males (category one) internalize the ideal and exhibit behavior congruent with the ideal. Black males most likely to be characterized in this manner typically are middle class, although they can be found throughout the Black social stratification. When such males come from the lower socioeconomic classes, they have usually acquired the necessary means for actualizing the ideal. Entertainers and sports figures who, after years of poverty, suddenly acquire great wealth are highly visible examples of lower class Black males who become socially mobile and, therefore, are able to actualize the internalized Prince Charming ideal. Other less visible Black males in this category include those who become socially mobile through education, hard work, and rare opportunities.

Category two calls attention to those Black males who, for a variety of reasons related to their socialization experience (both formal and informal), *do not* internalize the Prince Charming ideal, but rather act in a ritualistic manner regarding the ideal. These males, then, act in accordance with the ideal and may superficially resemble those Black males in category one. The characteristic that distinguishes the Black male category two from all of the others is a tendency to actualize his resentment of the roles he performs. In addition, when the oppor-

Black Male Responses to the Prince Charming Ideal

		BLACK MALE INTERNALIZATION RESPONSE RELATED TO THE PRINCE CHARMING IDEAL	
		Internalize	Failure to Internalize
Black male action responses related to the Prince Charming ideal	Act in accordance with the ideal	1	2
	Fail to act in accordance with the ideal	3	4

tunity presents itself, such Black males are extremely likely to discard the "performing" role. We contend that some unknown proportion of Black males who reject parental and spousal obligations fall into this category. However, not all Black men who initially act on the ideal but who do not subsequently continue to do so should be characterized as having failed to internalize the Prince Charming ideal, as we show later.

A third response category in which we feel a large number of poor Black males can be placed is category three. Black males in this category *do* internalize the Prince Charming ideal, but the behaviors which they exhibit are not congruent with the internalized values. Many of these Black males, we feel, come from the lower Black social stratum, while the remainder have experienced *downward social mobility*. The distinguishing feature of the males in this category is the high probability that they will engage in self-destructive behavior as well as anti-social behavior, that is, physically abusive behavior toward their mates. Such behavior, when viewed by the uninformed, is likely to be perceived as a failure to internalize the ideal. To the contrary, we believe that such behavior reflects feelings of poor self-esteem due to the lack of means by which to actualize the internalized and societally supported Prince Charming ideal. Additionally, such feelings and the resulting anti-social behavior may

be increased when the Black female in such a relationship also holds expectations for the Black male that are congruent with the ideal.

The fourth Black male response category describes the Black male who does not internalize the ideal and who fails to act in accordance with the ideal. These Black males can include two types: (1) those who appear to be estranged from Black females (and females in general), often by exhibiting boorish behavior and an apparent lack of respect for women; and (2) those Black males who in the vernacular seemingly "have it all together," but who refuse to allow Black females to become emotionally dependent upon them or to act in a protective, condescending, and generally patriarchal manner toward Black females. Because of the influence and pervasiveness of the Prince Charming ideal, however, we believe that Black males falling into this category are relatively few in number in comparison to those in the other three categories.

The Implications of Black Male Responses for Black Male–Black Female Relations

By now, the implications of Black male responses to the Prince Charming ideal for social interaction between Black males and Black females are probably apparent. Black males who interact with Black females from the vantage point of category one (internalization of the ideal and action in accordance with the ideal) usually do so with a minimum of difficulty. Both the male and the female generally experience a positive interaction. This is to be expected, since both individuals have similar expectations about the roles of Black males and Black females involved in social interaction. Moreover, hidden resentment is less likely to characterize the male involved in the interaction. In this case, Black Prince Charming is meeting his own expectations as well as the expectations of the Black Cinderella.

But, what happens to Black male–Black female relationships when Prince Charming does *not* internalize the Prince Charming ideal (category two)? Such relationships can superficially appear to be positive for years. This is true because the Black male's visible behavior under these circumstances may be no different from that of the true Black Prince Charming. However, the possible exception is that the Black male in category two strictly fulfills the overt behavioral requirements of his role and *demands* that Black Cinderella fulfill the requirements of her role. In such instances, the Black male is likely to be hypercritical of the Black female—making extreme demands on her and placing her in impossible situations (Goldberg, 1976). Her inability to meet these demands or to extricate herself from such situations provides the needed excuse for him not to *fulfill* his own and her expectations of his role. When this occurs, the Black male is inclined to leave the relationship. If he remains in the relationship, the situation usually becomes intolerable for the Black female and she is forced to flee the relationship. When both remain, the relationship becomes an overtly conflict-ridden one with both parties feeling that the expectations for the other are not being met.

Black male–Black female relationships are most visibly conflict-ridden when Black males fall into category three . . . (when they have internalized the Prince Charming ideal, but do not have the means by which to act on the ideal). Black males in these situations suffer from poor self-esteem *and* a loss of respect from Black females. These men are much more likely than are those in any other category to be physically abusive toward the Black female, who is perceived as demanding, nagging, domineering, and aggressive. On another level, however, such males feel that they are not adequately fulfilling their self-internalized roles. The Black female who also has accepted the definition of the Black male's role as that of "Prince Charming" and who exhibits behavior congruent with this acceptance is viewed by this Black male as a constant reminder of his failure to live up to his own ideals. Hostilities which Black males in this category direct toward these women may be construed as efforts to eradicate the "reminder."

Category four characterizes Black males who neither internalize nor act upon the Prince Charming ideal. The implications of this Black male response for Black male–Black female relationships take two diverse directions. One direction leads to unstable relationships between Black males in this category and Black females. The other direction, given modifications in the expectations for Black males held by many Black females, can lead to stable and positive relationships between these Black males and Black females.

With respect to the first direction, Black males who have neither internalized nor acted upon the ideal include those who visibly shirk all responsibility and act contrary to the male role ideal. Such men indicate verbally and by their actions that they have no intention of participating in a stable relationship with any Black female. Obviously, a proliferation of Black males who perform their roles in this manner foretells doom for Black male–Black female relationships.

Yet, there is a small and growing cadre of Black males who epitomize category four, but who believe that Black females should renounce many elements of the Cinderella complex and, therefore, modify their expectations of the role of Black men in Black male–Black female relationships. Such men *are* responsible and behave responsibly toward Black females, respecting Black females as mature adults. When these males form relationships with Black females who have modified their conceptions of the Black male's role in Black male–Black female relationships, stable relationships between the two may be obtained. Men and women who begin their relationship in this manner can be characterized in sex-role parlance as having an androgynous sex-role orientation. Moreover, we suggest that such relationships can be fulfilling to both parties. Given the fact that support exists in our society for less dependent, more assertive women and for less aggressive, less domineering men, those possessing an androgynous sex-role orientation may increase the probability that the relationships they form are both positive and powerful.

Conclusion

A latent but persistent theme in our analysis of Black male responses to the Black male's role in Black male–Black female relationships has been that Black men may respond in several ways. In addition, we indicated that there may not be a linear relationship between internalization of the traditional male role and the exhibition of behavior which is congruent with that role. Societal constraints on acting upon the Prince Charming ideal, noninternalization of the ideal, and an inability to act upon the ideal, among the factors, may all be responsible for Black male behavior which appears to be contrary to the Prince Charming ideal.

An additional feature of our analysis is that both the Prince Charming ideal and the Cinderella complex lock persons into social roles, which may be difficult to fulfill in a modern society. The Black male role may be the most difficult of all to fulfill, given the complexities of, and the contradictions inherent in, his role in a society which is often diametrically opposed to his interests.

Given the above statements, social scientists (both theoreticians and practitioners) should begin to view Black male responses in terms of the multiplicity of possible meanings of the responses. Traditionally, Black male responses deemed to be inappropriate in Black male–Black female relationships have been defined as meaning noninternalization of what we call the "Prince Charming ideal." As we have seen, this perception may or may not be accurate. Morever, when disruptive responses are defined in this way, measures designed to alter the responses may be inadequate. Certainly, the model presented in this paper to represent possible meanings underlying Black male responses is simplistic. Some Black males, for example, may partially internalize the ideal, act upon the ideal only part of the time, and so forth. Yet, we believe that approaching a particular case from the framework presented—with whatever modifications may be required by that case—may improve the rate of problem resolution between Black males and Black females. This undoubtedly will contribute to the unification of Black men and Black women in America.

References

Dowling, Colette
1981 *The Cinderella Complex*. New York: Summit Books.

Goldberg, Herb
1976 *The Hazards of Being Male*. New York: New American Library.

Grier, William H., and Price M. Cobbs
1968 *Black Rage*. New York: Basic Books.

Noble, Jeanne
1978 *Beautiful Also Are the Souls of My Black Sisters*. Englewood Cliffs, N.J.: Prentice-Hall.

Porter, John R.
1979 *Dating Habits of Young Black Americans*. Dubuque, Ia.: Kendall/Hunt.

Wallace, Michelle
1979 *Black Macho and the Myth of the Superwoman*. New York: Dial Press.

AN ALTERNATIVE ANALYSIS OF SEXISM:
Implications for the Black Family

Betty Collier-Watson · Louis N. Williams · Willy Smith

Gender differences are viewed as both favorable and unfavorable to women. In a systemic sense, women lose because of the inequalities that characterize the operation of social institutions. Conversely, in a vitalistic manner, men lose because their morbidity and mortality rates are higher than those of women. It is demonstrated that when men lose, Black men lose the most. When women lose, Black women lose the most. Thus, sexism is seen as a two-edged sword. Women gain in some areas and lose in others. It is concluded that Black men and women gain the least and lose the most of the sex–race groups.

Introduction

Over the past two decades since the mid-sixties, it has become quite popular for Black writers to engage in debunking of myths concerning the Black family. The reasons are obvious. The ideational content of knowledge is always socially determined and human thought has historically served as a critical instrument in the institutionalization of inequality. Thus, it has been incumbent on Black social scientists to inquire, explicate, and reiterate thoughts, ideas, and analyses towards a more accurate understanding of the Black family.

Such a task is, however, a difficult one. In societies characterized by inequalities, an epistemological catch-22 exists. On the one hand, various groups within the society may seek to be involved in the advocacy of measures to ameliorate social dysfunction to the degree that such a state is socially produced. Yet, in order to intermediate, a body of knowledge must exist that accurately reflects the magnitude and nature of the dysfunction so that programs and policies can be teleologically related to causes. However, when inequality exists within a society, the inequalities are so far-reaching that the disadvantaged groups are also underrepresented in the production and distribution of knowledge about their own condition. Furthermore, their disadvantaged status is often so psychosocially entrenched that they often fall victim to the same epistemological myopia that tailors the knowledge produced and distributed by the dominant group. The thesis herein is that over the last two decades the stability of the Black family and of Black male/female relationships has been reduced because Black social scientists have failed in promoting accurate discourse about the interactive relationship of race, gender, and class. Indeed, not only white but also Black social scientists have promoted the axiomatic view that race and sex have operated and continue to operate as parallel systems of oppression. Such a view has not leapt into Black consciousness. Rather, Black scholarship regarding sexism and sex role modeling has tended to play the role of passive beneficiary to the models and paradigms of sexism that have been promoted by white scholarship.

Previously unpublished paper, 1985. Printed by permission.

Accordingly, the tasks herein are several. At the first level, the objective of this discussion is that of examining the functioning of sexism between Black males and females. To accomplish this task, however, it is necessary to reanalyze and reconceptualize the functioning of sex role asymmetry in U.S. society.

Sex Role Asymmetry: A Contemporary Profile

For the most part, Black social scientists have adopted what can be called a unilateral model of sexism. A unilateral conception of the operation of sexism postulates that U.S. society is characterized by sex role asymmetry (inequality). Implicit within this conception is the view that this asymmetrical arrangement is one in which females lose and males gain. Indeed, inequalities of sex are viewed as constituting a system of male dominance. United States society is also characterized by forms of asymmetry based on race and class. These phenomena are similarly viewed as operating in such a fashion that inequalities emerge with gains accruing to the dominant race and/or class. For the purposes of the analysis herein, inequalities emerging as a consequence of the operation of sex, class, and/or race within a society will be separated into two separate but related categories. Those inequalities that characterize the operation of social institutions can be denoted as systemic inequalities. In contrast, those inequalities that characterize the chances of survival among the members of a given society will be called vitalistic.

Societies exist to enhance the chances of survival of its members. *Thus, the ultimate test of the impact of asymmetry on a given group in a society cannot be completely measured by an examination of the asymmetrical functioning of social institutions. Rather, the ultimate impact of asymmetry in that society reveals itself through the impact on the length and quality of survival.* Such a statement implies that systemic and vitalistic inequalities are *directly* related. That is, systemic gains are reflected in vitalistic gains. Conversely, systemic losses are reflected in vitalistic losses.

Empirical data support this assumption when asymmetries based on social class are examined. In U.S. society individuals of the lower classes experience systemic inequalities. Indeed, they receive unequal benefits from the major pivotal institutions. Such groups receive less income and wealth (Krauss, 1976; Miller and Roby, 1977). Additionally, members of the lower classes have less political power and influence (Turner and Starnes, 1976). Such a pattern extends itself into the educational institutions. Children of lower-class families relative to children from higher-class families graduate from high school 250% less often, attend college 400% less often, graduate from college 600% less often, and receive postgraduate training 900% less often (Sewell, 1971). Also, the lower classes have more children and more divorces (Krauss, 1976). Such systemic inequalities are directly correlated with a similar vitalistic trend. Lower classes in the United States have lower life expectancies and higher death rates (Tumin, 1967; U.S. Department of Health, Education, and Welfare, 1976). Similarly, individuals within these classes experience a higher incidence of psychosis (Faris and Durham, 1939; Hollingshead and Redlich, 1958). Surveys reveal that lower-class individuals report less happiness (Bradburn and Caplovitz, 1965) and more job boredom and dissatisfaction (Chinoy, 1955; Wooten, 1974). Lastly, lower-class individuals experience higher rates of crime as victim and victimizer and higher death rates from all major diseases (Collier and Smith, 1981). Indeed, when class asymmetry is examined, the direct relationship between systemic and vitalistic inequalities is most apparent.

Without detailing the data, it can be said that a similar direct relationship between systemic and vitalistic variables exists by race. Not only do minority groups have lower median family incomes, higher levels of unemployment, and disproportionate rates of poverty, but they also have: (1) lower life expectancies, (2) higher rates of crimes as victims and victimizers, (3) higher rates of criminal conviction, (4) higher divorce rates, (5) higher death rates from all major diseases, and so on, than do nonminority groups (Collier and Smith, 1981).

When sex role asymmetry is examined from such a perspective, however, and systemic as well as vitalistic variables are considered, a dual system of asymmetry becomes apparent. Systemically, females, for the most part, lose and males gain. Vitalistically, females gain and males lose. When these dual areas are interlocked, there emerges a unique type of asymmetry. More specifically, a bilateral relationship is revealed. Again, a detailed review of data supports these assertions.

The U.S. economy epitomizes an area in which systemic inequalities based on sex prevail. In 1983, for example, median weekly earnings for all families was $470. When the data are stratified by sex, however, significant differences emerge. Married couple families had median family incomes of $27,286. While single householders of both sexes had median weekly earnings less than those of married couple families, families maintained by women had median family incomes of only $11,789.[1] Similarly, in 1984 34% of female-headed families existed below the poverty level and 44.2% below 125% of poverty, in contrast to 13.1% and 19.8% of all families respectively.[2]

When employment by sex and occupational category is examined, a slightly different form of asymmetry emerges—females in contemporary U.S. society are disproportionately white-collar workers and males are disproportionately blue-collar workers. Whereas the overall earnings of males in these various occupational categories exceed those of females, it is not often pointed out that vitalistic losses are incurred by males. In one year, for example, males experienced 92.6 work-related accidents and injuries per 1,000 persons in contrast to 12.8 per 1,000 persons for females.[3] A similar pattern exists when occupational category is further disaggregated by sex. Females constitute only 13.4% of physicians, dentists, and related practitioners, for example.[4] Whereas such occupations are overwhelmingly male, such statuses carry with them one of the highest rates of suicide of all occupational categories as well as average life expectancies below those of males in general.

A brief glance at other pivotal institutions reveals a clear pattern of systemic inequalities from which males gain. Before the 1980 national elections, for example, 417 representatives were male and only 16 were female, and 99 senators were male and only 1 was female. State and local public offices followed a similar pattern. Some 3% of state executive and judiciary officials, 9.2% of state legislators, 3.1% of county commissioners, and 7.8% of mayors and city councilpersons were female.[5] This asymmetrical holding of statuses and roles by males extended itself into the religious institution, in which 89% of all religious workers were male.

The educational institution, however, displayed an asymmetrical pattern that was less clear in terms of gains and losses. Some 70% of all non-university and college teachers were female. Again, a disaggregation of the data reveals that 96.8% of prekindergarten and kindergarten, 85.1% of elementary, 49.6% of secondary, and 36.6% of college and university teachers were female.[6] Yet males were disproportionately represented in higher statuses within the educational institution; over 72% of college professors were male.

When this systemic data is conjoined with vitalistic data, the existence of a bilateral pattern of sex role asymmetry becomes most apparent. During the same time period, the life expectancy of females was 78.3 years in contrast to 71.1 years for males.[7] In addition, males died from diseases of the heart 129% more often, from malignant neoplasms 126% more often, from pneumonia 123% more often, from cirrhosis of the liver 200% more often, and from suicide 295% more often than females did (percentages calculated by authors). Indeed, males suffered from all major diseases except cardiovascular diseases, diabetes mellitus, and arteriosclerosis at a greater rate than that for females.[8]

The asymmetry extends itself into other areas. In this same period males were victims of all crimes except rape at a greater rate than that of females. Males were victims of robbery with injury 300% more often, robbery without injury 350% more often, aggravated assault 300% more often, simple assault 172% more often, and personal larceny 128% more often than females.[9] Lastly, males were victims of homicide 300% more often than females. Not only does asymmetry exist in victimization rates, it also exists in rates of arrest and convictions. Males were arrested for crimes 594% more often than females. Finally, since 1979 males have been sentenced to death 8000% more often than females.[10]

Parallel patterns exist in other areas. In 1980, 129% more males than females were in mental hospitals and residential treatment centers. As the disproportionate victims of lung diseases, 240% more males were in tuberculosis hospitals. Similarly, 129% more males were in homes and schools for the mentally handicapped, 266% more males were in homes and schools for the physically handicapped, 147% more males were in homes for dependent and neglected children, and 378% more males were in detention homes. Additionally, as would be expected, 5020% more males were in military barracks.[11] The only institutions with disproportionately higher female populations were homes for the aged and dependent and homes for unwed mothers.

Other data could be introduced. However, the data discussed is sufficient to lend validity to the hypothesis that U.S. society is characterized by an asymmetry from which males benefit systemically while losing vitalistically. In contrast, females lose systemically while gaining vitalistically. It is this aspect of sexism that is often underdeveloped in existing literature in the area. Additionally, it is this aspect of sexism that supports an assertion that unlike social asymmetries based on class and race, the phenomenon of sexism operates as a bilateral process. Before an analysis of the relations among sex, race, and class can be presented, it is necessary to address another thematic thread that emerges from the use of the explicit and implicit assumptions of models of sexism that focus on systemic asymmetries. Specifically, the existence of systemic asymmetries is viewed as implying the operation of a system of male dominance. Indeed, many social scientists have exonerated white females from responsibility for racial oppression by arguing that white females were merely victims of male dominance.

The notion that the history of women is a history of male dominance is so widely accepted that it too has become an axiom. Examples from literature and religion are used to demonstrate the existence of cultures imbued with sexist ideology (Campbell, 1959; Diner, 1973; Janeway, 1971). Male dominance is also viewed as not only reflecting itself in male control of the major pivotal institutions but also in the generally disproportionate accrual of prestige, power, and privilege to males. Indeed, male dominance is viewed by many as being so thorough and so indisputedly present in all relationships between males and females that sex, like race and class, has come to be viewed as another form of social stratification characterized by the oppression of females by males. This view is well summarized by Sheila Rowbotham (1974:35–46):

> *The social situations of women and the way in which we learn to be feminine is peculiar to us. Men do not share it, consequently we cannot be simply included under the heading of "mankind." The only claim that this word has to be general comes from the dominance of men in society. As the rulers they presume to define others by their own criteria.*

Accordingly, the implications or our bilateral conceptions of sexism for the male dominance thesis must be explored before the relationships between sex, race, and class can be examined. Although the primary focus of the analysis herein is upon the operation of sexism among Blacks, the concepts of sex role asymmetry and male dominance have become central themes in Black male/female relationships.

Sex Role Asymmetry: Male Dominance within a Bilateral Conception of Sexism

The existence of systemic sex role asymmetry is widespread in human societies. Similarly, the view that such societies are characterized by male dominance is widespread. The anthropologist W. M. Stephens (1963), in a study of forty-one societies, concluded that males were dominant in 65% of the societies studied, males and females shared power in 26%, and females were dominant in only 7%. Such findings have been confirmed in other studies (Gough, 1971; Hunt, 1973; Romney, 1965). Indeed, the analyses of George Murdock's world ethnographic sample by D'Androde (1966) indicated that

66% of a sample of 565 societies throughout the world were patrilocal, whereas only 14% were matrilocal. Some 80% of the cultures sampled were patrilineal and 99% permitted polygyny but not polyandry. The substantial body of literature on the phenomenon of male dominance from a cross-cultural perspective has been adequately reviewed elsewhere (Parker and Parker, 1979).

An additional glance at the literature reveals that social scientists have also sought to locate the causes of systemic asymmetry and male dominance. A relatively widespread view is that male dominance is a consequence of biological factors (Goldberg, 1973; Tiger and Shepher, 1975). A less well accepted explanation of the alleged existence of male supremacy is the idea that prestate warfare is the causal factor (Divale and Harris, 1974; Hirschfeld, Howe, and Levin, 1978; Lancaster and Lancaster, 1978). The most prevalent explanations, however, view biological factors that emerged into a division of labor by sex as having led to male dominance (Brown, 1970; Murdock and Provost, 1973). This view can be examined in greater detail.

For both Blacks and whites, sex role asymmetry fulfills several systemic functions. On the one hand, sex roles provide the basis for a division of labor and economic specialization. Additionally, critical social functions are fulfilled by the existence of sex roles. Importantly, sex role differentiation functions as the foundation of marriage and the family. This function is implicit in the definition of a family, which has been described as "a social arrangement based on marriage and the marriage contract, including recognition of the rights and duties of parenthood, common residence for husband, wife, and children and reciprocal economic obligations between husband and wife" (Stephens, 1963:8). The systemic functions of sex role asymmetry via its relationship to the family cannot be overemphasized because such functions relate directly to the themes of sex and class. These points can be examined more closely.

Not only is the family traditionally the basic unit of a society, it and the educational institution are the central mechanisms for preserving the value system of that society (Bell and Vogel, 1968). The division of labor by sex traditionally assigned to females the responsibilities for the socialization of children while assigning to males primary responsibility for the satisfaction of physical and biological needs of the family (e.g., food, shelter, and protection). These functions of males and females within the family interact in support of the family's role in another critical aspect of the society. Specifically, males and females within a family act out roles that cause the family to act as a major agent for creating and maintaining the existing systems of social stratification. Males are assigned the responsibilities for acquiring the artifacts of production and artifacts of power for placement within stratified hierarchy. Similarly, females are assigned the task of socializing the young into those beliefs, values, and practices that correlate to the family's position within the social hierarchy. Thus, both males and females are coparticipants in class- and race-based oppression. Such statements do not imply the application of a structural functionalist (Parsons, 1955) approach to sex role asymmetry and the concept of male dominance. The oversimplification implicit in such a position has been adequately discussed elsewhere (Aronoff and Crano, 1975).

Indeed, a rejection of the view that sex role asymmetry emerged as a functional adaptation of the species as a whole has led to the adoption of other overly simple analyses. Some theorists have suggested that systemic asymmetry and male dominance emerged as a correlate of the development of economic surplus (Gough, 1971). Still others have viewed systemic inequality and male dominance as emerging from a fear of rape (Brownmiller, 1975). Independent of the causes of the emergence of sex role asymmetry, the accepted position is that sex role asymmetry cross-culturally has led to the emergence of a system of social stratification characterized by male dominance. This system of social stratification is viewed as (1) operating in the interest of males and (2) maintained and supported by males. Additionally, this system of male dominance is viewed, like social stratification based upon race and class, as being supported by sanctions, myths, and other social psychological mechanisms that reinforce existing inequalities. Accordingly, the issue of whether systemic inequalities constitute a system of male dominance is actually subsumed by the issue of whether sex role asymmetry constitutes a system of social stratification. More importantly, it is critical to understand how sex role asymmetry is linked with race and class asymmetries.

Systems of social stratification have been recognized as consisting of inequality in three major components: (1) rights over property, (2) differential power or control, and (3) differential prestige or esteem (Weber, 1958). Such inequalities we have characterized as *systemic* inequalities. In addition, we have demonstrated that systemic inequalities in a system of social stratification are reflected in a direct relationship with *vitalistic* inequalities. When a system of social stratification exists, systemic and vitalistic inequalities together delineate a set of *class interests* for the dominant and subordinate groups.

Our analysis of U.S. society, however, demonstrated clearly an inverse relationship between systemic and vitalistic asymmetries for males and females. Although data is not available for measuring and correlating vitalistic asymmetry with systemic asymmetry in traditional societies, *existing data support the conclusion* that even in traditional societies, females and males do *not* have separate class interests. Males and females do not separately compete for either property and/or power. Whereas it is true that greater prestige accrues to males, it is critical to our analysis to note that the benefits of property, power, and prestige accrue differentially to family units. *Although intrafamilial relationships may be characterized by various inequalities, these are not so intense as to create a separate set of class interests for males and females.*

As other systems of social stratification emerge, such as racism, such systems become sex and gender linked. First, the physical attributes of the sex role model for that society are determined by the physical attributes of the dominant race and/or class. Second, gender role expectations and behaviors are dictated by standards derived from the dominant race and/or class. Thus, an *interactive* relationship exists between sex role asymmetry and other forms of social stratification. Importantly, neither males nor females as a *class* are the beneficiaries of a sex-based system of social stratification. *Rather, the family unit becomes the intervening variable through which sex-based roles provide benefits.* The family continues to function as the basic unit of social organization based on division of labor and specialization. Each family defends its position in the hierarchy in the struggle for property, power, and privilege. Males and females *share* class interests. Between males and females, males are allotted legitimate power while females share in other forms of power. An asymmetry does exist. This asymmetry produces benefits and losses for males and females within the family unit and thus must be more appropriately viewed as a system of exchange based on common goals and common interests. Thus, male/female interaction can be more appropriately characterized as cooperative and accommodative. *In contrast, males and females within families jointly cooperate in a competitive and conflicting interaction with families from other strata (e.g., Black versus white families).*

Thus, the position herein is that the prevalent view of sex role asymmetry as a system of social stratification characterized by male oppression of females represents tremendous oversimplification. Rather, the positions taken herein can be summarized as follows: (1) Different forms of sex role asymmetry exist for both males and females. (2) Under conditions of stable family units, such asymmetry constitutes a division of labor and specialization that is functional to the survival of the family members. (3) Similarly, when stability of the family exists, male/female asymmetry does not constitute a system of stratification based upon sex, but rather the male/female units act to preserve, in unity, their own race/class interests.

In contemporary U.S. society, however, sex and gender roles are being detached from their function as the foundation of the family unit. Indeed, the numerous factors leading to an increase in single family households has undermined the functioning of sex role asymmetry as a bilateral system of exchange. Within this context, the existence of sex roles achieves an additional importance beyond their impact on the self-actualization of males and females.

The increasing shift away from the family as the basic unit of social organization creates a basis for the emergence of class interests by sex. Males and females who choose to exist without attachment to a family unit become responsible for the total need satisfaction of self. Each individual, then, regardless of sex, must be expressive and instrumental in the tasks performed. Each individual must compete for limited social statuses and scarce economic resources. Because family units benefit from increasing returns to scale, the emergence of one-person social units, as well as single male- or female-headed households, places an additional burden on limited economic resources (e.g., housing, energy, and transportation). Accordingly, it is accurate to conclude that sex-based class interests may be emerging in U.S. society. How such a social phenomenon relates to existing forms of stratification has important implications for social change movements in the United States.

Class, Race, and Sex

If sex role asymmetry is beginning to emerge as a struggle for resources between males and females, the U.S. system of social stratification, already based on class and race, becomes even more complex. For the most part, unilateral models of sexism view the oppression of females by males as a separate phenomenon that operates across class and across race lines (Beal, 1975). In addition, unilateral models of sexism promote the viewpoint that women experience an oppression that parallels racial and class oppression. Such concepts have led many writers to conclude that in U.S. society, black females, for example, often suffer a triple oppression (Beal, 1975:2–3).

> *Since her arrival on these alien shores, the black woman has been subjected to the worst kinds of exploitation and oppression. As a black, she has had to endure all the horrors of slavery . . . ; as a worker, she has been the object of continual exploitation. . . . In addition, besides suffering the common fate of all oppressed and exploited people, the Afro-American woman continues to experience the age old oppression of woman by man.*

Although the assertion is often made in the literature that both sexism and racism are products of capitalism (Lewis, 1977; Rowbotham, 1974; Staples, 1979) and some efforts have been made to point out essential differences in the functioning of class, race, and sexism (Rowbotham, 1974), few systematic efforts have been made to identify the precise relations that exist between asymmetrical relations based on sex and those based on race and class. Thus, the task within this section is that of using our bilateral conceptualization of sexism to examine the interrelations among all three systems of social stratification.

As mentioned earlier, the ideals embodied in sex and gender role models are neither class nor race neutral. Sex- and gender-based role models prescribe ideal physical and behavioral attitudes for each sex. It has been asserted that losses and gains differentially accrue to individuals on the basis of how closely their physical and behavioral attributes fit the model for their sex. Also, a type of stratification occurs as males and females who more closely fit the model choose each other as mates (Collier and Williams, 1981). If sex role models are intrinsically race and class based, it follows that the interactive relationship between these three factors function so as to promote and sustain existing patterns of inequality. Studies on similarity attraction not only document that dating and/or marriage occurs disproportionately between those of similar class and race, but also between similar males and females as measured by other criteria. For example, Maslow (1963) pointed out that self-actualizing males tend to marry self-actualizing females. This tendency has since been confirmed by other investigators (King, 1974). Similarly, attraction has also been demonstrated by still other investigations. Males and females of parallel abilities are attracted to each other (Zander and Havelin, 1960). Of course, males and females of comparable socio-economic classes more often marry (Byrne, Cleve, and Worchel, 1966). In addition, physically beautiful females marry economically successful males (Elder, 1969).

Again, such data assume particular importance since inequalities by class and race are built into the sex role models that operate within U.S.

society. Additionally, such data imply that beyond their socialization function, marriage and the family are mechanisms through which class and racial inequalities are perpetuated. Racial and class exploitation, then, serve the interests of both males and females of the dominant race and class. *If such a thesis is correct, it would then follow that sexism reinforces patterns of inequality based on class and race.* That is, using the assumptions of our bilateral model, we can conclude that sex, race, and class would function in such a way that if the three are interactive, in those areas where males gain, males of the minority race and subordinate class will gain less. Conversely, in those areas in which males lose, the greatest losses would accrue to the victims of social stratification. Similarly, in those areas in which females gain, females of the minority race and subordinate class would gain less and in those areas in which females lose, the converse would occur. Similarly, in those physical and behavioral standards defining sex role models, males and females of the minority race and subordinate class would fall the greatest distance from the norm. Thus, it can be said that sex, race, and class form a comprehensive and interactive system of social stratification within U.S. society. This thesis can also be tested by a brief review of the empirical data. Because the data are unavailable by sex, race, and class, only the interactive effects of sex and race will be examined.

It was mentioned earlier that while men as a class gain systematically from sex role asymmetry, males as a class lose vitalistically. If there exists an interactive relation between stratification by sex and race, this pattern should be evident in vitalistic data by race and sex. And the data are quite clear. When life expectancy data are stratified by sex and race, a telling statistical portrait emerges. White females have a life expectancy 106% greater than that of minority females, 111% higher than that of white males, and 120% higher than that of minority males. Similarly, the age-adjusted mortality rate for minority males is 134% greater than that of white males, 169% greater than that of minority females, and 244% greater than that of white females.[12]

When other vitalistic data are included, the interactive effects of race and sex are even more apparent. Minority males die from diseases of the heart 101% more often than white males, 157% more often than minority females, and 217% more often than white females. Minority males die from malignant neoplasms 128% more often than white males, 168% more often than minority females, and 190% more often than white females.[13] When social causes of death such as homicide are included, the pattern continues. Minority males are victims of homicide 682% more often than white males, 480% more often than minority females, and 2072% more often than white females.[14]

When data on crime and crime victimization are examined in greater detail by sex and race, the interactive effects of these two forms of social stratification are equally distinct. Minority males in 1978 were robbed without injury 200% more often than white males, 200% more often than minority females, and 200% more often than white females. Similarly, minority males were robbed with injury 200% more often than white males, 250% more often than minority females, and 600% more often than white females.[15] While males in general are victims of all crimes except rape at greater than the rate for females, the data indicate that minority males in general are more often the victims of serious crime. For example, white males suffer from simple assault 105% more often than minority males, but minority males suffer from aggravated assault 106% as often as white males. In the area of criminal justice administration, this trend is also apparent. Over the period from 1930 to 1979, 3,862 persons were executed. Within this group, 54% of those executed were black, 45% were white, and 1% were members of other races. Less than one-tenth of 1% of those executed were females of either race.[16] Indeed, the data quite clearly support our thesis that in those vitalistic areas in which males lose, the interactive effects of race and sex create additional losses for Black males.

As mentioned earlier, sexual asymmetry affects females negatively from a systemic perspective. Again, the data support the assertion that sex and race are interactive social forces. The median income of minority males more nearly approximates that of white males than does the median income of white females. In contrast, the differential between minority females and white males is greatest of all. Similarly, minority male-headed, white female-headed, and minority female-headed families exist in poverty more often than Black male-headed families. If the analysis is extended to the political institution, a parallel trend is seen.

Even when systemic asymmetries are examined in combination with vitalistic asymmetries to demonstrate that sex and race are interactive forces, the portrait of the impact of this interaction is incomplete. Sex role models negatively affect the lives of males and females by (1) constraining self-actualization, (2) skewing the distribution of systemic and vitalistic losses and gains, (3) creating a system of rewards and punishments that differentially accrue to individuals on the basis of their physical and behavioral closeness to the ideal. When race and sex are operative forces, individuals are confronted with constraints to self-actualization as a consequence of race and sex. As has been demonstrated, systemic and vitalistic losses are compounded. Finally, however, the psychosocial impact of sex role models creates additional trauma for Black individuals. Such persons are permanently constrained from being able to achieve the physical and sometimes behavioral attributes of the ideal standard. Thus, additional trauma is created as such persons aspire to the unobtainable while their worth is measured by an implicitly biased model.

Conclusions and Implications

Several different yet related reconceptualizations in the area of sexism have been highlighted herein.

These can be summarized as follows. The first task was that of statistically demonstrating that sex role asymmetry functions in such a manner that females lose systematically while males gain. Simultaneously, data were introduced in support of the thesis that females gain vitalistically from sex role asymmetry while males lose. Second, this bilateral system of gains and losses does not tautologically cause a system of social stratification. Rather, in order for a system of social stratification to emerge, males and/or females as a group must have separate *class interests*. Third, the point was made that the changing patterns regarding organization of the family have caused a breakdown in the division of labor function of sex roles and have led to a struggle for resources between males and females. Fourth, it was concluded that this struggle for resources does not define sexism as a *separate* form of social stratification from race and class but rather as an *interactive* one based on race and class. Fifth, the thesis was introduced that race and class variables condition those attributes incorporated into sex role models. Thus, sexist standards are implicitly racist and class biased. Sixth, it was empirically demonstrated that in those areas in which females lose, Black females lose most and that in those areas in which males lose, Black males lose most. Finally, it was pointed out that the existence of sex role models creates special psychosocial problems for those who are Black.

In other words, both Black males and females are victims of a triple and interactive system of oppression. This interactive system poses psychological, sociological, and economic barriers to Black family development and growth.

1*U.S. Department of Commerce, Bureau of the Census*, Statistical Abstract of the United States, 1986. *"Median Family Money Income by Number of Earners and Race of Householders, 1983," No. 757 (Washington, D.C.: Government Printing Office), 453.*

2*U.S. Department of Commerce, Bureau of the Census*, Statistical Abstract of the United States, 1986. *"Persons below Poverty Level and below 128 Percent of Poverty Level by Race of Householders and Family Status: 1959–1984," No. 767 (Washington, D.C.: Government Printing Office), 458.*

3*U.S. Bureau of the Census*, Statistical Abstract of the United States, *"Occupations of Work-Experienced Civilian Labor Force, by Sex: 1970 and 1980," No. 697 (Washington, D.C.: Government Printing Office), 600.*

4*Center for the American Woman and Politics*, Women in Public Office: A Biographic Directory and Statistical Analysis, 1980 *(New Brunswick, N.J.).*

5*Bureau of the Census, 1980 Census of Population.*

6*Op. cit.*

7*U.S. Department of Commerce, Bureau of the Census*, Statistical Abstract of the United States, 1986, *"Expectation of Life at Birth: 1920–1984," No. 106 (Washington, D.C.: Government Printing Office), 68.*

8*Percentages calculated from data in U.S. Bureau of the Census, Statistical Abstract of the United States, 1986, "Death Rates by Selected Cases and Selected Characteristics: 1960–1982," No. 115 (Washington, D.C.: Government Printing Office), 74.*

9*Percentages calculated by author from data found in U.S. Bureau*

[9] of the Census, Statistical Abstract of the United States, "Victim-ization Rates for Crimes against Persons: 1973–1983," No. 284 (Washington, D.C.: Government Printing Office), 169.

[10] Percentages calculated from data taken from the U.S. Department of Justice, Bureau of Justice Statistics, Capital Punishment, 1982.

[11] U.S. Bureau of the Census, Statistical Abstract of the United States, "Population in Institutions and Other Group Quarters, by Sex, Race, and Type of Quarters: 1960–1980," No. 73 (Washington, D.C.: Government Printing Office), 48.

[12] Percentages calculated by the author from data in the U.S. Department of Commerce, Statistical Abstract of the United States, 1986, "Expectation of Life at Birth: 1920–1984," No. 106 (Washington, D.C.: Government Printing Office), 68.

[13] Percentages calculated by the author from U.S. Bureau of the Census, Statistical Abstract of the United States, "Death Rates by Selected Cases and Selected Characteristics," No. 115 (Washington, D.C.: Government Printing Office), 74.

[14] Percentages calculated from U.S. Bureau of the Census, "Victim-ization Rates for Crimes against Persons: 1973–1983," Statistical Abstract of the United States, No. 284 (Washington, D.C.: Government Printing Office), 169.

[15] Ibid.

[16] Percentages calculated from data taken from the U.S. Department of Justice, Bureau of Justice Statistics, Capital Punishment, 1982.

References

Alberle, David

1966 *The Peyote Religion among the Navaho.* Chicago: Aldine.

Aronoff, Joel, and William D. Crano

1975 "A Re-examination of the Cross-Cultural Principles of Task Segregation and Sex Role Differentiation in the Family." *American Sociological Review* 40 (February):12–20.

Beal, Frances M.

1975 "Slave of a Slave No More: Black Women in Struggle." *The Black Scholar* 6 (6, March):2–10.

Bell, Norman W., and Ezra F. Vogel

1968 "Towards a Framework for Functional Analysis of Family Behavior." In *A Modern Introduction to the Family,* pp. 1–34. New York: Free Press.

Bradburn, Norman M., and David Caplovitz

1965 *Reports on Happiness: A Pilot Study of Behavior Related to Mental Health.* Chicago: Aldine.

Brown, J. K.

1970 "A Note on the Division of Labor by Sex." *American Anthropologist* 72:1073–1078.

Brown, Radcliffe, and Alfred Reginald

1948 *The Andamon Islanders.* Glencoe, Ill.: Free Press.

Byrne, D.

1971 *The Attraction Paradigm.* New York: Academic Press.

Byrne, D., G. Cleve, and P. Worchel

1966 "Effects of Economic Similarity–Dissimilarity on Interpersonal Attraction." *Journal of Personality and Social Psychology* 19:155–161.

Campbell, J.

1959 *The Masks of God: Primitive Mythology.* New York: Viking.

Center for the American Woman and Politics

1980 *Women in Public Office: A Biographic Directory and Statistical Analysis.* New Brunswick, N.J.: Author.

Chinoy, Ely

1955 *Automobile Workers and the American Dream.* Garden City, New York: Doubleday.

Collier, Betty J., and Louis N. Williams

1981 "Towards a Bilateral Model of Sexism." *Human Relations* 34 (2):127–139.

Collier, Betty J., and Willy Smith

1981 "Racism, Sexism and the Criminal Justice System." *National Urban League Review* 6 (1, Fall):46–54.

D'Androde, Roy G.

1966 "Sex Differences and Cultural Institutions." In *The Development of Sex Differences,* Eleanor D. Maccoby, ed., pp. 174–204. Stanford: Stanford University Press.

Diner, H.

1973 *Mothers and Amazons? The First Feminine History of Culture.* Garden City, New York: Anchor.

Divale, W., and M. Harris

1974 "Population, Warfare, and the Male Supremist Complex." *American Anthropologist* 78:521–538.

Duberman, Lucille

1976 *Social Inequality: Class and Caste in America.* Philadelphia: Lippincott.

Elder, G. H.

1969 "Education in Marriage Mobility." *American Sociological Review* 34:519–533.

Faris, Robert, and Warren Durham

1939 *Mental Disorders in Urban Areas.* Chicago: University of Chicago Press.

Goldberg, Steven

1973 *The Inevitability of Patriarchy.* New York: Morrow.

Gough, Kathleen

1971 "The Origin of the Family." In *The Human Experience* (1st ed.), David H. Spain, ed., pp. 181–191. Homewood, Ill.: Dorsey Press.

Hirschfeld, Lawrence A., James Howe, and Bruce Levin

1978 "Warfare, Infanticide, and Statistical Inference: A Comment on Divale and Harris." *American Anthropologist* 80:110–115.

Hollingshead, Hugh, and Frederick C. Redlich

1958 *Social Class and Mental Illness.* New York.

Hunt, Robert C.

1973 "Power in the Domestic Sphere." *Science Journal* 6:68–72.

Janeway, E.

1971 *Man's World, Woman's Place.* New York: Dell.

King, Mark

1974 "Sex Differences in Self-Actualization." *Psychological Reports* 35:602.

Krauss, Irving

1976 *Stratification, Class and Conflict.* New York: Free Press.

Lancaster, Chet, and Jane Beckman Lancaster

1978 "On the Male Supremacist Complex: A Reply to Divale and Harris." *American Anthropologist* 80:115–117.

Lenski, Gerhard

1966 *Power and Privilege: A Theory of Social Stratification.* New York: McGraw-Hill.

Levinson, Andrew

1974 *The Working Class Majority.* New York: Coward, McCann and Geoghegan.

Lewis, Diane K.

1977 "A Response to Inequality: Black Women, Racism and Sexism." *Signs* (Winter):339–361.

Maslow, A. H.

1963 "Self-Actualizing People." In *The World of Psychology* (Vol. 2), G. G. Levitz, ed. New York: Braziller.

McKee, J. P.

1959 "Men's and Women's Beliefs, Ideals, and Self Concepts." *American Journal of Sociology,* p. 64.

Miller, S. M., and Pamela A. Roby

1977 *The Future of Inequality.* New York: Basic Books.

Murdock, G. P.

1937 "Comparative Data on the Division of Labor by Sex." *Social Forces* 15:551–553.

Murdock, George P., and Catherine Provost

1973 "Factors in the Division of Labor by Sex: A Cross Cultural Analysis." *Ethnology* 12:203–225.

Parker, Seymour, and Hilda Parker

1979 "The Myth of Male Superiority: Rise and Demise." *American Anthropologist* 81 (2, June):289–308.

Parsons, Talcott

1955 "Family Structure and the Socialization of the Child." In *Family Socialization and Interaction Processes*, Talcott Parsons and Robert F. Bales, eds., pp. 35–131. Glencoe, Ill.: Free Press.

Romney, A.

1965 "Variations in Household Structure as Determinants of Sex-Typed Behavior." In *Sex and Behavior*, F. Beach, ed., pp. 208–220. New York: Wiley.

Rowbotham, Sheila

1974 *Woman's Consciousness, Man's World.* Harmondsworth: Penguin Books.

Sewell, William H.

1971 "Inequality of Opportunity for Higher Education." *American Sociological Review*, pp. 793–809.

Sexton, Patricia, and Brendan Sexton

1971 *Blue Collars and Hard Hats: The Working Class and the Future of American Politics.* New York: Random House.

Smelser, Neil J.

1963 *The Theory of Collective Behavior.* New York: Free Press.

Staples, Robert

1979 "The Myth of Black Macho: A Response to Angry Black Feminists." *The Black Scholar* (March/April):24–36.

Stephens, William M.

1963 *The Family in Cross-Cultural Perspective.* New York: Holt, Rinehart & Winston.

Tiger, L., and J. Shepher
1975   *Women in the Kibbutz.* New York: Harcourt Brace Jovanovich.

Tumin, Melvin M.
1967   *Social Stratification: The Forms and Functions of Inequality.* Englewood Cliffs, N.J.: Prentice-Hall.

Turner, Jonathan H., and Charles Starnes
1976   *Inequality: Privilege and Poverty in America.* Pacific Palisades, Calif.: Goodyear.

U.S. Bureau of Prisons
1978   *Annual Statistical Report Series.* Washington, D.C.

U.S. Bureau of the Census
1979/   U.S. Department of Commerce, Current Popu-
80   lation Reports Consumer Income Services P-60, No. 125. *Money Income and Poverty Status of Families and Persons in the United States* (October), p. 7.

U.S. Department of Health, Education, and Welfare
1975   Public Health Service Publication No. 100, Series 10, No. 58. *Vital and Health Statistics.* Washington, D.C.: U.S. Government Printing Office.
1976   Public Health Service. *Health-Status of Minorities and Low Income Groups.*

U.S. Department of Justice
1978   *National Crime Survey.* Washington, D.C.: Law Enforcement Administration.

1979   *Capital Punishment.* Washington, D.C.: Bureau of Justice Statistics.

U.S. Department of Labor
        Employment and Earnings 27 (9):28. Washington, D.C.: Bureau of Labor Statistics.

U.S. Federal Bureau of Investigation
1978   *Uniform Crime Reports for the United States.* Washington, D.C.

U.S. Law Enforcement Assistance Administration
1979   Criminal Victimization in the United States.

U.S. National Center for Health Statistics
1978   *Vital Statistics of the United States.* Washington, D.C.

Weber, Max
1958   "Class, Status and Party." In H. H. Gerth and C. Wright Mills, eds., *From Max Weber: Essays in Sociology,* New York: Oxford University Press/Galaxy Books.

Wooten, James T.
1974   "Pre-Election Mood: There's No Time for Dreams." *New York Times,* October 17.

Zander, A., and A. Havelin
1960   "Social Comparison and Interpersonal Attraction." *Human Relations* 13:121–132.

Zimbardo, P., and R. Formica
1963   "Emotional Comparison and Self-esteem." *Journal of Personality* 31:141–162.

SEX ROLES AND SURVIVAL STRATEGIES IN AN URBAN BLACK COMMUNITY

Carol B. Stack

The existence of a viable network of relationships between the single Black parent and other persons is shown. The author finds that in spite of disruptive forces on the single parent family, a variety of creative solutions are available to the parent. She shows how these survival strategies help maximize the lone parent's independence.

The power and authority ascribed to women in the Black ghettos of America, women whose families are locked into lifelong conditions of poverty and welfare, have their roots in the inexorable unemployment of Black males and the ensuing control of economic resources by females. These social-economic conditions have given rise to special features in the organization of family and kin networks in Black communities, features not unlike the patterns of domestic authority that emerge in matrilineal societies, or in cultures where men are away from home in wage labor (Gonzalez, 1969, 1970). The poor in Black urban communities have evolved, as the basic unit of their society, a core of kinsmen and non-kin who cooperate on a daily basis and who live near one another or co-reside. This core, or nucleus, has been characterized as the basis of the consanguineal household (Gonzalez, 1965) and of matrifocality (Abrahams, 1963; Moynihan, 1965; Rainwater, 1966).

The concept of "matrifocality," however, has been criticized as inaccurate and inadequate. Recent studies (Ladner, 1971; Smith, 1970; Stack, 1970; Valentine, 1970) show convincingly that many of the negative features attributed to matrifocal families—that they are fatherless, unstable, and produce offspring that are "illegitimate" in the eyes of the folk culture—are not general characteristics of low-income Black families in urban America. Rather than imposing widely accepted definitions of the family, the nuclear family, or the matrifocal family on the ways in which the urban poor describe and order their world, we must seek a more appropriate theoretical framework. Elsewhere I have proposed an analysis based on the notion of a domestic network (Stack, 1974). In this view, the basis of familial structure and cooperation is not the nuclear family of the middle class, but an extended cluster of kinsmen related chiefly through children but also through marriage and friendship, who align to provide domestic functions. This cluster, or domestic network, is diffused over several kin-based households, and fluctuations in individual household composition do not significantly affect cooperative arrangements.

In this paper I shall analyze the domestic network and the relationships within it from a woman's perspective—from the perspective that the women in this study provided and from my own interpretations of the domestic and social scene. Many previous studies of the Black family (e.g., Liebow, 1967, and Hannerz, 1969) have taken a male perspective emphasizing the street-corner life of Black men and

From *Woman, Culture, and Society*, ed. Michelle Z. Rosaldo and Louise Lamphere (Stanford University Press, 1974). Adapted from *All Our Kin: Strategies for Survival in* viewing men as peripheral to familial concerns. Though correctly stressing the economic difficulties that black males face in a racist society, these and other studies (Moynihan, 1965; Bernard, 1966) have fostered a stereotype of Black families as fatherless and subject to a domineering woman's matriarchal rule. From such simplistic accounts it is all too easy to come to blame juvenile delinquency, divorce, illegitimacy, and other social ills on the Black family, while ignoring the oppressive reality of our political and economic system and the adaptive resiliency and strength that Black families have shown.

My analysis will draw on life-history material as well as on personal comments from women in The Flats, the poorest section of a Black community in the Midwestern city of Jackson Harbor.[1] I shall view women as strategists—active agents who use resources to achieve goals and cope with the problems of everyday life. This framework has several advantages. First, because the focus is on women rather than men, women's views of family relations, often ignored or slighted, are given prominence. Second, since households form around women because of their role in child care, ties between women (including paternal aunts, cousins, etc.) often constitute the core of a network; data from women's lives, then, crucially illuminate the continuity in these networks. Finally, the life-history material, taken chiefly from women, also demonstrates the positive role that a man plays in Black family life, both as the father of a woman's children and as a contributor of valuable resources to her network and to the network of his own kin.

I shall begin by analyzing the history of residential arrangements during one woman's life, and the residential arrangements of this woman's kin network at two points in time, demonstrating that although household composition changes, members are selected or self-selected largely from a single nework that has continuity over time. Women and men, in response to joblessness, the possibility of welfare payments, the breakup of relationships, or the whims of a landlord, may move often. But the very calamities and crises that contribute to the constant shifts in residence tend to bring men, women, and children back into the households of close kin. Newly formed households are successive recombinations of the same domestic network of adults and

children, quite often in the same dwellings. Residence histories, then, are an important reflection of the strategy of relying on and strengthening the domestic kin network, and also reveal the adaptiveness of households with "elastic boundaries." (It may be worth noting that middle-class whites are beginning to perceive certain values, for their own lives, in such households.)

In the remainder of the paper, the importance of maximizing network strength will be reemphasized and additional strategies will be isolated by examining two sets of relationships within kin networks—those between mothers and fathers and those between fathers and children. Women's own accounts of their situations show how they have developed a strong sense of independence from men, evolved social controls against the formation of conjugal relationships, and limited the role of the husband-father within the mother's domestic group. All of these strategies serve to strengthen the domestic network, often at the expense of any particular male–female tie. Kin regard any marriage as a risk to the woman and her children, and the loss of either male or female kin as a threat to the durability of the kin network. These two factors continually augment each other and dictate, as well, the range of socially accepted relationships between fathers and children.

Residence and the Domestic Network

In The Flats, the material and cultural support needed to sustain and socialize community members is provided by cooperating kinsmen. The individual can draw upon a broad domestic web of kin and friends—some who reside together, others who do not. Residents in The Flats characterize household composition according to where people sleep, eat, and spend their time. Those who eat together may be considered part of a domestic unit. But an individual may eat in one household, sleep in another, contribute resources and services to yet another, and consider himself or herself a member of all three households. Children may fall asleep and remain through the night wherever the late-evening visiting patterns of the adult females take them, and they may remain in these households and share meals perhaps a week at a time. As R. T. Smith suggests in an article on Afro-American kinship (1970), it is sometimes difficult "to determine just which household a given individual belongs to at any particular moment." These facts of ghetto life are, of course, often disguised in the statistical reports of census takers, who record simply sleeping arrangements.

Households in The Flats, then, have shifting memberships, but they maintain for the most part a steady state of three generations of kin: males and females beyond child-bearing age; a middle generation of mothers raising their own children or children of close kin; and the children. This observation is supported in a recent study by Ladner (1971:60), who writes, "Many children normally grow up in a three-generation household and they absorb the influences of a grandmother and grandfather as well as a mother and father." A survey of eighty-three residence changes among welfare families, whereby adult females who are heads of their own households merged households with other kin, shows that the majority of moves created three-generation households. Consequently, it is difficult to pinpoint structural beginning or end to household cycles in poor Black urban communities (Buchler and Selby, 1968; Fortes, 1958; Otterbein, 1970). But it is clear that authority patterns within a kin network change with birth and death; with the death of the oldest member in a household, the next generation assumes authority.

Residence changes themselves are brought on by many factors, most related to the economic conditions in which poor families live. Women who have children have access to welfare, and thus more economic security than women who do not, and more than all men. Welfare regulations encourage mothers to set up separate households, and women actively seek independence, privacy, and improvement in their lives. But these ventures do not last long. Life histories of adults show that the attempts by women to set up separate households with their children are short-lived: houses are condemned; landlords evict tenants; and needs for services among kin arise. Household composition also expands or contracts with the loss of a job, the death of a relative, the beginning or end of a sexual partnership, or the end of a friendship. But fluctuations in household composition rarely affect the exchanges and daily dependencies of participants. The ... chronology of residence changes made by Ruby Banks graphically illuminates these points [Table 1].

Ruby's residential changes, and the residences of her own children and kin, reveal that the same factors contributing to the high frequency of moving also bring men, women, and children back into the households of close kin. That one can repeatedly do so is a great source of security and dependence for those living in poverty.

A look in detail at the domestic network of Ruby's parents, Magnolia and Calvin Waters, illustrates the complexity of the typical network and also shows kin constructs at work both in the recruitment of individuals to the network and in the changing composition of households within the network, over less than three months [Table 2].

These examples do indeed indicate the important role of the Black woman in the domestic structure. But the cooperation between male and female siblings who share the same household or live near one another has been underestimated by those who have isolated the female-headed household as the most significant domestic unit among the urban Black poor. The close cooperation of adult siblings arises from the residential patterns typical of young adults (Stack, 1970). Owing to poverty, young women with or without children do not perceive any choice but to remain living at home with their mothers or other adult female relatives. Even when young women are collecting welfare for their children, they say that their resources go further when they share food and exchange goods and services daily. Likewise, the jobless man, or the man working at a part-time or seasonal job, often remains living at home with his mother—or, if she is dead, with his sisters and brothers. This pattern continues long after such a man becomes a father and establishes a series of sexual partnerships with women, who are in turn living with their own kin or friends or are alone with their children. A result of this pattern is the striking fact that households almost always have men around: male relatives, affines, and boyfriends. These men are often intermittent members of the households, boarders, or friends who come and go—men who usually eat,

TABLE 1

AGE	HOUSEHOLD COMPOSITION AND CONTEXT OF HOUSEHOLD FORMATION
Birth	Ruby lived with her mother, Magnolia, and her maternal grandparents.
4	To be eligible for welfare, Ruby and Magnolia were required to move out of Ruby's grandparents' house. They moved into a separate residence two houses away, but ate all meals at the grandparents' house.
5	Ruby and Magnolia returned to the grandparents' house and Magnolia gave birth to a son. Magnolia worked and the grandmother cared for her children.
6	Ruby's maternal grandparents separated. Magnolia remained living with her father and her (now) two sons. Ruby and her grandmother moved up the street and lived with her maternal aunt Augusta and maternal uncle. Ruby's grandmother took care of Ruby and her brothers, and Magnolia worked and cooked and cleaned for her father.
7–16	The household was now composed of Ruby, her grandmother, her grandmother's new husband, Augusta and her boyfriend, and Ruby's maternal uncle. At age sixteen Ruby gave birth to a daughter.
17	Ruby's grandmother died and Ruby had a second child, by Otis, the younger brother of Ruby's best friend, Willa Mae. Ruby remained living with Augusta, Augusta's boyfriend, Ruby's maternal uncle, and her daughters.
18	Ruby fought with Augusta and she and Otis moved into an apartment with her two daughters. Ruby's first daughter's father died. Otis stayed with Ruby and her daughters in the apartment.
19	Ruby broke up with Otis. Ruby and her two daughters joined Magnolia, Magnolia's "husband," and her ten half-siblings. Ruby had a miscarriage.
19½	Ruby left town and moved out of state with her new boyfriend, Earl. She left her daughters with Magnolia and remained out of state for a year. Magnolia then insisted she return home and take care of her children.
20½	Ruby and her daughters moved into a large house rented by Augusta and her mother's brother. It was located next door to Magnolia's house, where Ruby and her children ate. Ruby cleaned for her aunt and uncle, and gave birth to another child, by Otis, who had returned to the household.
21	Ruby and Otis broke up once again. She found a house and moved there with her daughters, Augusta, and Augusta's boyfriend. Ruby did the cleaning, and Augusta cooked. Ruby and Magnolia, who now lived across town, shared child care, and Ruby's cousin's daughter stayed with Ruby.
21½	Augusta and her boyfriend have moved out because they were all fighting, and the two of them wanted to get away from the noise of the children. Ruby has a new boyfriend.

and sometimes sleep, in these households. Children have constant and close contact with these men, and especially in the case of male relatives, these relationships last over the years. The most predictable residential pattern in The Flats is that individuals reside in the households of their natal kin, or the households of those who raised them, long into their adult years.

Welfare workers, researchers, and landlords in Black ghetto communities have long known that the residence patterns of the poor change frequently and that females play a dominant domestic role. What is much less understood is the relationship between household composition and domestic organization in these communities. Household boundaries are elastic, and no one model of a household, such as the nuclear family, extended family, or matrifocal family, is the norm. What is crucial and enduring is the strength of ties within a kin network; the maintenance of a strong network in turn has consequences for the relationships between the members themselves, as demonstrated in the following discussion of relationships between mothers and fathers and between fathers and their children.

Mothers and Fathers

Notwithstanding the emptiness and hopelessness of the job experience in the Black community, men and women fall in love and wager buoyant new relationships against the inexorable forces of poverty and racism. At the same time, in dealing with

TABLE 2

HOUSEHOLD	DOMESTIC ARRANGEMENTS, APRIL 1969	DOMESTIC ARRANGEMENTS, JUNE 1969
1	Magnolia, her husband Calvin, their eight children (4–18).	Unchanged.
2	Magnolia's sister Augusta, Augusta's boyfriend, Ruby, Ruby's children, Ruby's boyfriend Otis.	Augusta and boyfriend have moved to #3 after a quarrel with Ruby. Ruby and Otis remain in #2.
3	Billy (Augusta's closest friend), Billy's children, Lazar (Magnolia's sister Carrie's husband, living in the basement), Carrie (from time to time—she is an alcoholic).	Augusta and boyfriend have moved to a small, one-room apartment upstairs from Billy.
4	Magnolia's sister Lydia, Lydia's daughters Georgia and Lottie, Lydia's boyfriend, Lottie's daughter.	Lottie and her daughter have moved to an apartment down the street, joining Lottie's girl friend and child. Georgia has moved in with her boyfriend. Lydia's son has moved back into Lydia's home #4.
5	Ruby's friend Willa Mae, her husband and son, her sister, and her brother James (father of Ruby's daughter).	James has moved in with his girl friend, who lives with her sister; James keeps most of his clothes in household #5. James's brother has returned from the army and moved into #5.
6	Eloise (Magnolia's first son's father's sister), her husband, their four young children, their daughter and her son, Eloise's friend Jessie's brother's daughter and her child.	Unchanged.
7	Violet (wife of Calvin's closest friend Cecil, now dead several years), her two sons, her daughter Odessa, and Odessa's four children.	Odessa's son Raymond has fathered Clover's baby. Clover and baby have joined household #7.

everyday life, Black women and men have developed a number of attitudes and strategies that appear to militate against the formation of long-term relationships. Even when a man and woman set up temporary housekeeping arrangements, they both maintain primary social ties with their kin. If other members of a kin network view a particular relationship as a drain on the network's resources, they will act in various and subtle ways to break up the relationship. This is what happened in the life of Julia Ambrose, another resident of The Flats.

When I first met Julia, she was living with her baby, her cousin Teresa, and Teresa's "old man." After several fierce battles with Teresa over the bills, and because of Teresa's hostility toward Julia's boyfriends, Julia decided to move out. She told me she was head over heels in love with Elliot, her child's father, and they had decided to live together.

For several months Julia and Elliot shared a small apartment, and their relationship was strong.

Elliot was very proud of his baby. On weekends he would spend an entire day carrying the baby around to his sister's home, where he would show it to his friends on the street. Julia, exhilarated by her independence in having her own place, took great care of the house and her baby. She told me, "Before Elliot came home from work I would have his dinner fixed and the house and kid clean. When he came home he would take his shower and then I'd bring his food to the bed. I'd put the kid to sleep and then get into bed with him. It was fine. We would get a little piece and then go to sleep. In the morning we'd do the same thing."

After five months, Elliot was laid off from his job at a factory that hires seasonal help. He couldn't find another job, except part-time work for a cab company. Elliot began spending more time away from the house with his friends at the local tavern, and less time with Julia and the baby. Julia finally had to get back "on aid" and Elliot put more of his things back in his sister's home so the social worker wouldn't know he was staying with Julia. Julia noticed changes in Elliot. "If you start necking and doing the same thing that you've been doing with your man, and he don't want it, you know for sure that he is messing with someone else, or don't want you anymore. Maybe Elliot didn't want me in the first place, but maybe he did 'cause he chased me a lot. He wanted me and he didn't want me. I really loved him, but I'm not in love with him now. My feelings just changed. I'm not in love with no man, really. Just out for what I can get from them."

Julia and Elliot stayed together, but she began to hear rumors about him. Her cousin, a woman who had often expressed jealousy toward Julia, followed Elliot in a car and told her that Elliot parked late at night outside the apartment house of his previous girl friend. Julia told me that her cousin was "nothing but a gossip, a newspaper who carried news back and forth," and that her cousin was envious of her having an "old man." Nevertheless, Julia believed the gossip.

After hearing other rumors and gossip about Elliot, Julia said, "I still really liked him, but I wasn't going to let him get the upper hand on me. After I found out that he was messing with someone else, I said to myself, I was doing it too, so what's the help in making a fuss. But after that, I made him pay for being with me!

"I was getting a check every month for rent from welfare and I would take the money and buy me clothes. I bought my own wardrobe and I gave my mother money for keeping the baby while I was working. I worked here and there while I was on aid and they were paying my rent. I didn't really need Elliot, but that was extra money for me. When he asked me what happened to my check I told him I got off and couldn't get back on. My mother knew. She didn't care what I did so long as I didn't let Elliot make an ass out of me. The point is a woman has to have her own pride. She can't let a man rule her. You can't let a man kick you in the tail and tell you what to do. Anytime I can make an ass out of a man, I'm going to do it. If he's doing the same to me, then I'll quit him and leave him alone."

After Elliot lost his job, and kin continued to bring gossip to Julia about how he was playing around with other women, Julia became embittered toward Elliot and was anxious to hurt him. There had been a young Black man making deliveries for a local store who would pass her house every day, and flirt with her. Charles would slow down his truck and honk for Julia when he passed the house. Soon she started running out to talk to him in his truck and decided to "go" with him. Charles liked Julia and brought nice things for her child.

"I put Elliot in a trick," Julia told me soon after she stopped going with Charles. "I knew that Elliot didn't care nothing for me, so I made him jealous. He was nice to the kids, both of them, but he didn't do nothing to show me he was still in love with me. Me and Elliot fought a lot. One night Charles and me went to a motel room and stayed there all night. Mama had the babies. She got mad. But I was trying to hurt Elliot. When I got home, me and Elliot got into it. He called me all kinds of names. I said he might as well leave. But Elliot said he wasn't going nowhere. So he stayed and we'd sleep together, but we didn't do nothing. Then one night something happened. I got pregnant again by Elliot. After I got pregnant, me and Charles quit, and I moved in with a girl friend for a while. Elliot chased after me and we started going back together, but we stayed separate. In my sixth month I moved back in my mother's home with her husband and the kids."

Many young women like Julia feel strongly that they cannot let a man make a fool out of them, and they react quickly and boldly to rumor, gossip, and talk that hurts them. The power that gossip and information have in constraining the duration of sexual relationships is an important cultural phenomenon. But the most important single factor affecting interpersonal relationships between men and women in The Flats is unemployment. The futility of the job experience for street-corner men in a Black community is sensitively portrayed by Elliot Liebow in *Tally's Corner*. As Liebow (1967:63) writes, "The job fails the man and the man fails the job." Liebow's discussion (p. 142) of men and jobs leads directly to his analysis of the street-corner male's exploitive relationships with women: "Men not only present themselves as economic exploiters of women but they expect other men to do the same." Ghetto-specific male roles that men try to live up to at home and on the street, and their alleged round-the-clock involvement in peer groups, are interpreted in *Soulside* (Hannerz, 1969) as a threat to marital stability.

Losing a job, then, or being unemployed month after month debilitates one's self-importance and independence and, for men, necessitates sacrificing a role in the economic support of their families. Faced with these familiar patterns in the behavior and status of men, women call upon life experiences in The Flats to guide them. When a man loses his job, that is the time he is most likely to begin "messing around."

And so that no man appears to have made a fool of them, women respond with vengeance, out of pride and self-defense. Another young woman in The Flats, Ivy Rodgers, told me about the time she left her two children in The Flats with her mother and took off for Indiana with Jimmy River, a young man she had fallen in love with "the first sight I seen." Jimmy asked Ivy to go to Gary, Indiana, where his family lived. "I just left the kids with my mama. I didn't even tell her I was going. My checks kept coming so she had food for the kids, but I didn't know he let his people tell him what to do. While he was in Gary, Jimmy started messing with another woman. He said he wasn't, but I caught him. I quit him, but when he told me he wasn't messing, I loved him so much I took him back. Then I got to thinking about it. I had slipped somewhere. I had let myself go. Seems like I forgot that I wasn't going to let Jimmy or any man make an ass out of me. But he sure was doing it. I told Jimmy that if he loved me, he would go and see my people, take them things, and tell them we were getting married. Jimmy didn't want to go back to The Flats, but I tricked him and told him I really wanted to visit. I picked out my ring and Jimmy paid thirty dollars on it and I had him buy my outfit that we was getting married in. He went along with it. What's so funny was when we come here and he said to me, 'You ready to go back?' and I told him, 'No, I'm not going back. I never will marry you.'"

Forms of social control in the larger society also work against successful marriages in The Flats. In fact, couples rarely chance marriage unless a man has a job; often the job is temporary, low-paying,

and insecure, and the worker is arbitrarily laid off whenever he is not needed. Women come to realize that welfare benefits and ties within kin networks provide greater security for them and their children. In addition, caretaker agencies such as public welfare are insensitive to individual attempts for social mobility. A woman may be immediately cut off the welfare rolls when a husband returns home from prison or the army, or if she gets married. Unless there is either a significant change in employment opportunities for the urban poor or a livable guaranteed minimum income, it is unlikely that urban low-income Blacks will form lasting conjugal units.

Marriage and its accompanying expectations of a home, a job, and a family built around the husband and wife have come to stand for an individual's desire to break out of poverty. It implies the willingness of an individual to remove himself from the daily obligations of his kin network. People in The Flats recognize that one cannot simultaneously meet kin expectations and the expectations of a spouse. Cooperating kinsmen continually attempt to draw new people into their personal network; but at the same time they fear the loss of a central, resourceful member in the network. The following passages are taken from the detailed residence life history of Ruby Banks. Details of her story were substantiated by discussions with her mother, her aunt, her daughter's father, and her sister.

"Me and Otis could be married, but they all ruined that. Aunt Augusta told Magnolia that he was no good. Magnolia was the fault of it, too. They don't want to see me married! Magnolia knows that it be money getting away from her. I couldn't spend the time with her and the kids and be giving her the money that I do now. I'd have my husband to look after. I couldn't go where she want me to go. I couldn't come every time she call me, like if Calvin took sick or the kids took sick, or if she took sick. That's all the running I do now. I couldn't do that. You think a man would put up with as many times as I go over her house in a cab, giving half my money to her all the time? That's the reason they don't want me married. You think a man would let Aunt Augusta come into the house and take food out of the icebox from his kids? They thought that way ever since I came up.

"They broke me and Otis up. They kept telling me that he didn't want me, and that he didn't want the responsibility. I put him out and I cried all night long. And I really did love him. But Aunt Augusta and others kept fussing and arguing so I went and quit him. I would have got married a long time ago to my first baby's daddy, but Aunt Augusta was the cause of that, telling Magnolia that he was too old for me. She's been jealous of me since the day I was born.

"Three years after Otis I met Earl. Earl said he was going to help pay for the utilities. He was going to get me some curtains and pay on my couch. While Earl was working he was so good to me and my children that Magnolia and them started worrying all over again. They sure don't want me married. The same thing that happened to Otis happened to many of my boyfriends. And I ain't had that many men. I'm tired of them bothering me with their problems when I'm trying to solve my own problems. They tell me that Earl's doing this and that, seeing some girl.

"They look for trouble to tell me every single day. If I ever marry, I ain't listening to what nobody say. I just listen to what he say. You have to get along the best way you know how, and forget about your people. If I got married they would talk, like they are doing now, saying, 'He ain't no good, he's been creeping on you. I told you once not to marry him. You'll end up right back on aid.' If I ever get married, I'm leaving town!"

Ruby's account reveals the strong conflict between kin-based domestic units and lasting ties between husbands and wives. When a mother in The Flats has a relationship with an economically nonproductive man, the relationship saps the resources of others in her domestic network. Participants in the network act to break up such relationships, to maintain kin-based household groupings over the life cycle, in order to maximize potential resources and the services they hope to exchange. Similarly, a man's participation is expected in his kin network, and it is understood that he should not dissipate his services and finances to a sexual or marital relationship. These forms of social control made Ruby afraid to take the risks necessary to break out of the cycle of poverty. Instead, she chose the security and stability of her kin group. Ruby, recognizing that to

make a marriage last she would have to move far away from her kin, exclaimed, "If I ever get married, I'm leaving town!" While this study was in progress, Ruby did get married, and she left the state with her husband and her youngest child that very evening.

Fathers and Children

People in The Flats show pride in all their kin, and particularly new babies born into their kinship networks. Mothers encourage sons to have babies, and even more important, men coax their "old ladies" to have their babies. The value placed on children, the love, attention, and affection children receive from women and men, and the web of social relationships spun from the birth of a child are all basic to the high birthrate among the poor.

The pride that kinsmen take in the children of their sons and brothers is seen best in the pleasure that the mothers and sisters of these men express. Such pride was apparent during a visit I made to Alberta Cox's home. She introduced me to her nineteen-year-old son Nate and added immediately, "He's a daddy and his baby is four months old." Then she pointed to her twenty-two-year-old son Mac and said, "He's a daddy three times over." Mac smiled and said, "I'm no daddy," and his friend in the kitchen said, "Maybe going on four times, Mac." Alberta said, "Yes you are. Admit it, boy!" At that point Mac's grandmother rolled back in her rocker and said, "I'm a grandmother many times over, and it make me proud." A friend of Alberta's told me later that Alberta wants her sons to have babies because she thinks it will make them more responsible. Although she usually dislikes the women her sons go with, claiming they are "no-good trash," Alberta accepts the babies and asks to care for them whenever she has a chance.

Although Blacks, like most Americans, acquire kin through their mothers and fathers, the economic insecurity of the Black male and the availability of welfare to the mother–child unit make it very difficult for an unemployed Black husband-father to compete with a woman's kin for authority and control over her children. As we have seen women seek to be independent, but also, in order to meet everyday needs, they act to strengthen their ties with their kin and within their domestic network. Though these two strategies, especially in the context of male joblessness, may lead to the breakup of a young couple, a father will maintain his ties with his children. The husband-father role may be limited, but, contrary to the stereotype of Black family life, it is not only viable but culturally significant.

Very few young couples enter into a legal marriage in The Flats, but a father and his kin can sustain a continuing relationship with the father's children if the father has acknowledged paternity, if his kin have activated their claims on the child, and if the mother has drawn these people into her personal network. Widely popularized and highly misleading statistics on female-headed households have contributed to the assumption that Black children derive nothing of sociological importance from their fathers. To the contrary, in my recent study of domestic life among the poor in a Black community in the Midwest (Stack, 1972), I found that 70 percent of the fathers of 1,000 children on welfare recognized their children and provided them with kinship affiliations. But because many of these men have little or no access to steady and productive employment, out of the 699 who acknowledged paternity, only 84 (12 percent) gave any substantial financial support to their children. People in The Flats believe a father should help his child, but they know that the mother cannot count on his help. Community expectations of fathers do not generally include the father's *duties* in relation to a child; they do, however, assume the responsibilities of the father's kin. Kinship through males in The Flats is reckoned through a chain of acknowledged genitors, but social fatherhood is shared by the genitor with his kin, and with the mother's husband or with her boyfriends.

Although the authority of a father over his genealogical children or his wife's other children is limited, neither the father's interest in his child nor the desire of his kin to help raise the child strains the stability of the domestic network. Otis's kin were drawn into Ruby's personal network through his claims on her children, and through the long, close friendship between Ruby and Otis's sister, Willa Mae. Like many fathers in The Flats, Otis maintained close contact with his children, and provided goods

and care for them even when he and Ruby were not on speaking terms. One time when Otis and Ruby separated, Otis stayed in a room in Ruby's uncle's house next door to Ruby's mother's house. At that time Ruby's children were being kept by Magnolia each day while Ruby went to school to finish working toward her high school diploma. Otis was out of work, and he stayed with Ruby's uncle over six months helping Magnolia care for his children. Otis's kin were proud of the daddy he was, and at times suggested they should take over the raising of Otis and Ruby's children. Ruby and other mothers know well that those people you count on to share in the care and nurturing of your children are also those who are rightfully in a position to judge and check upon how you carry out the duties of a mother. Shared responsibilities of motherhood in The Flats imply both a help and a check on how one assumes the parental role.

Fathers like Otis, dedicated to maintaining ties with their children, learn that the relationship they create with their child's mother largely determines the role they may assume in their child's life. Jealousy between men makes it extremely difficult for fathers to spend time with their children if the mother has a boyfriend, but as Otis said to me, "When Ruby doesn't have any old man then she starts calling on me, asking for help, and telling me to do something for my kids." Between such times, when a man or a woman does not have an ongoing sexual relationship, some mothers call upon the fathers of their children and temporarily "choke" these men with their personal needs and the needs of the children. At these times, men and women reinforce their fragile but continuing relationship, and find themselves empathetic friends who can be helpful to one another.

A mother generally regards her children's father as a friend of the family whom she can recruit for help, rather than as a father failing his parental duties. Although fathers voluntarily help out with their children, many fathers cannot be depended upon as a steady source of help. Claudia Williams talked to me about Harold, the father of her two children. "Some days he be coming over at night saying, 'I'll see to the babies and you can lay down and rest, honey,' treating me real nice. Then maybe I don't even see him for two or three months.

There's no sense nagging Harold. I just treat him as some kind of friend even if he is the father of my babies." Since Claudia gave birth to Harold's children, both of them have been involved in other relationships. When either of them is involved with someone else, this effectively cuts Harold off from his children. Claudia says, "My kids don't need their daddy's help, but if he helps out then I help him out, too. My kids are well behaved, and I know they make Harold's kinfolk proud."

Conclusions

The view of Black women as represented in their own words and life histories coincides with that presented by Joyce Ladner: "One of the chief characteristics defining the Black woman is her [realistic approach] to her [own] resources. Instead of becoming resigned to her fate, she has always sought creative solutions to her problems. The ability to utilize her existing resources and yet maintain a forthright determination to struggle against the racist society in whatever overt and subtle ways necessary is one of her major attributes" (Ladner, 1971:276–77).

I have particularly emphasized those strategies that women can employ to maximize their independence, acquire and maintain domestic authority, limit (but positively evaluate) the role of husband and father, and strengthen ties with kin. The last of these—maximizing relationships in the domestic network—helps to account for patterns of Black family life among the urban poor more adequately than the concepts of nuclear or matrifocal family. When economic resources are greatly limited, people need help from as many others as possible. This requires expanding their kin networks—increasing the number of people they hope to be able to count on. On the one hand, female members of a network may act to break up a relationship that has become a drain on their resources. On the other, a man is expected to contribute to his own kin network, and it is assumed that he should not dissipate his services and finances to a marital relationship. At the same time, a woman will continue to seek aid from the man who has fathered her children, thus building up her own network's resources. She also expects something of his kin, especially his mother and sisters. Women continually activate these lines to bring kin and friends into the network of exchange and obligation. Most often, the biological father's female relatives are also poor and also try to expand their network and increase the number of people they can depend on.

Clearly, economic pressures among cooperating kinsmen in the Black community work against the loss of either males or females—through marriage or other long-term relationships—from the kin network. The kin-based cooperative network represents the collective adaptations to poverty of the men, women, and children within the Black community. Loyalties and dependencies toward kinsmen offset the ordeal of unemployment and racism. To cope with the everyday demands of ghetto life, these networks have evolved patterns of co-residence, elastic household boundaries; lifelong, if intermittent, bonds to three-generation households; social constraints on the role of the husband-father within the mother's domestic group; and the domestic authority of women.

---

[1]This work is based on a recent urban anthropological study of poverty and domestic life of urban-born Black Americans who were raised on public welfare and whose parents had migrated from the South to a single community in the urban North (Stack, 1972). Now adults in their twenties to forties, they are raising their own children on welfare in The Flats. All personal and place names in this paper are fictitious.

References

Abrahams, Roger

1963 *Deep Down in the Jungle*. Hatboro, Pa.

Bernard, Jessie

1966 *Marriage and Family among Negroes*. Englewood Cliffs, N.J.

Buchler, Ira R., and Henry A. Selby

1968 *Kinship and Social Organization: An Introduction to Theory and Method*. New York.

Fortes, Meyer

1958 "Introduction." In *The Developmental Cycle in Domestic Groups*, Jack Goody, ed. Cambridge, England.

Gonzalez, Nancie

1965 "The Consanguineal Household and Matrifocality." *American Anthropologist* 67:1541–1549.

1969 *Black Carib Household Structure: A Study of Migration and Modernization*. Seattle.

1970 "Toward a Definition of Matrifocality." In *Afro-American Anthropology: Contemporary Perspectives*, N. E. Whitten and J. F. Szwed, eds. New York.

Hannerz, Ulf

1969 *Soulside: Inquiries into Ghetto Culture and Community*. New York.

Ladner, Joyce

1971 *Tomorrow's Tomorrow: The Black Woman*. Garden City, N.Y.

Liebow, Elliot

1967 *Tally's Corner*. Boston.

Moynihan, Daniel Patrick

1965 *The Negro Family: The Case for National Action*. Washington, D.C.

Otterbein, Keith F.

1970 "The Development Cycle of the Andros Household: A Diachronic Analysis." *American Anthropologist* 72:1412–1419.

Rainwater, Lee

1966 "Crucible of Identity: The Negro Lower-Class Family." *Daedalus* 95 (2):172–216.

Smith, Raymond T.

1970 "The Nuclear Family in Afro-American Kinship." *Journal of Comparative Family Studies* 1 (1):55–70.

Stack, Carol B.

1970 "The Kindred of Viola Jackson: Residence and Family Organization of an Urban Black American Family." In *Afro-American Anthropology: Contemporary Perspectives*, N. E. Whitten and J. F. Szwed, eds. New York.

1972 "Black Kindreds: Parenthood and Personal Kindreds Among Blacks Supported by Welfare." *Journal of Comparative Family Studies* 3 (2): 194–206.

1974 *All Our Kin: Strategies for Survival in a Black Community*. New York.

Valentine, Charles

1970 "Blackston: Progress Report on a Community Study in Urban Afro-America." Mimeo. Washington University, St. Louis.

5 / Male/Female Relationships

BEYOND THE BLACK FAMILY:
The Trend toward Singlehood

Robert Staples

A majority of adult Blacks are unmarried. The author examines the sociocultural forces behind this unprecedented situation. A look at unmarried, college-educated Blacks reveals that being single poses unexpected problems for members of this group. Changes in cultural values and lack of institutional support creates barriers to finding a mate. It is concluded that the consequences of singlehood impact on the entire Black community.

Although the times are changing, it is hard to imagine a society in which large numbers of people reject the idea of marriage. In fact, one can hardly envision such a society being able to perpetuate itself. America's forefathers obviously considered singlehood a threat when it imposed a special tax on men who insisted on remaining bachelors. Contemporary America has come a long way from the days when birth, marriage, and death were the three supreme experiences in life.

Circa 1975, the proportion of adults that had never married in the United States reached a new high. In the 1960s, the average American got married between the ages of 20 and 24. The year 1975 finds 40 percent of the women in that age-range still single. In 1960, only 28 percent were still unmarried. About 60 percent of the men today are still bachelors at the age of 24, compared to 53 percent in 1960. It would be easy and comforting to assume that Americans are delaying marriage until a later age. But the proportion of single persons has also increased for the age group 25 to 29. While many will eventually marry, it is conceivable that a large proportion will remain single throughout their entire lives. Moreover, considering the number of individuals divorced, separated, or widowed, there are over 34 million Americans who are theoretically in the state of singleness, or about a third of all people over the age of 18 (U.S. Bureau of the Census, 1975a:1).

Obviously, attitudes toward marriage have changed in the past nineteen years. Some of the

---

From the *Western Journal of Black Studies* 3 (Fall 1979):150–157. Reprinted by permission.

reasons and forces responsible for this transformation are well known. If these changes in marital patterns are surprising, it may be even more shocking when one looks at the fact of singlehood and marriage among Blacks. Perhaps this writer assumes too much knowledge on the part of the readers when asserting that the large proportion of single Blacks will astonish them. Many may believe that Blacks never took marriage seriously, rarely formalized their relationships, or casually dissolved their marriages at will.

If such is their understanding, it could hardly be further from the truth. It is known that Blacks were not allowed to have a legal marriage during the period of slavery. Marriage was, and is, essentially a contractual relationship, and slaves were not permitted to consummate legal contracts for any purpose. However, there were relationships between male and female slaves that were socially, if not legally, recognized. After slavery ended, the freedmen went to great lengths to have their relationships legalized. A legal marriage was a status symbol to a group deprived of such rights for two centuries. They married in record numbers; by far the majority of Blacks were lodged in nuclear families by the beginning of the twentieth century (Staples, 1976:116–122).

As further evidence of the Black value of marriage, the census data indicate that a higher percentage of Blacks than whites eventually entered into marital relationships (U.S. Bureau of the Census, 1974). The question which begs an answer is what happened and why. It is easier to reply to what happened than the reasons behind it. The statistics cited earlier were for the general American population without regard to race. Looking at Blacks separately, the trend toward singleness and away from marriage is more pronounced. Over two-thirds of all Black males and 53 percent of Black females are still unmarried between the ages of 20 and 24. More significantly, one out of every three Black males is still single at the age of 30, and one out of every four Black women has not married (U.S. Bureau of the Census, 1975a:10–11).

As unexpected as those figures may be, they do not tell the entire story. Individuals who are separated, divorced, or widowed must be counted as single. When these Blacks are included with the never-married, it is found that at any given point in time, about 54 percent of all adult Black females are not married and living with a spouse. Based on the present trend, one can realistically predict that by the year 1980, the majority of adult Blacks, male and female, will be unmarried. Hence, this is not an esoteric group of people. Perhaps more important than why it has happened is how significant it is to the functioning of the Black community.

Before exploring the answers to those questions, the writer wishes to make his own position clear. A white colleague has conducted a study of white singlehood as a viable alternative to marriage (Stein, 1976). However, this is not this writer's perspective. Most Blacks do not see their singleness as a viable choice, but as a condition forced upon them by certain vicissitudes of life in America. This situation does not mean that Black singlehood is a pathological form or that Black marriages are that happy or functional. What it does signify is that being single and Black is problematic. It requires coping with certain problems that either do not occur in the conjugal state, or happen with less frequency, and for which solutions are more readily available.

It should be made clear at the outset that not all people are single in the same way. Some may be living with another person, and the relationship takes on all the qualities of a marriage; others have children who occupy their time and satisfy certain emotional needs; and a number of them may be wedded to a career. At the same time there are those who are actively involved in the dating game and ardently pursuing a spouse. At the bottom line of all these different configurations are conflicts in the male-female relationship. Remaining unmarried, or dissolving a marriage, is the most fundamental expression of an inability or unwillingness to resolve these conflicts.

Despite some misgivings, this writer will confine this analysis to what might be called the Black middle class. By excluding lower-income Blacks the writer does not have to deal with the economic forces which affect so much of their existence. It is also this writer's feeling that singlehood is handled in the lower-income class in a very different and perhaps more effective way than in the middle class.

As to the significance of Black singlehood for the functioning of the Black community, there are certain ramifications which are felt collectively. In contrast to the ideology of singlehood as a viable alternative, it must be interpreted as a symbol of role failure in the normative sense. Perhaps there needs to be some redefinition of roles. But, no one has yet offered a known workable alternative. Alternative family substitutes have been tried, such as open marriage, communal living, heterosexual cohabitation, etc., and found wanting. And, Blacks never adopted those family substitutes anyway. Being single and living alone is not a role that relates to any other role. It is the ultimate expression of individuality within a society that is based on organic togetherness. This is one reason why the society is geared toward families, not single individuals. There are few social rewards that go to the perpetually single, and there are quite a few punishments.

There is also the problem of emotional stability. Singles do have the recurrent problems of loneliness and other emotional crises, situations which they often have to endure without a buffer to cushion their impact. This is not to say that all married persons have an accessible person to provide them emotional support and that no single persons do. Many married people are lonely and frustrated, and a number of single individuals have an informal network of support structures. The writer is not juxtaposing marriage to singlehood as a sum-zero proposition. Indeed, it is the opposition to the problems of marriage that constitutes the raison d'être for much Black singleness. In a way similar to the last three presidential elections, people are voting against, rather than for, a particular option. Perforce, some are willing to settle for a troublesome life of singleness than accept a conflict-ridden marriage.

These problems of singlehood are cited with the clear knowledge that many marriages are unfulfilling to a number of Americans. This writer, particularly, realizes that women seem to suffer greatly when living in the institution of marriage. Many of the difficulties, however, arise from the unrealistic expectations people have about what marriage can provide. Whether marriage ever provided much personal happiness for its members is questionable.

As far as Blacks are concerned it did serve certain functions which have not been filled by other groups or institutions. Among those needs serviced were the rearing and socializing of children, and the sanctuary from a racist and hostile society. While those functions can be carried out in a structure other than marriage, there is no evidence that this is happening in the Black middle class.

Some of these statements will not set well with feminists and other ideologues. This writer is not a partisan of the traditional nuclear family, nor does he advocate a return to woman's domestic and subservient role. All that is being said here is that certain vital cooperative and sharing functions of marriage are being eroded for an individualistic singlehood. It is not certain that Blacks as an oppressed racial minority can afford that luxury. Witness, for instance, the increase in the gap between Black and white family incomes. From 1970 to 1973, Black family income declined from 61 percent to 58 percent of white family income. In part, this decrease was a result of the reduction in the proportion of Black families with two or more workers. Chances are that there are fewer Black families with dual workers because of the decrease in the number of Blacks married and living with a spouse (Thurow, 1976:4–5).

The income of individual Black workers vis-à-vis individual white workers has actually increased, albeit slowly. What, too, is the significance of the finding that Blacks are more likely to live alone than whites? The fact that this trend is becoming so pronounced has its own implications. How is the Black community to develop when its most educated members fail to marry, and those who are married have such a low fertility rate that they are not reproducing themselves? Using a cost-benefit analysis, what are the costs to the Black community from the benefits of individual expression and gratification?

Given the gradual resurgence of racism and the erosion of Black gains in the sixties, the price may be higher than Black people want to pay. There is no easy solution to this complex dilemma. Marriage is often a very fragile and conflict-ridden institution. From the writer's observations, many of the Black singles enjoy a higher level of education, income, and emotional well-being than some of their married counterparts. This situation seems particularly true of the women. But, this is not a study of Black marriages. Somehow and somewhere one must find a happy medium between the two evils.

As was true of white families, Black families were primarily an economic unit in the nineteenth century. Unlike many white families, particularly in the South, Black wives worked outside the home. In 1900, approximately 41 percent of Black women were in the labor force, compared with 16 percent of white women (Logan, 1965:162). A notable exception were middle-class Black families who preferred that the wife stay home in order to avoid the licentious behavior of white men. During the nineteenth century, most Blacks were concentrated in the rural South. The middle class was a very tiny and specialized segment of the Black community. Most were schoolteachers, morticians, doctors, or ministers. A college degree was essential for most Blacks aspiring to middle-class status. A significant deviation from the white culture was the large number of Black women who went to college. One of the reasons for this unusual pattern was the limited options open to Black women. Either they received college educations and became school teachers or worked as domestic servants in white households. Black men had a greater range of occupations open to them.

In the twentieth century Blacks migrated to the cities of the South and the North. In the Northern states Blacks increased their numbers in the middle class as more opportunities were opened to them. It was not until the 1960s that any significant economic gains were made by Blacks. As a result of the Civil Rights movement, Black student protests, and affirmative action programs, the middle class underwent a great expansion. By 1974, about 20 percent of all Black families had incomes over $15,000 a year. Twenty percent of Blacks between 25 and 35 had completed four or more years of college (U.S. Bureau of the Census, 1975b).

Today's Black middle class is primarily an urbanized group. Many of them will have their roots in the South and received their education in a predominantly Black college. They will be found in a number of different occupations rather than the traditional ones of teacher, social worker, or doctor.

The greatest concentration is still in the helping professions, although some are newscasters, architects, journalists, etc. As a result of certain historical factors, the majority of them will be women. They will have incomes ranging from $10,000 to $50,000 a year.

The social structure of middle-class Blacks in cities such as New York, Chicago, Los Angeles, and San Francisco is considerably more complex than was found in the rural or urban areas of the South. With their move to the urban North and exposure to higher education and different cultural values have come different behavioral modalities. They are by far the most acculturated of the Black population. In fact, many of the problems in Black singlehood are no different than the ones whites are also facing. There are, however, unique problems for the Black single person. As one observer noted, the problem has changed from living in a racist, segregated society to coping with a racist, integrated society (Robinson, 1976:24).

Living under different constraints and facing another set of cultural imperatives, many middle-class Blacks have adopted the life styles and value system of middle-class whites. Among these values is the subordination of group needs to individual desires. This value is easily maintained in an urban setting where the social sanctions on individual conduct are negligible. So, each individual is doing his or her own thing. A primary reason for the Black involvement in individualism is the decline of the Black movement. Without a leader, ideology, or movement to guide their behavior, many Blacks have been forced to fashion their life style and values on their own. Hence, they have acquired the ones presented to them by the dominant culture as representing the good life.

In conjunction with those changes have been the influence of the women's movement and ideology. Few Black women consider themselves feminist, and a lesser number are actively involved in the women's movement. But, the influence of feminist ideology is pervasive and obviously reflected in the rapid increase in Black women's organizations, consciousness-raising groups, and the everyday resistance of Black women to what they perceive as Black male chauvinism. It is possible that this situation may be the paramount factor in Black male–female conflict. While a factor, it may be more a result of sex-role conflict rather than a cause. Whatever the relationship between it and Black singlehood, it is very much evident in the changing relationship between the sexes.

Now that the implications of singleness for Blacks have been discussed, there are, in addition, certain structural conditions which make singlehood such a vexatious status for this group. One must point to the past history of racism, and even to its present form, for the existence of some of these conditions. It is the legacy of racism which has created the imbalance in the sex ratio among middle-class Black singles. Upwardly mobile Black families were forced to send their daughters, instead of their sons, to college to save them from the degradation of domestic work. The end result of this practice is substantially more Black female college graduates. There are approximately 85 college-educated Black males available for marriage to every 100 Black female college graduates over the age of 25.

This low sex ratio was formerly dealt with by college-educated Black women marrying men of lesser education. In one study conducted over twenty years ago, it was found that over half of these women were married to men employed at a lower socioeconomic level (Noble, 1956:108). A generation later it is found that college-educated Black women are much less willing to cross class lines in seeking a mate. One finds a curious pattern in the characteristics of never-married Blacks. There are actually a larger number of men who are never married between the ages of 25–35 than women; but, the largest proportion of those men are at the lowest socioeconomic level, while the greatest proportion of single women are at the higher socioeconomic level. Moreover, the divorce rate has increased most among high-status Blacks, and the women in that group are least likely to remarry (Glick and Mills, 1974).

Adding the two factors together—the high number of college-educated Black women who never marry and an equally large proportion who are divorced—the sex ratio in the eligible pool of mates for college-educated Blacks is as low as five women for every man.

There are other forces which tend to lower this ratio even further. Although there are no reliable data on Black homosexuality, it is generally agreed that the overwhelming majority of Black homosexuals are male. Fewer cases of Black lesbianism are known to the community. Another decrease in the eligible male poll occurs through the much larger proportion of Black men who marry women of other racial groups. While the percentage of Blacks married to whites is estimated to be less than 5 percent, it is known to occur more often in the high-status group (Heer, 1974). The tendency of college-educated Black males to marry women without college educations reduces the men available even further.

Racial tokenism in employment plays its share in creating impediments in matching up Black singles. One study of white singles found work was the most frequently cited institutional setting for meeting persons of the opposite sex (Starr and Carns, 1973). Due to the practice of many white employers to hire a token Black to prove they are equal opportunity employers, a number of Blacks work in settings where there are no other Blacks. The more educated and talented a Black is, the more likely is this to be the case.

In many large cities, particularly outside the South, there is literally no central place where middle-class Black singles can meet each other. Unlike whites they do not frequent singles bars or live in predominantly Black singles apartments. There are few Black organizations where singles are likely to encounter each other. Whereas whites have formed dating services, singles' organizations, and even advertise for mates in newspapers and magazines, much of Black dating is circumscribed. Because contacts are limited, many Blacks find themselves dating people in a very small clique and unable to broaden their options.

Changes in Black residence patterns have heightened the isolation of Black singles from each other. Although Los Angeles and San Francisco have a sizable Black population, the middle-class group is beginning to be dispersed in predominantly white apartments throughout the two areas. Moreover, where there is no large concentration of Blacks in a given setting there are likely to be few facilities that cater to them. Thus, in San Francisco, which has a very diffused Black middle class, one is hard-pressed to point out one place where they congregate. Class and racial boundaries are rarely crossed by middle-class Blacks, especially the women.

There are other forces at work, some too complex to delineate in this brief overview. Problems in finding a compatible mate are much more complex than in times gone by. The interests and values of Blacks were much more similar in the past. Nowadays, they may be looking for somebody who is interested in opera, skiing, or Zen Buddhism. Some of them in specialized occupations may want somebody who can relate to their field of endeavor. Thus, a woman banker may seek a man who understands the intricacies of international finance. These changes, coupled with the other barriers to a successful interpersonal relationship, complicate the exodus out of singlehood for many Blacks.

What is being witnessed in the year 1979 is the end product of the Black liberation movements that probably reached a peak around 1973. It is the formation of a small, elite class that has behaviorally assimilated the values of the dominant majority. At best they form about 10 percent of the Black population in the United States. They are not the inauthentic Black bourgeoisie that E. Franklin Frazier wrote of so pejoratively twenty years ago (Frazier, 1957). A number of them have gone to the top white and Black universities. Some have traveled and studied abroad, mostly in Europe. They occupy, in part, the role of native elites in a colonized nation. This writer categorizes them as elites because their status and way of life are vastly different from that of the Black masses who remain undereducated, poorly clothed, fed, and sheltered.

They are estranged from the Black majority not only in terms of education and income, but in life styles. However, their assimilation is not a completed process. To wit, they are still part of a separate Black community, but it is a milieu that, with a few exceptions, has not developed any institutions or values of its own. They are truly marginal people who exist on the cultural borders of both the Black and white community. This is not a role they have chosen but one forced upon them by the peculiar

character of American society. The Black majority still has many of its traditions and values. In the Black community, or ghetto, the stores, restaurants, and nightclubs belong to them. They also have other support institutions that sustain them, such as their churches, extended family system, and friendship networks.

Many of these changes are endemic to the urban North. In the cities of the South, middle-class Blacks are a more cohesive group. Due to the hard lines of racial segregation in that area, the Black middle class is more likely to live in the same environment and to have developed organizations and facilities to cater to their special needs. Many of the elite Blacks in the South attended predominantly Black colleges and joined fraternities and sororities which serve as social centers after graduation. This, too, is changing as the Black middle class in the South is beginning to disperse into former white enclaves. Some are frequenting predominantly white recreation and amusement centers. Of course, too many Blacks in these settings often change their racial character as whites respond to their presence by moving into other settings.

The basic perspective on the world of Black singles is that it constitutes a market, or exchange, system. In concrete terms this system means that men and women form relationships on the basis of their ability to bargain or negotiate for certain values. Traditionally, the most common transaction was the exchange of female sexual access for male economic resources. This negotiation occurred on many levels of society, despite the ideology that people dated and married on the assumption that strong affection or love was present. However, it is a complex process which takes on a number of different dimensions, depending on who does the buying and selling and which values are most highly desired in a partner (Goode, 1963:8).

What is seen is that bargaining still occurs between men and women who come together in the dating game. The traditional exchange values have been supplanted by another set of priorities. As a result of changes in the American society, men have much greater access to female sexuality, and the economically independent woman has much less need for the financial support of men. Thus, the parties involved may be bargaining for the satisfaction of certain psychological and physiological needs. Certain characteristics of the exchange system remain constant. Particular attributes are still more or less valuable in that market, and a certain class of individuals has more options than others.

The conditions under which middle-class Blacks select their mates, and the standards, have changed. The two are not unrelated. In the 1980s, the number of Black female college graduates will far excel the number of comparable males. Yet, most of these women will accept nothing less than a mate of similar educational level. This is a function of their acceptance of Euro-Americans' emphasis on status homogeneity as the basis for marriage. Not too long ago, less-educated males were acceptable as mates if they were hardworking and possessed other positive qualities. The middle-class Black male also falls victim to the lure of Euro-American values in his standards for a wife. As he rises into the middle class, acquires some power, and income, his standards begin to mirror those of his white counterpart. What he wants is a woman who fits into the Euro-American definition of womanhood, dependent and submissive. But the majority of Black women did not have these role models as children, nor did the imperatives of Black survival allow for them to acquire such traits.

Hence, the crisis of the Black family stems from more than poverty alone. It is also due to the problem of acculturation, the acceptance of values—alien values—that do not conform to the structural context of Black society. Despite all that was said about the lack of acculturation being the major cause of Black family weakness, it is becoming all too clear that Blacks' unique cultural moorings were functional for their situation. Now, Blacks stand at the crossroads of a major decision about which way they will proceed to order their lives. Will it be the organic family unit built on a Black ethos, or the materialism and individualism of Euro-American culture? Whatever that decision may be, Black people should not be deluded into believing that the consequences are individual ones. The future of the race may be at stake.

References

Frazier, E. Franklin
1957 *Black Bourgeoisie*. New York: Collier Books.
Glick, Paul C., and Karen M. Mills
1974 *Black Families, Marriage Patterns and Living Arrangements*. Atlanta, Ga.: Atlanta University.
Goode, William
1963 *World Revolution and Family Patterns*. New York: Free Press.
Heer, David
1974 "The Prevalence of Black-White Marriage in the United States, 1960 and 1970." *Journal of Marriage and the Family* 36 (May):246–259.
Logan, Rayford
1965 *The Betrayal of the Negro*. New York: Collier.
Noble, Jean
1956 *The Negro Woman College Graduate*. New York: Columbia University Press.

Robinson, Charlotte
1976 "Black Marriages—Victims of the Affluent Rat Race." *San Francisco Examiner,* April 25.
Staples, Robert
1976 *Introduction to Black Sociology*. New York: McGraw-Hill.
Starr, Joyce R., and Donald E. Carns
1973 "Singles in the City." In *Marriage and Families*, H. Lopata, ed., pp. 148–153. New York: Van Nostrand.
Stein, Peter
1976 *Single*. Englewood Cliffs, N.J.: Prentice-Hall.
Thurow, Lester
1976 "The Economic Status of Minorities and Women." *Civil Rights Digest* 8 (Winter-Spring):4–5.

U.S. Bureau of the Census

1974   *The Social and Economic Status of the Black Population, 1973.* Washington, D.C.: U.S. Government Printing Office.

1975a   Current Population Reports, Series P-20, No. 287. *Marital Status and Living Arrangements,* March 1975. Washington, D.C.: U.S. Government Printing Office.

1975b   *The Social and Economic Status of the Black Population, 1974.* Washington, D.C.: U.S. Government Printing Office.

BLACK MALE–BLACK FEMALE CONFLICT:
Individually Caused and Culturally Nurtured

Clyde W. Franklin II

A review of recent literature suggests that most authors writing on the subject agree that Black male–Black female relationships today are destructive and potentially explosive. The author explores two major sources of Black male–Black female conflict that have been identified: (1) noncomplementarity of sex role definitions internalized by Black males and Black females, and (2) structural barriers in the environments of Black males and Black females. Finally, the author offers some suggestions for attenuating the Black male–Black female conflict.

Who is to blame? Currently, there is no dearth of attention directed to Black male–Black female relationships. Books, magazine articles, academic journal articles, public forums, radio programs, television shows, and everyday conversations have been devoted to Black male–Black female relationships for several years. Despite the fact that the topic has been discussed over the past several decades by some authors (e.g., Frazier, 1939; Drake and Cayton, 1945; Grier and Cobb, 1968), Wallace's *Black Macho and the Myth of the Superwoman* has been the point of departure for many contemporary discussions of the topic since its publication in 1979.

Actually, Wallace's analysis was not so different in content from other analyses of Black male–Black female relationships (e.g., Drake and Cayton's analysis of "lower-class life" in *Black Metropolis*). But Wallace's analysis was "timely." Coming so soon on the heels of the Black movement in the late 1960s and early 1970s, and, at a time when many Black male-inspired gains for Blacks were disappearing rapidly, the book was explosive. Its theme, too, was provocative. Instead of repeating the rhetoric of the late 1960s and early 1970s that blamed conflictual relationships between Black men and Black women on White society, Wallace implied that the blame lay

From *Journal of Black Studies* 15 (2, December 1984): 139–154. © 1984 Sage Publications, Inc. Reprinted by permission of Sage Publications, Inc.

with Black males. In other words, the blame lay with those Black warriors who only recently had been perceived as the "saviors" of Black people in America. Wallace's lamenting theme is captured in a quote from her book: "While she stood by silently as he became a man, she assumed that he would finally glorify and dignify Black womanhood just as the White man has done for White women." Wallace goes on to say that this has not happened for Black women.

Wallace updates her attack on Black men in a later article entitled "A Black Feminist's Search for Sisterhood" (1982:9). Her theme, as before, is that Black men are just as oppressive of Black women as White men. She states:

> *Whenever I raised the question of a Black woman's humanity in conversations with a Black man, I got a similar reaction. Black men, at least the ones I knew, seemed totally confounded when it came to treating Black women like people. . . . I discovered my voice and when brothers talked to me, I talked back. This had its hazards. Almost got my eye blackened several times. My social life was like guerilla warfare. Here was the logic behind our grandmother's old saying, "A nigga man ain't shit."*

Wallace, however, is not alone in placing the blame on Black men for deteriorating relations between Black men and Black women. Allen (1983:62), in a recent edition of *Essence* magazine, states:

> *Black women have a tendency to be male-defined, subjugating their own needs for the good of that fragile male ego. . . . The major contradiction is that we Black women, in our hearts, have a tendency to believe Black men need more support and understanding than we do. We bought the Black Revolutionary line that a woman's place was three paces behind the man. We didn't stomp Stokeley when he made the statement that the only position for a woman in the movement was prone.*

Such attacks on Black men have been met with equally ferocious counterattacks by some Black authors (both Black men and Black women). A few months following the publication of Wallace's book, an entire issue of the *Black Scholar* was devoted to Black male–Black female relationships. Of the responses to Wallace by such scholars as Jones (1979), Karenga (1979), Staples (1979), and numerous others, Karenga's response is perhaps the most controversial and maybe the most volatile. Karenga launches a personal attack on Wallace suggesting that she is misguided and perhaps responding from personal hurt. Recognizing the complexity of Black male–Black female relationships, Karenga contends that much of it is due not to Black men but to the White power structure. Along similar lines, Moore (1980) has exhorted Black women to stop criticizing Black men and blame themselves for the disintegrating bonds between Black men and Black women.

Staples, in his response to Wallace and others who would place the blame on Black men for disruptive relationships between Black men and Black women, points out that while sexism within the Black culture may be an emerging problem, most Black men do not have the institutionalized power to oppress Black women. He believes that the Black male's "condition" in society is what bothers Black males. Staples devotes much attention to the institutional decimation of Black men and suggests that this is the reason for Black male–Black female conflict. Noting the high mortality and suicide rates of Black men, the fact that a half a million Black men are in prison, one-third of urban Black men are saddled with drug problems and that 25% to 30% do not have steady employment, Staples implied that Black male–Black female conflict may be related to *choice*. This means that a shortage of Black men may limit the choices that Black women have in selecting partners. As Braithwaite (1981) puts it, the insufficient supply of Black men places Black women at a disadvantage by giving Black men the upper hand. In a specific relationship, for example, if a Black woman fails to comply with the Black man's wishes, the Black man has numerous other options, including not only other Black women but also women of other races.

In a more recent discussion of Black male–Black female relationships, Alvin Poussaint (1982:40) suggests that Black women "adopt a patient and creative approach in exploring and creating new dimensions of the Black male–Black female bond." Others, like Ronald Braithwaite, imply in their analyses of relationships between Black men and Black women that Black women's aggressiveness, thought to be a carryover from slavery, may be partly responsible for Black male–Black female conflict.

Succinctly, by and large, most Black male and Black female authors writing on the subject seem to agree that many Black male–Black female relationships today are destructive and potentially explosive. What they do not agree on, however, are the causes of the problems existing between Black men and Black women. As we have seen, some believe that Black men are the cause. Others contend that Black women contribute disproportionately to Black male–Black female conflict. Still others blame White racism solely, using basic assumptions that may be logically inadequate (see Franklin, 1980). Many specific reasons for the conflict often postulated include the notions that Black men are abusive toward Black women, that Black men are irresistibly attracted to White women (despite the fact that only approximately 120,000 Black men were married to White women in 1980), that too many Black men are homosexual, that Black women are too aggressive, that Black women don't support Black men—the list goes on. Few of these reasons, however, really explore the underlying cause of the conflict. Instead, they are descriptions of the conflict-behaviors that are indicators of the tension between Black men and Black women. But what is the cause of the behavior—the cause of the tension that so often disrupts harmony in Black male–Black female relationships?

Given the various approaches many Black authors have taken in analyzing Black male–Black female relationships, it is submitted that two major sources of Black male–Black female conflict can be identified: (1) the noncomplementarity of sex-role definitions internalized by Black males and Black females; and (2) structural barriers in the environments of Black males and Black females. Each source is explored separately below.

Sources of Conflict between Black Men and Black Women

Sex-Role Noncomplementarity among Black Males and Black Females

Much Black male–Black female conflict stems directly from incompatible role enactments by Black males and Black females. Incompatible role enactments by Black men and Black women occur because they internalize sex-role definitions that are noncomplementary. For example, a Black woman in a particular conflictual relationship with a Black male may feel that her Black man is supposed to assume a dominant role, but she also may be inclined to exhibit behaviors that are opposed to his dominance and her subordination. In the same relationship, the Black man may pay lip service to assuming a dominant role but may behave "passively" with respect to some aspects of masculinity and in a dominant manner with respect to other aspects.

One reason for role conflict between Black men and Black women is that many contemporary Black women internalize two conflicting definitions of femininity, whereas many contemporary Black men internalize only a portion of the traditional definition of masculinity. Put simply, numerous Black women hold attitudes that are both highly masculine and highly feminine. On the other hand, their male counterparts develop traits that are highly consistent with certain aspects of society's definition of masculinity, but that are basically unrelated to other aspects of the definition. Thus, in a given relationship, one may find a Black woman who feels and behaves in ways that are both assertive and passive, dominant and subordinate, decisive and indecisive, and so on. Within that same relationship, a Black man may exhibit highly masculine behaviors, such as physical aggressiveness, sexual dominance, and even violence, but behave indifferently with respect to the masculine work ethic—assuming responsibility for family-related activities external to the home, being aggressive in the work place, and the like.

The reason these incongruent attitudes and behaviors exist among Black men and Black women is that they have received contradictory messages during early socialization. It is common for Black women to have received two messages. One message states, "Because you will be a Black woman, it is imperative that you learn to take care of yourself because it is hard to find a Black man who will take care of you." A second message frequently received by young Black females that conflicts with the first message is "your ultimate achievement will occur when you have snared a Black man who will take care of you." In discussing early socialization experiences with countless young Black women in recent years, I have found that most of them agree that these two messages were given them by socialization agents and agencies such as child caretakers, relatives, peer group members, the Black church, and the media.

When internalized, these two messages often produce a Black woman who seems to reject aspects of the traditional female sex role in America such as passivity, emotional and economic dependence, and female subordinance while accepting other aspects of the role such as expressiveness, warmth, and nurturance. This is precisely why Black women seem to be more androgynous than White women. Black women's androgyny, though, may be more a function of necessity than anything else. It may be related to the scarcity of Black men who assume traditional masculine roles in male–female relationships.

Whatever the reason for Black women's androgynous orientations, because of such orientations Black women oftentimes find themselves in conflictual relationships with Black men or in no stable relationships at all. The scenario generally can be described as follows. Many Black women in early adulthood usually begin a search for a Black Prince Charming. However, because of the dearth of Black men who can be or are willing to be Prince Charmings for Black women, Black women frequently soon give up the search for such a Black man. They give up the search, settle for less, and "like" what they settle for even less. This statement is important because many Black women's eventual choices are destined to become constant reminders that the "female independence" message received

during the early socialization process is the correct message. But, because Black women also have to deal with the second socialization message, many come to feel that they have failed in their roles as women. In an effort to correct their mistakes, Black women often choose to enact the aspect of their androgynous role that is decidedly aggressive and/ or independent. They may decide either to "go it alone" or to prod their Black men into becoming Prince Charmings. The first alternative for Black women often results in self-doubt, lowered self-esteem, and, generally, unhappiness and dissatisfaction. After all, society nurtures the "find a man" message far beyond early socialization. The second message, unfortunately, produces little more than the first message because Black women in such situations usually end up in conflictual relationships with Black men, who also have undergone a rather complicated socialization process. Let us explore briefly the conflicting messages numerous Black men receive during early socialization.

One can find generally that Black men, too, have received two conflicting messages during early socialization. One message received by young Black males is "to become a man means that you must become dominant, aggressive, decisive, responsible, and, in some instances, violent in social encounters with others." A second message received by young Black males that conflicts with the first is, "You are Black and you must not be too aggressive, too dominant, and so on, because the *man* will cut you down." Internalization of these two messages by some Black men (a substantial number) produces Black men who enact a portion of the traditional definition of masculinity but remain inactive with respect to other parts of traditional masculinity. Usually those aspects of traditional masculinity that can be enacted within the Black culture are the ones exhibited by these Black men. Other aspects of the sex role that require enactment external to the Black culture (e.g., aggressiveness in the work place) may be related to impassively by Black men. Unfortunately, these are aspects of the male sex role that must be enacted if a male is to be "productive" in American society.

Too many Black men fail to enact the more "productive" aspects of the male sex role. Instead, "being a man," for many Black males who internalize the mixed messages, becomes simply enacting sexual aggression, violence, sexism, and the like—all of which promote Black male–Black female conflict. In addition, contributing to the low visibility and low salience of "productive" masculine traits among Black men is the second socialization message, which provides a rationale for nonenactment of the role traits. Moreover, the "man will get you" message serves to attenuate Black men's motivations to enact more "positive" aspects of the traditional male sex role. We must keep in mind, however, that not all of the sources of Black male–Black female conflict are social-psychological. Some of the sources are structural, and in the next section these sources are discussed.

Structural Barriers Contributing to Black Male–Black Female Conflict

It is easy to place the blame for Black male–Black female conflict on "White society." Several Black authors have used this explanatory approach in recent years (e.g., Anderson and Mealy, 1979). They have suggested that Black male–Black female conflict is a function of America's capitalistic orientation and White society's long-time subjugation of Black people. Certainly historical conditions are important to understand when discussing the status of Black people today. Often, however, too much emphasis is placed on the historical subjugation of Black people as the source of Black male–Black female conflict today. Implicit in such an emphasis is the notion that independent variables existing at some point in the distant past cause a multiplicity of negative behaviors between Black males and Black females that can be capsulized as Black male–Black female conflict. A careful analysis of the contemporary environments of Black men and women today will show, instead, that factors responsible, in part, for Black male–Black female conflict are inextricably interwoven in those environments. In other words, an approach to the analysis of conflict between Black men and Black women today must be ahistorical. Past conditions influence Black male–Black female relationships only in the sense that

vestiges of these conditions exist currently and are identifiable.

Our society today undoubtedly remains structured in such a manner that the vast majority of Black men encounter insurmountable barriers to the attainment of a "masculine" status as defined by most Americans (Black and White Americans). Black men still largely are locked within the Black culture (which has relatively limited resources), unable to compete successfully for societal rewards—the attainment of which defines American males as "men." Unquestionably, Black men's powerlessness in society's basic institutions such as the government and the economy contributes greatly to the pathological states of many Black men. The high mortality and suicide rates of young Black men, the high incarceration rates of Black men, the high incidence of drug addiction among Black men, and the high unemployment rate of Black men are all functions of societal barriers to Black male upward mobility. These barriers render millions of Black males socially impotent and/or socially dysfunctional. Moreover, as Staples has pointed out, such barriers also result in a scarcity of functional Black men, thereby limiting Black women's alternatives for mates.

While some may be tempted to argue for a psychological explanation of Black male social impotence, it is suggested here that any such argument is misguided unless accompanied by a recognition of the role of cultural nurturance factors. Cultural nurturance factors such as the rigid castelike social stratum of Blacks in America foster and maintain Black men's social impotence. The result is powerless Black men primed for conflictual relationships with Black women. If Black men in our society were not "American," perhaps cultural nurturance of Black people's status in our society could not be translated into cultural nurturance of Black male–Black female conflict. That Black men are Americanized, however, is seen in the outcome of the Black movement of the last decade.

The Black movement of the late 1960s and early 1970s produced little structural change in America. To be sure, a few Black men (and even fewer Black women) achieved a measure of upward mobility; however, the vast majority did not reap gains from the Black movement. What did happen, though, was that Black people did get a glimpse of the rewards that can be achieved in America through violence and/or aggression. White society did bend when confronted by the Black movement, but it did not break. In addition, the few upward mobility doors that were ajar during the height of the movement were quickly slammed shut when the movement began to wane in the middle and late 1970s. Black men today find themselves in a position similar to the one Black men were in prior to the movement. The only difference this time around is that Black men are equipped with the psychological armor of aggression and violence as well as with a distorted perception of a target—Black women, the ones who "stood silently by."

Wallace's statement that Black women "stood silently by" must not be taken lightly. Black women did this; in addition, they further internalized American definitions of masculinity and femininity. Previously, Black women held modified definitions of masculinity and femininity because the society's definition did not fit their everyday experiences. During the Black movement they were exhorted by Black men to assume a sex role that was more in line with the traditional "feminine" role White women assumed in male–female relationships. Although this may have been a noble (verbal) effort on the part of Black men to place Black women on pedestals, it was shortsighted and doomed to fail. Failure was imminent because even during the peak of the Black movement, societal resistance to structural changes that would benefit Black people was strong. The strength of this resistance dictated that change in Black people's status in America could come about only through the united efforts of both Black men and Black women.

Unfortunately, the seeds of division between Black men and Black women were sown during the Black movement. Black men bought the Moynihan report (1965) that indirectly blamed Black women for Black people's underclass status in America. In doing so, Black men convinced themselves that they could be "men" only if they adopted the White male's sex role. An examination of this role reveals that it is characterized by numerous contradictions. The traditional White masculine role requires men to assume protective, condescending, and generally patriarchal stances with respect to women. It also requires, ironically, that men display dominant, aggressive, and often violent behaviors toward women. Just as important, though, is that White masculine role enactment can occur only when there is full participation in masculinist American culture. Because Black men continue to face barriers to full participation in American society, the latter requirement for White male sex-role assumption continues to be met by only a few Black men. The result has been that many Black men have adopted only a part of the culture's definition of masculinity because they are thwarted in their efforts to participate fully in society. Structural barriers to Black male sex-role adoption, then, have produced a Black male who is primed for a conflictual relationship with Black women. In the next section, an exploration is presented of some possible solutions to Black male–Black female conflict that arise from the interactive relationship between the noncomplementarity of sex-role internalization by Black men and Black women and structural barriers to Black men's advancement in American society.

Toward Solving Black Male–Black Female Conflict

Given that societal conditions are extremely resistant to rapid changes, the key to attenuating conflict between Black men and Black women lies in altering three social psychological phenomena: (1) Black male and Black female socialization experiences; (2) Black male and Black female role-playing strategies; and (3) Black male and Black female personal communication mechanisms. I first propose some alterations in Black male and Black female socialization experiences. . . .

Black female socialization must undergo change if Black men and Black women are to enjoy harmonious relationships. Those agents and agencies responsible for socializing young Black females must return to emphasizing a monolithic message in young Black female socialization. This message can stress warmth, caring, and nurturance, but it must stress simultaneously self-sufficiency, assertiveness, and responsibility. The latter portion of this message requires that young Black females must be cautioned against sexual freedom at relatively early ages—not necessarily for moral reasons, but because sexual freedom for Black women seems to operate against Black women's self-sufficiency, assertiveness, and responsibility. It is important to point out here, however, that this type of socialization message must be imparted without the accompanying castigation of Black men. To say "a nigger man ain't shit" informs any young Black female that at least one-half of herself "ain't shit." Without a doubt, this strategy teaches self-hate and sets the stage for future Black male–Black female conflict.

Young Black males, on the other hand, must be instructed in self-sufficiency, assertiveness, and responsibility without the accompanying warning opposed to these traits in Black males. Such warnings serve only to provide rationales for future failures. To be sure, Black men do (and will) encounter barriers to upward mobility because they are Black. But, as many Black men have shown, such barriers do not have to be insurmountable. Of course it is recognized that innumerable Black men have been victims of American racist policies, but some, too, have been victims because they perceived only that external factors hindered their upward mobility and did not focus on some internal barriers that may have thwarted their mobility. The former factors are emphasized much too often in the contradictory socialization messages received by most young Black males.

Along with the above messages, young Black males must learn that the strong bonds that they establish with their mothers can be extended to their relationships with other Black women. If Black men perceive their mothers to be symbols of strength and perseverance, they must also be taught that most other Black women acquire these same qualities and have done so for generations. It must become just as "cool," in places like urban Black barbershops, to speak of Black women's strength and dignity as it is now to hear of Black women's thighs, breasts, and hips.

On an issue closely related to the above, few persons reading this article can deny that Black men's attempts to enact the White male sex role in America are laughable. Black men are relatively powerless in this country, and their attempts at domination, aggression, and the like, while sacrificing humanity, are ludicrous. This becomes apparent when it is understood that usually the only people being dominated and aggressed against by Black men are Black women (and other Black men). Moreover, unlike White males, Black males receive no societal rewards for their efforts; instead, the result is Black male–Black female disharmony. Black men must avoid the tendency to emulate the nauseatingly traditional male sex role because their experiences clearly show that such a role is counterproductive for Black people. Because the Black man's experiences are different, his role-playing strategies must be different and made to be more complementary with Black females' altered role-playing strategies. The Black females' role-playing strategies, as we have seen, are androgynous, emphasizing neither the inferiority nor the superiority of male or female sex roles.

On a final note, it is important for Black people in our society to alter their personal communication mechanisms. Black men and Black women interact with each other in diverse ways and in diverse situations, ranging from intimate to impersonal. Perhaps the most important element of this diverse communication pattern is empathy. For Black people in recent years, this is precisely the element that has undergone unnecessary transformation. As Blacks in America have accepted increasingly White society's definition of male–female relationships, Black men and Black women have begun to interact with each other less in terms of empathy. While Black women have retained empathy in their male–female relationships to a greater degree than Black men have, Black men have become increasingly nonexpressive and nonempathic in their male–female relationships. Nearly 60% of Black women (approximately 25,000) in a recent *Essence* survey cited nonexpressiveness as a problem in male–female relationships; 56% also pointed out that Black male nonempathy was a problem (Edwards, 1982). It seems, then, that as Black males have attempted to become "men" in America they have shed some of the important qualities of humanity. Some Black women, too, who have embraced the feminist perspective also have discarded altruism. The result of both phenomena, for Black people as a whole, has been to divide Black men and Black women further. Further movement away from empathic understanding in Black male–Black female relationships by both Black men and Black women undoubtedly will be disastrous for Black people in America.

References

Allen, B.
1983   "The Price for Giving It Up." *Essence* (February):60–62, 118.

Anderson, S. E., and R. Mealy
1979   "Who Originated the Crisis: A Historical Perspective." *Black Scholar* (May/June):40–44.

Braithwaite, R. L.
1981   "Interpersonal Relations between Black Males and Black Females." In *Black Men*, L. E. Gary, ed., pp. 83–97. Beverly Hills, Calif.: Sage.

Drake, S. C., and H. R. Cayton
1945   *Black Metropolis*. New York: Harcourt.

Edwards, A.
1982   "Survey Results: How You're Feeling." *Essence* (December):73–76.

Franklin, C. W., II
1980   "White Racism As a Cause of Black Male–Black Female Conflict: A Critique." *Western Journal of Black Studies* 4 (1):42–49.

Frazier, E. F.
1939   *The Negro Family in the United States*. Chicago: University of Chicago Press.

Grier, W. H., and P. M. Cobb
1968   *Black Rage*. New York: Basic Books.

Jones, T.
1979   "The Need to Go beyond Stereotypes." *Black Scholar* (May/June):48–49.

Karenga, M. R.
1979   "On Wallace's Myth: Wading through Troubled Waters." *Black Scholar* (May/June):36–39.

Moore, W. E.
1980   "Black Women, Stop Criticizing Black Men—Blame Yourselves." *Ebony* (December):128–130.

Moynihan, D. P.
1965   *The Negro Family: The Case for National Action*. Washington, D.C.: U.S. Department of Labor, Office of Planning and Research.

Poussaint, A. F.
1982   "What Every Black Woman Should Know about Black Men." *Ebony* (August):36–40.

Staples, R.
1979   "The Myth of Black Macho: A Response to Angry Black Feminists." *Black Scholar* (March/April):24–32.

Wallace, M.
1979   *Black Macho and the Myth of the Superwoman*. New York: Dial.
1982   "A Black Feminist's Search for Sisterhood." In *All the Blacks Are Men, All the Women Are White, but Some of Us Are Brave*, G. T. Hull et al., eds., pp. 5–8. Old Westbury, N.Y.: Feminist Press.

6 / Husbands and Wives

MATE SELECTION DIFFERENTIALS BETWEEN WHITES AND BLACKS IN THE UNITED STATES

Graham B. Spanier · Paul C. Glick

The greater excess of women among Blacks than among whites during the years in which mate selection and first marriage most typically occur is documented. The extent to which this imbalance has implications for differential patterns of mate selection and marital history is explored through the use of data from the U.S. Bureau of the Census Current Population Survey for June 1975. The data are weighted to reflect estimates of the resident civilian, noninstitutional population of the United States age 14 and over. Specifically, the paper establishes that demographic necessity requires Black females to have a more restricted field of marriage eligibles than white females. It is demonstrated that Black women enlarge their field of eligibles by marrying males who tend to be older, who have lower educational attainment, and who have previously been married. The findings suggest that the "marriage squeeze" young marriageable Black women experience may have important consequences for courtship during adolescence, entrance into marriage, and marital dissolution.

Increasing interest during recent years in the study of Black families has led to the publication of numerous studies concerning the history, economics, and social psychology of Black family life. Considerably less attention has been given to the social demography of Black families and how some unique characteristics of the Black population influence patterns of mate selection, marital disruption, and family relationships.

This paper focuses on mate selection differentials between Black and White husbands and their wives. The paper receives its impetus from a finding rarely observed in research on Black families—namely, the relatively unbalanced ratio of males to

Reprinted from *Social Forces* 58 (March 1980): This article was prepared while the first author was on a visiting research appointment at the U.S. Bureau of the Census. The Current Population Survey data on which this analysis is based was in part funded by the National Institute of Child Health and Human Development. The authors thank Arthur J. Norton for his helpful comments on an earlier draft of this paper. Copyright © The University of North Carolina Press.

females in the age range in which most first marriages occur.

The high marital disruption rate among Blacks has been documented adequately (Spanier and Glick, 1980; U.S. Bureau of the Census, 1978b), and demographic surveys have established other relevant characteristics of the Black population that differ from those of the White population. For example, there is a higher proportion of Black women in the labor force compared to Whites, and Black women tend to marry earlier, have more children, and carry a greater proportion of the economic burden in their families (U.S. Bureau of the Census, 1976; Spanier and Glick, 1980).

Blacks have higher mortality rates than do Whites, and men have higher mortality rates than do women. But Black men have disproportionately high mortality rates compared to Black women at every age. Thus, there is an increasingly large discrepancy within given birth cohorts between the sex ratio for Black men and women and the sex ratio for White men and women (U.S. Department of Health, Education, and Welfare, 1977; U.S. Bureau of the Census, 1977b).

This paper hypothesizes that imbalanced sex ratios between Blacks and Whites account in part for some differentials in their patterns of mate selection and marriage. The purpose of the analysis, then, is to throw light on the degree to which Black females encounter a relatively restricted field of eligibles for marriage, and then to assess the consequences, if any, of this phenomenon. This purpose is accomplished through analysis of statistics on three readily available demographic characteristics—age, educational attainment, and marital history. White–Black differentials with respect to these variables are discussed.

Statement of the Problem

Estimates of the resident population of the United States as of July 1, 1975, indicated that there were 11 percent more Black females than Black males in the 20–24 year age group. Among Whites, there were approximately equivalent numbers of males and females. For persons in the 25–29 year age group,

Black females were 16 percent more numerous than Black males. The percentage increased to more than 19 percent for Blacks in the 30–34 year age cohort. Yet the ratio of White males to females remained nearly constant across these age groups, close to 1.0 (U.S. Bureau of the Census, 1977b). Due to higher age-specific mortality rates among males, the sex ratio tends to decrease with age. But among Whites, the sex ratio does not drop below 100 until 32 years of age, whereas for Blacks, women outnumber men beginning at age 18 (U.S. Bureau of the Census, 1977b). Thus, the sex ratio, which favors males at birth (about 105 White males for every 100 White females, and about 102 Black males for every 100 Black females), reverses at significantly different times in the life spans of Blacks and Whites.

Another way of considering these data is that for every 11 Black females in their early twenties, there are only 10 Black males in this age group. For every seven Black females in their late twenties, there are only six Black males. And for every six Black females in their early thirties, there are only five Black males. This trend continues in the same fashion through the life course. However, while the same phenomenon is also applicable to Whites, the sex ratio for Whites changes well after the typical mate selection years, and the rate of change is slower.

The above figures are based on independent estimates of the population developed by the U.S. Bureau of the Census. The decennial census enumerations which are updated by the independent population estimates are subject to undercounting, which is especially characteristic of young Black males, one group of interest in this study (U.S. Bureau of the Census, 1977a). The Census Bureau has published estimates of the undercount and therefore has developed correction factors which may be used to adjust for such undercounting, but which are not reflected in the figures presented above.

Census Bureau studies of completeness of coverage in the 1970 census (U.S. Bureau of the Census, 1977a) provide estimates of the ratio of census-level population to population adjusted for estimated net census undercount by age, sex, and race. White 15–19-year-old males had a coverage ratio of .99, compared to a ratio of .96 for Black 15–19-year-old males; for White and Black females the ratios were .99 and .97, respectively. The magnitude of the undercount is greater for persons age 20 and older, and the differences between Whites and Blacks become more pronounced for these older cohorts. The estimated completeness of coverage reached a low of .95 for White males ages 25–29, and a low of .97 for White females ages 25–29. However, for 25–29-year-old Black males and females, ratios as low as .81 and .92, respectively, were found (U.S. Bureau of the Census, 1977b).

When adjustments for the undercount are applied to sex ratios, the magnitude of the difference in numbers of Black males and females is diminished, thus substantially detracting from—although not eliminating—the merits of hypotheses that might follow from differences in sex ratios for males and females at similar ages. Differentials still remain, although slight. But it must also be noted that males tend to marry females who are, on the average, in younger age groups. Thus, sex ratios comparing men and women who are possible marriage eligibles ought to consider both adjustments for undercount and population distributions in appropriate age categories.

The two limitations in the use of same-age sex ratios cited above were considered in a recalculation of the sex ratios using 1970 census data adjusted for the undercount and comparing males between ages 20 and 34 with females who are in younger age categories. Using gross 5-year age intervals for illustration, the ratios were found to be *greater* than those presented earlier. Although this calculation probably overestimates the relevant sex ratios (the actual ratios undoubtedly are between the underestimated and overestimated figures), and although it is not possible to calculate precisely the numbers of males and females of each race who can be considered part of a given field of eligibles, the available data do suggest that Black males and females have an imbalance that White males and females do not.

One additional limitation in the data should be mentioned. The tables presented in this article were derived from the June 1975 Current Population Survey, which does not include the institutional population in its coverage. Because of the larger proportion of young adult Black than White persons, especially men, residing in institutions, a part of the differences by race discussed below may be attributed to this factor.

Thus, although differentials in sex ratios between Whites and Blacks are probably overestimated by routine application of Current Population Survey (CPS) data, the patterns of the differentials are believed to be valid when actual fields of eligibles are considered. Moreover, several other factors pertaining to the completeness of coverage of the population from CPS data still argue for using unadjusted estimates of the population: first, the precise extent of undercounting for subgroups of the population is uncertain (U.S. Bureau of the Census, 1977a); second, the social characteristics of those not counted that are relevant in connection with their eligibility for marriage are undoubtedly different from those counted; third, the institutional population, not enumerated in the CPS, is small and realistically outside of the field of the pool of marriage eligibles for those in the noninstitutional population.

Given the conclusion that an imbalance exists in the numbers of Black males and females in similar age cohorts, important questions about mate selection and marriage emerge. First, what consequences do such differences have for Black men and women approaching typical marriageable ages? Since Black women have a more restricted field of eligibles, one reasonably may hypothesize that a relatively large proportion of Black women either will marry men with lower social status or will remain unmarried. For example, differences in educational homogamy may be expected between Blacks and Whites, with a larger proportion of Black women marrying men with lower educational levels than would be predicted on the basis of their educational distributions. Second, since the field of eligibles in the woman's own age cohort is too small to accommodate all women in that cohort, a larger proportion of Black women than White women would be expected to marry men significantly older or significantly younger than themselves or to remain unmarried. In other words, Black couples would be expected to differ in age by a greater amount than would White couples. A third hypothesis is that never married Black women are more likely than their White counterparts to marry men who have been married previously.

The norms surrounding mate selection in the United States are powerful ones. Earlier analyses have demonstrated the relative stability over this century in events such as age at first marriage and age at the birth of the first child (Glick, 1977; Spanier and Glick, 1980). The hypotheses presented above are potentially important because they suggest that Black men and women may violate these norms more often than White men and women do. If it is correct that normative mate selection is a precursor to relatively functional marital interaction and marital stability (Lewis and Spanier, 1979), then the differentials in mate selection that Blacks face by necessity may account in part for the greater incidence of marital instability that characterizes this racial group.

Confirmation of these hypotheses might also contribute to an understanding of other Black–White differences in adolescent behavior and courtship. For example, Zelnik and Kantner (1977) report that 63 percent of Black females 15–19 years old are sexually experienced, compared to 31 percent of White females in this age group. Although a direct link may not exist between [these percentages and] the availability of males for intimate dating or marriage, an indirect connection may be suggested by the process of social pressure.

Adolescent Black females may learn that they will be faced with a restricted field of eligibles when they reach marriageable ages. To prepare for this relative dearth of men, the young Black female may experience greater pressures than White females from others their age to maintain close relationships with young men. Such pressures may account partially for their greater willingness to become sexually active at relatively young ages, inasmuch as such activity may be seen by the adolescent as a sign of commitment to and from the partner. Moreover, adolescent males may encourage such relationships by threatening to terminate the involvement if the female does not consent. If Black females anticipate greater pressure than White females to maintain intimate relationships, they may be more willing to engage in such behavior.

The inevitable "marriage squeeze" among Black women most likely results in other types of behavior that differ from the norm. Although the speculative analysis presented above would be difficult to test empirically, it does serve to highlight the potential diversity of consequences which might be related to imbalances between the numbers of males and females available for mate selection.

Data Source

Data for this study are from the June 1975 Current Population Survey. Each month, the U.S. Bureau of the Census conducts a survey consisting of a national probability sample of about 100,000 adults living in approximately 50,000 households. These surveys are used to estimate national employment and unemployment patterns, characteristics of the labor force, education, migration, fertility, and other important demographic characteristics of the population. Every 4 years since 1967, a marital history supplement has been appended to the survey conducted during the month of June. Data from the supplement provide an opportunity to consider the marital histories of the respondents and allow for comparisons of husbands and wives. The sample is weighted so as to be consistent with estimates for the entire noninstitutional population (U.S. Bureau of the Census, 1978a). However, the data do not take into account the previously identified problem of undercounting.

Profile of the Field of Eligibles

The analysis begins with an examination of the marital status of men and women in the United States by age and race. Table 1 shows the number and proportion of males and females by marital status in consolidated age groups from ages 14 to 54. In effect, of course, each age group is a birth cohort. Distributions are presented for the population of all races, for Whites, and for Blacks. Because women tend to marry men who are older than they are, the proportion of married or previously married females at the younger ages is considerably greater than the corresponding proportion for males. With some fluctuations, this imbalance tends to diminish progressively with advancing age.

TABLE 1   Ages of Men and Women 14–54 Years Old at Survey Date by Marital Status and Race: June 1975
(numbers in thousands)

MARITAL STATUS, SEX, AND RACE	AGE AT SURVEY DATE (YEARS)							
	14–19	20–24	25–29	30–34	35–39	40–44	45–49	50–54
All Races								
Never married	23,266	9,215	2,903	1,214	642	516	546	563
Percent:								
Males	51.7	56.8	59.3	56.6	56.8	53.4	55.6	52.8
Females	48.3	43.2	40.7	43.4	43.2	46.6	44.4	47.2
Married once, in intact marriage[1]	1,318	8,068	11,959	11,012	9,495	9,333	9,656	9,707
Percent:								
Males	21.5	40.0	47.4	49.5	49.3	50.3	50.9	50.6
Females	78.5	60.0	52.6	50.5	50.7	49.7	49.1	49.4
Married once, not in intact marriages[2]	112	921	1,495	1,387	1,190	1,191	1,471	1,599
Percent:								
Males	14.4	29.9	35.4	32.3	31.1	31.1	28.5	29.9
Females	85.6	70.1	64.6	67.7	68.9	68.9	71.5	70.1
White								
Never married	19,721	7,723	2,344	960	499	441	468	481
Percent:								
Males	52.0	58.5	61.1	58.5	58.8	53.1	55.9	52.6
Females	48.0	41.5	38.9	41.5	41.2	46.9	44.1	47.4
Married once, in intact marriage[1]	1,185	7,268	10,826	9,936	8,539	8,388	8,753	8,906
Percent:								
Males	22.1	39.7	47.8	49.4	49.3	50.3	50.9	50.6
Females	77.9	60.3	52.2	50.6	50.7	49.7	49.1	49.4
Married once, not in intact marriage[2]	98	744	1,175	1,016	891	849	1,132	1,257
Percent:								
Males	14.8	31.9	36.7	35.8	33.4	32.8	28.1	29.2
Females	85.2	68.1	63.3	64.2	66.6	67.2	71.9	70.8

Since the focus of the analysis is on the process of mate selection, perhaps the most appropriate group of persons to consider initially are those who had not yet married by the survey date. Males and females must be compared both at similar age levels and across age levels, since males typically marry females who are younger than they are. Looking first at never married Whites, one can see that never married males outnumber never married females in every age group. This differential increases across the first five categories presented—the range within which virtually all first marriages take place. Among Blacks, the trend is reversed across four of the first five age categories. Thus, an initial examination of these data immediately demonstrates the contrast in the respective field of eligibles. However, this is not the whole picture.

One must also consider currently and formerly married individuals. Part of the differential seen in the numbers of persons never married is

TABLE 1   continued
(numbers in thousands)

MARITAL STATUS, SEX, AND RACE	AGE AT SURVEY DATE (YEARS)							
	14–19	20–24	25–29	30–34	35–39	40–44	45–49	50–54
Black								
Never married	3,209	1,287	474	211	126	71	70	64
Percent:								
Males	50.1	47.4	49.7	45.8	46.8	56.6	52.3	52.1
Females	49.9	52.6	50.3	54.2	53.2	43.4	47.7	47.9
Married once, in intact marriage[1]	113	693	926	873	794	794	765	690
Percent:								
Males	15.3	44.3	46.2	51.9	49.9	50.3	51.9	51.8
Females	84.7	55.7	53.8	48.1	50.1	49.7	48.1	48.2
Married once, not in intact marriage[2]	14	166	302	352	277	329	315	328
Percent:								
Males	—[3]	22.6	31.1	23.1	25.3	27.1	30.4	32.7
Females	—[3]	77.4	68.9	76.4	74.7	72.9	69.6	67.3

[1]Married (except separated) persons married once.
[2]Separated, divorced, or widowed persons married once.
[3]Base too small to be reliable.

diminished among Whites but increased among Blacks by the phenomenon of many females selecting partners from the age cohort above them. The picture is complicated additionally by the opportunity formerly married persons have to marry someone who has never been married. However, it has been established that remarriage rates are higher for males than for females, and Blacks have lower remarriage rates than do Whites (U.S. Department of Health, Education, and Welfare, 1973).

An example helps illustrate the contrasting situations for Black and White women. Most of the never married White women age 20–24 (42 percent of all persons in this age group) can be expected to choose marital partners from among the abundant supply of never married males in their age group (59 percent) and in the 25–29 age group (61 percent). Most of the males in the 20–24 age category who do not marry women in the same age cohort will marry females shown in the 14–19 age group. Among Blacks, however, such choices are not pos-

sible across the population involved. Since there are fewer males than females in the younger unmarried age cohorts, some females only can be left with the options of marrying below their age cohort (in violation of the norm), marrying a previously married male, or not marrying at all. Of course, the majority of females may marry according to the same norms which apply to Whites, but it is not possible demographically for as many Black females to follow these norms as it is for their White counterparts.

Thus, it can be concluded that during the years in which most first marriages occur, Black females encounter a relatively restricted field of eligibles compared to White females. It also may be suggested that remedies to this situation are limited. The Black female may be more likely to marry a male who is significantly different from her in age, and possibly educational status. She also may be more likely to marry a man who has previously been married. These hypotheses will be examined.

The situation in which a Black female marries a man who is not Black is rare and thus does not merit treatment in this context (Glick and Spanier, 1980).

Mate Selection Differentials between Husbands and Their Wives

Table 2 shows the mean age at first marriage and mean educational attainment for husbands and their current wives by race and age at survey date. In addition, the mean differences between husbands and their wives with respect to age at marriage and education were calculated. The differences shown are absolute values. In other words, the means take into account the magnitude of the

differential between each husband and wife, regardless of the direction of the difference. These figures, then, are reflections of the gross magnitude of differences between wives and husbands in regard to age and education. The figures differ from those typically presented in analyses of mate selection, since *net* differences are usually presented; the net differences reflect the averages for all males and all females in the population without respect to individual couple differences. In fact, such net differences can be observed in Table 2 by comparing means for males and females.

Although the differences are not great, they show that Black females report earlier ages at marriage than White females, and Black males report later ages at marriage than White males. Among both Black and White females, a study of relevant

TABLE 2   Age at First Marriage and Education of Husbands and Wives 20 to 54 Years Old at Survey Date by Race and Age: June 1975

AGE AT FIRST MARRIAGE, YEARS OF SCHOOL COMPLETED, AND RACE	ALL HUSBANDS AND WIVES 20–54	AGE AT SURVEY DATE (YEARS)						
		20–24	25–29	30–34	35–39	40–44	45–49	50–54
White								
Mean age at first marriage:								
Husbands	23.1	20.4	22.1	22.8	23.1	23.7	24.3	24.5
Wives	20.2	18.2	19.8	20.1	21.1	20.4	20.9	21.4
Mean absolute difference[1]	4.1	3.0	3.1	3.7	4.3	4.6	4.7	5.0
Mean years of school completed:								
Husbands	12.5	12.3	13.1	12.9	12.5	12.3	12.0	11.8
Wives	11.8	11.3	12.2	12.1	11.9	11.6	11.7	11.3
Mean absolute difference[1]	1.9	1.8	1.7	1.8	1.9	2.0	2.0	2.0
Black								
Mean age at first marriage:								
Husbands	23.7	20.7	22.1	23.2	24.3	24.3	25.3	25.8
Wives	20.0	16.8	19.6	19.5	20.9	20.8	20.7	21.3
Mean absolute difference[1]	5.5	5.0	3.9	4.7	5.3	5.8	6.8	7.4
Mean years of school completed:								
Husbands	10.9	11.8	12.0	11.8	11.2	10.7	9.5	9.1
Wives	10.9	10.2	11.6	11.2	11.4	10.9	10.5	9.9
Mean absolute difference[1]	2.3	2.5	1.9	2.0	2.1	2.4	2.7	2.9

[1]Computed for each married couple, disregarding direction of difference.

statistics in Table 2 suggests that ages at marriage may be disturbed somewhat by a likely tendency for some never married mothers to report themselves as separated and hence to report an age at "marriage" earlier than their age at the birth of their first child. Also, both Black males and Black females appear to have lower educational attainment than do Whites in every age group. Furthermore, the data show that the older White males and Black females tend to have higher educational attainment than their spouses, but in the younger cohorts, Black males join the White males in having reached a higher level of education than their wives, on the average.

The most important finding from the analysis presented in Table 2, however, is the magnitude of the difference between Black and White husbands and their current spouses with respect to age and education. As hypothesized, the extent of the difference between both age at first marriage and education is shown to be greater for Blacks than for Whites. For all persons age 20–54, the mean difference in age at first marriage was 4.1 years for Whites and 5.5 years for Blacks. The mean difference in education was 1.9 years for Whites and 2.3 years for

Blacks. It can be concluded, therefore, that Black husbands and wives tend to differ in age at first marriage and education more than do White husbands and wives.

Having established these differentials between the races, it is necessary to explore the extent to which wives marry husbands of lower age and education—in short, the degree to which traditional norms of mate selection in these respects do not apply. Furthermore, the nature of male–female differentials can be related to marital history.

Age at First Marriage and Marital History

Table 3 presents the cross-classification of husband's marital history by differentials in ages at first marriage for husbands and their current wives. Table 4 substitutes the joint husband–wife marital status for the husband's marital history. Both tables allow for some added insight into the nature of mate selection for Black and White couples. A few comparisons may be highlighted.

TABLE 3   Difference between Ages of Husband and Wife at First Marriage by Marital History and Race of Husband, for Married Couples with the Husband 35–64 Years Old at Survey Date: June 1975

MARITAL HISTORY AND RACE OF HUSBAND	ALL MARRIED COUPLES		HUSBAND OLDER			
	Number (in thousands)	Percent	5 years or more	2–4 years	Less than 2 years	Wife older
White						
Total	24,152	100.0	34.3	22.8	23.3	19.5
Married once	20,266	100.0	30.4	24.9	25.7	19.1
Married more than once:						
Divorced after first marriage	3,318	100.0	55.7	12.1	11.3	20.8
Widowed after first marriage	568	100.0	59.3	10.2	10.4	20.1
Black						
Total	2,034	100.0	43.8	17.0	19.5	19.7
Married once	1,548	100.0	37.2	20.0	21.8	20.7
Married more than once:						
Divorced after first marriage	405	100.0	64.8	8.9	12.2	14.0
Widowed after first marriage	81	100.0	58.1	3.2	9.9	28.9

First, looking at couples in which the husband has been married once (Table 3, line 2) or in which the husband and wife have both been married once (Table 4, line 2), one may see that Black couples are considerably more likely than White couples to include husbands who are at least 4 years older than their wives. Thus, as hypothesized, Blacks are more likely to display greater age differences, but these differences are most often in the direction of older husbands. This difference persists across all combinations of marital status shown in Table 4. Yet, both racial groups have about the same proportion of wives who are older than their husbands.

For White and Black couples alike, the wife is more likely to be older than the husband if she had never been married before than if she had been previously married. The wife also has a relatively good chance of being older than her husband if both have remarried. A point deserving emphasis, however, is the fact that in one of every five or six marriages in the United States, the wife was older than the husband at the time of first marriage. Thus, to define any pattern of mate selection as normative, one must take into account the considerable variation evident in the population.

To summarize, Tables 3 and 4 demonstrate partial support for the hypothesis that Blacks are more likely than Whites to vary from traditional patterns of mate selection with respect to age homogamy. However, this variation is most pronounced among couples in which the husband is at least 4 years older than the wife. Black females are no more likely than White females to marry males who are younger than they are.

Education and Marital History

An earlier analysis made use of 1970 census data to support the conclusion that individuals tend to marry at the same educational level; that when persons marry across educational levels, the wife is likely to marry up; and that education remains a major factor in mate selection and potentially a major source of differences in marital patterns (Rock-

TABLE 4   Difference between Ages of Husband and Wife at First Marriage by Marital History of Husband and Wife and Race of Husband, for Married Couples with the Husband 35–64 Years Old at Survey Date: June 1975

MARITAL HISTORY OF HUSBAND AND WIFE AND RACE OF HUSBAND	ALL MARRIED COUPLES		HUSBAND OLDER			
	Number (in thousands)	Percent	5 years or more	2–4 years	Less than 2 years	Wife older
White						
Total	24,152	100.0	34.3	22.8	23.3	19.5
Husband and wife married once	18,790	100.0	30.9	25.8	26.3	17.0
Husband married once, wife more than once	1,476	100.0	23.8	13.4	17.2	45.6
Husband married more than once, wife once	1,507	100.0	67.9	11.3	8.5	12.3
Both married more than once	2,379	100.0	46.5	12.3	12.9	28.2
Black						
Total	2,034	100.0	43.8	17.0	19.5	19.7
Husband and wife married once	1,342	100.0	38.0	22.0	22.0	18.0
Husband married once, wife more than once	201	100.0	32.8	7.0	20.9	39.3
Husband married more than once, wife once	272	100.0	72.6	9.0	9.1	9.2
Both married more than once	219	100.0	53.3	5.7	15.3	25.8

well, 1976). This analysis found that nonwhite couples were more likely than White couples to include wives who exceeded their husband's level of education. But the study also found homogamy to be highest for nonwhite couples. Some of the results in this section tend to differ somewhat from the earlier results. This may result from the different universe used in the earlier study (*all* married couples were considered).

Table 5 presents the education of husband by education of wife for couples in which the husband was between 35 and 64 at the survey date in June 1975. This age range was regarded as optimum for the study of race differences in marital history. Al-

though the tendency to marry at one's own level of educational attainment can be seen, clearly a considerable amount of variation in joint husband–wife educational characteristics exists. Only 45 percent of the Whites and 46 percent of the Blacks marry someone at their level of education, in terms of the levels shown in the table. Thus, a majority of persons of both races marry up or down in educational level, according to the measures used here. When educational heterogamy exists, then, to what degree and in what direction do Blacks and Whites differ?

Tables 6 and 7 clearly support the hypothesis that Black women are more likely than White women to marry a man of lower educational attain-

TABLE 5 Education of Husband by Education of Wife by Race, for Married Couples with the Husband 35–64 Years Old at Survey Date: June 1975

| EDUCATION AND RACE OF HUSBAND | ALL MARRIED COUPLES | | EDUCATION OF WIFE | | | | | |
| | Number (in thousands) | Percent | Elementary | High school | | College | | |
			0–8 years	1–3 years	4 years	1–3 years	4 years	5 or more
White								
Total	24,152	100.0	13.2	17.0	47.5	12.4	6.7	3.2
Elementary:								
0–8 years	4,347	18.0	7.9	4.5	4.8	0.6	0.2	0.1
High school:								
1–3 years	3,734	15.5	2.3	5.7	6.3	0.8	0.2	0.1
4 years	8,704	36.0	2.3	5.4	23.7	3.3	1.0	0.4
College:								
1–3 years	3,104	12.9	0.4	1.0	6.8	3.4	0.9	0.4
4 years	2,257	9.3	0.1	0.3	3.7	2.5	2.2	0.6
5 or more	2,007	8.3	0.1	0.1	2.2	1.9	2.2	1.8
Black								
Total	2,034	100.0	24.9	24.8	36.1	7.4	3.9	3.0
Elementary:								
0–8 years	773	38.0	19.0	9.5	8.3	0.9	0.3	—[1]
High School:								
1–3 years	487	23.9	3.6	9.6	8.8	1.1	0.2	0.6
4 years	501	24.6	1.9	4.5	13.9	2.5	1.3	0.5
College:								
1–3 years	175	8.6	0.2	1.2	3.4	2.0	0.9	0.8
4 years	56	2.8	0.1	0.1	1.4	0.5	0.6	0.1
5 or more	42	2.1	—[1]	—[1]	0.2	0.4	0.5	1.0

[1]Zero or rounds to zero.

ment. Both Blacks and Whites, as previously noted, have similar proportions of couples at the same educational level. Among Whites, the husband is in a higher level in 31 percent of the couples, and in a lower one in 24 percent. Among Blacks, however, the husband is higher in only 18 percent of the couples, whereas the wife is higher in 36 percent. Stated differently, for Black couples where there is a difference in educational level, the wife is twice as likely as the husband to be more highly educated.

How is this educational differential related to marital history? The first block of data in Table 6 for Black couples shows that having a wife with a higher educational level is considerably more characteris-

tic of remarried husbands (44 percent) than once married husbands (34 percent). Among Whites the difference is negligible (24 percent versus 23 percent). The other blocks of data in the table, however, show that subdividing the sample into categories of husbands with high school education or less and husbands with at least some college greatly clarifies the nature of this relationship. This cross-tabulation suggests that husbands with a relatively low educational attainment are most likely to marry up in education, whereas husbands with a relatively high educational attainment are most likely to marry down.

Table 7 shows educational differentials by

TABLE 6   Differences between Educational Level of Husband and Wife by Marital History and Race of Husband, for Married Couples with the Husband 35–64 Years Old at Survey Date: June 1975

MARITAL HISTORY AND RACE OF HUSBAND	WHITE				BLACK			
	All married couples	Husband's education higher	Same level	Wife's education higher	All married couples	Husband's education higher	Same level	Wife's education higher
Total (in thousands)	24,152	7,565	10,827	5,760	2,034	365	937	731
Percent	100.0	31.3	44.8	23.8	100.0	18.0	46.1	35.9
Married once	100.0	31.4	45.5	23.1	100.0	17.9	48.6	33.5
Married more than once:								
Divorced after first marriage	100.0	30.9	40.4	28.7	100.0	19.3	37.7	43.1
Widowed after first marriage	100.0	29.9	47.3	22.9	100.0	13.4	40.5	46.1
Husband with no college education:								
Total (in thousands)	16,785	2,427	9,027	5,331	1,761	203	864	693
Percent	100.0	14.5	53.8	31.8	100.0	11.6	49.1	39.4
Married once	100.0	14.0	55.0	31.0	100.0	11.3	52.0	36.7
Married more than once:								
Divorced after first marriage	100.0	17.2	46.5	36.3	100.0	12.2	39.8	48.0
Widowed after first marriage	100.0	14.4	55.1	30.5	100.0	13.6	41.2	45.2
Husband with at least some college education:								
Total (in thousands)	7,376	5,138	1,801	429	273	162	74	38
Percent	100.0	69.7	24.4	5.8	100.0	59.2	27.0	13.8
Married once	100.0	69.4	24.8	5.9	100.0	58.2	27.9	13.9
Married more than once:								
Divorced after first marriage	100.0	72.3	21.7	6.0	100.0	65.1	23.8	11.1
Widowed after first marriage	100.0	71.9	25.9	2.2	100.0	—[1]	—[1]	—[1]

[1]Base too small to be reliable.

joint husband–wife marital status. According to this table, the wife tends to have more education than the husband if the husband has been married more than once but the wife only once. Nevertheless, for all combinations of marital status and at all levels of education for the husband, Black couples are more likely than White couples to include a wife with a higher educational level than her husband.

In conclusion, the data confirm the hypothesis that Black women are more likely than are White women to marry men who have less education than they have. Furthermore, data pertaining to Blacks suggest that educational heterogamy in which the wife has more education than the husband is particularly associated with second and subsequent marriages.

TABLE 7 Difference between Educational Level of Husband and Wife by Marital History of Husband and Wife and Race of Husband, for Married Couples with the Husband 35–64 Years Old at Survey Date: June 1975

MARITAL HISTORY OF HUSBAND AND WIFE AND EDUCATION OF HUSBAND	WHITE				BLACK			
	All married couples	Husband's education higher	Same level	Wife's education higher	All married couples	Husband's education higher	Same level	Wife's education higher
Total (in thousands)	24,152	7,565	10,827	5,760	2,034	365	937	731
Percent	100.0	31.3	44.8	23.8	100.0	18.0	46.1	35.9
Husband and wife married once	100.0	31.1	45.6	23.3	100.0	17.5	47.3	35.2
Husband married once, wife more than once	100.0	35.7	43.7	20.6	100.0	20.4	57.5	22.1
Husband married more than once, wife once	100.0	25.4	42.0	32.6	100.0	15.7	31.5	52.8
Both married more than once	100.0	34.1	41.0	24.9	100.0	21.5	46.4	32.2
Husband with no college education:								
Total (in thousands)	16,785	2,427	9,027	5,331	1,761	203	864	693
Percent	100.0	14.5	53.8	31.8	100.0	11.6	49.1	39.4
Husband and wife married once	100.0	13.2	55.3	31.4	100.0	10.3	51.0	38.7
Husband married once, wife more than once	100.0	22.3	51.8	25.9	100.0	17.5	58.2	24.3
Husband married more than once, wife once	100.0	11.6	47.7	40.6	100.0	8.4	34.0	57.6
Both married more than once	100.0	20.1	47.8	32.1	100.0	17.5	47.6	34.9
Husband with at least some college education:								
Total (in thousands)	7,376	5,138	1,801	429	273	162	74	38
Percent	100.0	69.7	24.4	5.8	100.0	59.2	27.0	13.8
Husband and wife married once	100.0	68.9	25.1	6.0	100.0	58.9	25.9	15.2
Husband married once, wife more than once	100.0	76.4	19.2	4.3	100.0	—[1]	—[1]	—[1]
Husband married more than once, wife once	100.0	67.7	24.3	8.0	100.0	—[1]	—[1]	—[1]
Both married more than once	100.0	75.0	21.2	3.8	100.0	—[1]	—[1]	—[1]

[1]Base too small to be reliable.

Patterns of First Marriage and Remarriages

It was hypothesized that never married Black females are more likely than White females to include previously married males in their field of eligibles for marriage. Table 8 summarizes the distribution of husband's and wife's marital status by race for couples with the husband 35 to 64 years old. Whereas only 6 percent of White couples include a wife married once and a husband married more than once, the corresponding figure is twice as great—13 percent—for Black couples. In other words, married Black women married only once were more than twice as likely as White women married once to be wedded to a man who had previously been married. Thus, it can be concluded that Black women are more likely than White women to consider formerly married men as belonging in their field of eligibles and subsequently to marry these men.

Summary

Mortality rates for males are considerably higher than those for females, and this difference is much greater for Blacks than for Whites. Moreover, larger proportions of young adult Blacks than Whites are not counted in census enumerations or are residing in institutions; these differences are greater for males than for females. For these and other reasons, census data show that the sex ratio falls below 100 males per 100 females for Blacks before the most typical years for mate selection (at age 18) but does not do so for Whites until well beyond that period (at age 32). Much of the difference would still persist if adjustments were made for the inadequacies in the basic data.

The impact of these differences between the sex ratios for Blacks and Whites are believed to produce unlike effects on the two racial groups with respect to mate selection, anticipatory socialization for it, and the consequences of it. In order to examine the plausibility of this belief, three hypotheses were tested.

First, it was hypothesized that the imbalance in the number of young Black men and women will cause an especially large proportion of Black women to marry men who are significantly older than the typical age at marriage for the population as a whole or to remain unmarried. This hypothesis was confirmed. Virtually all of the difference between the races in this regard, however, is accounted for by couples in which the man is at least 4 years older than the woman. Although Black couples are more divergent in age than White couples, the Black women are no more likely than the White women to have partners who are younger than they are.

Second, it was hypothesized that Black couples are more likely to differ in education than are White couples and that Black women would be more likely to marry men of a lower educational level. This hypothesis was also confirmed. Black couples are more divergent than White couples in educational attainment, and Black women are significantly more likely than White women to marry men at lower educational levels.

Third, it was hypothesized that never married Black women would be more likely than their White counterparts to marry men who had been married previously. This hypothesis was confirmed. Approximately twice as large a proportion of couples among Blacks as among Whites includes a wife married once and a husband married more than once.

These findings representing the population of the United States during June 1975 confirm significant racial differences in the selection of marriage partners. The present analysis does not demonstrate that these differentials are in turn related to the amount of marital instability, but the data do lend preliminary support for the speculation that higher rates of marital instability among Blacks may be associated with their higher incidence of deviation from normative mate selection patterns.

In the future, mortality rates of Blacks may be expected to approach those of Whites, and in other relevant ways the two racial groups may be expected to become more nearly alike. Consequently, the contrasts in patterns of mate selection may also be expected to diminish through the application of the principle of supply and demand. From a demo-

TABLE 8   Marital History of Husband and Wife by Race of Husband, for Married Couples with the Husband 35–64 Years Old at Survey Date: June 1975

MARITAL HISTORY OF HUSBAND AND WIFE	WHITE		BLACK	
	Number (in thousands)	Percent	Number (in thousands)	Percent
All married couples	24,152	100.0	2,034	100.0
Husband and wife married once	18,790	77.8	1,342	66.0
Husband married once, wife more than once	1,476	6.1	201	9.9
Husband married more than once, wife once	1,507	6.2	272	13.4
Both married more than once	2,379	9.9	219	10.8

graphic standpoint, a marriage squeeze exists for marriageable Black men and women, and the associated imbalances have direct implications for mate selection. An alternative explanation is that marriage norms of the subculture may be giving rise to these differences, but perhaps the best explanation is that these norms develop within the subculture to support the realities generated by the demographic differences. To the extent that marriage continues to be a more attractive status than lifelong singlehood, women (especially Black women) may be expected to attempt to enlarge their field of marriage eligibles by continuing to consider for marriage more of the men who are of divergent social status, age, marital history—or possibly race.

The scarcity of the pool of marriage eligibles among Black men could be alleviated through an increase in interracial marriage, but the prospects for this solution are not very likely today. In 1975, about 4.4 percent of married Black men and about 2.4 percent of married Black women had partners of a different race, almost always White. Among Whites the percentages are even smaller—seven-tenths of one percent for both married men and women, with less than half of such intermarriage

involving Blacks. With interracial marriage almost twice as characteristic of Black men as it is of Black women, the current tendency among racial intermarriages actually works against reversing the imbalanced sex ratio among the young adult marriage eligibles.

In conclusion, this paper has provided evidence that the unique demographic composition of the Black population has implications for one central social institution—marriage. The data show the nature of the problem and suggest a partial explanation for some of the racial differences in the formation, maintenance, and dissolution of marriage relationships. More speculatively, the analysis suggests a possible basis for racial differences in childbearing outside of marriage. Looking ahead, the most plausible expectation is that social and economic conditions among Blacks and Whites will gradually converge. One significant consequence would likely be that the number of young Black men would gradually come closer to the number of young Black women. Such a convergence has been occurring gradually but continuously in mortality rates (U.S. Department of Health, Education, and Welfare, 1977) and seems likely to continue.

References

Glick, Paul C.
1977   "Updating the Life Cycle of the Family." *Journal of Marriage and the Family* 39:5–13.

Glick, Paul C., and Graham B. Spanier
1980   "Married and Unmarried Cohabitation in the United States." *Journal of Marriage and the Family* 42(1):19–30.

Lewis, Robert A., and Graham B. Spanier
1979   "Theorizing about the Quality and Stability of Marriage." In *Contemporary Theories about the Family,* Wesley R. Burr, Reuben Hill, F. Ivan Nye, and Ira L. Reiss, eds., pp. 268–294. Glencoe, Ill.: Free Press.

Rockwell, Richard C.
1976   "Historical Trends and Variations in Educational Homogamy." *Journal of Marriage and the Family* 38:83–96.

Spanier, Graham B., and Paul C. Glick
1980   "The Life Cycle of American Families: An Expanded Analysis." *Journal of Family History* (Spring):98–112.

U.S. Bureau of the Census
1976   Current Population Reports, Series P-23, No. 58. *A Statistical Portrait of Women in the United States.* Washington, D.C.: U.S. Government Printing Office.
1977a   Current Population Reports, Series P-23, No. 65. *Developmental Estimates of the Coverage of the Population of States in the 1970 Census: Demographic Analysis.* Washington, D.C.: U.S. Government Printing Office.
1977b   Current Population Reports, Series P-25, No. 643. *Estimates of the Population of the United States, by Age, Sex, and Race: July 1, 1974 to 1976.* Washington, D.C.: U.S. Government Printing Office.
1978a   Technical Paper 40. *The Current Population Survey: Design and Methodology.* Washington, D.C.: U.S. Government Printing Office.
1978b   Current Population Reports, Series P-20, No. 323. *Marital Status and Living Arrangements: March 1977.* Washington, D.C.: U.S. Government Printing Office.

U.S. Department of Health, Education, and Welfare
1973   Vital and Health Statistics, Series 21, Data from the National Vital Statistics System, No. 25. *Remarriages.*
1977   *Life Tables.* Vital Statistics of the United States: 1975. Volume II, Section 5. National Center for Health Statistics.

Zelnik, Melvin, and John Kantner
1977   "Sexual and Contraceptive Experience of Young Unmarried Women in the United States, 1976 and 1971." *Family Planning Perspectives* 9:55–71.

MARITAL STATUS AND POVERTY AMONG WOMEN

United States Commission on Civil Rights

■ *This government report is a compendium of studies and statistical data on the relationship between poverty and marital status: Women with children and no husband have considerably lower incomes than married couples. For Black women, marital disruption virtually determines economic hardship. Fewer Black women remarry, and poverty is likely to be a permanent condition as long as they remain unmarried. Other problems of being a female household head are described.*

For American women, the correlation between marital status and economic well-being has become an increasingly harsh reality in the latter half of the 20th century. For some women, marital status matters more than labor market status as an indicator of financial well-being.[1] Mothers who do not marry and women who are separated, divorced, or widowed may face the prospect of financial insecurity more often than married women.

This chapter discusses the relationship between marital status and economic well-being for women. It examines trends in marital disruption (separation and divorce), child care, and the consequences of teenage childbearing. One of the principal Federal assistance programs that poor women rely on, aid to families with dependent children, is also reviewed.

Trend toward Female-Headed Families

The increase in the number and proportion of women heading households was small between 1960 and 1970, but has changed markedly since then. In 1960 female-headed families were 10 percent of all families;[2] in 1970, 10.8 percent.[3] By 1981 female-headed families were 18.8 percent of all families with children under 18 years of age, and the number of female-headed families had increased by 2.8 million (97 percent) since 1970.[4]

Female-headed families continued to be a larger proportion of the black family population than in any other subgroup. By 1981, 47.5 percent of black families with children present were headed by women, a rise from an already high 30.6 percent in 1970.[5] Among Hispanics, women headed 21.8 percent of all families in 1981, an increase from the 16.9 percent figure of 1970.[6] For whites, the proportion was smallest and the increase greatest: Women headed 14.7 percent of white families with children present in 1981, compared to 7.8 percent in 1970.[7]

Women with children but no husbands may lack the economic resources of husband-wife families for various reasons that include inadequate child support, lack of marketable skills, or job discrimination. Table 1 depicts not only the low median income of female householders when compared to husband-wife families, but also the increasing disparities between the two since 1970.[8]

From the report *A Growing Crisis: Disadvantaged Women and Their Children* (Washington, D.C.: U.S. Government Printing Office, 1983), pp. 5–14. Tables and footnotes have been renumbered.

TABLE 1 Median Income by Race and Type of Family

	1970	1981	INCREASE, 1970–1981
Type of family			
Husband-wife families[1]	$10,516	$25,065	138%
Wife in labor force	12,276	29,247	138
Female householder, no husband present	5,093	10,960	115
Male householder, no wife present	—	19,889	—
White families			
Husband-wife families	$10,723	$25,474	138
Wife in labor force	12,543	29,713	137
Female householder, no husband present	5,754	12,508	117
Male householder, no wife present	—	20,421	—
Black families			
Husband-wife families	$ 7,816	$19,624	151
Wife in labor force	9,721	25,040	158
Female householder, no husband present	3,576	7,506	110
Male householder, no wife present	—	14,489	—

---

[1]This item may be read as follows: Median income earnings for female householder families with no husbands present rose from $5,093 to $10,960, an increase of 115 percent, between 1970 and 1981.

Sources: U.S., Department of Commerce, Bureau of the Census, *Consumer Income: Income in 1970 of Families and Persons in the United States,* series P–60, no. 80, pp. 33, 35, and 37; *Money Income and Poverty Status of Families and Persons in the United States: 1981* (Advance Data), series P–60, no. 134, pp. 6, 7, 8, and 10.

The distribution of family income has changed markedly since 1970. Median income differences between all female householder families and all husband-wife families widened over the decade. When median family income of female householders is compared with median income of couples with wives in the labor force, the disparities are even greater. Total female householder median income as a proportion of working couple income declined from 41.4 to 37.4 percent between 1970 and 1981.

Among black families, median income of female householders grew 110 percent between 1970 and 1981, but median income of husband-wife families grew 151 percent, a striking difference. Median income growth among black couples with wives in the labor force grew 158 percent. The decline in black female householder median income relative to black husband-wife median income was 7.5 percent between 1970 and 1981.

Among all Hispanic families, median family income rose from $7,348 to $16,401 between 1969 and 1981, an increase of 123 percent.[9] Median income among female-headed Hispanic families increased 107 percent, from $3,654 to $7,586, during this period.[10] Also between 1969 and 1981, Hispanic female householder median income as a percentage of all Hispanic median family income decreased from 49.7 percent to 46.2 percent. These data indicate that Hispanic female-headed families experienced income losses during the 1970s relative to all Hispanic families.

Much, if not all, of the income growth during this period was dissipated by an increase in the cost of living. For example, in 1981 median income for all families was $22,388. However, in 1970 median family income expressed in 1981 dollars was $23,111.[11] While inflation has eroded the value of all families' purchasing power by about 3.5 percent, female householders, being poorer, have suffered the most.

Single Mothers

Whether by choice or circumstance, growing numbers of mothers have no husbands. Increased separation, divorce, and out-of-wedlock childbearing account for most of this trend. Between 1970 and 1981, for example, the divorce rate climbed from 47 to 109 finalized divorces per 1,000 married couples.[12] During the same period, families headed by never-married mothers climbed to 3.4 million, an increase of 356 percent.[13] As a result of this overall trend, 12.6 million children (20 percent of all children) lived with one parent; in 90 percent of these situations, that parent was the mother.[14] "In 1981, of the children who lived only with their mothers, 43 percent had a mother who was divorced, 27 percent had a separated mother and 16 percent had a mother who had never married."[15]

Regardless of why they are single parents, female householders earn less than male householders. For the categories shown in Table 2, female median earnings range between 52 and 74 percent of male householder earnings.

High poverty rates among female householders have not been changing much. Table 3 shows that about one-third of all female householders were poor in 1969, 1978, and 1981; slight declines in the poverty rate in 1978 were erased by 1981. Hardest hit were black and Hispanic female householders: Consistently more than half were poor.[16] Overall, women headed about half of all poor families in 1981.[17]

Poverty among male householders and husband-wife families was significantly less, ranging in 1981 from a low of 6.0 percent of white husband-wife families to highs of 19.1 and 19.2 percent of black and Hispanic male householders, respectively. These highs were still more than 8 percentage points below the lowest female householder poverty rate of 27.4 percent, for white female house-

TABLE 2	Householder Median Income, 1981
MALE HOUSEHOLDERS:	
Married, wife absent	$14,582
Widowed	10,157
Divorced	18,806
Single	15,640
FEMALE HOUSEHOLDERS:	
Married, husband absent[1]	$ 7,612
Widowed	7,324
Divorced	12,380
Single	11,496

[1]This item may be read as follows: Median income for female householders without husbands was $7,612 in 1981.
Source: U.S., Department of Commerce, Bureau of the Census, *Money Income and Poverty Status of Families and Persons in the United States: 1981* (Advance Data), series P–60, no. 134, pp. 6, 7, 8, and 10.

holders. In overall terms, the poverty rate for all female householders in 1981 was more than three times that for male householders (34.6 percent compared to 10.3 percent) and more than five times that for husband-wife families (6.8 percent).[18]

The apparent persistence of poverty among black female-headed families suggests to some a culture of poverty that recycles from one generation to another.[19] One writer who subscribes to this view noted recently: "Among the economically weakest segment of Afro-Americans—perhaps 35 percent of black households—there is ample evidence of structural and cultural ingredients that transmit poverty across generations."[20] The author argues that income and employment deficiencies of increasing numbers of black female-headed families usually result in bad housing and schooling, which "translate into cross-generational disadvantages for disproportionately larger numbers of black children."[21] This author, among others, uses a traditional research approach to studying the poverty population, namely, working with overall data on different groups collected at different points in time that show fluctuations in the numbers and types of impoverished persons, but cannot show whether the same individuals are affected.

TABLE 3   Female and Male Poverty Rates

	1969	1978	1981
All female householders[1]	32.3	31.4	34.6
White female householders	25.4	23.5	27.4
Black female householders	53.2	50.6	52.9
Hispanic female householders	—	53.1	53.2
All male householders	—	5.3	10.3
White male householders	—	4.7	8.8
Black male householders	—	11.8	19.1
Hispanic male householders	—	—	19.2
All husband-wife families[2]	6.9	5.2	6.8
White husband-wife families	6.0	4.7	6.0
Black husband-wife families	17.8	11.3	15.4
Hispanic husband-wife families	—	—	15.1

[1]This item may be read as follows: The poverty rates for all women heading families with no husband present were 34.6 in 1981, 31.4 in 1978, and 32.3 in 1969.

[2]Data for husband-wife families in 1969 were collected as "families with male head" and include some male householders with no wives present.

Sources: U.S., Department of Commerce, Bureau of the Census, *Twenty-Four Million Americans, Poverty in the United States, 1969,* series P–60, no. 76 (1970), p. 46; *Characteristics of the Population below the Poverty Level: 1978,* series P–60, no. 124 (1980), pp. 83–86; *Families Maintained by Female Householders: 1970–1979,* series P–23, no. 107, p. 37; and *Money Income and Poverty Status of Persons in the United States: 1981* (Advanced Data), series P–60, no. 134, p. 21.

When examined from a longitudinal perspective, however, the poverty population, including blacks, has been shown to be dynamic, rather than static.[22] In other words, a significant segment of the poverty population in one year was not impoverished in subsequent years. Bearing in mind that individuals move into and out of poverty, one of the limitations of even longitudinal research is that young persons, after forming nonpoor households, may subsequently fall into poverty. The conclusion that increasing numbers of black female-headed families transmit poverty to their offspring when they attain adulthood is less certain, although this group appears to be more vulnerable to intergenerational transmission than any other.

Divorced and Separated Mothers

The increase in divorce is one of the most significant social trends in America. In 1940 six marriages occurred for every divorce; by 1975 two marriages occurred for every divorce.[23] By 1981 the divorce ratio of 109 divorces per 1,000 active marriages was more than twice that of 1970.[24] Provisional reports from the National Center for Health Statistics suggest that the long-term increase in divorce may be leveling off or even falling slightly.[25] The higher divorce ratio among women (129 divorces versus 88 for men per 1,000 active marriages) indicates that divorced men generally remarry more quickly than divorced women.[26]

Divorce patterns among black, white, and Hispanic women differed between 1970 and 1981. During those 11 years, the black female divorce ratio increased from 104 to 289 divorced persons per 1,000 persons in active marriages.[27] In other words, by 1981 there were nearly 3 divorced black women to every 10 living with their husbands. The white female divorce ratio increased from 56 to 118 divorced persons per 1,000 persons in active marriages.[28] Hispanic women experienced the smallest rate of increase, from 81 to 146 divorced persons per 1,000 persons in active marriages between 1970 to 1981.[29] For women as a group, divorce occurred most frequently between the ages of 30 to 44, child-rearing years for perhaps the majority of American households.[30]

Income and Poverty

Should marital disruption occur, women with children, regardless of their previous economic circumstances, are usually poorer after the marriage fails. One longitudinal study found that among middle-aged women with children whose marriages ended between 1967 and 1972, the proportion of families below the poverty level increased from about 10 percent to over 25 percent for whites and from 44 percent to almost 60 percent for blacks.[31]

In assessing the relationship between family composition change and economic well-being, one researcher concluded that marriages and remarriages have the most beneficial effects whereas marital disruptions are the most harmful for women and children.[32] More recent research found similarly that changes in family composition increased the number of families below the poverty level. Families maintained by women tended to have much higher poverty rates than those maintained by men.[33]

Marital disruption significantly increases white women's chances for being poor and virtually determines economic hardship for black women. Using the standard definition of poverty,[34] one researcher found that:

> *about one white family out of four became poor after marital disruption. . . . About 40 percent of all white women who did not remarry over the seven-year [study] period were poor at least once; probably 15 to 20 percent were continuously poor or close to poverty.*[35]

For black women, the economic results of marital disruption were more severe:

> *At any one time 55 to 60 percent of the sample studied were poor by the standard definition and 70 percent were poor or relatively poor. If they did not remarry [and that likeli-*

> *hood is greater for black women than for white], the probability that they would remain poor was high.*[36]

When marital disruption occurs to couples with children, the children typically remain with the mother.[37] The new female householder presumably can rely upon a variety of sources that include her own earnings, alimony, child support, public assistance, personal savings, and division of community property; but these sources may not mean much. . . .

Child Support

Commitments to pay child support are frequently broken. In 1978 approximately 60 percent of the 7.1 million women with children from an absent father were awarded or had an agreement to receive child support payments.[38] The proportion of women awarded child support payments was higher for white women (71 percent) than for Hispanic women (44 percent) or for black women (29 percent).[39] Of the women awarded child support by a court, roughly one-quarter received no payments, another quarter received less than the full amount awarded, and one-half received the agreed-upon amount.

Alimony

Divorced and separated women eligible for alimony or spousal support receive it infrequently. Only 14 percent of ever-divorced or separated women in 1979 were awarded or had an agreement to receive maintenance payments or alimony.[40] Nearly 70 percent of the women due payments actually received them, with the average annual payment being $2,850.[41] "The mean total money income for women receiving payments ($11,060) was higher than that for women due payments but not receiving them ($7,270)."[42]

Child Care

In previous factfinding efforts in the area of sex discrimination, the Commission has recognized the relationship between child care and equal opportunity and the need for a revised Federal role.[43]

Educational and employment opportunities that women cannot pursue due to inadequate child care are opportunities effectively denied.

Women of different socioeconomic strata rely upon different resources for child care. Those with higher family incomes are more able to afford and, therefore, tend to utilize child care services.[44] Unmarried women of more meager means tend to rely upon the extended family as they have in the past. Mothers without mates, adequate income, or extended family support face a dilemma in finding affordable, reliable, and convenient child care, access to which may be the difference between supporting themselves partially, if not totally, or depending upon public assistance.

The increased number of mothers participating in the labor force provides some indication of the national need for child care. "Between 1950 and 1980, the labor force participation rates for wives with children under 18 increased from 18 to 54 percent, while the rate for other ever-married women with children increased from 55 to 69 percent."[45] "Among women with a child under 1 year old, 31 percent of currently married women and 40 percent of all other women were in the labor force" by 1980.[46]

Although many mothers of preschool children are working, still more would be in the labor force if they could find adequate child care. One study found that between 17 and 23 percent of mothers with preschool children who were neither employed nor looking for work would be working if work were available and if they had access to adequate child care facilities.[47] If already working, these mothers would be working more hours if suitable child care could be found.[48]

> Women who are most in need of employment are most likely to report that the unavailability of satisfactory child care at reasonable cost affects their labor force participation: the young mother (18–24), the

> unmarried mother, the black mother, the woman who did not graduate from high school, and the woman whose family income is less than $5,000.[49]

. . . .

Summary

During the last several decades, many women and their dependent children have experienced economic hardship. The phenomenal growth of female householder families, stemming in part from increasing marital disruption and out-of-wedlock births, has forced many women to be both chief parent and chief provider. The continuing trend in teenage childbearing out of wedlock is cause for concern. Teenage mothers often must interrupt or discontinue their education, thereby making the acquisition of marketable employment skills more difficult. If unable to find adequate and affordable child care, the teenage mother and those who experience marital disruption may be forced to rely upon public assistance for basic needs.

Female-headed families are disproportionately impoverished. Families headed by women with no husband present constituted 47 percent of all families below the poverty line in 1981. Minority female heads of household experience even higher levels of deprivation. More than half (53 percent) of all female-headed black and Spanish-origin families were below the poverty line. The vulnerability of female-headed families, particularly minorities, to economic adversity and the surprising number of households having some recent contact with welfare programs underline the importance of these programs.

Disproportionate numbers of America's poor in the early 1980s are women. The demographic data that reflect these trends suggest that more of the same may lie ahead.

[1]Isabel V. Sawhill, "Comments," in U.S., Department of Commerce, Bureau of the Census, conference on Issues in Federal Statistical Needs Relating to Women, series P–23, no. 83 (December 1979), p. 21.

[2]U.S., Department of Commerce, Bureau of the Census, Special Studies: Female Family Heads, series P–23, no. 50 (July 1974), p. 6 (hereafter cited as Special Studies: Female Family Heads). Data for 1960 were not collected in terms of families with children under 18.

[3]U.S., Department of Commerce, Bureau of the Census, Families Maintained by Female Householders, 1970–1979, series P–23, no. 107, p. 7 (hereafter cited as Families Maintained by Female Householders, 1970–1979). Data for 1970 were not collected in terms of families with children under 18.

[4]U.S., Department of Commerce, Bureau of the Census, Household and Family Characteristics: March 1981, series P–20, no. 371, p. 7 (hereafter cited as Household and Family Characteristics: March 1981).

[5]Ibid., p. 7.

[6]Special Studies: Female Family Heads, p. 6; Household and Family Characteristics: March 1981, p. 12.

[7]Household and Family Characteristics: March 1981, p. 7.

[8]In this report, "female householder families" refers to those families headed by women with no husbands present. Hence, female-headed families and female householder families are used interchangeably. Male householders are men heading households without wives present.

[9]U.S., Department of Commerce, Bureau of the Census, 1970 Census of the Population: Persons of Spanish Origin, PC(2)–1C, p. 121 (hereafter cited as Persons of Spanish Origin: 1970); and Money Income and Poverty Status of Families and Persons in the United States: 1981 (Advance Data), series P–60, no. 134, p. 8 (hereafter cited as Money Income: 1981).

[10]Persons of Spanish Origin: 1970, p. 121; and Money Income: 1981, p. 9.

[11]Money Income: 1981, p. 10.

[12]U.S., Department of Commerce, Bureau of the Census, Marital Status and Living Arrangements: March 1981, series P–20, no. 372 (June 1982), p. 1 (hereafter cited as Marital Status and Living Arrangements: March 1981).

[13]Household and Family Characteristics: March 1981, p. 7.

[14]Marital Status and Living Arrangements: March 1981, p. 5.

[15]Ibid.

[16]Money Income: 1981, p. 21.

[17]Ibid., p. 4.

[18]Ibid., p. 21.

[19]Daniel P. Moynihan and Oscar Lewis, among others, have hypothesized about the culture of poverty and its hold on minority female-headed families.

[20]Martin Kilson, "Black Social Classes and Intergenerational Poverty," The Public Interest, no. 64 (Summer 1981), p. 68.

[21]Ibid., p. 62.

[22]Greg Duncan and James Morgan, eds., "Introduction, Overview, Summary, and Conclusions," in Five Thousand American Families—Patterns of Economic Progress (Ann Arbor: Institute for Social Research, Univ. of Michigan, 1976), vol. IV, pp. 1–22.

[23]U.S. Department of Health, Education, and Welfare, Social Security and the Changing Roles of Men and Women (1978), p. 2.

[24]Marital Status and Living Arrangements: March 1981, pp. 3–4.

[25]The divorce rate declined from 5.3 per 1,000 population to 5.1 from January through August 1982, as compared to the same period in 1981 (94,000 and 100,000 divorces, respectively). U.S., Department of Health and Human Services, Public Health Service, "Births, Marriages, Divorces, and Deaths for August 1982," Monthly Vital Statistics Report, vol. 31, no. 8 (Nov. 15, 1982), p. 3.

[26]Marital Status and Living Arrangements: March 1981, p. 4.

[27]Ibid., p. 3.

[28]Ibid.

[29]Ibid.

[30]Ibid.

[31]Lois Shaw, "Economic Consequences of Marital Disruption," National Longitudinal Study of Mature Women (contract paper for U.S. Department of Labor, June 1978), p. 8.

[32]James N. Morgan, "Family Composition," in Duncan and Morgan, eds., Five Thousand American Families—Patterns of Economic Progress (1974), vol. I, pp. 99–121.

[33]U.S., Department of Commerce, Bureau of the Census, Changing Family Composition and Income Differentials, by Edward Welniak and Gordon Green (August 1982), p. 13.

[34]See chap. 1 for standard definition of poverty.

[35]L. Shaw, "Economic Consequences of Marital Disruption," p. 18.

[36]Ibid.

[37]Male householders increased by 95 percent to 666,000 between 1970 and 1981. Female householders with children under 18 years old increased by 97 percent to 5,634,000, although divorces alone do not account for all of this increase.

[38]U.S., Department of Commerce, Bureau of the Census, Child Support and Alimony: 1978 (Advance Report), series P–23, no. 106, p. 1.

[39]Ibid.

[40]Ibid.

[41]Ibid.

[42]Ibid.

[43]Ibid.

[44]Ibid.

[45]See U.S. Commission on Civil Rights reports: Women and Poverty, staff report (1974); Women—Still in Poverty (1979); and Child Care and Equal Opportunity for Women (1981) (hereafter cited as Child Care and Equal Opportunity).

[46]U.S., Department of Commerce, Bureau of the Census, Trends in Child Care Arrangements of Working Mothers, series P–25, no. 117 (June 1982), p. 3 (hereafter cited as Trends).

[47]Ibid. U.S., Department of Labor, Children of Working Mothers, Special Labor Force Report 217 (March 1977), p. A–30.

[48]Trends, p. 3.

[49]Harriet Presser and Wendy Baldwin, "Child Care as a Constraint on Employment: Prevalence, Correlates, and Bearing on the Work and Fertility Nexus," American Journal of Sociology, vol. 85, no. 5 (March 1980), p. 1205.

MARRIAGE: CONDUCIVE TO GREATER LIFE SATISFACTION FOR AMERICAN BLACK WOMEN?

Richard E. Ball

Objective differences between Black and white families (such as median income and illegitimacy rate) are well documented. It has been argued that because of social and economic pressures faced by Black families, such objective indicators are not appropriate measures of their functioning; rather, subjective impressions should be used. This study examines the life satisfaction of a sample of 373 Black women. Satisfaction was highest for the currently married, the widowed, and the divorced—and was significantly lower for the single and the separated.

Introduction

Differences between black and white families in the United States are well documented. Median family income for blacks is only 57 percent of that of whites, and the illegitimacy rate for blacks has reached 50 percent, as opposed to 8 percent for whites. Whereas 12 percent of white children reside in families headed by their mothers, 42 percent of black children are similarly situated (Bianchi and Farley, 1979; U.S. Bureau of the Census, 1980).

Disparities in objective indicators such as these have been viewed by some social scientists as well as by the general public as reflecting weaknesses in the structure and functioning of the black family. In response, other writers have attacked this perspective as having reversed the relationship between economic and social handicap and the structure and functioning of black families (Billingsley, 1968, 1970; Rainwater and Yancey, 1967; Staples 1969, 1971a, 1971b, among others). In fact, the entire approach of using objective indicators to compare the functioning of black families vis-à-vis those of whites has been criticized strongly.

One of the most articulate of these critics has been Robert Staples, who has indicated that comparing black families with those of whites inevitably has resulted in the minority being seen as inferior. Other writers such as Andrew Billingsley and Robert B. Hill have pointed out that because of their disadvantaged place in society, black families have developed alternative family forms as mechanisms for survival. Therefore, it is argued that black families should be evaluated in terms of their own strengths and weaknesses (Billingsley, 1968; Hill, 1972; Hill and Shackleford, 1975; Staples, 1971b).

A variable of major interest when addressing family composition and functioning is marital status. Although increasing numbers of Americans are delaying or eschewing matrimony[1] and divorce rates are rising, marriage still is the expectation for the overwhelming majority of adults. Handicaps

Unpublished paper originally presented at the annual meeting of the National Council on Family Relations, Washington, D.C., October 13–16, 1982. Reprinted by permission of the author. The research on which this paper reports was supported partially by NIMH grant RO12740. The author thanks Lynn Robbins, Department of Psychiatry, University of Florida, for her generous research assistance.

for those who are not married can be severe. For example, median income for female-headed black households is only 53 percent of that of black husband-headed households (Bianchi and Farley, 1979).

In spite of objective data such as these indicating certain disadvantages that may be suffered by those who are not married, a contrary viewpoint sometimes is expressed regarding the utility of marriage for at least some low-income black Americans.

Some research has indicated that marital failure almost seems predestined for a substantial proportion of poor black Americans. The inability of many men to obtain steady employment at a living wage causes strains within the marriage and creates expectations of marital failure (Liebow, 1967; Parker and Kleiner, 1969; Rubin, 1978; Schulz, 1969). Other research has shown that some low-income black mothers believe that they are better off without a husband at home (McIntyre, 1966; Rainwater, 1971). Heiss's study (1975) found that fewer than one-third of currently married or unmarried black mothers believed that most men make good husbands, and about one-half agreed that women's best time is when they are married. Slightly over two-thirds indicated that they would marry again. It appears that for some black Americans, at least, marriage is viewed as a losing status.

As pointed out by Billingsley, students of the black family have concentrated on its instrumental functioning (1968). As a result, there is a paucity of empirically backed data regarding the *expressive* functioning of the American black family. The vital subjective dimension all too often has been ignored. In addition, black families that are *not* poor generally have been neglected.

The expressive realm is the focus of this research. The dependent variable for investigation is level of life satisfaction, which is indicative of perceived well-being. The independent variable of greatest interest is marital status. The study is designed to bring data from a representative sample of a black population to bear on the question: What is the impact of marital status on black satisfaction levels? Because of the comparatively high levels of attenuation among American black families, this research focuses on black women.[2]

Literature Review

Research assessing subjective well-being within the normal population has increasingly been emphasized since the mid-1950s. However, most of this study has been directed toward the white population, with nonwhites either excluded or forming a small subsample of little interest to the researchers.

Most frequently used as indicators of perceived well-being have been responses to items assessing overall happiness or life satisfaction. One of the most consistent findings regarding the general (or white) population is that those currently married and residing with spouse report higher levels of well-being than do those who are not residing with spouse. Intermediate in well-being may be the widowed and the single, with the separated and the divorced lowest in perceived well-being (Bradburn, 1969; Bradburn and Caplovitz, 1965; Campbell et al., 1976; Clemente and Sauer, 1976; Glenn, 1975; Glenn and Weaver, 1979; Gurin et al., 1960; Palmore and Luikart, 1972; Spreitzer and Snyder, 1974).[3]

Much less is available on perceived well-being among black Americans. The comprehensive study of a national sample conducted by Campbell, Converse, and Rodgers (1976) found that among their black subsample both the married and the widowed were equally high in happiness and life satisfaction. Much lower were the single and the separated/divorced (together). A study that included only blacks aged 45 through 74 found marital status and happiness not to be significantly related (Wray, 1974). Gerontological study of only the elderly found little difference in satisfaction levels between married and unmarried blacks (Jackson et al., 1977–1978).

Prior research has shown that a number of variables other than marital status have potential impact on subjective well-being. These variables include income, education, age, social participation, and health.

Research findings on black Americans regarding the effect of income and education are contradictory. Some studies have found positive correlations, others a curvilinear relationship. Contradictory findings also are found in regard to age, although a slight preponderance of evidence indicates that age and well-being are related positively for black Americans. For the general population, self-evaluated health and well-being are positively correlated, and the scant research available indicates that this also holds for blacks. Social participation has been measured in a variety of ways. Generally, it pertains to voluntary contacts outside the home or workplace. Although for the general population social participation tends to be positively correlated with well-being, little and contradictory evidence is available in regard to blacks (Alston et al., 1974; Bradburn, 1969; Campbell et al., 1976; Jackson et al., 1977–1978; Wray, 1974). It is clear that more research is needed on the relations of these variables to subjective well-being among black Americans.

Method

Data used for this study were collected in four counties of central Florida. Although primarily rural and agricultural, the area includes a number of small towns and two minor standard metropolitan statistical areas (SMSAs). Multistage cluster sampling and the randomization technique developed by Kish (1965) were used to ensure representativeness of respondents. The overall sample consisted of 3,674 persons 18 and over, of whom 626 (17 percent) were black. Of the black respondents, 373 (60 percent) were female. These female black respondents are the subsample for this study. A comprehensive interview schedule was administered in the respondents' homes by trained interviewers. The overall response rate was 86 percent. Comparison of the overall sample to census data on standard socioeconomic variables showed it to be representative (Warheit et al., 1976).

The dependent variable of life satisfaction is measured by responses to the Cantril Self-Anchoring Striving Scale, one component of a series of items designed to help respondents establish their own frames of reference regarding their personal situations. The scale is designed to be "symbolic of the 'ladder of life'" (Cantril, 1965:22). It has ten rungs and allows eleven possible responses, ranging from 0, the lowest possible, to 10, the high-

est. Those scoring 10 indicate that they have the best possible life for themselves. Other variables investigated are income, education, age, social participation, and health.

An adjusted indicator is used for family/household income. Termed *welfare ratio*, it is determined by dividing a family's total income by its federally determined poverty level. A welfare ratio of 1.0 or lower indicates that the family officially is "in poverty." Poverty levels for the period of data collection were used. Due to the family size and age–sex composition adjustment inherent in the poverty level for any family, this ratio better indicates economic standard of living than does raw income.

Education data are in seven categories (none through college graduate). Age is age at last birthday. Social participation is determined by a composite score on three items. Item one requests frequency of interaction with nearby relatives, including use of the telephone. Item two requests frequency of getting together with nearby friends. Item three asks how often the main worship service of her church is attended. Total possible individual scores range from 0 through 14. Self-evaluated health is indicated by response to an item requesting the individuals' assessment of her current health. Scores range from 1 through 5 (very bad through excellent).

ANOVA is used for bivariate analysis, with multiple correlation and regression with stepwise inclusion of variables used for the multivariate analysis. In order for all calculations to involve the same universe of data, a case with a missing value on any variable has been eliminated completely from the multivariate analysis. Being categorical, marital statuses are coded as dummy variables.

The major hypothesis to be investigated involves testing for differences in life satisfaction levels between black women with different marital statuses. In addition, the impact of other variables previously discussed is studied.

Research Findings

Table 1 shows life satisfaction scores in bivariate relationship with the independent variables.

TABLE 1   Life Satisfaction, Bivariate Analysis[1]

VARIABLE	N	$\overline{X}$[2]	SD	F	P
Sample	351	6.09	2.68		
(Not available)	(22)				
Marital status	351	6.09	2.68	5.53	.001
Single	51	4.98	2.66		
Married	153	6.28	2.51		
Widowed	70	6.84	2.87		
Separated	53	5.30	2.68		
Divorced	24	6.75	2.25		
(Not available)	(22)				
Welfare ratio	269	6.09	2.66	2.42	.05
0.0–0.5	49	5.10	2.88		
0.5–1.0	84	6.42	2.83		
1.0–1.5	55	6.07	2.73		
1.5–2.0	31	6.00	2.39		
2.0 +	50	6.56	2.13		
(Not available)	(104)				
Age	351	6.09	2.60	5.09	.001
18–19	21	5.24	2.68		
20–29	71	5.35	2.13		
30–39	64	5.38	2.68		
40–49	60	6.42	2.48		
50–59	54	6.13	2.76		
60–69	52	7.08	2.83		
70 +	29	7.55	2.85		
(Not available)	(22)				
Education	346	6.07	2.65	1.27	n.s.
None	9	6.11	3.69		
1–4 years	44	6.64	3.10		
5–8	69	6.39	2.69		
9–11	122	5.80	2.74		
High school graduate	68	6.04	2.28		
1–3 college	22	5.14	1.86		
College graduate	12	6.67	2.02		
(Not available)	(27)				
Social participation	351	6.09	2.68	6.02	.001
0–2	5	5.20	4.44		
3–5	36	4.50	2.97		
6–8	74	5.64	2.74		
9–11	123	6.24	2.32		
12–14	113	6.76	2.61		
(Not available)	(22)				
Health	351	6.09	2.65	3.28	.01
Very bad	5	2.60	1.82		
Poor	25	5.48	3.34		
Fair	101	5.87	2.57		
Good	142	6.24	2.75		
Excellent	78	6.51	2.34		
(Not available)	(22)				

[1]Ns vary due to missing data. n.s. = not significant.

[2]Range possible: 0 to 10.

Highest mean level of life satisfaction is found for widows (6.84 of a possible 10.0), followed closely by the divorced (6.75). Slightly lower are the married (6.28), and considerably lower are the separated (5.30). Lowest of all are the single (4.98). The extreme differences are significant at $p < .001$.

Excluding the separated category, life satisfaction levels are higher for the formerly married than for the currently married. However, these differences are slight.

Also statistically significantly related to life satisfaction in bivariate analysis are welfare ratio, age, social participation, and health, as shown in Table 1. Only education lacks significance.

As shown in Table 2, zero-order correlations between control variables are statistically significant in most instances. However, only for age and education and for welfare ratio and education are the R^2 values high enough to indicate the potential for distortion of multivariate findings due to multicollinearity.

Table 3 shows the multiple stepwise regression and correlation matrices. Only those in the marital status categories of single and separated show significant variance in satisfaction from the married (the suppressed category). Controlling other variables in the equation, the single and the separated show lower satisfaction levels than do the married ($p < .05$). The widowed and the divorced vary little from the married. Thus, those who never have been married or who are separated, perhaps recently, are lower in life satisfaction than are the currently married, the widowed, or the divorced, independent of levels of the other variables investigated.

Of the other variables in the equation, social participation, age, and perceived health are significantly related to satisfaction. Those who are more involved in interaction outside the home, those who are older, and those who feel that they are in good health tend to be more satisfied.[4] Income and education are not significant, controlling the other variables. Of all variables investigated, social participation has the greatest impact on satisfaction, as shown by its regression coefficient (B) and standardized coefficient (B^*).

The null hypothesis of no difference in mean satisfaction levels among women in different marital status categories is rejected at $p < .05$. The overall equation is significant at $p < .001$, and the multiple R^2 of .209 indicates that about one-fifth of total variance in satisfaction involves linear relationship with these variables.

Discussion

It appears that marriage is no more conducive to life satisfaction for these black women than is being divorced or widowed. The impact on life satisfaction of having a husband appears to be minimal, except for those who have never had one (the single) or who have recently lost one (often the separated). Those who have had a husband, but who lost him or left him—often some time ago (the divorced or widowed)—are as satisfied as are the currently married.

It might be conjectured that the lower satisfaction scores of the separated than those of the divorced are an artifact of younger age, as the younger tend to be less satisfied. Also, it might be argued that this difference reflects socioeconomic status (SES) differentials, with those with higher SES more likely both to be satisfied and to formalize separation through divorce. However, as age and SES (here income and education) are controlled in the multivariate equation, it appears that recency of marital dissolution is a more plausible explanation for the disparity in satisfaction between the divorced and the separated.

Single women's low satisfaction levels may reflect the desire of many single women to be married. These generally low-income Southern black women, none of whom resides in a large city, may view singlehood as resulting from rejection, rather than from choice.

The comparatively high satisfaction levels of widows may involve several factors, at least two of them unique to this status. As with the divorced, marital dissolution in many cases no doubt occurred some time previous. However, in addition, two other circumstances may be of importance. First, marital dissolution for widows is an "act of God," rather than an event that usually follows an acrimonious relationship. Thus, fault is not an issue, although for the separated or divorced it may lead

TABLE 2 Zero-Order Pearson Product-Moment Correlations (R) among Control Variables[1]

VARIABLE	WELFARE RATIO	AGE	EDUCATION	SOCIAL PARTICIPATION
Age	− .15**			
Education	.40***	− .58***		
Social participation	.02	.06	.08	
Health	.13**	− .10*	.12*	.13**

[1]Significance levels, direction unpredicted: * = $p < .05$, ** = $p < .01$, *** = $p < .001$. Ns vary between 373 and 285 because of missing data.

TABLE 3 Life Satisfaction and Marital Status, Multiple Stepwise Regression Model

VARIABLE	B	B*	SEB	F	P
Social participation	.219	.248	.050	19.424	.001
Age	.038	.246	.013	9.029	.01
Health	.368	.128	.163	5.114	.05
Welfare ratio	.167	.068	.158	1.108	n.s.
Single	− 1.163	− .135	.534	4.750	.05
Separated	− .899	− .123	.448	4.031	.05
Education	.102	.050	.148	0.479	n.s.
Widowed	− .060	− .009	.447	0.018	n.s.
Constant: includes married; divorced deleted ($B = .003$, $F = .002$)	.577				

	df	SUM OF SQUARES	MEAN SQUARE	F	P
Regression	8	389.342	48.668	8.497	.001
Residual	257	1472.00	5.728		
Standard error of the estimate: 2.393					

VARIABLE	R	MULTIPLE R	MULTIPLE R^2	R^2 CHANGE	ADJUSTED R^2
Social participation	.290	.290	.084	.084	.081
Age	.275	.384	.147	.063	.141
Health	.140	.411	.169	.022	.159
Welfare ratio	.118	.431	.186	.017	.174
Single	− .191	.442	.195	.009	.180
Separated	− .178	.456	.208	.013	.189
Education	− .052	.457	.209	.001	.188
Widowed	.149	.457	.209	.000	.185

to self-denigration and, thereby, dissatisfaction.[5] Second, although age is controlled in the multivariate analysis, because there are comparatively few young widows this control may not function adequately.

That having a husband is not particularly conducive to satisfaction for some women may be tied to exchange theory. One of the basic tenets of this theory is that relationships are discontinued if they appear unprofitable to the actor in comparison with perceived alternatives. In regard to marriage among black Americans, often advanced is the economic perspective that because of racial discrimination, black men have difficulty competing in the labor market. Thus, their economic input into the family sometimes is minimal, or even negative.[6] Perhaps because of this, other inputs, such as those of the expressive realm, may be lessened as well (Liebow, 1967).[7] Thus, after having experienced it, some may not evaluate marriage in retrospect as having been particularly satisfying. After an adjustment period, again being unmarried may seem as satisfying as being married had been.

In the introduction it was stated that some writers believe that black Americans have developed a number of coping mechanisms, including adaptability in family roles. This research indicates that in fact this contention may have validity. Many black women seem as satisfied going it alone as are others who are married and residing with their husbands.[8]

Further study may find variables such as the recency of the separation, divorce, or widowhood and stages of the family life cycle to offer avenues for fruitful research on well-being.[9] Also, although some research has been conducted on satisfaction and happiness levels for specific domains of life in addition to overall well-being, much study remains to be done in the area of domain satisfaction.[10]

Additional opportunities for further research include multivariate investigation of the relationship between marital status and perceived well-being for black men and detailed comparisons between the perceived well-being of black men and women.

---

[1]Currently, a record low proportion of black Americans under age 25 report being married (Bianchi and Farley, 1979).

[2]In 1978, 42.7 percent of all black families were female headed, and 82 percent of these families contained minor children (Bianchi and Farley, 1979; U.S. Bureau of the Census, 1979).

[3]Many of these findings lack comparability not only due to varying methods and analyses, but also because marital status categories are constituted in different ways in separate studies. The separated may be included with the married, placed with all others not currently married, placed with the divorced, or viewed as a unique category.

[4]As might be expected, social participation is important particularly for separated women. Separate analysis shows that it alone accounts for 42 percent of the variance in their satisfaction scores. However, social participation appears much less important for the divorced and the widowed in this context.

[5]It might be hypothesized that life satisfaction leads to marital "success," as evidenced by the higher satisfaction levels of the married and the widowed. This reversal of the cause–effect relationship pursued here is plausible, but is brought into question by the equally high satisfaction levels of the divorced.

[6]Punitive welfare regulations in many states prohibit aid to families in which the husband-father is present, thus exacerbating the situation.

[7]It must be noted that the relationships between marital status and life satisfaction shown in this research hold both in bivariate and multivariate analyses. Thus, regardless of income level, the divorced and the widowed are as satisfied as are the married. For this sample, at least, the economic perspective lacks explanatory power. It appears that discrimination may have taken its toll in additional ways, perhaps involving the fostering of negative self-images.

[8]It should be noted that a consistent research finding is that blacks score lower on happiness and satisfaction scales than do whites, even when variables such as income are controlled. In addition, where investigated, black women have been shown to perceive lower well-being than do black men (Alston et al., 1974; Bradburn, 1969; Campbell et al., 1976; Clemente and Sauer, 1976; Lewinski, 1977; Wray, 1974).

[9]In addition to marital status and age, the life cycle component of having a minor child at home was investigated in this research. Overall, and for each marital status separately, having a child at home did not have statistically significant impact on life satisfaction for these women.

[10]Campbell, Converse, and Rodgers addressed the domain satisfaction of black Americans in their comprehensive study, but primarily relied on bivariate analysis (1976).

References

Alston, Jon P., G. Lowe, and A. Wrigley
1974 "Socioeconomic Correlates for Four Dimensions of Perceived Satisfaction, 1972." *Human Organization* 33:99–102.

Bianchi, Suzanne M., and R. Farley
1979 "Racial Differences in Family Living Arrangements and Economic Well-Being: An Analysis of Recent Trends." *Journal of Marriage and the Family* 41:537–551.

Billingsley, Andrew
1968 *Black Families in White America*. Englewood Cliffs, N.J.: Prentice-Hall.
1970 "Black Families and White Social Science." *Journal of Social Issues* 26:127–142.

Bradburn, Norman
1969 *The Structure of Psychological Well-Being*. Chicago: Aldine.

Bradburn, Norman, and D. Caplovitz
1965 *Reports on Happiness*. Chicago: Aldine.

Campbell, Angus, P. Converse, and W. Rodgers
1976 *The Quality of American Life*. New York: Russell Sage.

Cantril, Hadley
1965 *The Pattern of Human Concerns*. New Brunswick, N.J.: Rutgers University Press.

Clemente, Frank, and W. Sauer
1976 "Life Satisfaction in the United States." *Social Forces* 54:621–631.

Glenn, Norval
1975 "The Contribution of Marriage to the Psychological Well-Being of Males and Females." *Journal of Marriage and the Family* 37:594–600.

Glenn, Norval, and C. Weaver
1979 "A Note on Family Situation and Global Happiness." *Social Forces* 57:960–967.

Gurin, Gerald, J. Veroff, and S. Feld
1960 *Americans View Their Mental Health*. New York: Basic Books.

Heiss, Jerrold
1975 *The Case of the Black Family: A Sociological Inquiry*. New York: Columbia University Press.

Hill, Robert B.
1972 *The Strengths of Black Families*. New York: Emerson Hall.

Hill, Robert B., and L. Shackleford
1975 "The Black Family Revisited." *Urban League Review* 1:18–24.

Jackson, James S., J. Bacon, and J. Peterson
1977– "Life Satisfaction among Black Urban Elderly."
1978 *Journal of Aging and Human Development* 8:169–179.

Kish, Leslie
1965 *Survey Sampling*. New York: Wiley.

Lewinski, Robert E.
1977 "A Study of Job Satisfaction and Life Satisfaction in the Mid-Seventies." M.A. thesis, Department of Sociology, University of Florida.

Liebow, Elliot
1967 *Tally's Corner*. Boston: Little, Brown.

McIntyre, Jennie J.
1966 Illegitimacy: A Case of Stretched Values? Ph.D. Dissertation, The Florida State University. Ann Arbor, Mich.: University Microfilms.

Palmore, Erdman, and C. Luikart
1972 "Health and Social Factors Related to Life Satisfaction." *Journal of Health and Social Behavior* 13:68–80.

Parker, Seymour, and R. Kleiner
1969 "Social and Psychological Dimensions of the Family Role Performance of the Negro Male." *Journal of Marriage and the Family* 31:500–506.

Rainwater, Lee
1971 *Crucible of Identity: The Negro Lower-Class Family*. In *Black Matriarchy: Myth or Reality?*, John H. Bracey, Jr., A. Meier, and E. Rudwick, eds., pp. 76–111. Belmont, Calif.: Wadsworth.

Rainwater, Lee, and W. Yancey, editors
1967 *The Moynihan Report and the Politics of Controversy*. Cambridge, Mass.: The M.I.T. Press.

Rubin, Roger H.
1978 "Matriarchal Themes in Black Family Literature: Implications for Family Life Education." *The Family Coordinator* 27:33–41.

Schulz, David
1969 *Coming Up Black*. Englewood Cliffs, N.J.: Prentice-Hall.

Spreitzer, Elmer, and E. Snyder
1974   "Correlates of Life Satisfaction among the Aged." *Journal of Gerontology* 29:454–458.

Staples, Robert
1969   "Research on the Negro Family: A Source for the Family Practitioner." *The Family Coordinator* 18:202–209.

Staples, Robert, editor
1971a   *The Black Family: Essays and Studies.* Belmont, Calif.: Wadsworth.

Staples, Robert
1971b   "Toward a Sociology of the Black Family: A Theoretical and Methodological Assessment." *Journal of Marriage and the Family* 33:119–138.

U.S. Bureau of the Census
1979   *Statistical Abstract 1979.* Washington, D.C.: U.S. Government Printing Office.

1980   Current Population Reports, series P–60, No. 125. *Money Income and Poverty Status of Families and Persons in the United States, 1979.* Washington, D.C.: U.S. Government Printing Office.

U.S. Department of Labor, Office of Policy Planning and Research
1965   *The Negro Family: The Case for National Action.* Washington, D.C.: Department of Labor.

Warheit, George J., C. Holzer, R. Bell, and S. Arey
1976   "Sex, Marital Status, and Mental Health: A Reappraisal." *Social Forces* 55:459–470.

Wray, Stephen D.
1974   "The Social Factors Associated with the Happiness and Mental Health of People in the Middle Years and Early Old Age." Ph.D. dissertation, Department of Sociology, University of Florida. Ann Arbor, Mich.: University Microfilms.

PART THREE

The Family

Childbearing

The bearing of children has traditionally been a very important function in the Black community. The sacrifices of Black mothers for their children have been legendary for hundreds of years. While children are still regarded as a strong value to Blacks, attitudes toward having large numbers of them have changed dramatically since 1965. Contributing to this change are the beliefs of many Black women that the responsibility for rearing large numbers of children is destructive to their personal freedom and job mobility, the different problems faced in raising children in urban centers, the decline in biparental households, and the necessity of raising children alone. Around 1983, the lifetime births expected by single Black women aged 18–24 years were the same as that of comparable white women. Women in both groups expected to have fewer than two children in their lifetime (U.S. Bureau of the Census, 1984).

One of the most significant changes in the period 1970–1979 was the change in the Black fertility rate. In 1978, the Black birth rate continued to decline. However, the white birth rate declined even more rapidly (11 percent versus 2 percent), and the total fertility rate in 1979 of 21.5 children per thousand Black women was still higher (14.4 per thousand) than that of white women (U.S. Bureau of the Census, 1984). The Black fertility rate is influenced by a number of factors including regional variations, rural–urban differences, and, most importantly, socioeconomic levels. In 1979, Black women in the South had more children than those who lived in the North, and the birth rate of urban Black women was lower than that of Black women in rural areas. Significantly, college-educated Blacks have the lowest fertility rate of almost every demographic category in the United States, whereas middle-class Catholics and Mormons have the highest. College-educated Black women actually have a lower birth rate than college-educated white women (U.S. Bureau of the Census, 1984).

One of the more significant events since the mid-1970s was the steady increase in the out-of-wedlock births of Black women; at the same time, the birth rate among married Black women showed a steady decline. The illegitimacy rate among whites went from 1.7 to 7.3 per 1,000 unmarried women 15–44 years old between 1950 and 1975, while the rate among Blacks increased from 17.9 to 48.6 during the same time span (Bianchi and Farley, 1979). Some of this racial difference in the illegitimacy rate increase can be attributed to the more frequent and effective use of contraceptives, abortions, and shotgun weddings among white women. The official data show that Black women married before their child was born in only 32 percent of the cases, whereas white women married before their child was born in 63 percent of the cases (U.S. Bureau of the Census, 1984). Another reason has been the substantial decrease in legitimate fertility rates among married Black women over the age of 24. Almost a third of all births to Black women occur to those under the age of 19, the majority of them illegitimate. In 1978, 34 percent of Black mothers only households were maintained by never-married women (U.S. Bureau of the Census, 1984).

The selection by McKay provides us with valuable information on sex ratios at births to Black women. In a study of Black families with incomes between $13,000–17,000, she learned that two-thirds of them had families with only one child. Even more interesting was the secondary sex ratio of 83 male children to every 100 female children at birth. The obvious implication of her study, if generalized to the rest of the middle-class Black population, is that the shortage of Black males will continue to be a critical problem for the Black community.

In another article, Barnett examines some of the antecedent factors that have an adverse impact on the health and well-being of the Black adolescent mother and her child. It illustrates that teenage pregnancy has consequences in addition to the problems that arise from an immature woman taking on the responsibility of raising a child alone. Childbirth in the adolescent years tends to have negative health consequences for both the mother and child.

Parental Roles

Raising a Black child is not, and has never been, an easy task. In light of the obstacles they face, Black parents have done a more than adequate job. Generally, they have more children to rear, with fewer resources, than white parents. They must also socialize their children into the values of mainstream culture in order to adapt successfully to majority group requirements and institutions. At the same time they must teach the children the folkways of their own culture and what it means to be Black in a racist society. Given the poor social conditions under which most Black children are raised, it is not surprising that some fail in life. What is even more surprising is that so many succeed in the face of the adverse circumstances they encounter.

Child-rearing practices do not differ significantly by race. Variations in socialization techniques are more a function of class membership. Middle-class parents, Black and white, are more likely to use verbal than physical punishment to discipline a child. Lower-class Black mothers are often regarded as ineffective parents because of their reliance on physical punishment techniques to control their children. What is not considered in that assessment is the tendency of many Black mothers to combine physical measures with very heavy doses of emotional nurturance. This combination of spankings and affection may be more beneficial for a child's development than the middle class parents' threat of withdrawal of love if the child does not behave correctly. Many observers of the Black family have noticed how children in the lower-class Black community are well treated and seem emotionally and psychologically healthy.

The attitudes and behavior of many Black parents are changing. Fewer children are being born per family and there are indications that those children who are brought into this world are not as well treated. The same trend is also evident in the white community and seems to be part of the tendency of mothers to put their own wishes and goals ahead of everything and everyone else. There are also certain tensions in our society, particularly in urban areas, that affect behavior toward children. Corresponding to an increase in those tensions has been an elevation of the incidence of child abuse in Black families and a decline in the respect of Black children for their elders. Certain changes in the Black fertility pattern are responsible for some of the inadequate parenting that exists today. While there have been overall declines in the Black birth rate, there has been a significant increase in out-of-wedlock pregnancies, primarily to teenaged women. With the decline in the Black extended family system, immature mothers and one-parent households have fostered the arrogance and negativism emerging among many Black youth.

Although there may be problems stemming from the one-parent household, one study of fatherless Black families found that boys in these homes do not see themselves as less worthwhile than boys who reside in father-present homes (Rubin, 1974). One reason for their high self-esteem is the availability of male role models outside the home and the significance of adult males in the family. Still, one cannot underestimate the importance of the mother and father to the child's development. Those parents provide the necessary aid, values, and encouragement for their children's mobility aspirations. In their survey of female-headed households, Peters and de Ford note that it is not an easy task to raise children alone but that the households were generally coping well in their circumstances and were a viable form of the family. The paper by Hampton discusses findings that child abuse in Black families may have been overstated by the tendency of health personnel to label Black families as abusive because of their personal characteristics.

The Extended Family

Kinship bonds have always been important to the Black population. In African societies kinship was and is the basis of the social organization. During the period of slavery many of the bondsmen were organized into an extended family system based on biological and nonbiological standards. Most research studies of Black kinship networks generally indicate that they are more extensive and significant to the Black community than to the white community (Adams, 1970). Whatever the reason, there is little doubt that kinsmen play an important role in the Black family system.

Among the valuable services provided by kin is the sharing of economic resources, child care, advice, and other forms of mutual aid. Those are acknowledged functions of a kinship network, but members of the extended family also serve to liberate children from the confines of the nuclear family unit. Children have someone other than a mother or father to relate to and from whom to receive emotional nurturance. The network also helps socialize children more effectively into values that Blacks held more strongly in rural and southern settings. The function of kinship groups to Blacks is so important that many nonblood relatives are referred to and regarded as kinsmen. Usually, this is a special friendship in which the normal claims, obligations, and loyalties of the kin relationships are operative, such as those of godmothers or play brothers (McAdoo, 1981).

One of the problems the Black family is facing today is a decline in the extended family system. This has occurred, in large part, as a result of Black mobility patterns. Many Blacks have moved from their place of origin to large cities where they have few, if any, kin. Fairly large numbers of Blacks are moving to suburban areas, where they often lack friends or relatives in their immediate neighborhood or community. Changes in the attitudes of Black youth toward their elders have also weakened the role of some older kin. The antiauthority attitudes of many youth have made many of them less responsive to the wisdom and guidance of grandparents and other kin.

The article by Hill and Shackleford takes a look at the contemporary extended family pattern among Blacks. They found that the characteristics of Black families over the years remain the same and the informal adoption of children is an important and overlooked function of the extended family. It is an institution that has been a source of strength and resilience in the Black community for generations. Jackson details more closely the role that Black grandparents perform in the urban setting. She found they were needed because of the affectional closeness, value consensus, and role identification they provided.

Adolescence and Personality Development

The period of adolescence has been generally regarded as a time of identity acquisition and liberation from parental control. For Black youth the problem of transition from adolescence to adulthood has been compounded by their unique status in the society. Many, for example, do not have a carefree period in which to acquire their identity as do middle-class white youth. Because they come from relatively poor families, large numbers must find jobs to help in the support of their families. Finding employment in today's job market is not an easy task. Without any special skills and with little education, the majority of Black youth are without regular employment of any kind. In the inner cities of the United States as many as 65 percent of Black teenagers are unemployed (Glasgow, 1979).

Because of that high unemployment rate Black youth are overrepresented in the crime statistics, in the volunteer army, among drug addicts, and in other negative social indexes. There has been a tendency to place the responsibility for the problems of Black youth on their disorganized family system. Although it is true that a slight majority of Black youth are now living in one-parent homes, there is reason to question that those types of families produce uneducable and delinquent children. One-parent households are generally poor families and it is the relationship between poverty and negative youth behavior that bears watching. Taylor's article investigates the general sociohistorical context within which the psychosocial development of Black youth occurs. His purpose was to look at role model identifications for these youth and their function in molding their psychosocial identity. What he found was that these youth had at their disposal a rich variety of social and psychological supports as well as a fund of experience on which to rely for the formation of their identity. Mayfield's paper looks at the adaptation of adolescent mothers to their position as mothers of a child. The cultural traditions of the Black community are supportive of unwed motherhood and the young mother often finds support within her extended family and leads a relatively normal life in many ways.

Socioeconomic Characteristics

It is necessary to understand the influence of economics on Black families' lives in order to conceptualize the conditions under which they function—or fail to function—as a viable system. Ever since the release from slavery, economic deprivation has been a fact of life for Black people. Since the forties the rate of unemployment among Blacks has been steadily twice that of whites. The National Urban League's (1974) hidden unemployment index shows the real unemployment rate of Black men to be around 25 percent. Men who can not find work not only have trouble maintaining a stable marital

and family life but often can not find a woman willing to marry them in the first place. Only 55 percent of all Black men with incomes of less than $5,000 a year are married, compared to 80 percent of those earning $15–20,000. As incomes rise so does the number of Black men who marry (Glick and Mills, 1974).

Black families have a median income of $13,598 a year compared to $24,603 a year for white families (U.S. Bureau of the Census, 1984). Not only is Black family income 56 percent that of white family income, but that figure indicates a drop in the ratio from 61 percent in 1969. If adjustments for inflation are made, Black families were slightly worse off five years later (National Urban League, 1974). This does not even consider the fact that many more Black families (two-thirds) derive their family income from multiple earners than white households (one-half). The implications of those economic facts are obvious when we observe that the higher the income of Blacks the more likely we will find a biparental family. When we look at Black families headed by women, we see that they had an average income of only $7,510 a year, approximately 38 percent of the earnings of intact Black families in 1981 (U.S. Bureau of the Census, 1984).

Charles Willie's article examines Black family life styles at three different class levels. He found that styles of life do vary by social class but that, in general, Black and white families do share a common value system. The report by Joe and Yu describes the large number of Black males presently out of the labor force and suggests that the percentage of Black families headed by women is strongly correlated with the employment status of Black men. The Alliance Against Women's Oppression also declares that the poverty of Black women is shared by Black males, that not all women are poor, and many white women share the affluence of white males while many Black men have a common economic status with Black women.

References

Adams, B.
1970 "Isolation, Function and Beyond: American Kinship in the 1960s." *Journal of Marriage and the Family* 32 (November):575–598.

Bianchi, S., and R. Farley
1979 "Racial Differences in Family Living Arrangements and Economic Well-Being: An Analysis of Recent Trends." *Journal of Marriage and the Family* 41 (August):537–552.

Glasgow, D.
1979 *The Black Underclass.* San Francisco: Jossey-Bass.

Glick, P., and K. Mills
1974 *Black Families: Marriage Patterns and Living Arrangements.* Paper presented at the W. E. B. Du Bois conference on American Blacks, Atlanta, Ga.

Marshall, G.
1972 "An Exposition of the Valid Premises Underlying Black Families." In *The Black Family. Fact or Fantasy,* Alyce Gullatte, ed., pp. 12–15. Washington, D.C.: National Medical Association.

McAdoo, H.
1981 *Black Families.* Beverly Hills, Calif.: Sage.

National Urban League Research Department
1974 *Inflation and the Black Consumer.* Washington, D.C.: Author.

Rubin, R. H.
1974 "Adult Male Absence and the Self-Attitudes of Black Children." *Child Study Journal* 4 (Spring):33–45.

United States Bureau of the Census
1984 Series P–20, No. 386. *Fertility of American Women: June 1983.* Washington, D.C.: U.S. Government Printing Office.

7 / Childbearing

ONE-CHILD FAMILIES AND ATYPICAL SEX RATIOS IN AN ELITE BLACK COMMUNITY

Ruth McKay

The author provides several explanations for the large number of one-child families among a sample of Blacks who are solidly upper-middle class. Attention is also given to the significant number of female offspring in comparison to male offspring in this setting.

My original intention in writing this paper had been to discuss some of the cultural factors affecting family size in the Black Elite and Ghetto communities I had studied between 1960 and 1967. In the course of examining the Elite data recently for numbers and ratios of children, which had not been done when the material was analyzed previously for socialization trends, a number of surprising relationships involving disproportionate numbers of one-child families and female children came to light. Today's presentation will focus exclusively on the Elite material.

The Elite Black community data was collected in Border City[1] during a two-year field study of socialization practices, six months of which were devoted to a definition of the social class structure as it was perceived by the members of the Black community. The criteria for determining social class placement most frequently mentioned by my informants were: education, occupation, income, and "old family" affiliation. The best perspective on the distribution of Elite status characteristics within the Black community can be gained by looking at some 1960 U.S. census findings for Border City. In that year, it had a total population approaching one million (939,024), of which two thirds were classed as "White" (610,608), and one third were classed as "Non-White" (328,416). All but 2,800,[2] or more than 99% of the "Non-Whites" were Negro. (The 1960 Census Report figures do not differentiate Negroes from other "Non-Whites.")

Six per cent, or 3,900 "Non-White" families had an annual income of $10,000 or more. Three per cent, or 5,929 "Non-White" individuals had completed four or more years of college. (In our community survey, more Negro females than males had completed college.) 7,760 "Non-Whites" were

---

Reprinted by permission. Footnotes have been renumbered.

engaged in occupations falling in the two highest occupational categories of "Professional and Technical" and "Managerial and Proprietary." Of the "Non-Whites" engaged in high status occupations, 47% (3,685) were male, 53% (4,075) were female. Given the fact that more Black women than men possessed high status educational and professional credentials, some Elite status Black women married Black men with less education and less prestigious occupations than they themselves possessed.

The Elite Black Border City family in the early 1960's typically consisted of parents who were college educated. The family income typically ranged from $13,000 to $17,000 in families in which both husband and wife worked (81%), although incomes over $50,000 were reported. In descending order, the occupations represented in the Elite Black community sample studied were: elementary school teacher, secondary school teacher; social worker; physician; college professor; clerical worker; postal clerk; judge; junior high school principal; clergyman; engineer; building contractor; newspaper reporter; investment broker; business manager; chemist; nurse; policeman; pharmacist; and college dean. Although some of the families had achieved Elite status in their own lifetimes, many of the Elite adults were themselves children of Elite parents whose names could be found in the first edition of "Who's Who in Colored America," published in the 1920's.

In the course of conducting the study of socialization practices, the author experienced extreme difficulty in locating families with at least one young child of each sex. At the end of the two-year study, the Intensive Study Sample of twenty-five families included seven one-child families because no other families with young children of opposite sex could be found. In attempting to get greater breadth to the observations derived from the twenty-five family sample, the author was fortunate in being given access to the membership roster of a mothers' and children's organization with which all but a handful of the Elite Black families were associated. In the course of two years of attending parties, barbecues, dances, club meetings, and other social and community events, I encountered only two Elite women who did not belong to this organization. I shall call this elite club the "Lads and Lassies."

TABLE 1 Family Size, Elite Black Community Sample

CHILDREN PER FAMILY	NUMBER OF FAMILIES	% OF TOTAL
1	102	63
2	39	24
3	16	10
4	4	2.4
5	1	0.6
Total	162	100

Excluding a few families with adopted children, and mothers who were not natives of the United States, the "Lads and Lassies" provided a sample of 162 mothers and 249 children. In looking at family size in this larger sample, I was surprised to learn that almost two thirds of the Elite Black families consisted of families with one child. Of a total of 162 families, 102 (63%) had one child, 39 (24%) had two children, 16 (10%) had three children, 4 (2.4%) had four children, and 1 family (0.6%) had five children. (See Table 1.)

The great proportion of one-child families in this generation is in sharp contrast to the family size of the Elite mother's own family of orientation. In the Intensive Study Sample, the mothers reported up to eleven siblings, and an average family size of 5.2 children. The average family size for the 162 families in our "Lads and Lassies" sample was 1.54 children.

The findings of a majority of one-child families in the Elite Negro community also contrasts strongly with numbers of children born to Non-White married women in the Border City Standard Metropolitan Area. For a population of 6,686 Non-White married women, ages 45–49, 1,877 (28%) had borne one child, 1,333 (20%) had borne two children, 949 (14%) had borne three children, 721 (11%) had borne four children, 830 (12%) had borne either five or six children, and 966 (15%) had borne seven or more children. Although the "Lads and Lassies" mothers ranged in age from early thirties to late forties, we may still infer that few of the children in the one-child families would acquire younger siblings at some future time. Seventy of the 102 children in the one-child families were over ten years of age.

A closer look at the seven one-child families in the twenty-five [family] Intensive Study Sample revealed that five of the seven children in these one-child families were girls. In turning to the larger "Lads and Lassies" sample, I expected that the children in the 102 one-child families would be about evenly divided between boys and girls. I was startled to learn that there were almost twice as many girls as boys in this group of one-child families. The Elite Black population appeared to be a community in which girls and one-child families predominated. Both of these characteristics run counter to population trends for the United States and the world at large.

The secondary sex ratio, or the sex ratio at birth, is approximately 106 males to 100 females for United States Whites and 102.6 males for every 100 females among United States Negroes.[3] Urban sex ratios tend to run lower than rural ratios and national averages. The secondary sex ratio of White babies born in Border City in 1960 was 104.3; the secondary sex ratio of Negro infants born in that city in 1960 was 100.7. The sex ratio for Border City White youth, ages 3 to 19 years, in 1960 was 100.2; for Non-White youth, ages 3 to 19 years, was 95.7. The sex ratio in our "Lads and Lassies" sample of 249 children, ages 3 to 19, was 83.0 males to every 100 females. The sex ratio for the 102 children in the one-child families in the "Lads and Lassies" sample was 61.9.[4]

The "United Nations Report on the Role of Women," issued in November 1974, indicates a world trend in the direction of a growing increase of men over women which is expected to continue until the end of the century.[5] A community in which children run on the order of five girls for every four boys is, therefore, contrary to the expected ratio.

My first explanation for the preponderance of girls in the one-child families was that there must have been some sort of matrifocal influence at work. Once a mother had borne a female, she had the child of the desired sex and there was no need to bear additional children. If this were the case, in looking at the multi-child families, one would ex-pect to find a greater number with an oldest male child, leading the parents to try again for the desired female child. Actually, the sex of the first child in the multi-child families was evenly divided between the sexes. Twenty-eight of the multi-child families had had a son first; twenty-eight of these families had had a daughter first. Since there did not seem to be any greater inclination for the families with an only son to try for additional children in the hope of attaining the desired female child, another explanation would have to be found.

I am grateful to my physical anthropological colleagues for information about recent work in the field of Human Reproductive Biology which helps to explain the unusual sex ratio among the children in this community. We shall see how *a culture pattern has interacted with a biological trend to produce a situation in which the expected sex ratio of children is reversed.*

The culture pattern is an Elite social structure in which the full-time income of the wife is necessary for the maintenance of the desired standard of living. Typically, she interrupts her professional career just once, in order to bear one child, and then returns to full-time earning power for the balance of her professional life.

Studies of human reproduction have revealed that although the sex ratio of males to females is greater at conception and birth, there tends to be a reduction in the disparity of males over females as the age of the father increases and as the rank order of birth increases. "In nearly all populations, the ratio of males is highest for the first birth and decreases with successive births. Such a correlation . . . may be directly related to the birth order itself; or to the ages of the parents, which obviously increase with increasing birth order. . . . Analysis has shown that the age of the mother is not correlated with the sex ratio, but, curiously enough, the age of the father may be."[6]

Since the population with the atypical sex ratio is predominantly a population of one-child families, we may discount birth order as a likely explanation for the over-representation of girls. In turning to a more careful look at the timing of conception of the child or children in the Elite Black family, we see that child-bearing, which interferes with the wife's earning capacity, is usually post-

TABLE 2 Sex Ratios

	WHITE	NEGRO
U.S. secondary sex ratio, 1960	106.0	102.6
Border City secondary sex ratio, 1960	104.3	100.7
Border City youth, ages 3–19 years	100.2	95.7[1]
Lads and Lassies (total of 249 children, 3–19)		83.0
Lads and Lassies (102 "only" children, 3–19)		61.9

[1] A figure for Negro youth alone was not available. This ratio is based on total "non-white" youth in this age category in Border City, 1960.

poned for several years after marriage until the couple have completed professional training, acquired a home, furnishings, automobile, and other necessary accoutrements of elite life-style. For the small number of Elite families in which the age of the fathers at the time of the birth of the child is known, we learn that the mean age of the fathers was 32.66 years, with a range from 24 to 50 years of age. Thus, while the delay in child-bearing was caused by the women's wish to contribute to the families' nest eggs, the husbands had, perforce, aged along with their wives during the waiting period. Fathers moderately to well-advanced in their reproductive cycle might well tend to produce fewer male than female children in the first conception.

In the concluding section of this paper, I would like to consider some of the possible social structural implications our findings of large numbers of one-child families and of girls over boys may hold for the future of the Elite Black community. For a woman beginning her child-bearing career in 1960, Thompson[7] reckoned that an average of 2.38 children would be necessary to maintain the population at a stationary level. Although the greater number of females borne by Elite Black women may mean that a slightly lower number of children per mother would be required to maintain the population at a stationary level, the average of 1.54 children borne by mothers in our sample may not be high enough to replace the Elite population. We will look at replacement of population by recruitment a little later.

The greater ratio of males to females at birth

for most human populations means that the higher attrition rate for males through life will lead to parity in the sex ratio somewhere in the middle adult years. A population in which numbers of girls exceeds numbers of boys at birth is one in which there will be an increasing surplus of females or, stated differently, an increasing deficit of males, as the generation grows to maturity. We may foresee a future Elite adult population which is proportionately higher in females than was true for the generation of parents we studied in 1960. Recall that the Elite adult community of 1960, coming from good-sized families in which there was no marked overrepresentation of females, was one in which more women than men had completed college and more women than men occupied positions in the highest two occupational categories.

"No matter," some may say. "A community replaces itself not only by births within but through recruitment of individuals from outside of the community." This indeed happens. Every generation witnesses the ascent of some individuals from lower- to middle- and upper-class standing. The dilemma this process of recruitment poses for the Elite Black community is that, traditionally, more women than men have made the transition to Elite status. For a variety of historical and cultural reasons, ranging from differential patterns of discrimination within educational and occupational systems to differential expectations and socialization pressures for boys and girls within lower-class Black families, social mobility has been easier for the Black woman to achieve.

Until the social and psychological structures which serve to block the Black man's mobility are dismantled, a disproportionately female endogenous Elite of the future will be joined by a similar population of mobile newcomers to their community. All of which might very well lead the upper-class Black Border Citian of the 1980's to query, "Where did all these girls come from?"[7]

---

[1]*A fictitious name for a city on the mid-Atlantic coast.*

[2]*Other "Non-White" races included American Indian, Japanese, Chinese, Filipino, Korean, Asian Indian, and Malayan.*

[3]*Curt Stern,* Principles of Human Genetics *(San Francisco, W. H. Freeman, 1973), pp. 529–530.*

[4]*Human geneticist Curt Stern has stated that the "observed [secondary] sex ratios are empirical values which are subject to chance variation. . . . [In] a population of one hundred, the probability of observing a deviation from 106 as large as 158.1 or 71.4 or larger would be 5% (Ibid., p. 530). The only Black*

Elite population on which I could derive the secondary sex ratio, or the sex ratio at birth, was the sixty-child sample in the Intensive Study Sample of families. Their secondary sex ratio was 68.5. If there had been one hundred children in this sample, the sex ratio of 68.5 would probably border on the 5% probability range (see Ibid., chapter 20).

[5]Washington Post, *November 19, 1974, B3.*

[6]*Stern, op.cit., p. 538.*

[7]*Warner S. Thompson and Donald T. Lewis,* Population Problems *(New York: McGraw Hill, 1965), pp. 270–271.*

SOCIOCULTURAL INFLUENCES ON ADOLESCENT MOTHERS

Alva P. Barnett

This article explores some of the major health consequences and needs of the Black adolescent mother and her child. In the context of sociocultural and structural considerations, the discussion centers on antecedent factors likely to have an adverse affect on the health and well-being particularly of the Black adolescent mother and her child. These factors include inadequate family income and nutrition, lack of accessible quality health care services, and age. The author believes that in order to begin appropriate and effective intervention that is likely to have a positive impact on these young lives, a better understanding of the antecedent factors is needed. Such intervention will increase the functional capacities and optimal abilities of a major segment of our children and youth.

Introduction

This paper is intended to contribute to the understanding of the health problems and needs of the Black adolescent mother and the health effects associated with adolescent pregnancy and motherhood. Selected antecedent factors that adversely affect the health and well-being of the Black adoles-

---

Revised and adapted from an article originally published in *Pediatric Social Work* 3, (4, 1985). © 1985 by Eterna International. Reprinted by permission.

cent mother and her child will be discussed. These antecedent factors are age, inadequate nutrition, family income, changing family structure, and the lack of available and accessible quality health care services. If uncorrected, these factors could have far-reaching implications regarding the functional capacity and optimal ability of these mothers and their infants, who are a major portion of this nation's vital resources.

Quality health care, as a right, should be afforded every individual; it is necessary regardless of race, ethnic identity, social status or economic circumstances of an individual or group of individuals (Zastrow and Bowker, 1984). As Ramsey Clark reminds us, "Youth is the foundation on which quality health is built. If America is to be free and offer fulfillment to its people, it must guarantee every teenager a healthy body, a sound mind and a decent environment" (Clark, 1978).

This American guarantee is a noble gesture that—no matter how profoundly we hope, desire, and believe it to be—simply flies in the face of reality. That reality is supported by facts that are disturbing and warrant full attention, understanding, commitment, and action by all adults, practitioners, and, most importantly, Black Americans. These facts highlight some of the present conditions that affect the health and well-being of Black families, children, and youth. They include the steady growth of female-headed households; alarming rates of infant mortality; a growing number of poor persons and those below the poverty level as defined by the U.S. government; higher fertility rates, especially among younger adolescents; an increasing percentage of out-of-wedlock births and unemployment; and increasingly low levels of family income. Facts such as these strongly suggest a crisis situation for several reasons.

First, the effects are multiple and will have a negative impact on two subsequent generations of adults, adolescents, and their children. Secondly, adequate and effective intervention and prevention techniques have not been utilized to any measurable degree. The growing body of descriptive literature and statistical reports has not focused significantly on understanding the interactive, multidimensional nature of the situation, which

has a particular impact on Black lives. These dimensions include structural barriers to opportunities, cultural values, and individual coping and adaptive patterns in relationship to survival and individual development.

Present Conditions

In order to understand what the adolescent mother and her infant potentially face, some of the present conditions resulting in multiple effects that adversely impact the well-being mainly of Black families, children, and youth will be discussed in order to understand what potentially faces the adolescent mother and her infant.

The increasing rate of Black female-headed households: In 1982 over 47 percent of Black families with children under the age of 18 years were female-headed households; this represents almost a 40 percent increase of Black female-headed households from the 1950 rate of 8 percent. During this same time frame, white female-headed households increased 12 percent from 3 percent in 1950 to about 15 percent in 1982 (Raspberry, 1984:1; U.S. Bureau of the Census, 1983). These figures show that differences between Black and white family structures are widening, but particularly devastating is that the majority (56 percent) of poor families are female-headed households. It is estimated that 44.9 percent of Black children under 18 years of age live below the poverty line (Mathey and Johnson, 1983).

The gap between Black and white infant mortality rates is not closing but widening at a steady pace. In 1978, the Black infant mortality rate was 86 percent higher than the white infant mortality rate. Four years later, the Black infant mortality rate was 95 percent higher than the white counterparts. According to Dorothy Rice (1984), the federal government's goal to reduce Black infant mortality to no more than 12 infant deaths for each 1,000 live births by 1990 will not be realized if this emerging trend continues. Directly related to infant mortality is the high percentage of underweight babies being born and inadequate nutrition and health care. The most seriously underweight babies have disproportionately been born to Black mothers. For example, in 1981, 6 percent of all white infants were underweight at birth as compared to 31 percent of all Black babies who were underweight at birth (Avery, 1984).

There are many other related facts that have an impact on the level of health and well-being of Black adolescent mothers and their infants, two of which are the higher fertility rates and percentages of the out-of-wedlock births. Also included are higher unemployment levels and lower family income (see Figures 1 and 2 and Tables 1 and 2).

The data presented here disclose the continued lack of parity and, in many instances, the widening gap between minority and majority group circumstances that adversely affects the health and well-being of Black children and youth. The social, health, and structural conditions of which these facts are representative are ultimately surrounded by the issues of wealth and income opportunities.

Current Knowledge

Since the 1960s, the occurrence of adolescent pregnancy and motherhood has continued to receive an enormous amount of national attention from a variety of disciplines and professional audiences. The steady attention given to adolescent pregnancy and

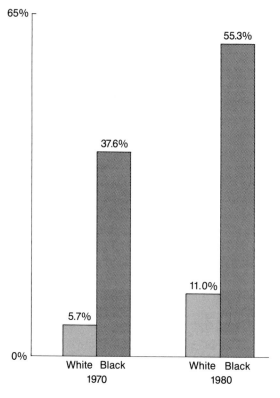

FIGURE 1 Percent of Births Born Out of Wedlock by Race: 1970 and 1980.
Source: National Center for Health Statistics.

TABLE 1   Fertility Rates among Women under Twenty by Age, Race and Marital Status of Woman: 1966, 1970, 1975, and 1978

	1966	1970	1975	1978
All women				
18–19	121.2	114.7	85.7	81.0
15–17	35.8	38.8	36.6	32.9
10–14	0.9	1.2	1.3	1.2
All unmarried women				
18–19	25.8	32.9	32.8	35.7
15–17	13.1	17.1	19.5	19.5
Unmarried white women				
18–19	14.3	17.6	16.6	19.5
15–17	5.4	7.5	9.7	10.5
Unmarried nonwhite women				
18–19	110.5	126.5	117.4	116.3
15–17	61.2	73.3	72.0	64.9

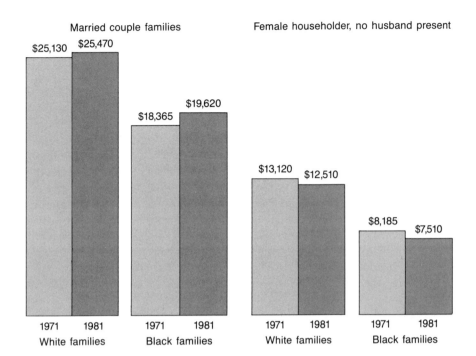

Married couple families   Female householder, no husband present

FIGURE 2 Median Family Income by Type of Family and Race of Householder: 1971 and 1981 (1981 dollars)

TABLE 2 Unemployment Rates

	1970	1975	1980	1982
All workers (16 years and over)	4.9	8.5	7.1	9.7
Black	—	14.8	14.3	18.9
Female	—	14.8	14.0	17.6
Male	—	14.8	14.5	20.1
White	4.5	7.8	6.3	8.6
Female	5.4	8.6	6.5	8.3
Male	4.0	7.2	6.1	8.8
Female-headed households	5.4	10.0	9.2	11.7
Black	7.5	14.0	14.9	18.7
White	4.8	8.9	7.1	8.6
Teens (16–19 years)	15.3	19.9	17.8	23.2
Black	—	39.5	38.5	48.0
White	13.5	17.9	15.5	20.4

motherhood has resulted in a plethora of descriptive literature and statistics.

Many of the studies have identified such related issues as health risks associated with adolescent pregnancy, childbearing, and the infant; the incidence of adolescent pregnancy and childbearing; and the negative economic social and educational consequences of adolescent motherhood affecting the quality of life (Brown, 1982; Klerman and Jekel, 1973; Ogg, 1976). Descriptive information has been important in learning about the prevalence of problems related to adolescent motherhood; aggregate statistics is also a significant part of this literature. As Resnick (1984) indicates, this type of statistics tends to hide more than it reveals, particularly the patterns and functions of behaviors. Some of the questions arising from these areas that have not been greatly explored are: What are the cultural patterns that must be understood in light of the structural barriers to opportunities afforded Black adolescents? What are the meanings of certain values and beliefs influencing functional behaviors that help to maintain family and community support of U.S. Blacks in light of numerous stresses, such as minimal economic resources? What are the adaptive patterns toward optimal functioning, given the structural nature of various environmental systems or subsystems in which Black adolescents interact? Have these sociocultural and structural issues been adequately addressed from a Black perspective? Have these issues been incorporated in significant numbers of the programs that provide services to Black adolescent mothers and their infants?

Program Issues

Over 300 programs have been developed to address these issues associated with adolescent pregnancy and motherhood, especially within the age group under fifteen years. Ironically, this growth in program development has occurred since the period of greatest increase of adolescent motherhood, 1960–1974 (Baldwin, 1976).

Many of these programs have been characterized as inadequate in meeting the diverse and multiple needs of the pregnant adolescent and young mother, in part because of the unidimensional as-

pect of the program (Brown, 1982; McKenry et al., 1979). For example, frequently a biological or physiological approach to intervention is taken without priority being given simultaneously to socioeconomic needs. The inaccessibility of programs and services has been clearly documented, especially in low income areas where inadequate public transportation, lack of child care services, and geographical distance to services represent barriers to the equal access of services (Chilman, 1980; Congressional Budget Office, 1978; Shannon et al., 1969; U.S. Department of Health, Education, and Welfare, 1980). The anticipated outcome goals of these programs are to reduce the incidence of adolescent pregnancy and to minimize the impact of aspects that affect the quality of life associated with adolescent motherhood, which include high morbidity and mortality rates and limited educational gains and employment skills (Russ-Eft et al., 1979). These expected goals, with the general objective of improving the health and well-being of the adolescent mother and her child, have not been realized in any appreciable measure (Bolton, 1980).

This lack of goal attainment is evidenced by the increasing birthrate since 1960 among adolescents younger than 14 years of age and the steady birthrate among adolescents 14–17 years of age (Bogue, 1977; Guttmacher Institute, 1976). In 1980, almost 600,000 babies were born to adolescents under 20 years of age and over 10,000 of these births were to adolescents 14 years of age and younger (Edelman, 1984:3). Fifty-seven percent of all babies born to adolescents under 15 years of age are Black. For the Black adolescent female, the birthrate remains disproportionately higher than for white adolescents. For example, one out of every four babies is born to Black adolescents, whereas one out of seven babies is born to white adolescents (Meriwether, 1984).

As indicated, there has been an enormous amount of concentrated attention to the growth rates of our young who are having children and choosing to rear them. There has been an increase in the descriptive studies and statistics; also, numerous programs have been developed in hopes of reducing the number of babies that are born to adolescents. Moreover, the overall objective of these intervention strategies over the last few decades has been to improve the health and well-being of these youths and their infants. These efforts have been worthy and for some they have even been effective. However, for Black adolescent mothers, who have consistently had the highest mortality rates, minimal access to services, and disproportionately higher birthrates, these intervention efforts have not significantly altered the impact of adolescent pregnancy and motherhood.

Given this state of affairs, the question arises of why program goals and activities have not significantly improved the health and well-being of the population of adolescents who become pregnant and choose to rear their infants. There may be several reasons for this problem. However, only two major reasons will be discussed with alternative suggestions.

The first major reason that the stated goals are not fully realized might be that adolescent pregnancy and motherhood is viewed as an epidemic rather than a social problem. This perception does not view the problem as structural in nature, limiting targets for intervention. In recent years, this view has been discussed and debated (Klerman, 1980). Many have called into question the extent to which the incidence of adolescent pregnancy is a disease process. Such a view places emphasis on symptomatology and the individual as the problem, rather than broadening its perspective and priority to include the need for understanding antecedent causes that have severe consequences on the adolescent who becomes pregnant and chooses to rear her child, particularly the Black adolescent (Butts, 1981). For example, Lorraine Klerman (1980:777) states:

> This country is not faced with an epidemic but rather a continuing problem which will fluctuate with the size of the population at risk. . . . No magic bullet will solve the problem; rather its underlying causes must be examined and appropriate interventions designed.

The second reason for the failure to accomplish the identified program goals is the tendency to view adolescent mothers as a homogeneous group (Falk et al., 1981). For the Black adolescent,

this view can mean the difference between prevention and chronic or intractable health and socioeconomic problems. Clearly, the awareness of the cultural and historical context of which the adolescent is a part provides knowledge to the practitioner about her needs, resources, and obstacles to health care. It allows the practitioner to move beyond categorizing or compartmentalizing behaviors and lifestyles. With appreciation and the acceptance of uniqueness that allows the adolescent mother to adapt functionally, the practitioner can intervene and advocate appropriately and in ways that have a positive impact on existing adverse circumstances (Litsitzky, 1956).

Taking into account the need for effective programs to minimize the effects and consequences of adolescent pregnancy and motherhood, the following statement acknowledges issues that must be addressed:

> We need a new philosophy of health—nothing less. It must be seen in the context of a larger societal whole and the interactions between the person and the environment. Thus, if a better basic income or environment will produce a healthier individual or family, they should be part of the health strategy. (McNerney, 1975:411)

In further support for minimizing the impact of these areas that affect the quality of life of adolescent mothers and their infants, Karl Fox (1974) has suggested that "the success of a program in promoting well-being must be reflected in the life experiences of its members."

The Impact of Morbidity and Mortality

Maternal Effects

Research has shown that pregnant adolescents who choose to have their babies are more likely to experience an increased incidence of health problems than their older counterparts. For example, mothers between the ages of 15 and 19 years are twice as likely to die from hemorrhage and miscarriage than mothers over 20 years of age (Bogue, 1977). For this adolescent age group, the maternal death rate from pregnancy and its complications is sixty percent higher than for mothers in their early twenties (Planned Parenthood, 1979).

Similarly, these younger mothers are 23 percent more likely to experience a premature birth with complications such as anemia, prolonged labor, and nutritional deficiency and 92 percent more likely to have anemia than mothers in their twenties (Cooke and Dworkin, 1980; Edelman, 1984; Guttmacher Institute, 1981). Toxemia, hemorrhage, and infections have been identified as major medical determinants of maternal mortality (Minkler, 1979).

For the Black adolescent who chooses motherhood, an even higher incidence of health problems and medical complications is likely to occur when accompanied by adverse antecedent factors. These factors are largely due to the lack of equitable distributed resources and have been identified as inadequate nutrition, financial sources, and income and the lack of an opportunity to secure training, employment, and housing facilities to weather the natural elements, such as winter months; the factor that places Black adolescents in an extremely high risk group for medical complications is inaccessible quality health care (prenatal and postnatal) services (Edelman, 1984; Peoples et al., 1984; Somers and Somers, 1977;411–417). For example, a study by Rothenberg and Varga (1981) found that the health and development of children born to adolescent mothers were not disadvantaged when compared to the children of older mothers, if the socioeconomic backgrounds were similar.

Age, associated with biological immaturity, is being given less attention as an independent risk factor for pregnant adolescents and mothers over 15 years of age (Avery, 1984; Klerman, 1980). Death rates for these mothers are 60 percent higher than female counterparts in their early twenties; one in five adolescents in this age group receives late or no health care, compared to one in ten of pregnant adolescents in all age groups (Children's Defense Fund, 1982).

It is apparent that the risk of maternal morbidity and mortality to Black adolescents is dispropor-

tionately higher than that of the majority population. It seems that the adverse antecedent factors significantly contribute to these differences. As Aaron Antonovsky (1974) pointed out, class and race do affect the life chances of an individual. In order to improve the life chances of the Black adolescent mother who is at greatest risk, active attention to change needs to be given to the structural inequities that negatively impinge on the functional capacities of these young people, who are capable of becoming successful, contributing adult citizens.

Infant Effects

Health, security, and the opportunity to enter a world in which one can develop to maturity in the best possible state of health are considered the right of every child (U.S. Department of Human Resources, 1974). The measures most frequently used in regard to infants include rates of stillbirth, birth weights and birth lengths, and neonatal and infant mortality (Rothenberg and Varga, 1981). This section focuses primarily on infant mortality and the effects of underweight babies.

The infant mortality rate is considered to be the rate that is most sensitive to differences in health care and is inextricably related to social and economic factors. As a result, it is often described as a social indicator or measure determining the level of health. There has been a decrease in the infant mortality rates since the 1960s; however, the gap between Black and white rates has not narrowed. In fact, this widening gap in rates of infant mortality may potentially undermine the slow progress in reducing the nation's infant mortality rate. In the early eighties, almost 20,000 Black infants died during the first year of life who, according to David Anderson (1984:5), would not have died had their chance been equal to that of white infants. Statistics from the U.S. Bureau of the Census (1983) indicate that the cities with the highest infant mortality rates have a majority or near majority Black population.

In 1979, the Black infant mortality rate was 21.8 deaths under the age of one for every 1,000 births and the infant mortality rate for whites was 11.4; in 1982, the rate of Black infant mortality was 95 percent higher than the rate for whites. This is a

9 percent increase within a four year period (Reid, 1982). If this emerging trend continues it is likely to affect adversely the federal government goal of reducing Black infant mortality by 1990.

The most frequently cited adverse outcomes to the infants of young mothers are considered to be prematurity and low birth weight (Rothenberg and Varga, 1981). The high infant mortality is found to be directly related to the high percentage of underweight babies and this is linked to prematurity. In a study done at Johns Hopkins (Battaglia et al., 1963), it was found that the increase in low birth weights and prematurity were attributed to adolescents under 15 years of age. Two factors that have been frequently associated with premature infants are the inadequate prenatal care and nutrition received by adolescent mothers. Some of the potential outcomes of underweight in babies are epilepsy, cerebral palsy, other disabilities, and death.

Given possible outcomes such as these, it is clear that a combination of intervention strategies is needed. Some of the strategies needed are: (1) health care that is responsive to the needs of these infants and their mothers; (2) an aggressive outreach program that will familiarize mother with services as well as provide educational information and demonstration in such areas as nutrition and infant stimulation skills; (3) accessible and adequate health care service; (4) an adequate number of health care and social service providers whose attitudes about adolescent mothers and their infants are acceptance, high expectations, and encouragement toward self-sufficiency; (5) modification of the philosophy, policies, and practices in social welfare that provide options and resources based on individual needs and acknowledgment of the diversity of life-styles and cultural values; (6) program policy that automatically includes family members and other natural support systems; and (7) sufficient income for basic needs and the opportunity for these young mothers to gain self-sufficiency through job training and available job placements.

Given the information presented in this paper, it seems evident that the problems associated with the incidence of adolescent pregnancy and the prevalence of adolescent motherhood are not so much internal manifestations as results of interactions with a variety of external systems. Therefore, we must understand the individual dynamics within primary systems as well as institutional dynamics that interface with a diversity of people. There also is a need for commitment to prevention intervention along with a commitment to these adolescent mothers becoming self-sufficient and self-determining, and thus contributing, members of this society. The right of every child to health, security, and opportunity can be realized.

References

Anderson, David
1984 "Study: Black Infant Mortality Rates Not Declining." *National Leader,* January 19.

Antonovsky, Aaron
1974 "Class and the Chance of Life." In Lee Rainwater, ed., *Equality and Justice.* Chicago: Aldine.

Avery, Byllye
1984 "The Status of Black Women's Health." *Congressional Black Caucus Foundation* (Spring).

Baldwin, W.
1976 "Adolescent Pregnancy and Childbearing Growing Concern for Americans." *Population Bulletin* 31:3–21.

Battaglia, F., T. Frazier, and A. Hellegers
1963 "Obstetric and Pediatric Complications of Juvenile Pregnancy." *Pediatrics* 32:902.

Bogue, Donald, editor
1977 *Adolescent Fertility.* Chicago: University of Chicago Community and Family Study Center.

Bolton, Frank
1980 *The Pregnant Adolescent.* Beverly Hills, Calif.: Sage.

Brown, S.
1982 "Early Childbearing and Poverty: Implications for Social Services." *Adolescence* 17 (66, Summer):397–408.

Butts, June Dobbs

1981   "Adolescent Sexuality and Teenage Pregnancy from a Black Perspective." In T. Ooms, ed., *Teenage Pregnancy in A Family Context*, pp. 307–325. Philadelphia, Pa.: Temple University Press.

Children's Defense Fund

1982   *America's Children and Their Families*. Washington, D.C.: Author.

Chilman, C.

1980   *Adolescent Sexuality in a Changing American Society: Social and Psychological Perspectives*. Washington, D.C.: U.S. Government Printing Office.

Clark, Ramsey

1978   *Voices of Concern: Americans Speak Out for Teenage Health Services Pamphlet*. Atlanta, Georgia: Emory University Family Planning Program, Grady Memorial Hospital.

Congressional Budget Office

1978   *Health Differentials between White and Nonwhite Americans*. Washington, D.C.: U.S. Government Printing Office.

Cooke, Cynthia, and Susan Dworkin

1980   *The Ms Guide to a Woman's Health*.

Edelman, Marian W.

1984   "Remembering Our Youngest Mothers," *The Omaha Star*, May 10.

Falk, Ruth, Maria Gispert, and Donald Baucom

1981   "Personality Factors Related to Black Teenage Pregnancy and Abortion." *Psychology of Women Quarterly* 5 (5):737–746.

Fox, Karl

1974   *Social Indicators and Social Theory*. New York: Wiley.

Guttmacher Institute

1976   *Eleven Million Teenagers: What Can Be Done about the Epidemic of Adolescent Pregnancies in the United States*. New York: Planned Parenthood Federation of America.

1981   *Teenage Pregnancy: The Problem That Hasn't Gone Away*. New York: Alan Guttmacher Institute.

Klerman, Lorraine

1980   "Adolescent Pregnancy: A New Look at a Continuing Problem." *American Journal of Public Health* 70 (8):776–778.

Klerman, Lorraine, and James Jekel

1973   *School-Age Mothers: Problem, Programs and Policy*. Conn.: The Shoe String Press.

Litsitzky, Gene

1956   *Four Ways of Being Human*. New York: Viking Press, 1956.

Mathey, William, and Dwight Johnson

1983   "America's Black Population: 1970 to 1982." *The Crises* 90 (10, December).

McKenry, Patrick, Lynda Walters, and Carolyn Johnson

1979   "Adolescent Pregnancy: A Review of the Literature." *The Family Coordinator* (January):17–28.

McNerney, Walter J.

1975   Quoted in A. Somers and H. Somers, eds., *Health and Health Care: Policies in Perspective*. Maryland: Aspen Systems Corporation.

Meriwether, Louise

1984   "Teenage Pregnancy." *Essence* (April):94–96.

Minkler, Donald

1979   "Pregnancy and the Prevention of Undesirable Consequences." In R. Jackson, J. Morton, and M. Sierra-Franco, eds., *Social Factors in Prevention*, pp. 3–15. Calif.: University of California, School of Public Health.

Ogg, E.

1976   *Unmarried Teenagers and Their Children*. Public Affairs Pamphlet, No. 537.

Peoples, M., R. Grimson, G. Daughtry

1984   "Evaluation of the Effects of the North Carolina Improved Pregnancy Outcome Project: Implications for State-Level Decision-Making." *American Journal of Public Health* 74 (6, June): 549–554.

Planned Parenthood

1979   "Teenage Pregnancy: A Major Problem for Minors." In *Zero Population Growth*. Calif.: Planned Parenthood Association of San Diego.

Raspberry, William

1984   "New Interest in an Old Problem." *Chicago Tribune*, February 6.

Reid, John

1982   "Black America in the 1980's." Washington, D.C.: Population Reference Bureau.

Resnick, Michael

1984   "Studying Adolescent Mothers' Decision Making

about Adoption and Parenting." *Social Work* (January-February).

Rice, Dorothy
1984 A Report from the National Center for Health Statistics." *National Leader,* January 19.

Rothenberg, Pearlia, and Phyllis Varga
1981 "The Relationship between Age of Mother and Child Health and Development." *American Journal of Public Health* 71 (8, August).

Russ-Eft, Darlene, Marlene Springer, and Anne Beaver
1979 "Antecedents of Adolescent Parenthood and Consequences at Age 30." *The Family Coordinator* (April):173–178.

Shannon, G., et al.
1969 "The Concept of Distance as a Factor in Accessibility and Utilization of Health Care." *Medical Care Review* 26 (143, February).

Somers, Anne, and Herman Somers
1977 *Health and Health Care: Policies in Perspective.* Rockville, Maryland: Aspen Systems Corporation.

U.S. Bureau of the Census
1983 *Statistical Abstract of the United States 1984.* Washington, D.C.: U.S. Department of Commerce.

U.S. Department of Health, Education, and Welfare
1980 *Health Status of Minorities and Low Income Groups.* Rockville, Maryland: Office of Health Resources Opportunity.

U.S. Department of Human Resources
1974 *Children: The Resource of the Future.* Washington, D.C.: Government of the District of Columbia.

Zastrow, Charles, and Lee Bowker
1984 *Social Problems: Issues and Solutions.* Chicago: Nelson-Hall.

8 / Parental Roles

THE SOLO MOTHER

Marie Peters · Cecile de Ford

The recent growth of single-parent female-headed families is a well-documented phenomenon of U.S. society as a whole. Its existence among Blacks has been the subject of a number of controversial studies. The authors of this study focus on the viability of the Black mother-headed family and the mother's strategies for coping with this situation. Attention is given to the values and support of the larger Black community.

Introduction

It is usually assumed that the "biological parent team" of mother and father is the appropriate descriptive model for contemporary American families and a departure from that norm has been typically viewed as deviant. In an earlier day, the female who had no husband was referred to as a "poor widow" to be viewed with "sympathy and understanding." More recently, mother-headed families have been generally viewed as "indicative of breakdown and failure" and Black broken marriages have been officially considered to be pathological (Moynihan, 1965).

However, female-headed families in this country are growing at double the rate of husband–wife families and, as will be shown, there is beginning to be some recognition that the mother-and-children unit may be a viable family form.

How Many?

In 1973 there were over 6.6 million families who were headed by a woman. In over half (57.5%) of these families the mother had children under 18 years of age. Twenty-three percent of the families had children under age 6 (U.S. Bureau of the Census, 1974).

Four million, three hundred and twenty-six thousand (4,326,000) female-headed families with children under 18 years of age cannot be ignored; nor can 9,627,000 children under 18 years of age or 2,153,000 children under 6 years of age who live with their mothers be studied only from the perspective of some presumed pathological effects resulting from living in a household without a father. Brandwein et al. (1974:498–515) in a recent review of studies of divorced mothers and their families noted the "paucity of studies on mothers" and "the

Revised and reprinted by permission. Updated and condensed version of paper presented at the 1974 annual meeting of the National Council on Family Relations, St. Louis, Mo.

assumption throughout the literature that the female single-parent family is deviant and pathological." In fact, as they found, much of the literature on single-parent families focuses not on the mother at all, but on the effect of father absence on the children.

Several years ago, Herzog and Sudia (1968:181) made a similar observation. They wrote,

> *The fatherless home in the United States . . .*
> *deserves study as a family form in itself,*
> *rather than a mutilated version of some*
> *other form. It would be useful to give clearer*
> *recognition to the one-parent family as a*
> *family form in its own right . . . one that ex-*
> *ists and functions.*

The purpose of this study, then, is to examine solo-parent family as a viable family form, not to document pathology, but to learn about family functioning, patterns of living, and techniques for coping with problems. We will look for the strengths and diversity, as well as the stresses and strains. We will consider first the attitudes and values the Black community generally hold concerning the family roles of Black women. Then we will report the findings of interviews with solo female parents who through divorce, widowhood or by choice are raising families without husbands.

Understanding Black Female-Headed Families

Black women have been raising families successfully in this country for three hundred years, the result of having been snatched from their families in Africa and transported to America where for generations they were forced to propagate, but not always allowed to have husbands. (During slavery, the men were sold away from families. More recently, men were legislated out of their families when government-funded welfare programs routinely denied financial assistance to the families of unemployed fathers.)

The Black single female parent is part of a culture which understands that a woman may be either co-head of family as wife/mother, or head-of-family as solo mother. Each or both statuses are possible for female adults, and Black children are socialized accordingly.

Black families, then, unlike most families in the dominant culture, have subscribed to attitudes and values which include (1) commitment to employment in the labor force for women as well as men (Scanzoni, 1971; Jackson, 1973; Peters, 1974); (2) egalitarian relationship between husband and wife within the marriage (TenHouten, 1970; Mack, 1971; Hyman and Reed, 1969; Yancey, 1972); and (3) recognition that women who marry and bear children can not necessarily expect to raise children to adulthood in an intact family (although, of course, some do) and therefore there is acceptance within the Black community of single-parent status, whether by choice or by chance, as will be discussed below.

Divorce and Separation: Logical Adjustment When Marriages Flounder

The divorce rates in this country are rising steadily. We are approaching the ratio of one divorce per two marriages. Although marital breakup has been traditionally viewed as undesirable and many clergymen and marriage counselors in the traditional mold still counsel toward keeping marriage intact, there is [an] increasing acceptance of divorce in our society, especially if there are no children. There is also [an] increasing acceptance of divorce when there are children.

Nye and Hoffman (1963) concluded from their research that an unhappy "unbroken" family is psychologically more damaging to children than a happy "broken" family. Robert Bell (1971) also pointed out that research has shown that two parents are not necessarily better than one. LeMasters (1970:168) concluded in a review of the literature on the one-parent family that the one-parent family is not "inherently dysfunctional or pathological." He wrote,

> *It is obvious to any clinician that the two-*
> *parent system has its own pathology—the*

two parents may be in serious conflict as to how their parental roles should be performed; one parent may be competent but have his (or her) efforts undermined by the incompetent partner; the children may be caught in a "double bind" or crossfire between the two parents; both parents may be competent but simply unable to work together as an effective team in rearing their children; one parent may be more competent than the other but be inhibited in using this competence by the team pattern inherent in the two-parent system.

LeMasters suggests that there are problems inherent in the two-parent family system that will be absent in a one-parent family. For these and many other reasons, then, divorce, with or without remarriage, may then be viewed positively as a logical and sometimes necessary way to resolve family difficulties in a complex culture. If divorce has greater beneficial consequences to children as well as to parents than does continuing an unhappy family, then it may be functional to socialize both male and female children into a self-sufficiency which allows disruptions and changes in marital status to occur without demoralization or dependency, as is done in Black families.

Some time ago, J. Bernard suggested the startling idea that perhaps an intact home is not the norm for American families, as researchers had so long assumed. Many families exist (during some part of their life cycle) as a one-parent family. According to Bernard (1966:41), "Recently it [has] become clear that for a considerable proportion of the population, Negro or white, the female-headed family is a standard phenomenon—culturally acceptable, if not prescribed or preferred."

Many families will exist during some part of their life cycle as a one-parent family. They may be both one-parent and two-parent during the growing up years of the children.

An examination of the Census data confirms this. In 1974, over half the Black families with incomes under the poverty line were female-headed and more than one third (35%) of all Black families were female-headed (U.S. Bureau of Census, 1976). As Figure 1 shows, the number of Black female-

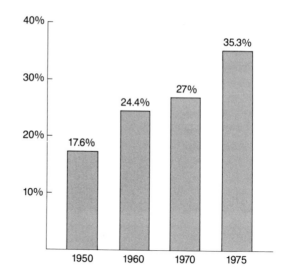

FIGURE 1 Percentage of Black Families Headed by a Woman (Source: U.S. Bureau of the Census, 1974; 1976)

headed families has been increasing rather rapidly over the past twenty years—the percentage, in fact, has doubled. . . .

Family Stability: A Matter of Definition

If the single parent family has historically been an adaptive life style within the Black subculture, one wonders why it has been widely viewed so negatively. Part of the problem is due, as J. Jackson (1973) has correctly observed, to the way social scientists measure family stability. Family stability is determined not from rating the quality of parent–child or family relationships, but from demographic data such as (1) proportion of female-headed households, coupled with data concerning (2) illegitimacy rates, (3) percentage of minor children residing with only one parent, and/or (4) separation and divorce rates. This is misleading. It is solving a social "problem" via teleology.

Sixty-five percent of single mothers require no welfare support. However, a working mother who is fully supporting her own child (and perhaps her own mother as well) but chose not to marry her children's father would be a statistic of instability because the family is female-headed, her child is illegitimate, and the child is residing with only one parent. Or, if she had married and divorced and is now working and self-sufficient (one third of divorced fathers make no payments and 80% are paying nothing by ten years later), she would be a statistic of instability because the family is female-headed, the child is residing with only one parent, and she is divorced. She becomes a statistic and placed into negative categories because of definitions used, although in fact the mother may be supporting and maintaining a "stable" home. As J. Jackson (1973) pointed out, the presence or absence of a male head is insufficient criterion for family stability.

In spite of the teleology involved, however, female-headed families continue to be viewed as unstable. There are several reasons for this. First, female-headed families are associated in the public mind with poverty (Jackson, 1973). Because women face discrimination in employment and in income when they are heads of families, they are often poorer.

As LeMasters (1970) points out, the one-parent family is more likely to be poor, Black, and over-represented on the public welfare rolls. This, perhaps, is to be expected in a society that has, through the years, discriminated against women and Blacks in the job world. Because solo-parent families are more likely than two-parent families to be poor, LeMasters (1970:168) suggests, does not demonstrate inadequacy. He maintains that poverty in single parent families "merely proves that our economic, political, and social welfare systems are not properly organized to provide adequate standard of living for the one-parent family."

However, in spite of discrimination against women and Blacks in the labor market, almost two thirds of single mothers are not on welfare (Helco et al., 1973). However, it is commonly assumed that female-headed families are dependent and on public assistance.

A second reason for instability to continue to be associated with the female-headed family, especially the Black female-headed family, is the associations which the term *matriarchy* brings to mind. Matriarchy connotes deviance in a society that val-ues traditional patriarchy or male dominance in the family. Female-headed families are almost by definition assumed to be pathological. So, in the "deviant" matriarchal family, sons are presumed to be inadequately socialized; they are expected to fall into juvenile delinquency. Daughters are presumed to perpetuate the cycle of intergenerational desertion of wives.

But this, too, is a myth. In Duncan and Duncan's (1969) national sample no relationship was found between the current marital status of the mother and the marital stability of her family of origin. Kriesberg's (1970) research reported a similar finding. Those low-income mothers who grew up in intact families were as likely to be separated or divorced as those who grew up in one-parent families. Most of the solo mothers came from complete families. Duncan and Duncan also found that sons (Black or white) who grew up in female-headed families were no more likely to be separated or divorced than sons from intact homes.

Finally, there is the factor of visibility (Jackson, 1973). Most poor female-headed families live in metropolitan areas (62%) and are therefore more visible and more involved with society's institutions (courts, welfare agencies, school social workers). Most poor male-headed families, on the other hand, live in rural (non-metropolitan) areas (U.S. Bureau of the Census, 1969).

One-Parent Families Do Survive

At any one time most Black families are managing pretty well: they are intact; they are self-supporting. At the same time there are other Black families that are also managing to survive pretty well: most are self-supporting;[1] but many are not intact. Not only do we need to know more about the functionings of Black families, but we need to know about the Black single-parent family, a variant form of the Black family. We need to understand its durability, in spite of its association with poverty and neglect. We need to study its survival and coping practices, its emotional maintenance, the social control and patterns of enculturation of children.

It has been suggested here that Black females are socialized to expect to be employed throughout a lifetime. If they marry they typically maintain an egalitarian relationship with their husbands. They are able to adjust competently to separation and/or divorce. Most seem to be able to consider solo parenthood without guilt or a lifetime of welfare dependency.

In the section that follows, a study of Black solo mothers who are raising children in stable one-parent families will be reported. In this study Black female-headed families are viewed as a viable form of the Black family.

The Study

Eleven solo Black mothers who are heads of families participated in this study. The mothers lived in a medium-sized New England city. They represented a socio-economic status from working class to middle class, as determined by their income, education, occupation, and life-style—ranging from welfare recipient to professional worker. The women spanned a generation: from 25 to 56. All shared, however, the double disadvantaged status in our society of being not only husbandless but also Black.

The sample was obtained in two ways: the middle-class mothers were secured by contacting eligibles within the researchers' personal acquaintances. The working-class mothers were those whose children attended Get Set for School,[2] a half-day pre-school program sponsored by the city Board of Education.

The mothers were interviewed in their own homes by one of the two interviewers, both of whom were Black. The interviews were informal, but at the same time they were structured. (An interview schedule was followed.) The interviews were also lengthy, taking from two to four hours, with the interviewers taking notes.

Sometimes family members (usually children) were present or on the periphery during most of the interview. In one case the respondent's mother was present during the entire interview (which stimulated general family discussion).

A special effort was made at the beginning of the interview to explain that the purpose of the study is to discover how women who are heads of families manage their families and their lives. We attempted to demonstrate our interest in them as individuals and, in turn, elicit their interest in our study. We also explained that we were interested in the positives as well as the negatives of single parenthood status, that we wanted to know about the good things, the advantages and the pleasures of single parenthood (if there were some) and the disadvantages, problems, and/or annoyances of single parenthood (if there were some).

All the women seemed to enjoy the interviews. In fact, for some it seemed to be therapeutic. They welcomed the chance to pause and view their lives from a different perspective.

The question occurs as to whether or not an individual's own statement about his/her attitudes or his/her values can be accepted as veridical. However, as Robin Williams (1951:378) observed:

> *No student of human conduct can accept uncritically, as final evidence, people's testimony as to their own values. Yet, actions may deceive as well as words, and there seems no reason for always giving one precedence over the other.*

As Williams points out, direct observations of these mothers' interacting with their children may also be somewhat unreliable in terms of revealing the parents' true feelings.

Findings

As this is an exploratory study attempting to assess parental conceptions of their own situation, the findings will be reported in summary form.

Two types of women emerged from this sample:

1. An older, middle-class woman, working at a professional job and making an adequate salary to support herself and three or four children, and
2. A younger, working-class woman managing with the financial support of public assistance and through her own resourcefulness (and support of family and friends) a family of three or four children.

Two types of housing patterns emerged:

1. Own or rented house in a good Black or integrated neighborhood (women who have been single for over five years), and
2. Good-sized rented apartment in a transitional neighborhood (women who have been single for less than five years).

Reaction to Divorced Status

The typical reaction of the families of the women in this study to divorce was to give emotional support (especially in the situation where the mother's parents had originally exerted pressure for the couple to marry because the girl was pregnant). Other families were noncommital, expecting the mother to make her own decisions in this matter without family interference.

Typically the children accepted the marital breakup, if they were old enough to understand, because it was the resolution of an unhappy, difficult, and tense situation.

The community typically was unconcerned or disinterested in the marital status of the mother. Her relationships with her friends continued pretty much as before. The loneliness some divorcees have reported because their social world is made up of couples did not appear to be a problem for these mothers.

Social life for the younger mother was hampered only if she had baby-sitting problems. Moreover, the children (especially as they became older) typically not only did not object to their mother's going out; they encouraged it. However, the older women encountered the problem described by J. Jackson [1971]—no men.

The modal woman in this study indicated that she did not feel overwhelmed when she assumed single parenthood and solo head-of-household status. The women typically recalled that, as adults, they always felt autonomous, rather than dependent. They felt competent as workers and believed that they had adequate resources within themselves to manage alone. Some mothers took on a second regular job. Others used public assistance for a while, until, as one mother expressed it, "I could

get on my feet." Others picked up extra employment here and there.

Although most of the mothers felt independent and capable of raising a family, the unpleasant reality of having your children welfare recipients or the awesome responsibility of being dependent solely upon oneself was sometimes more than some mothers wanted. Half of them indicated that at times they felt resentful or drained, and would have preferred having someone share their responsibilities with them—especially when there were important decisions to be made. However, some of the women had families they could talk to at critical times.

Single parenthood is not an easy job. Some of the mothers indicated that they were adapting somewhat reluctantly to the stresses of solo head-of-family. Others were more satisfied with their solo status.

Problems Solo Mothers Faced and How They Solved Them

Money, however, was always a problem in these families. Nevertheless, the children were adequately clothed, housed, fed, and generally were well-cared for. As employed workers in the labor force, the mothers of young children had to make substitute child-care arrangements. These mothers typically did not use day care facilities, nor did they find community agencies in general very helpful (except for the financial support some of the mothers received through AFDC).

Concerning child-care arrangements, most mothers stayed home while they had a young baby at home or had two or more pre-schoolers at home. If and when they returned to work, they used their own mothers, other relatives, or neighbors to baby-sit until their youngest children were of school age. By then, older children were expected to supervise their younger siblings. Emergencies were taken care of as they came along, knowing family and friends were available as a last resort.

In general, any problems the mothers had with the school authorities developed out of racial discrimination or prejudice, rather than over the issue of the absent father. The school personnel seemed comfortable dealing with mothers if a child presented a problem.

For the occasional mother whose child came in contact with the police, however, it was a different situation. Mothers would note a change in a policeman's treatment of a boy once he learned there was no father present in the home. Not only did the police become more harsh, but the mothers felt a "what-else-can-you-expect-from-a-boy-with-no-father" attitude. All the mothers, except one, reported that there were important male figures in the lives of these children, although they lived in a fatherless household. Sometimes it was the child's own father. Other important male figures reported were the child's uncle, cousin, or other male relatives, or the mother's boyfriend. Most of the children saw other people (grandparents or aunts or uncles or mother's boyfriend) in addition to their mother as an authority figure.

In the area of discipline, some mothers responded that one or more children were problems; more of the mothers reported no special discipline problems (beyond the youngest child being spoiled). Typically, the mothers reported that misbehavior is punished immediately by spanking. As children get older mothers do more talking, punishing by denial or restriction. Some mothers also emphasized the importance of verbalization about an offense and made a special point of explaining to a child why punishment was necessary.

Credit was a problem only during the time a mother was receiving public assistance and, according to these mothers, the credit problems they had were due to the fact of their welfare status, not their sex. These employed women had no trouble getting credit, nor did their single parenthood status affect their ability to obtain decent housing. Here, the problem was the number of children in the family. Landlords did not welcome "large" families with more than two children.

Single-Parent Families versus Two-Parent Families

When the mothers were asked about the advantages in their present situation compared to life with a husband (if they had been previously married) or the life of their married friends, all but one felt that there are actually a number of advantages. Most mothers said that their children were more independent and responsible. Most were happy that now the children no longer see their parents in constant conflict. (One mother observed that now the children don't see the father drunk.)

Some also expressed the strong feeling that their family now was closer, worked as a cooperative unit, and that family life was more flexible and more reflective of what the mother or the children want to do.

Each mother was asked about her plans for the future. Would she work? Would she marry? Mothers still home with pre-schoolers expected to take a job as soon as possible. Mothers in the labor force expected to continue to work. When asked if she expected to marry most mothers said no, although four answered with a tentative maybe. Only one responded yes.

Response to Questionnaire

A questionnaire was administered to the mothers at the end of the interview which contained seven questions about the children's response to father absence. Answers were varied and individualistic. About half the children were described as missing their father; half as not. Some children were too young to know their father. Similarly, when asked if they thought father absence affected their children's development, here again answers were diverse—some "not at all," some "very much," some "somewhat."

These mothers considered their sons to be somewhat more aggressive than their peers. They also felt that their sons were higher academic achievers and more mature than their age mates. Most daughters were also viewed as more aggressive than their peers.

It is of interest to note that when asked how the behavior problems they had with their children compared to the behavior problems they noticed in children in intact families, these mothers either felt that they had more behavior problems or that they had fewer behavior problems than other families.

Only one mother indicated that she thought her children were just about like other children in this respect.

Summary

In this study Black female-headed families were viewed as a viable form of the Black family, a flexible pattern of functioning that has developed within the Black community where there is (1) expectation of egalitarian relationships between competent females and males and (2) where there is a preponderance of females over males of marriageable age.

The life styles of eleven solo Black parents who are heads of families were examined. These parents were seen, in general, to be coping competently with their individual circumstances.

This study of solo Black mothers was exploratory. There needs to be continued research on the divorced, widowed, or single Black working-class and middle-class mother in order to find how they cope with the exigencies of single parenthood and head-of-family status. This would provide information which may be of use to other American female-headed families, which are becoming increasingly prevalent in American society. It could, perhaps, inform how communities can more effectively be supportive of single parents who are neither pathological nor dependent.

[1] *According to the Bureau of Census, 1971, 75% of Black and other races are self-supporting. Only 25% of all persons of Negro and other races received public assistance or welfare income.*

[2] *This is a pseudonym.*

References

Bell, Robert
1971 *Marriage and Family Interaction,* 3d ed. Homewood, Ill.: Dorsey Press.

Bernard, Jessie
1966 *Marriage and Family among Negroes.* Englewood Cliffs, N.J.: Prentice-Hall.

Brandwein, Ruth, Carol Brown, and Elizabeth Fox
1974 "Women and Children Last: The Social Situation of Divorced Mothers and Their Families." *Journal of Marriage and the Family* (August): 498–515.

Duncan, Beverly, and Otis Dudley Duncan
1969 "Family Stability and Occupational Success." *Social Problems* 16:273–285.

Helco, Hugh, Lee Rainwater, Martin Reiss, and Robert Weiss
1973 "Single-Parent Families: Issues and Policies." O.C.D. Working Paper. Washington, D.C.

Herzog, Elizabeth, and Celia Sudia
1968 "Fatherless Homes: A Review of Research." *Children* (Sept.–Oct.):177–182.

Hyman, Herbert, and John Reed
1969 "Black Matriarchy Reconsidered: Evidence from Secondary Analysis of Sample Surveys." *Public Opinion Quarterly* 33 (Fall):346–354.

Jackson, Jacquelyne J.
1971 "But Where Are the Men?" *The Black Scholar* 3 (4, December):30–41.

1973 "Black Women in a Racist Society." In Charles Willie, Bernard Kramer, and Bertram Brown, eds., *Racism and Mental Health.* Pittsburgh, Pa.: University of Pittsburgh Press.

Kriesberg, Louis
1970 *Mothers in Poverty.* Chicago: Aldine.

LeMasters, E. E.
1970 "Parents without Partners." In *Parents in Modern America,* pp. 157–174. Homewood, Ill.: Dorsey.

Mack, Delores W.
1971 "Where the Black Matriarchy Theorists Went Wrong." *Psychology Today* 4:24ff.

Moynihan, Daniel P.
1965 *The Negro Family: The Case for National Action.* Washington, D.C.: U.S. Department of Labor, Office of Policy, Planning and Research.

Nye, Ivan F., and Lois Hoffman

1963 *Employed Mothers in America.* Chicago: Rand McNally.

Peters, Marie F.

1974 "The Black Family—Perpetuating the Myths: An Analysis of Family Sociology Textbook Treatment of Black Families." *The Family Coordinator* (October):349–357.

Scanzoni, John

1971 *The Black Family in Modern Society.* Boston: Allyn and Bacon.

TenHouten, Warren

1970 "The Black Family: Myth and Reality." *American Journal of Sociology* (November):145–172.

U.S. Bureau of the Census

1970a PC (1)-C1. *Census of the Population's General Social and Economic Characteristics.* Washington, D.C.: U.S. Government Printing Office.

1970b "24 Million Americans: Poverty in the U.S. 1969." Washington, D.C.: U.S. Government Printing Office.

1971 *Negro Population, 1970.* Washington, D.C.: U.S. Government Printing Office.

1972 *The Social and Economic Status of the Black Population in the U.S., 1971.* Washington, D.C.: U.S. Government Printing Office.

1973 Series P–20, No. 258. *Household and Family Characteristics.* Washington, D.C.: U.S. Government Printing Office.

1974 *The Social and Economic Status of the Black Population in the U.S., 1973.* Washington, D.C.: U.S. Government Printing Office.

1976 *The Social and Economic Status of the Black Population in the U.S., 1975.* Washington, D.C.: U.S. Government Printing Office.

Williams, Robin

1951 *American Society.* New York: Alfred Knopf.

Yancey, William L.

1972 "Going Down Home: Family Structure and the Urban Trap." *Social Science Quarterly* 52 (4):893–906.

RACE, ETHNICITY, AND CHILD MALTREATMENT:
An Analysis of Cases Recognized and Reported by Hospitals

Robert L. Hampton

Using the National Study of the Incidence and Severity of Child Abuse and Neglect, the most comprehensive and reliable information available on this problem, it was discovered that Black children were more likely to be reported to child protection agencies as alleged victims of maltreatment than white children. Those data suggested that Black

families may be victimized by a process in which their personal characteristics rather than their alleged behavior define them as deviant.

Violence toward children has existed throughout recorded history. In the view of many historians and social theorists, it is deeply embedded in the social

Unpublished paper, 1985. Printed by permission. This research was supported by a grant from the National Center on Child Abuse and Neglect (90CA891), Department of Health and Human Services, Washington, D.C. The author served as a Rockefeller Foundation Postdoctoral Fellow during the period in which this research was conducted.

institutions and legal structures of industrialized societies. To combat this phenomenon, the child welfare movement was established in the United States during the middle and late nineteenth century, and societies for the prevention of child abuse have continued to operate in this country since that time.

Hospitals and families share a concern for the well-being of children, but there is little research that specifically addresses the interaction between hospitals and families with respect to child maltreatment. This paper addresses the role of hospitals as gatekeepers in reporting child maltreatment and examines the ethnic differences among reported cases.

Prevalence

The true prevalence of child abuse is unknown, although nationally reported cases of child abuse have increased 142 percent since 1976. In that year, 416,033 child maltreatment cases were reported to the child protective services (CPS) system. The number of reported cases has increased annually to a total of 1,007,658 in 1983, the latest year for which data are currently available. This increase can be attributed to a number of factors, but we must remember that it is impossible to determine to what extent the increase in reporting is directly associated with an increase in the number of maltreated children. Individual states continue to modify reporting legislation to encompass new reportable conditions, such as emotional maltreatment (American Humane Association, 1983). It is likely that the increase in reporting is due to increased public awareness and to improved accountability on the part of state reporting systems.

Official statistics on child abuse (and other forms of family violence) do not show the full extent of child maltreatment in families. For this reason, research has been conducted to obtain better estimates of the prevalence of child abuse. The National Study of the Incidence and Severity of Child Abuse and Neglect (1981) [abbreviated National Incidence Study] was designed from a conceptual model based on the iceberg metaphor: Although substantial numbers of abused and neglected children are recognized as such and are reported to protective services, the reported cases may represent only the tip of the iceberg.

The model assumes that additional children are known to other investigatory agencies such as police and public health departments, courts, and corrections agencies, and to professionals in other major community institutions: schools, hospitals, and social service and mental health agencies. Even a clear-cut case of child maltreatment may go unreported and consequently may never be included in the official record.

. . . .

Factors Associated with Family Violence

Child maltreatment and family violence may be considered most accurately as indicators of families in trouble. Many factors can place a family in jeopardy and lead to family violence, and this multiplicity of causes complicates the task of understanding the origins of family violence. To understand the etiology, one must take into account circumstances that might make a child, parent, or family more susceptible to the particular stresses associated with family violence.

In both empirical studies and reviews of literature, several factors are consistently related to the origins of family violence. Research and clinical findings indicate that parents who use violence against their children were frequently subjected to violence as children (Newberger et al., 1977; Straus et al., 1980). . . . Straus, Gelles, and Steinmetz (1980) not only found support for the hypothesis that "violence begets violence" but also provided data demonstrating that the greater the frequency of violence, the greater the chance that the victim will grow up to be a violent partner or parent. Even so, we must exercise caution in drawing deterministic conclusions from the often-reported association between violence experienced as a child and the subsequent use of violence. Many individuals who experienced violence in their childhoods are not violent adults.

. . . .

Discussions of social class differences in family violence alert us to many issues related to the family life experiences associated with social position. Households where the husband was unemployed or underemployed had the highest rates of violence between spouses and violence by parents toward a child (Straus et al., 1980). Unemployed men were twice as likely to use severe violence on their wives as were men employed full time. Among men employed part time, the rate of wife beating was three times the rate for men employed full time. The rate of child abuse among fathers employed part time was nearly twice as high as the rate for fathers employed full time. These findings raise the important issues of family resources acquired through fathers' full-time employment and time at risk. . . .

Another issue is the stress on families associated with lack of employment. A number of researchers have indicated the importance of stress for understanding family violence (Newberger et al., 1977; Straus, 1979). It has been suggested that overzealous physical punishment of children by parents may result as much from the various stresses experienced by the child's parents as from the actual desire or need to control the child's behavior. . . .

Race and Child Maltreatment

Examinations of the relation between family violence and race have yielded mixed results. In the first large-scale summary of national reports, Gil (1970) concluded that families reported for abuse were drawn disproportionately from the less educated, the poor, and ethnic minorities. Black children were overrepresented as victims of abuse. A more recent compilation of reports gave a similar picture: whites were underrepresented in reported cases of maltreatment, and lower-income families, in general, were overrepresented (Jason et al., 1982).

. . . .

Newberger and his colleagues (1977) believe that children from poor and minority families are more vulnerable to being labeled as abused than

are children from more affluent households; the latter are more likely to be classified as victims of accidents. Support for this proposition, particularly with respect to abuse cases seen in medical settings, comes from several sources. In research conducted among physicians, Gelles (1982) reported that when the physicians made a report of child abuse, they considered not only the child's physical condition but also the caretaker's occupation, education, race, and ethnicity. Five percent of a group of physicians surveyed ($N = 157$) stated that the caretaker's race and ethnicity were so important that they would file a child abuse report on the basis of those characteristics alone (Gelles, 1982).

Using a case vignette model, Turbett and O'Toole (1980) found that recognition of child abuse by physicians was affected by severity of injury and by the parents' socioeconomic status and ethnicity. When children were described as having a major injury, Black children were nearly twice as likely as white children to be recognized as victims of abuse. Physicians were 33 percent more likely to report Black children suffering from a major injury than children identified as white who were described in identical vignettes. Children described as lower-class whites suffering from major injuries were more likely to be classified as abused than white children with the same injury who were presented as members of an upper-class group (Turbett and O'Toole, 1980).

Data from the national survey of family violence (Straus et al., 1980) indicated little difference between Black and white families in the rates of abusive violence toward children (15 percent in Black families, 14 percent in white families). In a more detailed examination of the national survey data, Cazenave and Straus (1979) concluded that the aid and support, especially child care, provided by Black extended family kin seemed to reduce the risk of abusive violence toward children. These data included only two-parent families; consequently, we advise some caution in interpretation.

In the most complete attitudinal research to date on the topic of ethnicity and violence, Giovannoni and Becerra (1979) explored how the various ethnic and professional groups within the large city define child maltreatment. They presented a series of case vignettes that described specific incidents of child maltreatment, representing a range of behaviors that might be considered maltreatment and that varied in degree of severity. Respondents included professionals and lay people in the metropolitan Los Angeles area.

The respondents were asked to rate each vignette according to the seriousness of its impact on the welfare of the child. The sample population comprised 12 percent Blacks, 17 percent Hispanics, 65 percent white (Anglo), and 6 percent other.

The study sought to test the idea that ethnic minorities and people of lower socioeconomic status are "more tolerant of mistreatment and likely to have a higher threshold for considering actions as mistreatment" (Giovannoni and Becerra, 1979). The results, however, showed just the opposite: In 94 percent of the cases, Blacks and Hispanics were found to give more serious ratings to the vignettes than did the Anglos. Contrary to the authors' expectations, it was found that education and income (the prime indicators of socioeconomic status) were related inversely to ratings of seriousness. That is, the higher the education and income level of the respondent, the lower the seriousness rating. Ethnic differences among respondents were not merely a product of social class differences; ethnic differences persisted even within educational levels. Blacks across all educational levels rated categories of neglect as more serious than did others. The results of analysis by income show similar, though less consistent, trends.

This research suggests that poor and nonwhite families may not share similar attitudes toward maltreatment with white and more affluent families. Nonwhites and people of lower socioeconomic status tended to evaluate the vignettes as more serious (Giovannoni and Becerra, 1979).

The Framework

Several theoretical frameworks and propositions have been developed from the study of violence and aggression, and these are applicable to the issue of family violence. Gelles and Straus (1979) surveyed fifteen theories ranging from intrapsychic to macrosociological. Many of these approaches are simplistic, unicausal models that fail to articulate the complex, multidimensional process described in some of the earlier works on family violence (Gil, 1970).

To understand violence toward children within a family requires a perspective that takes into account multiple factors interacting within the family system. The ecological model of human development is particularly useful because it not only helps avoid the analytic limitations imposed by unitary theories, but also provides insights into the dynamics of child maltreatment (Garbarino, 1977, 1982a; Bronfenbrenner, 1979).

In its most general form, ecological analysis focuses on the activities of organisms in an environment. This approach locates the child in the setting of the family and explores ways in which the family is connected to other concrete settings and to more general social forces in the social environment (Bowles, 1983). It calls for the separate conceptualization of the environment or context, the characteristics of each actor, and the interaction of actors with each other and with the environment.

Anyone who is concerned with the causes of child maltreatment must be aware of the notion that agents outside the victim–perpetrator dyad have a significant, even controlling effect on the dynamics of maltreatment (Garbarino, 1977; Justice and Justice, 1976). The analysis of child maltreatment involves both the examination of factors within the family microsystem and the identification of other settings in which family members participate individually or collectively. Each setting can be described and analyzed in terms of activities in which people engage, relationships between people, and social roles that organize the activities of different participants and the relationships between participants (Bowles, 1983).

Social institutions such as schools, churches, and medical care facilities are important elements in the family's social environment. To date, little research has examined the connections among these systems with respect to child maltreatment. Gelles (1975) suggested that social agencies are major gatekeepers in the process of labeling and defining a child as abused and a caretaker as abusive. Therefore we must examine the gatekeepers who initially attach the label of abuser to a caretaker, pass this individual through the gate, and reinforce the label (Gelles, 1975).

Methodology

Data for this analysis were taken from the National Incidence Study mentioned earlier, the most comprehensive and reliable information available on the incidence and severity of child abuse and neglect. This study was conducted in a stratified random sample of twenty-six counties clustered within ten states. Each sample county had a known probability of selection, which provided the basis for computing national estimates. Data were collected on case reports received between May 1, 1979, and April 30, 1980. We reanalyzed data from that study with a specific focus on child maltreatment cases seen in hospitals.

Seventy of the ninety-two eligible hospitals (75 percent) participated in the study (National Incidence Study, 1981: Methodology). From these hospitals 805 cases of child abuse and neglect were brought to the attention of the study. Using an elaborate weighting system to extrapolate from study cases, the study investigators estimated that for the country as a whole, hospital personnel suspected a total of 77,380 cases of abuse and neglect. . . .

For the purpose of this study a child-abuse situation was defined as follows:

> *one where, through purposive acts or marked inattention to a child's basic needs, behavior of a parent/substitute or other adult caretaker caused forseeable and avoidable injury or impairment to a child, or materially contributed to unreasonable prolongation or worsening of an existing injury or impairment. (National Incidence Study, 1981:4)*

. . . Any particular child may have been reported to CPS more than once during the study year and/or may have been described to the study by any number or combination of sources. Enough identifying data were collected, however, to allow us to determine reliably whether or not any two data forms were describing the same child. Duplicate records were purged from the analysis file so that the case was counted only once. Whenever a particular child was identified to the study by a hospital, or whenever another non-CPS source also appeared in the CPS file, the CPS record was retained. In effect, non-CPS sources were given credit only for children who had not also been reported to CPS.

Results

Previous analyses have shown that in comparison to other agencies in the National Incidence Study, the hospital sample included children who were younger, who had younger mothers, who were more urban (65.8 percent versus 42.1 percent), and who were Black (25 percent versus 16 percent). There were no major differences among hospitals and other agencies with respect to income, mode of medical payment (public or private), proportion of single parents, or sex of child (Hampton and Newberger, 1985). Table 1 provides a summary of the hospital sample characteristics.

Some important differences existed among samples with respect to the type and severity of recognized maltreatment cases. Hospitals identified many more cases of physical abuse than did other agencies. The proportion of cases in this category alone exceeded the proportion of physical, sexual, and emotional abuse cases recognized by all other agencies; over half the hospital cases belonged to one or another category of abuse. Among hospital cases, the rated severity of injury also tended to be more serious. Twenty-four percent of the hospital cases were rated as serious compared to 13 percent for the rest of the sample (Hampton and Newberger, 1985).

Table 1 reflects maltreatment cases reported to the study either by CPS or directly by hospitals. Because we are concerned with the recognition and reporting process, we must examine carefully this latter set of cases.

As Table 2 shows, Black and Hispanic children were more likely than white children to be reported to child protection agencies as alleged victims of maltreatment. Children from higher-income families were also less likely to be reported.

Younger children were more than three times as likely as adolescents to be reported officially. Single-parent households and families receiving public assistance were also more likely to be reported.

TABLE 1 Total Sample Characteristics

CHARACTERISTIC	PERCENT[1]	CHARACTERISTIC	PERCENT[1]
Age of child (in years)		Receiving AFDC	
0–5	54.9	Yes	32.2
6–12	28.9	No	67.8
13–17	16.2	Type of maltreatment	
Sex of child		Physical abuse	35.2
Male	52.3	Sexual abuse	9.3
Female	47.7	Emotional injury	19.4
Mother's education[2]		Physical neglect	26.6
0–8 years	12.2	Miscellaneous	9.5
Some high school	44.4	Severity of maltreatment	
High school graduate plus	43.4	Serious	33.4
Mother's age (in years)		Moderate	36.0
Less than 19	10.8	Probable	30.6
20–24	21.5	Number of children	
25–29	15.9	1	35.3
30–34	18.3	2	22.2
Over 35	14.1	3	15.6
Don't know	19.4	4	7.9
Race		5 or more	19.0
White	66.7	City size	
Black	25.6	SMSA over 200,000	65.8
Hispanic	7.6	Other SMSA	18.4
Father present		Non-SMSA	15.8
Yes	54.2	Official report filed	
No	45.8	Yes	66.4
Family income[2]		No	33.6
Less than $7000	49.3	Weighted N = 77,380	
$7,000–14,999	36.6	Unweighted N = 805	
$15,000–24,999	9.3		
$25,000 or more	4.9		

[1]All percentages reflect weightings and may not add up to 100 percent because of rounding.

[2]Variable excludes missing data.

Physical abuse cases were more likely to be reported than unreported but cases of emotional abuse and neglect tended to be underreported. The latter finding is consistent with our expectation that when concrete evidence of injury is absent in cases of emotional maltreatment, professionals tend not to report.

Surprisingly, although hospitals identified more serious cases of child abuse and neglect than other agencies, serious injuries were often unreported.

Multivariate analyses (Table 3) yield a more detailed understanding of the differences between reported and unreported cases. A stepwise discriminant function procedure was used to select variables for inclusion. The variables in Table 3 appear in order of their selection. In our analysis, the following factors appeared to affect case reporting most powerfully: income, the role of the mother in maltreatment, race, emotional injury, sex of child, sexual abuse, and mother's education. Disproportionate numbers of unreported cases were victims

TABLE 2 Child Maltreatment Cases Seen in Hospitals by CPS Reporting (Hospital Survey) [1]

VARIABLE	REPORTED	NOT REPORTED	TOTAL PERCENT
Sex of child			
Male	41.7	58.3	52.3
Female	44.1	55.9	47.3
Age of child (in years)			
0–5	51.9	48.1	54.8
6–12	45.8	54.2	26.8
13–17	14.2	85.8	18.5
Race			
White	36.5	63.5	70.5
Black	48.3	51.7	21.7
Hispanic	85.5	14.5	7.8
Mother's education			
0–8 years	44.4	55.6	11.0
Some high school	57.7	42.3	37.2
High school graduate	58.8	42.0	51.8
Father present			
Yes	39.6	60.4	51.4
No	46.6	53.4	48.6
Family income			
$7,000 or less	56.1	43.9	47.9
$7,000–14,999	62.9	37.1	37.9
$15,000–24,999	36.8	63.3	8.2
$25,000 or more	3.3	96.7	6.0
Receiving AFDC			
Yes	53.5	46.5	28.4
No	46.5	53.5	

[1]Percentages may not add to 100 percent because of rounding. All percentages reflect case weights. Table reflects cases reported to study by sampled hospitals only and excludes cases reported to study by CPS only.

of emotional abuse in white families of higher income, whose mothers were alleged to be responsible for the injuries.

These data raise a number of important questions regarding the type of cases seen by hospitals and those selected for reporting. It suggests that socially marginal families may be victimized by a process in which their personal characteristics rather than their alleged behavior define them as deviant (Turbett and O'Toole, 1980). This discrimination not only subjects ethnic minority and lower socioeconomic status families to the stigma of being labeled as abusive, but may also subject them to interventions that may be both intrusive and puni-

tive. The same process discriminates in favor of white and high socioeconomic status families. (A latent consequence of this biased reporting may be a failure to address the needs of the many middle-class families who, surveys suggest, are at risk for child maltreatment.)

Another central question raised by this analysis concerns differences among the various ethnic groups in the hospital sample. Do they differ in their use of medical facilities? Do they differ in patterns of alleged maltreatment? To what extent might the medical encounter be different for members of different groups?

Table 4 provides an ethnic breakdown of the

TABLE 2 continued

VARIABLE	REPORTED	NOT REPORTED	TOTAL PERCENT
Type of maltreatment			
Physical abuse	52.2	47.8	30.9
Sexual abuse	45.8	54.2	5.7
Emotional injury	28.3	71.7	27.3
Physical neglect	42.7	57.3	26.8
Miscellaneous	59.8	45.2	5.2
Severity of maltreatment			
Serious	28.9	71.1	35.8
Moderate	33.5	66.5	39.5
Probable	45.9	54.1	29.6
Mother's role in maltreatment			
Maltreater	33.0	67.0	64.9
Not involved	70.4	29.6	26.6
Don't know	39.1	65.9	8.5
Number of children			
1	51.7	48.3	29.5
2	47.3	53.7	21.9
3	52.3	47.7	14.1
4	43.1	36.9	7.1
5 or more	25.4	74.6	27.4
City size			
SMSA over 200,000	46.0	54.0	66.2
Other SMSA	41.1	58.9	16.0
Non-SMSA	33.4	66.6	17.8
Total	93.0	57.0	100.00

Weighted N = 45,276
Unweighted N = 415

TABLE 3 Stepwise Discriminant Analysis Results for Hospital Reporting

VARIABLE	STANDARDIZED COEFFICIENT	VARIABLE	STANDARDIZED COEFFICIENT
Race	.507	Father in household	.264
Mother's role	.577	Number of children	.250
Income	.586	City size	.198
Mother's education	.294	Canonical R	.691
Sex of child	.372	Wilkes' lambda	.589
Emotional injury	.354	Percentage of cases	
Sexual abuse	.238	correctly classified	65%

sample. The groups show several differences in child and family characteristics, as well as in the type of alleged maltreatment. Black and Hispanic children were younger, had younger mothers, and were more likely to live in urban areas. Whereas 86 percent of the entire sample had incomes below $15,000, 93 percent of the Black and 76 percent of the Hispanic families had incomes below this level. Almost half the Black families were receiving Medicaid and AFDC assistance. Seventy-one percent of the Black households were female-headed.

When we look at differences among the groups with respect to type of maltreatment, we see that almost half the Hispanic children were alleged

TABLE 4   Ethnicity by Selected Household and Family Characteristics: National Incidence Study Hospital Sample[1]

VARIABLE	WHITE	BLACK	HISPANIC	TOTAL[3]
Age of child				
0–5	54.3	53.6	64.4	54.9
6–12	25.9	36.1	30.4	28.9
13–17	19.7	10.3	5.2	16.2
Sex of child				
Male	52.6	51.6	51.0	51.6
Female	47.4	48.4	49.0	48.3
Number of children in household				
1	36.0	34.7	31.2	35.3
2	24.3	16.7	21.6	22.2
3	14.3	14.8	29.9	15.6
4	7.8	9.7	2.7	7.9
5 or more	17.6	24.1	14.6	19.0
Age of mother				
Less than 20	10.6	9.5	16.7	10.8
20–24	16.5	33.6	24.3	21.5
25–29	16.3	13.7	19.1	15.9
30–34	19.3	13.2	26.9	18.3
35 and older	14.2	16.5	5.1	14.1
Don't know	23.1	13.5	7.9	15.4
Mother's education[2]				
0–8 years	10.5	9.8	29.5	12.2
9–11 years	39.8	58.6	35.9	44.4
High school graduates	49.7	31.7	34.6	43.4
Role of mother in maltreatment				
Perpetrator	49.9	47.2	63.2	50.2
Not involved	42.2	42.5	27.2	42.5
Don't know	7.9	5.3	9.5	7.3
Family income[2]				
Less than $7,000	42.9	62.8	30.8	49.3
$7,000–$14,999	38.1	30.2	46.6	36.6
$15,000–$24,999	12.7	3.6	2.6	9.3
$25,000 or more	6.3	3.3	0	4.9

[1]Percentages may not add to 100 because of rounding.
[2]Cases of unspecified ethnicity are excluded.
[3]Missing data excluded.

victims of physical neglect. The other largest category for Hispanics was miscellaneous maltreatment (21 percent), which included involuntary neglect due to caretaker hospitalization, financial problems, or other unspecified neglect.

Black maltreatment cases were primarily physical abuse (40.6 percent) and physical neglect (31.4 percent). Emotional injury was alleged only infrequently (10.8 percent).

Discussion

The ecological perspective suggests that one might approach the issue of child maltreatment and the

VARIABLE	WHITE	BLACK	HISPANIC	TOTAL[3]
TABLE 4 continued				
AFDC				
Yes	23.1	58.5	20.5	32.2
No	76.9	41.5	79.5	67.8
Medicaid				
Yes	22.1	57.4	4.2	29.5
No	77.9	41.6	95.8	70.5
Father in household				
Yes	62.9	28.4	65.0	54.1
No	37.1	71.6	35.0	45.9
Type of maltreatment				
Physical abuse	35.9	40.6	10.0	35.2
Sexual abuse	8.6	11.1	10.0	9.4
Emotional injury	23.8	10.8	9.7	10.4
Physical neglect	22.1	31.4	49.2	26.6
Miscellaneous	9.0	6.1	21.0	9.2
Severity of child's injury/impairment				
Serious	30.7	40.1	37.5	33.4
Moderate	40.8	27.7	17.6	36.0
Probable	28.5	32.2	44.9	30.6
Urbanicity				
SMSA over 2,000,000	60.3	73.4	88.4	65.8
Other SMSA	25.0	10.6	4.7	18.7
Non-SMSA	16.8	16.0	6.9	15.5
Substantiated (percent of reported)				
Yes	34.7	57.6	69.7	57.1
No	49.3	42.4	30.3	42.9

N = 75,274 (weighted)
N = 777 (unweighted)

reporting process by observing factors on different levels of analysis. One could ask which factors among those that directly affect the lives of families increase the risk for maltreatment. Such factors as mundane extreme environmental stress (Peters and Massey, 1983) may be regarded as a macrosystem variable. This factor, combined with the racist or sexist values that demean some minority parents and thus raise the level of stress for their children (Garbarino, 1982a, 1982b), places many children and families at risk. It provides a context of endemic stress (Belle, 1982; Fried, 1982) within which the family members must conduct their daily lives.

Similarly, any analysis of maltreatment in families must acknowledge factors at the institutional level that affect families. Factors that differentially affect the Black family include high unemployment rates, lower incomes, and an overall poverty rate that continues to be about three times as high for Black families as for all families (Glick, 1981; McAdoo, 1982; Pearce and McAdoo, 1981). These factors not only have a direct impact on the quality of family life for Black families, but also appear to have an indirect effect through such factors as marital disruption (Hampton, 1979, 1980), adolescent pregnancies, and mental health problems (Frerichs, Aneshensel, and Clark, 1981). It has been argued that child maltreatment in black families may be a secondary effect of societal violence against Black families (Daniel et al., 1983).

Although macrolevel variables obviously affect child maltreatment in families, the interaction between the family and other agencies is also important. No objective behavior is automatically recognized as child abuse (Gelles, 1975); the agencies that are confronted with suspected cases of maltreatment serve as gates and gatekeepers, which either admit selected cases as abuse or identify them as not being abuse and turn them away. The social process of defining abuse has important political and social implications both for the recipients of the label and for sevice providers.

Medical personnel have a legal mandate to report suspected cases of child maltreatment. All fifty states have enacted legislation that mandates reporting and defines not only the procedure for reporting but also the consequences for failing to report. . . . Nonetheless, reporting is inhibited by a variety of factors, including lack of clarity in defining child maltreatment, the reluctance to intervene in family privacy, and the time and emotional involvement associated with these cases (Newberger et al., 1977; Pfohl, 1977). . . . Our data indicate clearly that even in the presence of these laws, criteria for reporting are applied differentially, often along ethnic and social class lines.

The marginal economic position of many Black families cannot be overstated. Many U.S. Black families do not participate fully in the mainstream health care system and may prefer to use the emergency room as a source of care on an episodic basis. The emergency room is a significant element in the family's social environment not only because it can provide services to relieve acute suffering, but also because emergency services permit nonscheduled visits, often require shorter waiting times than outpatient departments, and are generally accessible by public transportation. These features approximate most closely the conveniences that private care offers to people who can afford it.

The medical encounter represents the interaction between two social systems, whether medical care is provided in the emergency room or in other clinics. This encounter is much more than the interaction between a clinician's expertise and a child's medical condition; most clinicians are majority group members, and the Black family often presents the white physician with socioeconomic differences as well as differences in racial experience (Daniel, 1985; Levy, 1985).

Ethnic families bring to the medical encounter general styles of interaction, attitudes toward authority figures, sex role allocations, and ways of expressing emotion and asking for help that may differ from those of the middle class. These sociocultural factors influence people's interaction in the medical encounter. It has been suggested that culturally based patterns of interaction between Blacks and whites may actually intrude in doctor–patient interactions involving members of those two racial groups (Daniel, 1985; Franklin, 1985; Jackson, 1981; Levy, 1985). Where cultural differences exist, they may affect both the process and the product of the medical encounter.

This encounter typically takes place among strangers who are unequal in ascribed and achieved status. Social distance is inherent in this relationship; the medical provider is always in a superordinate position because the family seeks his or her expertise with respect to the diagnosis and treatment of the child's symptoms. We have learned from labeling theory that the greater the social distance between the typer and the person singled out for typing, the broader the type and the more quickly it may be applied. In particular, the label of child maltreater is less likely to be applied if the diagnostician (gatekeeper) and the possible abuser share similar characteristics, especially socioeconomic status. This is particularly important when the child's injury is not serious or manifestly a consequence of maltreatment.

The assessment of alleged child maltreatment typically involves more than the evaluation of a child's physical symptoms. It implies an evaluation of the family's care-giving potential and behavior that might be related to the child's current symptoms. Although the family and the clinician are allied in a common concern for the child, the alliance is frequently broken by the clinician's responsibility to interrogate the family to determine to what extent their behavior may have caused the child's suffering.

Many of the Black families in our sample are poor, receive public assistance (58 percent), are young (43.1 percent under 25), and are single-parent households (71.6 percent). This combination of factors often leads to the confounding of two sets of variables: those that could make certain people likely to be labeled child abusers and those that previous research has suggested are causal factors in the act(s) of child abuse.

The medical encounter is frequently problematic in its own right and issues of race and ethnicity further complicate these matters. In light of the structured inequality that pervades the lives of Black families, including many factors that contribute to high-risk parenting, being labeled as an abuser holds both symbolic and real implications for child and family. For many families, the label of perpetrator extends beyond the parent–child dyad and can be traced to the larger social structure, which denies many families an opportunity to achieve a reasonable quality of life. Medical professionals frequently contribute to a negative cycle by overintrusion in the guise of help (Newberger, 1985). These practices not only blame the victim for his or her life circumstances but also visit additional cruelty and violence on the Black family and its children.

References

American Humane Association

1983 *Highlights of Official Child Neglect and Abuse Reporting, Annual Report.* Denver: Author.

Belle, Deborah

1982 *Lives in Stress.* Beverly Hills, Calif.: Sage Publications.

Bowles, R. T.

1983 "Family Well-Being, Family Violence and Rapid Community Growth: An Ecological Perspective." In *Proceedings of the Alaska Symposium on the Social, Economic and Cultural Impacts of Natural Resource Development,* S. Yarie, ed., 146–151. Fairbanks: University of Alaska.

Bronfenbrenner, U.

1979 *The Ecology of Human Development: Experiments by Nature and Design.* Cambridge, Mass.: Harvard University Press.

Cazenave, N., and M. A. Straus

1979 "Race, Class, Network Embeddedness and Family Violence: A Search for Potent Support Systems." *Journal of Comparative Family Studies* 10:281–300.

Daniel, J. H.

1985 "Cultural and Ethnic Issues: The Black Family." In *Unhappy Families,* E. H. Newberger and R. Bourne, eds., pp. 195–254. Littleton, Mass.: PSG Publishers.

Daniel, J., R. L. Hampton, and E. H. Newberger

1983   "Child Abuse and Accidents in Black Families: A Controlled Comparative Study." *American Journal of Orthopsychiatry* 53 (4):649–653.

Franklin, D. L.

1985   "Differential Clinical Assessments: The Influence of Class and Race." *Social Service Review* (March):45–61.

Frerichs, R., C. Aneshensel, and V. Clark

1981   "Prevalence of Depression in Los Angeles County." *American Journal of Epidemiology* 11 (6):691–699.

Fried, M.

1982   "Endemic Stress: The Psychology of Resignation and the Politics of Scarcity." *American Journal of Orthopsychiatry* 52 (January):4–19.

Garbarino, J.

1977   "The Human Ecology of Child Maltreatment: A Conceptual Model for Research." *Journal of Marriage and the Family* 39:721–736.

1982a *Children and Families in the Social Environment.* New York: Aldine.

1982b "Healing the Social Wounds of Isolation." In *Child Abuse,* E. H. Newberger, ed. 43–55. Boston: Little, Brown.

Gelles, R. J.

1975   "The Social Construction of Child Abuse." *American Journal of Orthopsychiatry* 45 (April): 363–371.

1980   "Violence in the Family: A Review of Research in the Seventies." *Journal of Marriage and the Family* 42 (4, November):873–885.

1982   "Child Abuse and Family Violence: Implications for Medical Professionals." In *Child Abuse,* Eli H. Newberger, ed. Boston: Little, Brown.

Gelles, R. J., and M. A. Straus

1979   "Determinants of Violence in the Family: Toward a Theoretical Integration." In *Contemporary Theories about the Family,* W. Burr et al., eds. New York: Free Press.

Gil, D.

1970   *Violence against Children: Physical Child Abuse in the United States.* Cambridge, Mass.: Harvard University Press.

Giovannoni, J. M., and R. M. Becerra

1979   *Defining Child Abuse.* New York: Free Press.

Glick, P. A.

1981   "A Demographic Profile of Black Families." In *Black Families,* Harriette McAdoo, ed. Beverly Hills: Sage.

Hampton, R. L.

1979   "Husbands' Characteristics and Marital Disruption in Black Families." *The Sociological Quarterly* 20:255–266.

1980   "Institutional Decimation, Marital Exchange and Disruption in Black Families." *Western Journal of Black Studies* 4 (2):132–139.

Hampton, R. L., and E. H. Newberger

1985   "Child Abuse Incidence and Reporting by Hospitals: The Significance of Severity, Class and Race." *American Journal of Public Health* 75 (1):56–60.

Jackson, J. J.

1981   "Urban Black American." In *Ethnicity and Medical Care,* A. Harwood, ed., 37–129. Cambridge, Mass.: Harvard University Press.

Jason, J., N. Amereuh, J. Marks, and C. Tyler, Jr.

1982   "Child Abuse in Georgia: A Method to Evaluate Risk Factors and Reporting Bias." *American Journal of Public Health* 72 (12):1353–1358.

Justice, B., and R. Justice

1976   *The Abusing Family.* New York: Human Sciences Press.

Levy, D. R.

1985   "White Doctors and Black Patients: Influence of Race on the Doctor–Patient Relationships." *Pediatrics* 75 (4):639–643.

McAdoo, H. P.

1982   "Demographic Trends for People of Color." *Social Work* 27 (1):15–23.

National Study of the Incidence and Severity of Child Abuse and Neglect

1981   Publication No. (OHDS) 81–030326. *Study Findings.*: Author.

Newberger, E. H.

1985   "The Helping Hand Strikes Again: Unintended Consequences of Child Abuse Reporting." In E. H. Newberger and R. Bourne, *Unhappy Families,* pp. 171–178. Littleton, Mass.: PSG Publishers.

Newberger, E. H., R. B. Reed, J. H. Daniel, J. N. Hyde, and M. Kotelchuck

1977 "Pediatric Social Illness: Toward an Etiologic Classification." *Pediatrics* 60:178–185.

Pearce, D. and H. P. McAdoo

1981 "Women in Poverty: Toward a New Understanding of Work and Welfare." In *Thirteenth Final Report*. Washington, D.C.: National Advisory Council on Economic Opportunity.

Peters, M., and G. Massey

1983 "Mundane Extreme Environmental Stress in Family Stress Theories: The Case of Black Families in White America." *Marriage and Family Review* 1 and 2:193–215.

Pfohl, S.

1977 "The Discovery of Child Abuse." *Social Problems* 24 (3):310–323.

Straus, M.

1979 "Stress and Physical Child Abuse." *Child Abuse and Neglect* 4:75–88.

Straus, M. A., R. J. Gelles, and S. Steinmetz

1980 *Behind Closed Doors: Violence in the American Family.* Garden City, New York: Doubleday.

Turbett, J. P., and R. O'Toole

1980 "Physician's Recognition of Child Abuse." Paper presented at the annual meeting of the American Sociological Association, New York.

9 / The Extended Family

BLACK GRANDPARENTS:
Who Needs Them?

Jacquelyne Jackson

*The transition from a rural to an urban set-
ting has had a strong impact on the traditional position of the elderly in the family.
The author examines the living situations of
older Blacks in urban areas and the impact
on family relations, particularly between
grandparents and grandchildren.*

This [chapter] focuses specifically upon . . . grandparental roles in a contemporary urban Southern
setting and certain implications of those roles relative to sociocultural conditions of aged blacks. . . .

Perhaps the most impressive finding about
the black grandparental roles is their striking similarity to comparable findings about non-black
grandparent–grandchild patterns. If so, the emphasis often placed upon the "peculiarity" of "Black
Grannies" may be unwarranted or unduly exaggerated. These findings tend to be in general agreement, e.g., with those of Shanas et al.,[1] Shanas and

Streib,[2] Townsend,[3] and Young and Willmott[4] in
such areas as (1) emphasis upon the usually vivid
presence of grandmothers especially in kinship networks, with an important task being involvement in
grandchild rearing; (2) more involvement of grandmothers than grandfathers in activities with grandchildren; (3) closer bonds among grandmothers,
daughters, and grandchildren than among grandfathers, sons, and grandchildren; and (4) the presence of extended or three-generational families
within urban areas.

Frazier's classic description of "Granny: The
Guardian of the Generations" depicted an ener-
getic, courageous, and devoted "Granny" whose
prestige and importance were great during and
after the Civil War. "Granny" continued watching
"over the destiny of the Negro families as they have
moved in ever increasing numbers to the cities during the present century," wrote Frazier, with the
gradual increase in patriarchal authority in family

Abridged from "Aged Blacks: A Potpourri in the Direction
of the Reduction of Inequities," *Phylon* 32 (1971):260–271.
Reprinted by permission. Footnotes have been renumbered. This paper was partially supported by the Center for
the Study of Aging and Human Development, Duke University Medical Center, Durham, North Carolina, Grant
5 T01 HD00164 of the National Institute of Child Health and
Human Development, and by the U.S. Public Health Service Grant #MH 1655402.

relations and in female economic subordination, decreasing "Granny's" prestige and importance. Frazier made no explicit mention of grandfathers.[5] A majority of the grandmother subjects in this study still resemble Frazier's "Granny." Grandmothers are still generally more important than grandfathers, but the importance of the latter within black urban kinship systems is increasing, necessitating a reassessment of black families and a burial of extant myths.

Kahana and Kahana[6] noted that most grandparental studies focused only upon them rather than upon both them and their grandchildren. This section is traditional in focusing upon grandparental perceptions only, but atraditional in focusing upon black grandmothers and grandfathers. Specifically, analytical data about *interactional* and *subjective* roles between (a) grandparents residing in predominantly low-income, urban renewal areas and the grandchildren they see most often, and (b) selected comparisons of the grandparental subgroupings are presented.

The subgroupings of the sampled 68 black grandparents, whose ages, marital statuses, and subgroupings are detailed in Table 1, . . . were as follows: (1) by sex, grandmothers and grandfathers; (2) by age, younger (i.e., under 50 years) and older (i.e., 50 + years); and (3) by household composition, grandparents living alone and grandparents not living alone. No significant age differences characterized the latter subgroup. Using t, both the grandfathers and older grandparents were significantly older than their subgroup counterparts ($p < .001$). The subjects reported approximately (a few were imprecise) 391 grandchildren, about 5.8 grandchildren per subject. Almost 12 percent had

---

TABLE 1   Black Grandparental Subgroupings by Age and Sample Size

SUBGROUPING	N	AGE (IN YEARS)	
		X	s
By sex:			
All grandmothers	54	59.4	13.6
Older, with spouse	6	66.7	7.5
Older, without spouse	33	66.5	7.6
Younger, with spouse	3	45.0	0.0
Younger, without spouse	12	40.0	6.7
Employed	9	49.4	12.4
Nonemployed	45	61.4	13.0
All grandfathers[1]	14	69.3	7.8
Older, with spouse	5	73.0	4.5
Older, without spouse	9	67.2	8.3
Employed	4	62.5	9.6
Nonemployed	10	72.0	4.8
By living arrangements:			
All grandparents			
Living alone	26	64.2	11.6
Not living alone	38	59.7	13.7
By age:			
Younger grandparents	15	41.0	6.4
Older grandparents	53	67.2	7.7

---

[1]No grandfathers were under 50 years of age.

no granddaughters; almost 15 percent no grand-sons. Table 2 contains selected background information of these grandchildren.

A modified form of the Adams Kinship Schedule[7] was used to collect data in personal interview settings within the subject's homes. Following Adams (1968),[8] *interactional characteristics* referred to the "frequency of interaction and kinds of or occasions for interaction with" grandchildren, including telephone contacts and letter writing, or the non-face-to-face means of keeping in touch. His eight "contact types" (i.e., home visiting, social activities, voluntary organizations, working together at the same occupation and location, rituals, communication, aid received from a specific relative, and aid given to a specific relative) were modified to seven: home visiting, social activities (including reading), church, luxury gifts, communication, aid received from grandchildren, and aid given to grandchildren. The subjective characteristics were affectional closeness, value consensus, identification, and obligation.

TABLE 2   Background Data on Grandchildren by Grandparental Subgroups

| | | | | GRANDPARENTAL SUBGROUPS | | | |
| | | | | Grandparents Living | | | |
CHARACTERISTIC[1]	Percent Base:	Grandmothers (N = 54)[1] 100.0	Grandfathers (N = 14)[1] 100.0	Alone (N = 26)[1] 100.0	Not Alone (N = 38)[1] 100.0	Grandparents Younger 100.0	Older 100.0
Number of grandsons							
None		14.3%	37.5%	13.0%	16.7%	23.1%	19.2%
One		16.3	0.0	8.7	13.3	30.8	7.7
Two		18.4	18.8	30.4	13.3	15.4	19.2
Three +		51.0	43.8	47.8	56.7	30.8	53.8
Number of granddaughters							
None		21.6	31.3	30.4	16.1	15.4	25.9
One		21.6	18.3	30.4	16.1	15.4	22.2
Two		9.8	6.3	8.7	12.9	15.4	7.4
Three +		47.1	43.8	30.4	54.8	53.8	44.4
Grandchildren's residence							
In same household as grandparent		30.4	0.0	0.0	34.5	46.2	16.7
In same city as grandparent		37.0	40.0	52.4	27.6	38.5	37.5
In northeastern states		19.6	40.0	38.1	20.7	15.4	14.6
Elsewhere		13.0	20.0	9.5	17.2	0.0	31.3
Ages of grandchildren							
Under 6 years		25.6	14.3	14.3	29.6	58.3	13.3
6–11 years		27.9	42.9	33.3	25.9	25.0	33.3
12–17 years		20.9	28.6	19.0	29.6	8.3	26.7
18 + years		25.6	14.3	33.3	14.8	8.3	26.7
Grandchildren's marital status							
Married		41.2	33.3	62.5	22.2	0.0	44.4

[1]Percentages were computed upon available responses, so *N* is sometimes less than given.

Determination of affectional closeness is in answer to the question: "How close would you say you feel to your . . . ?" Responses of "quite close" and "extremely close" are combined and designated as strong feelings of closeness. Value consensus is ascertained by the following question: "Do you and your . . . agree in your ideas and opinions about the things you *consider really important in life?" Answers of "yes, completely," and "yes, to a great extent" appear to indicate substantial value consensus, as distinct from value divergence. Idealization of or identification with the relative is determined by responses to this question: "Would you like to be the kind of person your . . . is?" Close identification is based upon the responses "yes, completely," and "in most ways." Feelings of obligation are ascertained . . . by asking . . . how important certain reasons for keeping in touch are in relation to a particular relative.*[9]

Findings

In general, when the data were controlled for grandparents with at least one son with offspring and at least one daughter with offspring, who either both resided elsewhere (i.e., not within the same locality as the subject) or within the same location as did the subject, the grandchild seen most often was the daughter's, as opposed to the son's, child, a finding consistent with Young and Willmott's observation that grandchildren usually interact more frequently with their mother's mother than with their father's mother.[10] Rare exceptions in this sample were among subjects whose son's offspring resided with them.

Interactional characteristics Possible responses for frequency of interaction between a grandparent and grandchild ranged from daily through "never during the past year." Percentage data in Table 3 depict frequency of interaction in five "contact types" for subjects interacting at least "once during the year" with the grandchild.

Grandparental subgroupings emerged Younger grandparents, grandparents living alone, and grand-

mothers were more likely to report home visiting than were their respective counterparts, true even when the data were controlled to exclude grandparents and grandchildren in the same household. Those living alone and those not living alone differed since the latter reported greater frequency of contact ($p < .05$).

The modal form of interaction in social activities was "shopping, exclusive of grocery shopping," with joint movie attendance especially rare. Reading was largely restricted to interaction with preschool grandchildren. Table 4 contains a rank ordering, in decreasing frequency, of these activities.

The data on church revealed that older grandparents, grandparents living alone, and grandfathers reported less frequent church activities (most often joint attendance at regular Sunday morning worship services) with grandchildren than their counterparts. Younger grandparents were far more likely to be accompanied by or to accompany a grandchild to church than were older grandparents ($p < .05$), attributable partially to greater shared residence among the former. Joint church activity decreased as the ages of the grandparents and grandchildren increased.

Excepting younger grandparents, subjects reported infrequent or no luxury gift-giving to their grandchildren, a finding explicable perhaps by such variables as (a) a greater likelihood of younger grandparents being employed; and (b) greater likelihood of grandparents providing younger grandchildren with luxury gifts and older ones with practical gifts.

Non-face-to-face communication patterns investigated were (a) telephoning grandparent–grandchild contacts; and (b) written communication among grandparent–grandchild pairs not residing within the same city. No more than one third of any grandparent subgroup reported writing to a grandchild within the preceding year. More had received correspondence from their grandchildren. Grandfathers, as well as grandparents living with others, were less likely to have had telephonic communication with grandchildren than grandmothers and grandparents living alone, but the differences were insignificant. Older grandparents were significantly more likely than younger grandparents to

TABLE 3   Responses to Interactional Items by Grandparental Subgroups

			GRANDPARENTAL SUBGROUPS			
				Grandparents Living		Grandparents
CHARACTERISTIC[1]	Percent Base:[1]	Grandmothers	Grandfathers	Alone	Not Alone	Younger	Older
		100.0	100.0	100.0	100.0	100.0	100.0
Frequency of contact with grandchild							
Daily, same household		29.3%	0.0%	0.0%	32.0%	50.0%	15.9%
Monthly, or more often		43.9	53.8	60.0	36.0	40.0	47.7
At least once during past year		24.4	30.8	35.0	24.0	10.0	29.5
Not at all during past year		2.4	15.4	5.0	8.0	0.0	6.8
Home visiting							
Yes		31.3	27.3	42.1	11.8	60.0	26.3
No		68.8	72.7	57.9	88.2	40.0	73.7
Social activities							
Going to the park		22.0	15.4	10.0	20.0	36.4	16.3
Attending the movies		4.8	0.0	0.0	3.8	0.0	4.5
Grocery shopping		35.7	15.4	15.0	42.3	54.5	25.0
Shopping, other than grocery		45.2	15.4	30.0	46.2	63.6	31.8
Local or other trips/vacation		28.6	7.7	15.0	26.9	27.3	22.7
Reading		14.3	7.7	5.0	11.5	18.2	11.4
Church		45.2	23.1	35.0	42.3	72.7	31.8
Luxury gifts							
Yes		32.4	33.3	15.8	47.4	75.0	23.7
No		67.6	66.7	84.2	52.6	25.0	76.3
Communication							
S writes out of town grandchild		28.6	25.0	27.3	33.3	0.0	28.6
S written by out of town grandchild		53.3	33.3	58.3	30.0	0.0	47.8
No telephone communication on special occasions or emergencies		42.3	21.4	31.3	38.9	0.0	42.4
Telephone communications monthly or more frequently		15.4	28.6	25.0	16.7	14.3	21.2

[1]All percentages based upon interaction having occurred at least once during the past year.

have such interaction ($p < .05$), an artifact, perhaps, of more grandchildren living with younger grandparents. While few subjects reported relatively frequent (i.e., monthly or more often) telephone contact, most reported at least one call (usually an emergency or a "special occasion" day) during the preceding year.

Table 5 contains responses concerning grandparent–grandchild aid patterns. A minority perceived their grandchildren as "not much help at all," a statement verbalized most often by grandfathers (50 percent), and less often by those who were not living alone (37 percent), older (33 percent), living alone (28 percent), grandmothers (25 percent), and younger (20 percent). But inquiry about specific aid revealed that a majority had received assistance from grandchildren during the preceding year. Their modal responses were not instru-

TABLE 4   Rank Order of the Frequency of Social Activities between Grandparents and Grandchildren

| | RANK ORDER[1] | | | | | |
| | | | Grandparents Living | | Grandparents | |
SOCIAL ACTIVITY	Grandmothers	Grandfathers	Alone	Not Alone	Younger	Older
Shopping other than grocery shopping	1	2	1	1	1	1
Grocery shopping	2	2	2.5	2	2	2
Going to the park and/or walking	4	2	4	4	3	4
Movies	6	6	6	6	6	6
Trips/vacations	3	4.5	2.5	3	4	3
Reading	5	4.5	5	5	5	5

[1] 1 = greatest frequency of occurrence; 6 = least occurring activity.

mentally, but affectively, oriented: disregarding the "not much help at all response," the modal response for younger grandparents and grandparents living alone was "visits"; for the remaining subgroups, "a feeling of usefulness." Those living alone received more visits from grandchildren than those not living alone ($p < .05$), while the latter received greater assistance with household and/or yard chores ($p < .05$) than the former. Younger grandparents also received more chore assistance than older grandparents ($p < .05$), and more advice from grandchildren as well ($p < .05$).

The modal form of grandparent–grandchild assistance was childcare; almost 44 percent of the grandmothers, 56 percent of grandparents living with others, and 82 percent of the younger grandmothers, had grandchildren residing with them. A smaller proportion of the subjects "babysat" with school-age children awaiting parental arrival at residences other than those of the grandparents. Younger, as contrasted with older, grandparents provided more direct financial assistance to a grandchild and/or his parents ($p < .01$); they were also more involved in patterns of luxury and practical gift-giving to grandchildren ($p < .01$), childcare ($p < .001$), and housing ($p < .05$). Grandmothers were more involved as childcare agents than grandfathers ($p < .05$), as were grandparents not living alone compared with those living alone ($p < .001$). Among the latter subgrouping, those not living

alone tended to engage in greater luxury and necessary gift-giving as well ($p < .05$).

While impressionistic judgments suggested that the older grandparents had been far more active in grandchild rearing earlier, it was quite clear that grandparental involvement in childrearing is directly related to the grandchild's familial structure: grandparental involvement, as Frazier[11] indicated, increased with the absence of the grandchild's parent.

Subjective characteristics   Qualitative data on affectional closeness, value consensus, identification with grandchild, satisfaction of present contact with grandchild, and the primary initiant of grandparent–grandchild contacts were available for analysis. A majority of the subjects verbalized strong affectional closeness between themselves and their grandchildren. Only grandmothers considered themselves significantly closer to grandchildren than did grandfathers ($p < .05$), but grandparents living with others and younger grandparents tended to report greater closeness than their counterparts, suggesting probably the importance of considering more closely sex, age, and residential proximity in future grandparent–grandchild studies.

Value divergence was more typical than substantial value consensus, but the greatest congruence of value consensus between grandparents and

TABLE 5   Mutual Aid Patterns between Grandchildren and Grandparents

CHARACTERISTIC[1]	Grandmothers	Grandfathers	Grandparents Living		Grandparents	
			Alone	Not Alone	Younger	Older
Aid received from grandchildren						
Financial assistance	12.5%	0.0%	10.5%	11.8%	20.7%	7.9%
Feeling of usefulness	35.3	36.4	26.3	42.1	57.1	31.6
House or yard chores	27.8	18.2	5.3	35.0	55.6	18.4
Visiting	31.3	27.3	42.1	11.8	60.0	26.3
Transportation	6.5	0.0	5.3	6.3	0.0	5.3
Gifts	18.8	9.1	15.8	23.5	20.0	15.8
Advice	12.5	9.1	10.5	11.8	40.0	7.9
Writing letters, reading, etc.	3.1	0.0	0.0	5.9	0.0	2.6
"Not much help at all"	25.0	50.0	27.8	36.8	20.0	33.3
Aid given to grandchildren						
Indirect financial assistance	15.2	0.0	0.0	17.6	50.0	5.3
Direct financial assistance	30.6	18.2	15.8	40.0	75.0	17.9
Necessary gifts	33.3	9.1	10.5	89.5	66.7	18.4
Housing	36.8	27.3	15.0	42.9	66.7	27.5
Assistance with illness	11.8	9.1	0.0	16.7	16.7	10.3
Child care	43.6	9.1	5.3	56.5	81.8	23.1
Took grandchild on a special trip	6.3	10.0	0.0	5.9	20.0	5.4
Advice	52.8	33.3	42.1	42.9	75.0	42.5
Keeping after school until parent arrives	8.8	9.1	0.0	15.8	16.7	7.7
Other	14.3	0.0	16.7	10.5	0.0	14.8

GRANDPARENTAL SUBGROUPS

[1]All percentages based upon interaction having occurred at least once during the past year.

grandchildren was found among grandfathers, which warrants an investigation of black generational transmission of political socialization and advocates for the aged. Older grandmothers displayed the most distance in grandchild–grandparent value consensus. In addition, less than five percent of the subjects closely identified with grandchildren. Almost 20 percent rejected any close identification (i.e., they would not like to resemble the grandchild in any way).

Obligatory kinship ties were apparent. Most subjects, and particularly younger grandparents and grandparents living with others, felt that the obligation of "keeping in touch" was very important. Excepting younger grandparents, all of the subjects placed greater emphasis upon the obligatory than upon the enjoyable aspect of "keeping in touch." Older grandparents and those living alone desired greater grandchild contact. Compared with their respective counterparts, they were significantly less likely to be satisfied with the present contact levels ($p < .05$). A very small percentage of older grandparents (2 percent) and grandparents not living alone (4 percent), however, felt that less frequent grandchild contact would be desirable.

Most subjects felt that grandchildren should live near (but not necessarily with) their grandparents, and provided rationalizations categorized as unilateral and bilateral need-fits (e.g., "Grandchildren can be a lot of help to their grandparents,"

"Grandparents can help parents with children," and "Because we need each other") and kinship obligations (e.g., "Everyone should be close around their family"). Equally important, almost 15 percent of the subjects feeling that grandchildren should not live near grandparents cited the necessity for physical generational separation so as to reduce problems for the grandparent (e.g., "Do not want to be worried with them") and/or the grandchild (e.g., "It tends to spoil the child") and emphasized parental responsibility. Almost 25 percent of the subjects stressed the primary responsibility of parents for rearing their own children in neolocal residences. Most were specifically concerned about possible detrimental effects of extremely close grandparent–grandchild residential proximity upon development of independence in a maturing grandchild; and, to a less extent, childrearing roles constraining grandparents with "other fish to fry," as they develop or maintain new roles as they aged.

In general grandchildren were not considered the initiants of the grandparent–grandchild contacts. Grandfathers also did not perceive themselves in this role, but considered a parent of the grandchild as the primary contact agent for them. Younger grandparents and grandparents living alone rarely regarded themselves as prime contact agents either, inasmuch as those younger grandparents with spouses felt that the spouses actually initiated the contact most often, and both groups felt that their own children also served as links between themselves and grandchildren. Younger grandparents and grandfathers, however, were more likely to telephone a grandchild than the reverse, whereas grandchildren were more likely to contact grandmothers, older grandparents, and grandparents not living alone. The only significant subgroup distinction occurred in that grandfathers were more frequent initiators of telephone calls with grandchildren than were grandmothers ($p < .05$).

Discussion

Apparently these grandparents prefer children's children to live near, but not with, them, and younger to older grandchildren.[12] Very old grandparents appeared more concerned about proximity

in the event grandchildren were needed for instrumental and affective support. Relationships among affectional closeness, value consensus, and identification were unclear, but they are probably related to such preferences as those mentioned above. Any postulation of a "generation gap" per se between black grandparents and their grandchildren is too vague. That is, far greater specificity and empirical data about those gaps which may exist are needed, with particular emphasis upon separation of spurious or superficial gaps (e.g., clothing or hairstyles) and substantial ones (e.g., divergence upon dominant values). Age is not a sufficient explication of generation gaps in dominant values.

The specific contact types investigated suggested relatively infrequent grandchild–grandparent interaction, due perhaps to an artifact of the study in focusing directly upon those rather than upon other contact types, and/or to such variables as inadequate income, transportation, and awareness of or free and friendly access to available resources. The general findings clearly point up some problem areas, a specific one being public housing.

In this connection, empirical data on relationships between housing and kinship patterns among blacks are clearly warranted. For example, grandparent–grandchild patterns may be affected positively and negatively by public housing policies for the aged. For blacks at least, alternative forms of housing (e.g., age-segregated and age-integrated) within the same locale are desirable. Telephone service should be available. Single blacks dependent upon public housing (and especially when such dependence is fostered through their involuntary relocation as a result of urban renewal and highway express programs) should not be forced (as is true in some localities) to accept one-room or efficiency apartments, but should be permitted to occupy at least one-bedroom apartments, if they prefer such an arrangement. Physical space permitting brief or extended visits from relatives should be available.

These findings about black grandparents and their grandchildren help to debunk myths of the deaths of the "Black Grannies"; the "powerful matriarchies" ruled by "Black Grannies"; and the disintegrating or ephemeral kinship ties between aged and aging blacks. They indicate that many black grandparents serve as a point of anchorage for grandchildren and provide kinds of supports for them unavailable from their own parents. In that sense, the grandparents take on the responsibilities of and function as individual departments of welfare. Many black families, in all probability, adhere to familial norms characteristic of the larger culture. Finally, these data are most significant in [pointing toward the] need for [more research about grandparental roles among Americans]. . . .

[1]*Ethel Shanas et al., Old People in Three Industrial Societies (Chicago, 1968).*

[2]*Ethel Shanas and Gordon Streib,* Social Structure and the Family: Generational Relations *(Englewood Cliffs, 1965).*

[3]*Peter Townsend,* The Family Life of Old People *(London, 1957).*

[4]*Michael Young and Peter Willmott,* Family and Kinship in East London *(London, 1957).*

[5]*E. Franklin Frazier,* The Negro Family in the United States *(Chicago, 1939), pp. 114–24.*

[6]*Boas Kahana and Eva Kahana, "Grandparenthood from the Perspective of the Developing Grandchild (Mimeographed, Washington University, St. Louis, Missouri, 1969).*

[7]*Bert N. Adams,* Kinship in an Urban Setting *(Chicago, 1968), pp. 10–14.*

[8]*Ibid., pp. 13–15.*

[9]*Ibid., pp. 14–15.*

[10]*Young and Willmott, op. cit.*

[11]*Frazier, op. cit.*

[12]*Cf. Kahana and Kahana, op. cit., and also Jacquelyne J. Jackson, "Kinship Relations among Older Negro Americans" (Paper read at the Eighth International Congress of Gerontology, Washington, D.C., August, 1969); Jacquelyne J. Jackson, "Urban Negro Kinship Relations" (Paper read at the annual meeting, American Sociological Association, San Francisco, California, September, 1969); Jacquelyne J. Jackson, "Changing Kinship Roles and Patterns among Older Persons in a Black Community" (Paper read at the annual meeting, American Psychological Association, Washington, D.C., September, 1969); Jacquelyne J. Jackson, "Kinship Relations among Urban Blacks," Journal of Social and Behavioral Sciences, 16 (Winter, 1970), 1–13.*

THE BLACK EXTENDED FAMILY REVISITED

Robert B. Hill · Lawrence Shackleford

The authors stress the importance of the extended Black family, in its variety of forms, as a stabilizer of otherwise fragmented urban families. They see the extended family pattern as a source of strength to the Black family.

One mechanism that has provided resilience to black families for generations has been the extended family—or the informal absorption of families and individuals by relatives. During slavery, for example, thousands of children of slave parents were often reared by elderly relatives, who served as a major source of cohesion and fortitude for many black families.[1]

The extended family pattern has also served historically as a means of pooling meager resources, particularly during periods of severe economic decline. For example, during the Great Depression of the 1930s, thousands of blacks moved in with other relatives until they were able to obtain a more secure economic position that permitted them to go out on their own. A disproportionate number of the families that were doubling up with

From *The Urban League Review* 1 (Fall 1975):18–24. Reprinted by permission.

relatives were female-headed families with dependent children. As a result of recent recessions, the proportion of black children living with only their mothers in subfamilies of households headed by relatives rose sharply from 22 to 33 percent between 1969 and 1974.[2]

The number of children being taken in by relatives is still exceedingly high. Today, about 3 million children under 18 years old are living in households headed by relatives and 45 percent (or 1.3 million) of these children are black.[3]

Despite the disproportionate number of blacks who have been reared by relatives throughout the history of blacks in America, it is surprising that there have been few systematic empirical studies of the distinctive characteristics of extended family arrangements, particularly those related to the informal adoption of children, and how they have adapted over time. Almost all the literature on black adoption relates to formal adoption, despite the fact that less than 10 percent of black children born out of wedlock each year are placed with formal adoption agencies.[4]

Extended Family Patterns

Although there have been few systematic studies that have focused solely or primarily on the black extended family, most of the classic studies on black families have underscored the significance of extended family patterns for the survival, stability and advancement of black families.[5]

Charles S. Johnson noted that the black extended family has the "semblance of a normal and natural family and functions as one, except that the members of the group are drawn into it by various circumstances rather than being a product of the original group."[6] Hortense Powdermaker also observes, "... stepchildren, illegitimate, adopted children, mingle with the children of the house. No matter how small or crowded the home is, there is always room for a stray child, an elderly grandmother, an indigent aunt."[7]

Some scholars, such as Herskovits, trace the origins of the black extended family to Africa: "The African immediate family, consisting of a father, his wives and their children, is but a part of a larger unit. This immediate family is generally recognized by Africanists as belonging to a local relationship group termed the "extended family."[8] Several anthropological studies of black families in the rural South have identified family patterns that closely correspond to those in patrilineal tribes of West Africa.[9]

Subfamilies

As Billingsley has noted, black extended families take many forms depending on the composition of the individuals and families that are absorbed by primary family units: subfamilies, families with secondary members and augmented families. Subfamilies, which consist of at least two or more related individuals, can be differentiated into the following extended family categories: (a) the "incipient" extended family, which consists of a husband–wife subfamily with no children of their own living in the household of relatives; (b) the "simple nuclear" extended family, which consists of a husband–wife subfamily with one or more own children living in the household of a relative's family; and (c) the "attenuated" extended family, which consists of a parent and child subfamily living in the household of a relative.[10]

Over the past decade, the proportion of black subfamilies has remained constant. Although the number of black subfamilies rose from 248,000 to 332,000 between 1965 and 1974, the proportion of black subfamilies of all black families remained unchanged at 6 percent. Basic characteristics of black subfamilies are essentially the same.

Black subfamilies are overwhelmingly attenuated families, i.e., they consist of one female parent and her children living in a relative's household. About three-fourths of black subfamilies are headed by women with at least one own child under 18. More than three-fourths of the women heading black subfamilies are living with one or both of their parents (or parents-in-law). About 10 percent of these women, however, are living in their sister's household.

The overwhelming majority of the women heads of black subfamilies were formerly married, but are currently separated, widowed or divorced.

There is an average of 1.8 children per black subfamily headed by a female and about half (45 percent) of these subfamilies consist of only one own child.

Secondary Members

In addition to taking in already existing families, black extended families take in four classes of relatives, or secondary members, who come alone: (a) minor relatives, including grandchildren, nieces, nephews, cousins and young siblings under 18; (b) peers of the primary parents, including siblings, cousins and other adult relatives; (c) elders of the primary parents, particularly aunts and uncles; and (d) parents of the primary family.

Dependent children are much more likely than elderly persons to be taken into black families as secondary members. Half the black families headed by women 65 and over have children under 18 not their own living with them. On the other hand, only 4 percent of black husband–wife families and families headed by women have persons 65 years and over living with them.

Most dependent secondary members of black extended families are grandchildren. Two-thirds of the 800,000 black children under 18 living in families without either parent are being reared by their grandparents or great-grandparents. The rest are mostly being reared by their aunts and uncles.

Augmented Families

Although the overwhelming majority of children informally adopted are relatives of the heads of household, a disproportionate number are not related at all. About 100,000 (or 6 percent) of black children living in families without either parent are not relatives of the heads of household. Nonrelated children make up 8 percent of all other than own children in husband–wife families, but only 3 percent of those in female-headed black families.

Since Census Bureau data fail to distinguish foster care nonrelated children from informally placed nonrelated children, it is not possible to precisely determine the extent to which nonrelated children were placed through formal or informal channels. HEW data on child care arrangements in-dicate that a total of 243,000 children were in foster care families in 1969. Since this would account for only a little over half of all unrelated children in families without their parents, it is safe to say that almost half the nonrelated children in families are not in foster care.[11]

Dependent children under 18 do not constitute the majority of unrelated persons taken into augmented extended families. Most of these unrelated individuals are adults living as roomers, boarders, lodgers or other relatively long-term guests. Over half a million (522,000) black persons live with families with whom they were not related by marriage, ancestry or adoption. Eighty percent of these nonrelated individuals are 18 years of age and over, and 56 percent of these nonrelated adults in black households are men.

In sum, black extended families are primary family units that take in: (a) two or more related persons (i.e., subfamilies); (b) one related person (i.e., secondary members); and (c) nonrelatives (i.e., augmented families). But all of these extended family types, according to Census Bureau definition, presuppose the existence of a primary family unit consisting of at least two or more related persons that takes in other relatives or nonrelatives.

These typologies fail to incorporate an extended family pattern that is one of the most prevalent of all—the informal adoption of individuals or subfamilies by relatives who live alone (e.g., widowed grandmothers or aunts). Forty-five percent of the 1.3 million black children living with kin are in households headed by female relatives, while 9 percent are living with male relatives who are without spouses. Thus over half of the black children living with kin are being reared by relatives who are without mates. There are numerous accounts in the literature of black children being taken into one-parent households of relatives.[12]

Grandparents

Most of the "adopting" relatives in black extended families are either grandparents (many of whom are not necessarily elderly) or aunts and uncles. Two-thirds of black children under 18 living with relatives today are grandchildren of the heads of household, while one-fifth are primarily nieces and nephews. The historic fortitude and self-reliance of the black elderly is vividly reflected in the fact that they are more likely to take others into their households than to be taken into the households of younger relatives.[13]

Frazier, in particular, took special note of the role of the grandmother in his classic work on black families in the United States in a chapter entitled "Granny: the Guardian of the Generations."[14] Some contemporary social scientists have distorted Frazier's original meaning of the matriarch and have incorrectly applied it to young black women with dependent children who "castrate" their husbands. But the "matriarch," according to Frazier, referred to a warm, compassionate, but resolute grandmother who inspired her children and grandchildren to achieve, and not to a domineering wife who continually competed with and ridiculed her husband.[15]

Many outstanding blacks have been reared by their grandparents or see them as having been major influences in their lives. Frederick Douglass, for example, wrote in his autobiography with deep affection of the impact that his grandmother had in the early stages of his life in slave quarters.[16]

As Frazier observed, "Granny" served many roles in black families, as nurse, midwife, mother, educator, minister, disciplinarian, and transmitter of the family heritage. Some grandparents were held in such high esteem by plantation owners that they often received favorable treatment, such as in Frederick Douglass's grandmother's case, receiving a special plot of land on which to live out their lives and to pass on to kin.[17]

Who Are Adopted?

What are the social characteristics of black children who are informally adopted? Are they more likely to be preschoolers or school-age? Were most of them born out of wedlock? Sixty percent of black children living with neither parent in the household of relatives today are 6 years and over, while 41 percent of them are 10 years and over. One-fourth of these informally adopted children are less than 3 years old.

As a result of declining birth rates among blacks, the proportion of informally adopted chil-dren under 3 has been steadily decreasing. In 1969, 35 percent of black children living with kin without their parents were under 3 years old, but by 1974 only 26 percent were under 3.

This does not mean that children who are informally adopted are more likely to be adopted when they are school-age than preschool. On the contrary, most studies of informal adoption patterns indicate that children are most likely to be taken in at very early ages. According to the Tuskegee Institute study of informal adoption patterns in rural counties of Alabama, 70 percent of the families reported that informally adopted children were less than 2 years old when taken in and 31 percent said that the children had been born there.[18]

Although a majority of informally adopted children were born in wedlock, a sizable minority were not. About two-fifths of black children living with relatives in 1970 had parents who were never married. This was particularly the case for children who lived in one-parent subfamilies in the household of relatives.

In a study of the six-year experience of unwed mothers, the Community Council of Greater New York found that 10 percent of 136 black mothers interviewed had placed their out-of-wedlock, first-born child in an informal adoption arrangement. Most of these children were being reared by one or both grandparents.[19] Similarly, in her study of kinship patterns of blacks in the Midwest, Carol Stack reported several instances of out-of-wedlock children being reared by grandparents, great-grandparents and great-aunts and -uncles.[20]

Reasons for Adoption

Why are these children taken in? There are a variety of circumstances that lead to informal adoption of children. One frequent factor is death or illness of the child's parents. Frazier gives an account of such a case by an elderly female who was a former slave:

> *I was 77 years old this last gone February.*
> *The two little orphan children. I raised them*
> *here with me. These little orphan children*
> *mother dead and father dead too. I'm they*
> *great aunt. Me being the oldest one and me*
> *being they mother's auntie and the oldest*

head, that's how I come by them. So me and my husband raised them children from little bit a things.[21]

Another factor often leading to informal adoption is separation or divorce of parents. Johnson describes such a situation with regards to the adoption of an older black child:

When Hesekie was 13 years old his mother and father separated. He does not know why. They never told him and he did not inquire. One day his mother just went off and did not come back. Later his father left for Illinois. Now both have remarried and Hesekie is living with his grandparents who, as tenants go in this section, are fairly well off.[22]

Many children who are born out of wedlock to young women are often informally adopted by older relatives because of the "immaturity" of an unwed mother.[23] A frequent reason for temporary or short-term informal adoption is to permit the parents to go to work or to attain a more secure economic footing:

Violet married and moved to another state with her husband and her two youngest children. She left her two older daughters with their grandmother. After about seven months Violet took the train back home in order to get her daughter and take them to a new home out of state.[24]

Proximity of a relative to a school is also a factor leading to informal adoptions. Shimkin described a case where a mother moved and wanted her son to continue at the same school he was attending. Since a great-aunt lived closer to the school, the child lived with her.[25] Johnson cites a case where a child was taken in by nonrelated family friends because they lived closer to the school that the parents wanted the child to attend.[26] Today, many children not only give the addresses of relatives who live within the boundaries of the schools that they would like to attend, but they often live with those relatives as well.

Many children are often taken in by relatives simply because they wanted a child to raise. In the Tuskegee study of informal adoptions, several respondents indicated: "I wanted a child and found out I could have this one; I needed company in the house; I needed someone to help me around the house, so I gave him a home."[27] According to the Tuskegee study, most of the reasons for informally adopting children were for "parental convenience" (i.e., work, illness, schooling, etc.) and feelings of family responsibility. In most instances, the taking in of the child just happened without any formal agreement as to the length of time that the child would live with relatives. Although many informal adoptions began as temporary arrangements, they became long-term. Even among those with a more definite understanding of how long they expected to keep the child, 90 percent said "until grown" or "as long as I live."

Most informally adopted children are aware that their parent surrogates are not their biological parents, and in many cases have periodic contact with their natural parents, especially their mothers. In the Tuskegee study about two-thirds of the parent surrogates reported that the mothers of the children were in contact with the children monthly or more frequently.[28]

Although it is frequently believed that informal adoptions are primarily a result of irresponsible males abandoning mother and child, case studies of informal adoption reveal numerous instances where the father or relatives on the father's side assumed a major responsibility for rearing the child. Stack describes a situation in which a two-year-old child was adopted by the mother's ex-boyfriend and family because of their deep affection for the child. She also cites several instances of informal adoption by paternal aunts and grandparents.[29] The Community Council of Greater New York also cites several cases where out-of-wedlock children were reared by relatives of the father.[30]

Economic Status

What is the economic status of these families? How do they cope financially? Although three-fifths of black families with related children are above the poverty level, they tend to have a disproportionate number below the poverty level. Over half of the female-headed black families with informally adopted children are poor, compared to only three out of ten husband–wife black families with other than own children.

The disproportionate poverty status of informally adopted children is most vividly reflected in the relatively low median income of their families. Although all black children under 18 lived in families with a median income of $4,256 in 1969, children under 18 living with kin were in families that had a median income of $2,592—only two-thirds of all black families. Moreover, although husband–wife black families with informally adopted children had a median income of $3,796, female-headed families with related children had a median income of only $1,632. Since almost half of these children live in female-headed families, it is clear that thousands of these children are being reared in economically disadvantaged settings.

Most financial support of informally adopted children comes from the adopting relatives. In the Tuskegee Institute study, the biological parents (primarily the mother) provided some support for the child in 43 percent of the families. The most frequent types of help provided by parents were money and clothes. Of those that reported specific amounts of money, over half gave less than $50 per month. Parent surrogates assumed the primary financial responsibility for rearing these children.

Despite their limited economic resources, most families with informally adopted children do not receive public assistance. Only one-third of the informally adoptive black families in the rural Alabama study indicated that they were receiving AFDC public assistance or food stamps. Over half of those who did receive AFDC received less than $80 a month. On the other hand, 62 percent of them said that the children were receiving free school lunches.

It is also surprising that while over half of the parent surrogates were 60 years and over, three-fourths of them did not receive any Social Security assistance. These findings of the Tuskegee study strongly suggest that many impoverished black families in rural areas are not receiving basic public benefits.

Despite the absence of some formal mechanisms of economic support, two-thirds of the respondents felt that they had enough clothes. The overwhelming majority reported that the children were in good health. Many of these parent surrogates are sufficiently resourceful to provide their informally adopted children with the basic necessities even at a low-income standard of living. There are mutual networks of assistance in many of these rural areas from churches, neighbors and other relatives.

The extended family has been a source of strength and resilience in the black community for generations. Much more research should be conducted on its patterns of adaptation in urban Southern and Northern areas as well as in rural settings. In-depth studies are also vitally needed to identify insensitive policies and programs at the national and local levels that have a negative impact on the functioning of kinship networks.

According to current federal income tax guidelines, child care deductions can only be made by working mothers whose children are cared for by nonrelatives or placed in a child care facility. But 40 percent of black women who work depend on responsible adult relatives to care for their children. Thus expenses made to those relatives (often an elderly grandmother or aunt of the child being cared for) are not tax deductible, despite the vital services being performed. What is needed are federal policies that reinforce and build on the strengths of extended families, not weaken them.

[1] E. Franklin Frazier, The Negro Family in the U.S. *(Chicago: University of Chicago Press, 1939); Charles S. Johnson,* Shadow of the Plantation *(Chicago: University of Chicago Press, 1934).*

[2] Hortense Powdermaker, After Freedom *(New York: Russell & Russell, 1939); National Urban League Research Department,* Black Families in the 1974–75 Depression *(Washington, D.C.: National Urban League, 1975); Committee for Children in New*

York, Children's Allowances and the Economic Welfare of Children.

[3] U.S. Bureau of Census, *"Marital Status and Living Arrangements: March 1974,"* Current Population Reports: Population Characteristics *(Washington, D.C.: U.S. Government Printing Office, 1975).*

[4]*Robert B. Hill*, The Strengths of Black Families *(Washington, D.C., National Urban League Research Department, 1971).*

[5]*Frazier*, Negro Family; *Johnson*, Shadow of the Plantation; *Powdermaker*, After Freedom.

[6]*Johnson*, Shadow of the Plantation.

[7]*Powdermaker*, After Freedom.

[8]*Melville Herskovits*, The Myth of The Negro Past *(Boston: Beacon Press, 1958).*

[9]*M. J. Herskovits et al., "The Physical Form of Mississippi Negroes,"* American Journal of Physical Anthropology 16 (1931):193–201.

[10]*Andrew Billingsley*, Black Families in White America *(Englewood Cliffs, N.J.: Prentice-Hall, 1968).*

[11]*U.S. Department of Health, Education and Welfare, Social and Rehabilitation Service, National Center for Social Statistics,* Child Welfare Statistics: 1969, *NCSS Report CW-1(69).*

[12]*Frazier*, Negro Family; *Johnson*, Shadow of the Plantation.

[13]*U.S. Bureau of the Census*, 1970 Census of Population: Persons by Family Characteristics, *Subject Report PC(2)–4, table 1; U.S. Bureau of the Census, "Marital Status"; Hill*, Strengths of Black Families.

[14]*Frazier*, Negro Family, *esp. chap. 8.*

[15]*Frazier*, Negro Family, *chap. 7; Daniel P. Moynihan*, The Negro Family: The Call for National Action *(Washington, D.C.: U.S. Department of Labor, 1965).*

[16]*Frederick Douglass*, My Bondage and My Freedom *(New York and Auburn, 1855).*

[17]*Ibid.*

[18]*Lewis W. Jones*, Informal Adoption in Black Families in Lowndes and Wilcox Counties, Alabama *(Alabama: Tuskegee Institute, 1975).*

[19]*Community Council of Greater New York*, The Six-Year Experience of Unwed Mothers *(New York: Community Council of Greater New York, Research Department, 1970).*

[20]*Carol B. Stack*, All Our Kin: Strategies for Survival in a Black Community *(New York: Harper & Row, 1974).*

[21]*Frazier*, Negro Family.

[22]*Johnson*, Shadow of the Plantation.

[23]*Stack*, All Our Kin.

[24]*Ibid.*

[25]*Demitri B. Shimkin, Gloria J. Louie and Dennis A. Frate, "The Black Extended Family: A Basic Rural Institution and a Mechanism of Urban Adaptation" (University of Illinois at Urbana-Champaign, 1975).* The Extended Family in Black Societies *(The Hague: Mouton, forthcoming).*

[26]*Johnson*, Shadow of the Plantation.

[27]*Jones*, Informal Adoption.

[28]*Ibid.*

[29]*Stack*, All Our Kin.

[30]*Community Council of Greater New York*, Six-Year Experience.

10 / Adolescence and Personality Development

BLACK YOUTH AND PSYCHOSOCIAL DEVELOPMENT:
A Conceptual Framework

Ronald L. Taylor

This article discusses the importance of role models for Black youth in their psychosocial development. The author feels that commitment is important to the success of Black youth in pursuing long-range goals.

While there exists a massive literature on the characteristics and problems of black Americans, few studies exist which take as the main focus of attention the black adolescent or youth and the problem of psychosocial development. Moreover, while there has been considerable genuine interest and concern for the psychosocial developmental problems of black youth, there has been little actual systematic or theoretically guided research in this area (Pettigrew, 1964; Proshansky and Newton, 1968). Indeed, a perusal of that small corpus of research which does exist suggests that many of the more fundamental and significant questions have not even been broached, much less subjected to empirical investigation. For example, the way in which black youth "construct" or cultivate their identities through the use of others as models has been virtually ignored, despite evidence from psychological, clinical, and sociological studies on the significance of role models as sources of psychosocial development (Bandura and Walters, 1963).

The dearth of research on psychosocial development among black youth, in contrast to the wealth of data on early self-identity development among black children, is all the more surprising when seen against the background of recent social change (both within and without the black community), the substantial growth and visibility of a black professional leadership class sufficiently available as models of achievement, and the dramatic growth in the number of black youth currently enrolled in traditionally white and black colleges and

From *Journal of Black Studies* 6 (June 1976):353–372. © 1976 by Sage Publications, Inc. Reprinted by permission of the publisher, Sage Publications, Inc.

universities. In view of these recent developments, together with new and expanded opportunities in employment and the apparent new level of self-awareness among black youth, it is reasonable to assume that these events have created new and unfamiliar developmental problems for not a few black youth.

The development of a relevant theoretical or conceptual framework is essential for a more thorough understanding and analysis of psychosocial identity development among black youth. The purpose here is to emphasize, through theoretical formulation and case study analysis, the utility of the role model approach as a conceptual framework for investigating the development of psychosocial identity among black youth. More specifically, this paper focuses upon the ways in which role models are selected and rendered useful by these youth in their various attempts to cultivate features of their personal and social identities. Such a focus allows observation of how the youth shapes his own identity through his own actions, rather than being acted upon by his social environment. While such an approach is subject to certain limitations, it is clearly a useful strategy to explore the theoretical possibilities opened up by considering the function of role models in black psychosocial development.

Theoretical and Conceptual Orientation

Psychosocial development, of which identity formation is of prototypical significance, has been the subject of considerable discussion and investigation by behavioral scientists in recent years. Nowhere has this subject received fuller treatment than in the numerous works of Erikson (1950, 1964, 1968). While his perspective is dictated by psychoanalytic theory, he has systematically reorganized that theory to take greater account of the sociocultural environment. For Erikson, the quintessential task of youth is the establishment of a sense of one's own identity as a unique person. Identity represents an evolving configuration gradually established through successive synthesis and resynthesis of psychosocial components, involving the articulation of

personal capacities, value, identifications, and fantasies with plans, ideals, expectations, and opportunities. Thus in Erikson's view, relative identity formation is not fully possible before late adolescence, when the body, "now fully grown, grows together into an individual appearance," when the fully developed cognitive structure enables the youth to envisage a career within an historical perspective, and when the emergence of the capacity for and interest in sustained heterosexual intimacy has been reached.

Most behavioral scientists are agreed that the youth stage of the life cycle is increasingly more problematic owing to social, psychological, and physical changes (Conger, 1973; Hauser, 1971). Youth find themselves in the position of having lost their former childhood status and yet not having acquired the full status of the adult. They are, as Hoffer (1965) suggests, in a traditional period between statuses and affiliations characterized by rootlessness and a high rate of change. The experience of status discontinuity confronts the youth with few clearly defined expectations or norms to guide his behavior.[1] At the social level, youth are expected to become more seriously committed to the acquisition of values, skills, and patterns of behavior appropriate to the adult world of experience, to enlarge the range of potential reference groups and significant others, and to become much more sophisticated in relating to others. These relationships in turn bring new expectations, demands, and opportunities to which the youth is expected to respond. As a psychological phenomenon, the youth perhaps for the first time attempts consciously and deliberately to conceptualize himself, to reconcile the external and internal world of experience, i.e., to come to terms with himself and his society (Douvan and Adelson, 1968; Erikson, 1968). The growth in cognitive capacity and the development of intellectual skills permit new ways of learning and incorporating behavior while simultaneously serving as liberating and motivating forces impelling the youth toward more active participation in his own socialization. These unprecedented changes create perturbations if not severe stress. The normative identity crisis so often referred to in connection with this period is a result of these multiple transformations and social pressures.

There is little to indicate that black youth escape the tensions and turbulence of this period, as numerous autobiographical accounts and essays would seem to suggest (Brown, 1965; Cleaver, 1968; Ellison, 1963; Malcolm X, 1965). Moreover, problems precipitated by minority status, cultural conflict, and caste victimization may result in complications of a somewhat different order and may be seen to take different forms and find quite different solutions among these youth (Brody, 1964; Clark, 1965; Rainwater, 1966).

The issues of crucial significance for youth are questions of choice and commitment (Erikson, 1968; Marcia, 1966). The need to develop a sense of identity from among all past, current, and potential relations compels the youth to make a series of increasingly more circumscribed selections of personal, occupational, and ideological commitments. His choice and commitment to the performance of certain social roles aids in the establishment of his social identity, while his commitment to certain personally relevant values and beliefs permits membership in a larger community through which extensions of his identity are fostered and solidified. The variety of social roles and values as available options open to the youth are not, however, unlimited. With each choice the breadth and variety of alternatives narrow. Such variables as race, religion, level of education, and community have the effect of reducing the range of possibilities. Furthermore, there is some reason to believe that the specific ways in which the youth attempts to resolve these issues is determined in part by his position or the position of his parents in the hierarchy of social classes (Musgrove, 1964; Schonfeld, 1971). That is, the status differentials among youth are highly related to the ways in which they orient themselves to the society at large and have a decided influence on the content, duration, and stressfulness of the period. Hence, youth of various classes may be expected to differ in their modes of response to problems encountered during this period in their development and to move at differing paces toward relative identity formation.

With the prospect of choice and decision, the youth is likely to be shopping around for behavioral models and clarifying definitions that offer the possibility of relative permanence and stability in personal organization. Parents may only ambivalently serve as acceptable models during this period given the youth's early dependency on them. Furthermore, the inability of parents to confer extrinsic personal status is well recognized by the youth, as is the knowledge that a sense of identity and personal worth as an adult requires a degree of social recognition that transcends the family. How parents are displaced as role models is revealed in a study by Havighurst and his associates (1946) in their analysis of essays written by children and youth on the theme, "The Kind of Person I Want to Be." In childhood the persons most clearly idealized are parents, while during early adolescence parents are partially displaced by various glamorous "personalities" such as movie stars, athletes, or fictional characters. But in late adolescence, the most idealized individuals tend to be attractive and visible individuals who exemplify certain valued competences or skills, and who are generally admired by adults in the community. Yet parents are not altogether rejected by the youth. Their significance and function as models tend to vary depending upon socioeconomic status and the nature of early parent–child relationships.

Perhaps at no other time is the tendency to rely on models more open to observation than during the adolescent period of development. The literature abounds in examples of youth seeking desperately for someone to have faith in, to look up to, someone to serve as a reliable and trustworthy model for experimentation and guidance into their new identities (Goethals and Klos, 1970). "To such a person," Erikson (1956) writes, "the late adolescent wants to be an apprentice or disciple, a follower . . . a patient." The phrase "in search of identity" quite appropriately describes the youth's experimentation with different models and value systems to find the ones of best fit. Since identity is something to be cultivated and not merely a function of social inheritance, there is the necessity of experimenting and choosing, and the possibility of making incorrect and inappropriate choices. Nonetheless, how the youth relates himself and is related to his society is revealed through these crucial choices.

To the extent that identity formation involves the activity of relating oneself to persons, values, and institutions in one's society, it invariably involves the process of identification. As the massive literature and research reveals, the process of identification is one of the principal media through which behavior, values, skills, and other identity elements are learned—the essential means by which identity grows in ever more mature interplay with the identities of the individual's models. The cultivation of identity through the process of identification inevitably gives to the individual's identity features which are common to the identities of others. Thus the youth identifies with others and those others become extensions of his identity, i.e., features or symbols of its content.

The selection and identification with role models may be determined by several factors. As Bandura and Walters (1963) have shown, models must be perceived as having high utility value for the realization of personal aspirations and goals. In addition, such variables as age, sex, social class, and racial and ethnic status are all important determinants in role model selection. Equally important are the potential identifier's own characteristics that affect his preferences and determine the types of models who are selected for observation and emulation (Bandura and Walters, 1970). Most youth may be assumed to have some plans regarding their personal futures, the outlines of which are only roughly sketched in. Hence, the youth's anticipations and aspirations may be said to serve as the reference ground for present conduct and stylizations of his identity (Hauser, 1971). In his choice of models he is likely to choose attributes or qualities that fit him, become him, those things that go with his other qualities. Again, much depends on how the youth sees himself and his future, for appropriateness and fit are only meaningful in terms of the ideal identity for which the qualities of the model are chosen.

In considering the role of models as they function in the service of relative identity formation, attention should be focused on relevant psychosocial tasks to be resolved at this stage in the life cycle. Among the tasks encountered during this period are those of instrumental and interpersonal competence, i.e., the development of role skills and styles of performance related to particular social roles. For male youth, choosing and preparing for a vocational role takes precedence in awareness,

since occupation plays a crucial defining role in his identity (Blau, 1963). The dominant theme in his choice of models is therefore likely to be work relevant. An equally important task has to do with the establishment of a set of personal values and, more generally, the commitment to an ideological system. Lane (1969) and Smith et al. (1956), among others, have demonstrated the important function of ideological commitments in the search for a personal sense of identity. The values to which the youth commits himself are not simply carbon copies of parental values, nor are they the result of internalization of disembodied rules, principles, or other abstractions; rather they are the outcome of discovery through experience of these ideals and principles appropriate to his circumstances.

From the foregoing, two types of role models can be conceptually distinguished. Models may be conceived as: (1) specific persons who serve as examples by means of which specific skills and behavior patterns are acquired, and (2) a set of attributes or ideal qualities which may or may not be linked directly with any one particular person as such, in which case the model is symbolic, representing a synthesis of diffuse and discrete phenomena. Hence, *exemplary* and *symbolic* models may be observed to serve different functions and to be invested with quite different meanings by the youth engaged in the process of cultivating various features of his social and personal identity.[2]

Exemplary models may be seen as persons who provide the technical knowledge, skills, or behavioral patterns that can be effectively utilized by the youth for developing certain competencies; in effect, they demonstrate for the youth how something is done (Kemper, 1968). A variety of exemplary models may be utilized for cultivating different features of identity and may reflect more clearly achievement strivings and identity goals. Symbolic models may be conceived as representing particular value orientations, ideal or ideological perspectives. We have in mind the tendency of cultures to embody abstract values, principles, and other "collective representations" in mythical, historical, and living figures (e.g., heroes), and the inclination of individuals to view certain figures as repositories of particular virtues, ideals, or esteemed attributes. As persons, symbolic models function as guides in the search for congenial ideology and values through their "personalization" of values and ideals. Through personal achievement, courage, or social activities, they serve to inspire adherence to certain ways of behaving and thinking.

The nature and extent of a given model's influence in the emerging psychosocial identity of youth may vary, and such a possibility must be taken into account. As a means of approach, the relationship between a given youth and his models may be conceptualized in terms of *type, content, and scope of* their relationship. *Type* refers to the quality or tone of the relationship and may be defined as *positive, negative, or neutral*. The quality of the relationship between the subject and the model can be established largely through an analysis of the content of the relationship. By *content* we refer to the nature of the model's influence as this is defined or described by the subject. Such influence may be described as having occurred on the level of overt behavior or conscious orientations, with respect to values, aspirations, beliefs, or goals. In addition, the influence of the model may be seen as general or specific, in which case we refer to the *scope* of the model's influence, that is, whether the youth is inclined toward appropriating specific behaviors or orientations of the model, or whether his desire is generally to "be like" the model in most respects. In those terms, the scope of the model's influence would indicate whether he functions in the capacity of exemplary or symbolic model.

This approach to psychosocial development attempts to remedy what Matza (1964) has termed the "hard determinism" perspective, which suffuses sociological and social psychological research at some levels with an emphasis on personal choice, commitment, and uniqueness as essential ingredients in identity formation. Hence, it seeks to focus attention on the interactional and constructive processes of psychosocial development in which the individual is an active participant. Its value lies in the potential for providing useful data on the content and character of black youths' evolving sense of identity as reflected in their choice of models. Its utility has already become apparent in a recent investigation carried out by the author (Taylor, 1973). Some of the more salient findings from that study are summarized below.

Black Youth and Role Models Identification

Thirty black male youth made up the total sample for the investigation. They ranged in age from 18 to 21 and represented a wide range of socioeconomic backgrounds and geographical locations. The sample is therefore a highly specific one. To begin with, it consists only of male college youths.[3] While this fact places an important limitation on the kinds of conclusions that can be drawn, the aim was to examine the lives of a certain segment of the youth population to discover the function of role models in their emerging psychosocial economies. The techniques of investigation consisted of the autobiography and the intensive interview. A number of topics empirically shown to be relevant to psychosocial development were explored, including the youth's early and more recent experiences in the family and community, his conceptions of the future as reflected in aspirations and plans, and his value orientations and self-definitions (Douvan and Adelson, 1968; Elder, 1968; Hauser, 1971). Data from these areas provided the basis upon which to establish the general sociohistorical context within which psychosocial development occurred, and it was within this context that role model identifications and their function in psychosocial identity were examined.

It is in the youth's striving to systematize and order the various and sundry influences on his life that his significant models can be observed to emerge. In fact, the clarity of self-concept can be seen to have been aided by the establishment of significant identifications; we found that such models could be isolated for most of these youth and that they were closely related to the quality of integration of their psychosocial organization.

Who are the figures that emerge in the imagery of these youth as they move toward engagement of identity-related issues and the task of evolving an identity ideal? When the data are analyzed for those models having a significant impact on the psychosocial identity of these youth, patterns of identification are centered primarily, though not exclusively, in the family. Parental models are observed to play powerfully active roles in the evolving sense of identity of these youth. To be sure, other models are also observed to have a significant impact on shaping their identities and tend to reflect certain styles of psychosocial development.

Most behavioral scientists seem to agree that the influence of one parent or the other tends to exceed the influence of any other one or two persons in our lives. Some students attribute the more formative and influential role to the mother whose early relationship with the child is assumed to be of crucial importance in subsequent development. In this connection, the role of the black mother has been given particular attention owing to her alleged dominant position in the family and the assumed consequences this seems to have for the child. A variety of empirical evidence would appear to support the view of the mother's influential role in the child's early development (Emmerich, 1956; Mussen, 1969; Winch, 1962). However, a somewhat different pattern of influence may emerge during later stages of development. For the male youth, the mother may continue to function as an object of moral and emotional support, while others, including the father, serve as models through whom he seeks to cultivate his social and personal identity. Indeed, this is precisely the pattern which emerges from the accounts of our subjects. The model who figures most prominently in their accounts of their more recent development is clearly the father or father surrogate.

From their various accounts it becomes clear that a considerable transformation has occurred over the years in their relationship with the father, growing stronger or weaker as the case may be, as each youth has gained in the capacity and knowledge to make critical judgments of the father's personal qualities, competences, and limitations. Changes at both the conceptual and perceptual levels have apparently resulted in changes in valuing and behaving toward the father as model, and more often than not these changes have revealed new and different aspects of his personal qualities previously overlooked or ignored. This may be seen to have important consequences for the father's role as model for his son.

At least several factors or conditions could be identified as having influenced the extent to which the father became a salient model for the youth. In general, the father's influence as a model stems from his ability to provide what may be called crucial resources, i.e., pertinent behavior patterns, general value orientations, and the like, which the youth has found, through experience, to be particularly effective in coping with certain developmental problems. Hence, the father's role as significant model was often contingent upon and expressed in terms of what he did or failed to do for the youth at various crucial periods in life. What emerges, then, is a general principle of "reciprocity," i.e., an exchange of resources for identification between father and son (compare Scanzoni, 1971).

For most youths the father functions generally as exemplary rather than as symbolic model. That is, few choose him as their identity ideal. Rather, a pattern emerges whereby the father, during various stages in the early life of the youth, functions as a powerful symbolic model, but growth and maturity lead to an apparent rejection of him at later stages, though he continues to serve the useful function of exemplary model. However, where appropriate opportunities for making critical judgments of the father's personal attributes or competences were not possible, or where such opportunities were severely limited, a transformation in this role frequently did not occur. This tendency was often observed in cases where the father was absent from the home through separation, divorce, or death, and where his place in the psychological economy of the youth became that of an unchanging figure whose personal characteristics and expectations were imagined to always be the same. Under these circumstances, the youth desired to become like this idealized image of the father (often encouraged by the mother and other relatives) and sought to cultivate his putative characteristics.

Just as the father may come to serve as a powerful object of positive identification, both admired and emulated by the youth, he was also observed to function in the capacity of "negative model," an evil prototype of identity features the youth should seek to avoid and of a potential future he should seek to prevent. This seeming rejection of the father as a relevant or useful model does not necessarily see the end of his influence, however. Indeed, he may "live on" in the shadows of the youth's consciousness, assuming the role of *rival*, and thus come to occupy a prominent place in the evolving identity. Implicit here, of course, is the notion that the perception and rejection of the father as appropriate model extends beyond simple nonacceptance of his modes of behavior, attitudes, or values, frequently encompassing the formation of counter-behavior and values. Hence, the father's role as negative model may often turn out to be just as influential in shaping the behavior, values, and identity aspirations of the youth as his function in a more positive sense.

In general, from these data it becomes clear that the father plays a highly significant role in the evolving identity of these youth. It seems that in one way or another, they are compelled to come to terms with the paternal figure. And since different motives may be seen to have driven the youth at different periods in life, the extent to which the father becomes a salient model may be governed by the relevance of certain of his personal attributes or qualities for coping with the central concerns of the youth during a given period, including the resolution of certain tasks related to identity formation. Thus our analysis suggests that the father's function as role model is never static or unchanging, except under conditions where he may be absent from the home during crucial periods in the life of the youth.

Other models are also observed to play active roles in the emergent identity of these youths. While these models are seen to come and go, to wax and wane in importance across the span of the youth's biographical career, they tend to fall roughly into two main categories: work relevant and value relevant models. Both are essential in the youth's ability to evolve an identity ideal, an interrelated set of images that have psychological significance for him. Almost all youth had strong work models, i.e., they had identified closely with someone in a vocational area in which they were interested. Although it is difficult to know whether the choice of an occupation preceded identification with a specific model, or whether the discovery of the model resulted in a strong interest in a given field, it is clear that the model often served to deepen vocational interests and inspire commitment of a significant nature. Indeed, the model was often said to have more clearly focused the interests and energies of the youth, a typical response being: "I became more serious

about my studies and more concerned about really preparing myself for a career."

Value relevant models come into focus as the youth moves toward setting priorities among his interests and preferences, as he seeks to give a certain structure and meaning to his life. Such attempts reflect a growing awareness of the diversity of human values, the complexity of human experience, and the relationship between values and the achievement of social purpose. Such value relevant models were both living and dead, and were frequently selected on the basis of their convictions, courage, and achievements. They provided values and beliefs about what is worthwhile in life and inspired hope in the future and in one's individual chance.

Perhaps one of the most serious and recurring problems encountered by many of these youth in evolving an identity ideal—that is, in selecting appropriate models for inclusion in the evolving pattern—has to do with the impermanence of potentially useful models which, in turn, renders significant and lasting identifications difficult, if not impossible. In recent years numerous popular black figures have appeared, persons with whom these youth have become familiar and to whom many have become attracted. Yet the failure of many such persons to withstand the press of events and changing times has often resulted in their failure to hold the imagination of these youth. Indeed, the emergence and demise of once popular models has at times been so incessant as to leave many youth confused, frustrated, and eventually unwilling to invest themselves, their admiration, and their trust in any and all models.

Here one may observe a strong skepticism toward popular and not so popular models. The attitude may be assumed that all models are constantly becoming out of date, beginning to decline even as they emerge, since things are in a state of flux. For some youth a solution is found in selecting as models more distant figures, those less vulnerable to change, e.g., the deceased. Thus it is not surprising that such figures as Martin Luther King, Malcolm X, Marcus Garvey, Frederick Douglass, or W. E. B. DuBois, all important black men of the past, are identified as the nearly most perfect models by these youth.

Since one's own fate may be thought to be linked with that of one's model in the sense that their failures and humiliations become one's own and, therefore, damaging to self-esteem, the selection of deceased figures may often be seen as "safer" investments, as less susceptible to the vicissitudes of contemporary life than are living models. In any case, one is less likely to be disappointed by such models in the future since their biographical careers have been terminated.

Summary and Conclusions

Although there are perhaps many ways of looking at the process of becoming an adult, that is, of achieving a mature and relatively stable sense of personal identity, we found it to be a useful strategy to see the process as one in which the youth gradually acquires a variety of commitments as revealed through his selections and identifications with certain role models who influence as well as constrain his psychosocial development. In effect, commitments create the conditions for stability in personal organization and thus permit the relative formation of identity. The extent to which a given youth was able to establish significant role model identifications was found to be intimately related to the character and quality of integration of his psychosocial organization. The notion of commitment allows us to focus upon the age at which it becomes possible to make serious choices of some lasting consequence. For example, it seems less likely that children are capable of making lasting commitments that more or less bind them to a future course of development than are youth about to enter upon a new and different status, youth who are not only encouraged to make serious commitments but who have at their disposal a rich variety of social and psychological supports as well as a fund of experience upon which to rely.

How the youth comes eventually to commit himself to achieving a certain identity requires a fuller analysis than we have given here. Investigations have only recently begun in this area of which the work of Hauser (1971) is a notable example. In his investigation of identity formation among black and white lower-class youth, he finds an identity

foreclosure pattern to be more prevalent among black youth. He attributes this identity variant to "model deprivation," frequent failure, and to their perception of limited opportunities. Hence, their view of the future, together with absent role models, had a decided effect on their ability to make future commitments, i.e., to stake themselves on achieving certain identities with a fairly confident expectation that such identities would be realized in the future. But what of other youth? What antecedent conditions give rise to their permanence of choice and commitment? Does environmental stability, including such things as changes in family structure, frequent changes in social conditions, and the impermanence of popular and potentially useful models, affect the permanence with which they are able or willing to make more or less lasting commitments? While these data suggest that environmental stability is indeed an important aspect influencing personal commitments, only a more rigorous investigation can produce evidence that would either confirm or deny the validity of this observation.

There would appear to be heuristic value in conceptualizing psychosocial identity as a constructive process, a process mediated by the youth's conception of the future which he may render tractable by choices made in the present. Stated differently, the youth's anticipation of a certain future is the reference point for present conduct and stylizations of identity. His role model identifications would expose the changing meaning of the future. Youth lacking a clear conception of the future, having failed to develop a tentative life plan, were observed to have less instrumental and realistic notions of steps toward their goals, including the selection of appropriate models who might help to bring about their realization. Future investigations might focus more fully on the sequence of models as indications of the youth's changing perspectives, values, and identity goals. In addition, stability and change in role model identifications may offer important insights into the nature of the youth's conception of future possibilities in terms of identity construction.

A thorough developmental analysis of personal and social identity among black youth is a major task that goes beyond the present undertaking. What is required is a comprehensive longitudinal portrayal of development, including description and explanation of the evolving relations between the processes of construction, interaction, and enculturation. We have attempted to develop a tentative conceptual framework which, it is hoped, will facilitate analysis and interpretation in this area, one which will enable us to see the function of role models as integral parts of the developmental and maturational process.

---

[1] While it is perhaps true that youth subcultures function as sources of interim status and social support, they are for most youth temporary solutions. It remains for the youth to come to grips with the adult world of experience where a mature (or more acceptable), permanent identity and status are to be found.

[2] Orrin Klapp uses the term "symbolic leaders" to describe such persons as movie stars, politicians, and other celebrities; see his Symbolic Leaders (1967). Bandura and Walters (1963) have used the term "symbolic and exemplary models" to describe persons presented through films to children. As these terms are used here, both take on a largely different meaning than those assigned by Klapp or Bandura and Walters.

[3] Black females were not included in the sample because it was assumed on the basis of some empirical evidence that females are normally presented with a somewhat different set of psychosocial problems and thus would have made the task of analysis more difficult.

References

Bandura, A., and R. H. Walters

1963　Social Learning and Personality Development. New York: Holt.

1970　Psychological Modeling. Chicago: Aldine.

Blau, P.

1963　"Occupational Choice: A Conceptual Framework." In Neil Smelser and William T. Smelser, eds., Personality and Social Systems. New York: Wiley.

Brody, E. B.

1964　"Color and Identity Conflict in Young Boys." Archives of General Psychiatry 10 (April):354–360.

Brown, C.

1965　Manchild in the Promised Land. New York: Macmillan.

Clark, K. B.

1965　Dark Ghetto: Dilemmas of Social Power. New York: Harper.

Cleaver, E.

1968　Soul on Ice. New York: Delta.

Conger, J. J.

1973　Adolescence and Youth. New York: Harper.

Douvan, E., and J. Adelson

1968　The Adolescent Experience. New York: Wiley.

Elder, G. H.

1968　Adolescent Socialization and Personality Development. Chicago: Rand McNally.

Ellison, R.

1963　The Invisible Man. Westminister, Md.: Modern Library.

Emmerich, W.

1956　"Parental Identification in Young Children." Genetic Psychology Monographs 60:257–308.

Erikson, E.

1950　Childhood and Society. New York: Norton.

1956　"The Problem of Ego Identity." Journal of the American Psychological Association 4:58–121.

1964　"Memorandum on Identity and Negro Youth." Journal of Social Issues 20:29–42.

1968　Identity: Youth and Crisis. New York: Norton.

Goethals, G., and D. S. Klos, editors

1970　Experiencing Youth: First Person Accounts. Boston: Little, Brown.

Hauser, S. T.

1971　Black and White Identity Formation. New York: John Wiley.

Havighurst, R., M. Robinson, and M. Dorr

1946　"The Development of the Ideal Self in Childhood and Adolescence." Journal of Educational Research 40:241–257.

Hoffer, E.

1965　"An Age for Juveniles." Harper's 6:18–21.

Kemper, T.

1968 "Reference Groups, Socialization and Achievement." *American Sociological Review* 33 (February):31–45.

Klapp, O. E.

1967 *Symbolic Leaders.* Homewood, Ill.: Dorsey.

Lane, R.

1969 *Political Thinking and Consciousness.* Chicago: Markham.

Malcolm X

1965 *The Autobiography of Malcolm X.* New York: Grove.

Marcia, J. E.

1966 "Development and Validation of Ego Identity Status." *Journal of Abnormal and Social Psychology* 3:551–558.

Matza, D.

1964 *Delinquency and Drift.* New York: Wiley.

McKinley, D. G.

1964 *Social Class and Family Life.* New York: Free Press.

Musgrove, F.

1964 *Youth and the Social Order.* London: Routledge & Kegan Paul.

Mussen, P. H.

1969 "Early Sex-Role Development." In David A. Goslin, ed., *Handbook of Socialization Theory and Research.* Chicago: Rand McNally.

Pettigrew, T. F.

1964 "Negro American Personality: Why Isn't More Known?" *Journal of Social Issues* 20 (April): 4–23.

Proshansky, H., and P. Newton

1968 "The Nature and Meaning of Negro Self-Identity." In Martin Deutsch, Irwin Katz, and Arthur R. Jensen, eds., *Social Class, Race, and Psychological Development.* New York: Holt.

Rainwater, L.

1966 "Crucible of Identity: The Negro Lower-Class Family." *Daedalus* 95 (Winter):172–216.

Scanzoni, J. H.

1971 *The Black Family in Modern Society.* Boston: Allyn & Bacon.

Schonfeld, W.

1971 "Adolescent Turmoil: Socioeconomic Affluence as a Factor." In Ralf E. Muuss, ed., *Adolescent Behavior and Society.* New York: Random House.

Smith, B. M., J. Bruner, and R. White

1956 *Opinions and Personality.* New York: Wiley.

Taylor, R. L.

1973 "The Function of Role Models in Social Development: Explorations in Black Identity." Ph.D. dissertation, Boston University (unpublished).

Winch, R.

1962 *Identification and Its Familial Determinants.* New York: Bobbs-Merrill.

EARLY PARENTHOOD AMONG LOW-INCOME ADOLESCENT GIRLS

Lorraine P. Mayfield

It has been believed that many women become trapped in poverty because of out-of-wedlock children born during their adolescence. Data are presented which show this to be more true for whites than for Blacks. Black adolescents who become mothers are less likely than whites to marry and move away from home and are more likely to be living with their parents and receiving assistance with child care. For the Black adolescent, motherhood is less likely to terminate education and preparation for the future.

Introduction

By 1980, two-thirds of female-headed families received child welfare and two-thirds of the long-term poor were women (U.S. Commission on Civil Rights, 1983). This rapid rise of female-headed families is due partly to the rising failure rate of marriage and the low income of women who were separated and divorced and partly to a massive rise in the number of babies born to unwed teenage mothers. The contemporary trend toward out-of-wedlock teenage motherhood is particularly striking in both Black and white low-income communities. Between 1975 and 1979, out-of-wedlock births to teenagers 15–19 years old increased from 223 to 253 per 1,000 live births (U.S. Department of Health and Human Services, 1981).

Many researchers have examined the implications of teenage childbearing for education, employment, and other factors related to poverty. Research shows that early motherhood has serious negative consequences for young women (Chilman, 1983; Furstenberg, 1976; Presser, 1975; Waite and Moore, 1978). Teenage mothers in these studies were much more likely to drop out of school because of pregnancy, be without employment experience, bear other children early, and be on public assistance after the birth, in comparison to youth who began childbearing in their early twenties.

Usually uneducated, unskilled, and unsupported, teenage mothers are in need of financial and emotional support. This paper examines the role of family support and family formation for low-income adolescent women who are coping with motherhood. I focus on poor teenagers because they are more likely to become pregnant and less likely to terminate an unwanted pregnancy than youth from affluent backgrounds (Chilman, 1983). In addition, youth from poor families are more likely to be vulnerable to the intergenerational transmission of poverty. In particular, this paper explores the family support available and attempts to explain young mothers' marital status. I hypothesize that family support and marital status vary by racial background. The following propositions are discussed in this study:

1. Low-income adolescent Black mothers have more role models of single-headed households

Paper prepared for presentation at the American Sociological Association Annual Meeting, San Antonio, Texas, August 28, 1984. Printed by permission.

than whites, which reduces the urgency of an early marriage.

2. Low-income adolescent Black mothers receive greater family support than whites because of strong kinship ties in the Black community.

3. Low-income young Black mothers marry later because they aspire to higher upward mobility aspiration than low-income young white mothers.

The implications of these hypotheses may provide important insights to process of whether or not poverty is transmitted across generations and assist with social policy geared to reduction of poverty in women's lives and their disadvantaged children.

Theoretical Overview and Review of Literature

Status Transition

The status transition perspective is used to assess whether young mothers view themselves as moving from one status to another, leaving adolescence to enter adulthood. The early entry into the role of parent is often synchronized with other role transitions that interfere with the normative central activity of adolescent years—that is, schooling. The single most evident consequence of early role transition is the depressing effect on schooling (Furstenberg, 1976; Hofferth and More, 1979; Presser, 1975; Waite and Moore, 1978). Whether or not young mothers aspire to remain in school and seek its completion provides evidence of how they view their status in the life course.

Some researchers (Ladner, 1972; Stack, 1974) report that low-income teenage Black mothers gain maturity, autonomy, and respect as mothers in the community after the birth of their first child. Ladner (1972), in her anthropological study of Black adolescent females in a St. Louis ghetto, advances the idea that a girl becomes a woman through having a baby; she performs motherhood functions and joins the community of experienced mothers. According to

Ladner, adolescence is not seen as a life stage and as a period of preparation for maturity; rather, children move directly into adulthood when they become parents, even though premarital birth of a first child is characteristically viewed as a mistake (Ladner, 1972:216). Stack (1974), in her anthropological study of a midwestern city of low-income Black families and youth, found that young Black mothers often stated that having a baby made them feel more mature and responsible. She found that within their homes, young Black mothers are granted freer social lifes. Although early and out-of-wedlock childbirths are not held to be desirable in the low-income Black community, it is usually accepted as an unfortunate but often inevitable event.

However, other researchers view early motherhood as an event that has serious negative consequences but does not necessarily propel youth into the adult role. Furstenberg (1976), in his longitudinal survey study of 400 predominantly Black and economically disadvantaged adolescent mothers in Baltimore, found that early motherhood may present no serious obstacles to continued high school education. Furstenberg's sample showed that young Black mothers were most apt to return to school if they held high educational goals and had help with child care. In his study, remaining single was highly correlated with more help from the teenagers' family in many ways, including child care. Presser (1975), in her study of 408 women in several age brackets from New York City, found that 60 percent of the first births were unplanned and that teenage mothers, although unprepared for motherhood, did not consider themselves adults.

The literature on young white mothers, especially from low-income family backgrounds, is scant. Rubin's (1976) in-depth study of white working-class families shows that marriage is viewed as an absolute requirement by both men and women if a girl becomes pregnant; thus, the white teenage mother is likely to enter the role of wife.

Value of Early Marriage

In conventional thinking, when a young woman marries she assumes the role of adult. Overall, the dominant U.S. cultural norms prescribe entry into the marital role during the youth's twenties. The costs of teenage marriage are great to individuals and society because early marriages are associated with higher fertility, economic difficulties, and greater risk of divorce.

In the blue-collar California families that Rubin (1976:41) describes in her study,

> *for most working-class girls getting married was, and probably still is, the singularly acceptable way out of an oppressive family situation and into a respected social status and the only way to move from girl to woman.*

For this group, premarital pregnancy automatically means marriage for both men and women (Rubin, 1976:67). Elder and Rockwell (1976) carried out an analysis of the causes and consequences of timing of marriage among white women born between 1925 and 1929. Using data from the National Fertility Studies of 1965 and 1970, they found that early-marrying women were more likely to come from low socioeconomic origins, especially if they failed to finish high school. Howell and Frese (1982:46) confirm this finding in their study of 945 southern teenagers in 1975, in which they found that white females tended to marry earlier and drop out of school at higher rates than Blacks. Kenkel (1981) reports in his study of 311 low-income southern high school girls that white girls were less willing to postpone marriage and were more likely to have goals of being wives and mothers only.

Within low-income Black communities, marriage to legitimize a child has often been seen as not practical (Ladner, 1972; Stack, 1974). Although fertility is highly valued in the Black community, early marriage to legitimize children is not the dominant practice (Furstenberg, 1976; Ladner, 1972). In addition, early marriages are perceived as having negative consequences on youths' educational achievement. All too often, the father of the baby is an unemployed or underemployed youth with little chance for financial improvement. The community usually holds that marriages should be entered into because they have a good chance of succeeding and because the couple wants to (and can) live together and establish its own home. Otherwise, the young

mother and her child can live with relatives. With the concept of status transition, we examine some of the social consequences, particularly as it relates to marriage and family support.

Data and Methodology

Data

The data for this study came from the Youth Incentive Entitlement Pilot Project (YIEPP), funded by the U.S. Department of Labor and managed by Manpower Demonstration Research Corporation. In response to high unemployment among young people, especially Blacks, Congress in 1977 enacted the Youth Employment and Demonstration Projects Act. YIEPP was one of the four experimental programs established under the act. The research design for this study of the program impact of YIEPP incorporated interviews with a sample of 7,553 youths at four locations and four matched comparison sites. The urban sites were Baltimore, Maryland; Cincinnati, Ohio; and Denver, Colorado. In Baltimore, only a third of the city was included in the area of study, whereas the entire cities of Cincinnati and Denver were included. The fourth study site consisted of eight rural counties in Mississippi (Adams, Claiborne, Covington, Franklin, Jefferson, Jones, Wayne, and Wilkinson). The four comparison sites chosen were Cleveland, Ohio; Louisville, Kentucky; Phoenix, Arizona; and a group of counties in western and eastern Mississippi (Clarke, Humphreys, Lauderdale, Shirley, Smith, and Washington).

The following criteria were used to choose eligible youth for the sample: (1) The youth must live in the geographic areas of the Entitlement project for 30 days prior to the survey, (2) the youth is aged 15–19, (3) the youth has not received a high school diploma or certificate of high school equivalency, and (4) the youth is economically disadvantaged, either by constituting a family of one or by being a member of one, and the family income is at or below the poverty level as determined by the Office of Management and Budget.

During 1978, household screening interviews were administered to a stratified random sample of about 130,000 households to determine the presence of youths. Interviewers subsequently returned to each eligible household and conducted baseline interviews with eligible youths and their parents.

The purpose of the baseline survey was to collect data on demographic characteristics, family background, and self-esteem of the youths as well as on the behavior of these youths with regard to their schooling, training, and work experience. The baseline survey was not officially identified with YIEPP demonstration program. The findings of the baseline survey are reported in *Schooling and Work among Youth from Low-Income Households* (Barclay et al., 1979).

The Full Sample

The entire sample consisted of 7,553 youths interviewed in their households in the areas listed previously. Minority representation was very high because of the southern locations and the greater minority populations in the inner city. The sample consisted of white, Black, and Hispanic youths ranging from 15-year-olds to 19-year-olds. Fourteen percent were age 15, 30 percent were 16, 27 percent were 17, 18 percent were 18, and 11 percent were 19.

The sample was 48 percent male and 52 percent female. The mean level of family income for the total sample was $6,395 in 1975. Over 50 percent of family income is derived from earned income in most sites, except Baltimore, Cleveland, and Cincinnati. In these study sites, the Aid to Families with Dependent Children (AFDC) component is high. Slightly more than 55 percent of all youths and their families were receiving some type of welfare assistance.

This YIEPP baseline survey sample was in no way identified with the demonstrations and included all youths eligible for the program. One strength of this data set is that it sheds light on an infrequently surveyed population—older teenagers from poverty families living either in inner cities or rural areas and who are making slow progress in school. In contrast to the National Longitudinal Study of High School Seniors of the Class of 1972,

this data set provides insights into the behavior of the U.S. poor in their formative years. Another advantage is that the large sample size makes it possible to categorize respondents by motherhood status and race. The effects of motherhood are inferred by comparing the outcome variables for the nonparenting groups.

For this paper, I focus the analysis on a sample of 3,832 Black and white female teenagers. This sample consists of 56 percent Black nonmothers, 21 percent white nonmothers, 17 percent Black mothers, and 6 percent white mothers. Much of the analysis focuses on the young mothers.

Methodology

Cross-tabular analysis of the outcome variables of family support and marital status were presented by racial and parenting status for comparison. Measures of family support included questions on residential, financial, and child care assistance. Respondents were asked "Do you live with parent/guardian now?" Unfortunately, if the teenager did not live with parent/guardians, no other question was asked about whom else she may be living with. Financial dependence on parents or guardians was determined from responses to the question "Do you receive any allowance or money from your parents or guardians on a regular basis?" Child care assistance was ascertained by the question "Is your child regularly cared for by someone else during the day?"

Measures for upward mobility aspirations related to educational status and were gleaned from the following questions: "Are you currently enrolled in a junior high school, or any kind of high school, or in a G.E.D. program?" "What was the highest grade you completed in school?" "How much education would you really like to get, if everything worked out just right?"

The girls' parents' current household status was taken from the parents' response to this question: "Are you currently married and living with your (husband/wife), widowed, divorced, separated, or have you never been married?"

Portrait of Teenage Mothers and Nonmothers

Table 1 shows how teenagers who are mothers differ in many respects from those who do not have children. Background factors (e.g., age, marital status, present living arrangements) are compared across race and parenting status. Table 1A shows the age range of the sample is 15 to 19 years old. Young mothers are slightly older than nonmothers and, regardless of race, youths tend to be mothers as their age increases.

From Table 1B, we learn that the overwhelming majority of Black mothers have never married, but the marital status of white mothers is quite different—40 percent of them were once married. Table 1C shows that older youths are more likely to marry than younger ones. This is especially the case for white mothers; 51 percent of the 19-year-old white mothers were previously married. Only 11 percent of the 19-year-old Black mothers were ever married.

Table 1D shows the present living arrangements of the teenagers, if the youth was living with parents/guardians at age 14. Black youth and white nonmothers are overwhelmingly likely to continue living with their parents and guardians. About 1 out

TABLE 1 Portrait of Teenage Mothers and Nonmothers by Age, Marital Status, Living Arrangements, and Child Care Support and by Race and Parenting Status

		BLACK MOTHERS	WHITE MOTHERS	BLACK NONMOTHERS	WHITE NONMOTHERS
A.	Age (in years)				
	15	8%	2%	21%	20%
	16	16	15	32	30
	17	27	25	26	26
	18	26	34	15	15
	19	24	24	6	9
		100%	100%	100%	100%
		(667)	(219)	(2,128)	(818)
B.	Never married	95%	60%	99%	86%
		(667)	(219)	(2,128)	(818)
C.	Never married by age (in years)				
	15	97%	—[1]	100%	100%
		(32)	(5)	(455)	(165)
	16	99%	70%	100%	98%
		(110)	(33)	(675)	(244)
	17	98%	57%	99%	95%
		(187)	(54)	(550)	(214)
	18	94%	65%	99%	91%
		(177)	(74)	(326)	(125)
	19	89%	49%	97%	87%
		(160)	(53)	(122)	(70)
D.	Living with parents *now*	83%	49%	98%	86%
		(391)	(159)	(1,197)	(450)

[1]Number of cases is too small for percentage.

of 2 white mothers live with parents/guardians. Unfortunately, the survey does not provide data on where youths live if they do not live with parents.

Table 2 presents some characteristics of the teenagers' family of origin. In particular, Table 2B shows that Black youths, both mothers and non-mothers, are more likely to live with parents who are without spouses than are white youths. Not only are Black youths more likely than whites to live in single-parent households, the young Black mothers also are more likely than any other category to live in a household in which their mothers have never married. Hence, the family structures of these low-income groups differ by race.

There are other variations in the households. The amount of deprivation varies within these low-income families. Table 2C shows that the young mothers' families, both Black and white, are more likely to receive public assistance than nonmothers' families.

Table 2D presents the distribution of the youths' parents' education. The mean grade completed for all the youths' parents is the ninth grade. Black parents are slightly more likely than white parents to have received more education, although few if any of the parents continued their education beyond high school. Table 2E shows that Black parents were not able to turn their slight education advantage into increased labor force participation. Approximately half of Black parents were out of the labor force in the past three years. In summary, young mothers' parents are little able to provide financial assistance and working role models as they struggle with poverty.

Results

Analyses of the Black/white differences in family formation for low-income adolescent girls are present in relationship to each of the three hypotheses.

1. Low-income adolescent Black mothers have more role models of single-headed households than whites, which reduces the urgency of an early marriage.

2. Low-income adolescent Black mothers receive greater family support than white mothers because of strong kinship ties in the Black community.
3. Low-income young Black mothers marry later because they aspire to higher upward mobility aspirations than low-income young white mothers.

The first proposition suggests that the family background and structure influence the type of future structure that young mothers may adopt. The profile of young mothers shows that a greater percentage of young Black mothers live in single-headed households than whites. This experience confirms previous research showing that young women brought up by female heads of household are less favorably disposed to traditional patterns of family structure (Crowley and Shapiro, 1982:414). Black youth, regardless of parenting status, are still living at home and may learn and value the viability of a single-parent home. Black adolescent mothers learn that the high rates of unemployment for Black men, particularly adolescent males, makes viable two-parent families difficult to achieve and maintain.

The second hypothesis concerning family support addresses the families' resources and strengths that low-income families can provide to their daughters. This section provides an analysis of the young women's continued dependence on their parents and society. Four types of dependence are examined: residential, financial, child care assistance provided by family, and welfare dependence on society (in particular, direct AFDC support to young mothers).

Table 3 shows the percentages of respondents who live at home with parents or guardians. The overwhelming majority of youths, regardless of parenting status, are more likely to live with their families.

Table 4 shows residential arrangement by marital status. As expected, never-married young women are more likely to live with their families. Of those youths who were previously married, 68 percent of Black mothers live at home and only 28 percent of white mothers live with their parents.

TABLE 2   Family Background Data by Race and Parenting Status

		BLACK MOTHERS	WHITE MOTHERS	BLACK NONMOTHERS	WHITE NONMOTHERS
A.	Relationship between parent and teenager, if teenager lives with parent				
	Mother	85%	83%	85%	82%
	Father	5	12	5	11
	Other relative	10	5	10%	7
		100%	100%	100%	100%
		(544)	(108)	(1,986)	(721)
B.	Parents' marital status				
	Married, living with spouse	26%	41%	31%	53%
	Widowed, divorced, separated	63	56	61	45
	Never married	11	3	8	2
		100%	100%	100%	100%
		(551)	(109)	(2,005)	(725)
C.	Percent of family receiving AFDC	63%	61%	47%	43%
		(550)	(109)	(2,002)	(725)
D.	Parents' education				
	8th grade or less	34%	53%	35%	47%
	9th grade	12	19	12	13
	10th grade	19	8	17	12
	11th grade	16	7	16	11
	12th grade	18	12	18	14
	Beyond high school	1	1	2	3
		100%	100%	100%	100%
		(538)	(108)	(1,950)	(707)
E.	Parents' time in labor force for past 3 years				
	All of the time	22%	24%	19%	16%
	Most of the time	8	9	9	9
	Some of the time	20	25	19	26
	None of the time	50	42	53	49
		100%	100%	100%	100%
		(551)	(109)	(2,004)	(725)

The percentages of single respondents who stay home is high, and marriage for white young mothers seems to be an impetus for moving away from home. On the other hand, motherhood for Blacks does not appear to be a compelling reason to leave home. In general, Black families continue to provide residential assistance to their daughters.

Another form of family support is financial assistance. Table 5A shows the percentage of respondents who receive regular financial support. Overall, nonmothers are more than twice as likely than young mothers to receive financial help. When young mothers do receive help, Blacks receive slightly greater financial assistance than their white counterparts, even when we take residential arrangements into account. Table 5B reveals that the

TABLE 3 Present Living Arrangements of Teenagers (If Teenagers Lived with Parents in the Past)

	BLACK MOTHERS	WHITE MOTHERS	BLACK NONMOTHERS	WHITE NONMOTHERS
Not living with parents	17%	51%	2%	14%
Living with parents	83	49	98	86
	100%	100%	100%	100%
	(391)	(159)	(1,197)	(450)

TABLE 4 Living with Parents/Guardian by Marital Status and by Race and Parenting Status

	BLACK MOTHERS	WHITE MOTHERS	BLACK NONMOTHERS	WHITE NONMOTHERS
Ever married	68%	28%	—[1]	1%
	(19)	(64)	(7)	(25)
Never married	85%	63%	99%	90%
	(371)	(95)	(1,190)	(425)

[1]Number of cases is too small for percentage.

youths' age influences whether or not they receive financial assistance. For all the categories of teenagers, as their age increases financial support decreases, especially for young mothers. The financial support for younger teenagers better enables them to continue their schooling; families may expect older adolescents to work or seek other means of support.

The availability of child care assistance is assessed by a number of indicators. Although these respondents were not directly asked who provides child care assistance, it is possible to speculate on possible candidates by examining their responses to the following questions:

1. "(Is/Are any of) your child(ren) regularly cared for by someone else during the day?"
2. "About how much does this care usually cost you per week?"

3. "About how many hours each day are they usually cared for?"
4. "How many miles, if any, do you have to travel to deliver your child(ren) to this care?"

Table 6A reports the percentage of young mothers who receive regular child care. Approximately half of Black mothers reported they can depend on someone else for child care assistance, whereas only a quarter of white mothers can do so. Black teenage mothers are more likely than white mothers to receive child care aid. Table 6B reveals that over three-fourths of Black mothers have child care assistance for five days of the week. Table 6C displays the percentages of the cost of child care to the young mothers. Black young mothers are more likely to receive free assistance than their white counterparts, and a larger percentage of white mothers pay a higher cost for child care than Blacks.

TABLE 5   Financial Help

		BLACK MOTHERS	WHITE MOTHERS	BLACK NONMOTHERS	WHITE NONMOTHERS
A.	Financial support from family by race and parenting status				
	Yes	14%	7%	33%	22%
	No	86	93	67	78
		100%	100%	100%	100%
		(663)	(216)	(2,121)	(813)
B.	Percentage of teenagers receiving financial aid from family by race, parenting status, and age				
	Age (in years)				
	15	39%	—¹	42%	33%
		(31)		(455)	(164)
	16	16%	19%	36%	26%
		(110)	(32)	(672)	(243)
	17	23%	13%	31%	19%
		(185)	(53)	(547)	(212)
	18	10%	1%	23%	12%
		(175)	(73)	(323)	(124)
	19	4%	2%	18%	8%
		(162)	(53)	(124)	(70)

¹Number of cases is too small for percentage.

Table 6D shows that all young mothers use child care assistance for the large portion of the day and that white mothers receive more hours per week.

Table 6E shows the miles traveled for child care help. Young mothers (both Black and white) often do not travel at all for child care assistance. Fewer than 5 percent of the mothers traveled beyond four miles for this help.

It is suggested by the extensive free child care, long hours provided, and lack of travel that parents or other relatives are providing help to these mothers. Black adolescent mothers who for the most part live at home receive more child care assistance than whites.

Although only 5 percent of all 3,832 youths— mothers and nonmothers—received any public assistance directly, Table 7 shows that Black young mothers were more likely than the other groups to receive this assistance. Because Black mothers come from homes that are more likely to be welfare-dependent, they may be more familiar with public assistance's eligibility criteria and procedures.

In summary, Black mothers are found to be more dependent on their families than their white counterparts. By living at home, Black adolescent mothers receive not only room and board but also regular financial help and child care assistance. For the very small percentage of youths who receive welfare support directly, Black mothers appear to be more dependent on societal resources than their white counterparts.

We next examine the hypothesis that low-income young Black mothers marry later than whites because they have high upward mobility aspirations. In particular, we explore educational attachment and aspirations as indicators of mobility aspirations.

TABLE 6   Child Care Assistance

		BLACK MOTHERS	WHITE MOTHERS
A.	Child care by someone else		
	Yes	48%	23%
	No	52	77
		100%	100%
		(658)	(214)
B.	Number of days child care used		
	1	1%	3%
	2	3	2
	3	2	5
	4	1	5
	5	78	59
	6	2	7
	7	13	19
		100%	100%
		(313)	(49)
C.	Cost of child care		
	$0	69%	51%
	$1–14	10	10
	$15 and over	21	39
		100%	100%
		(309)	(49)
D.	Child care hours used		
	1–7	23%	9%
	8	13	8
	9–24	64	83
		100%	100%
		(313)	(49)
E.	Miles traveled for child care		
	0	86%	80%
	1–3	10	15
	4 and over	4	5
		100%	100%
		(286)	(49)

Table 8A shows that the overwhelming proportion of Black nonmothers are currently enrolled in school; over half of white nonmothers and over two-fifths of Black mothers are attending school. White mothers are most likely to drop out—93 percent are not currently enrolled.

The highest grade completed provides a measure of school progress. Table 8B shows that white mothers made the least amount of educational progress; only 34 percent of them completed the ninth grade. Although white mothers are older than the other groups, they are less likely to be in the

TABLE 7   AFDC Income by Race and Parenting Status (from January 1977 to August 1984)

	BLACK MOTHERS	WHITE MOTHERS	BLACK NONMOTHERS	WHITE NONMOTHERS
Yes	69%	48%	26%	7%
No	31	52	74	93
	100%	100%	100%	100%
	(149)	(111)	(53)	(72)

TABLE 8   Educational Experiences and Aspirations

		BLACK MOTHERS	WHITE MOTHERS	BLACK NONMOTHERS	WHITE NONMOTHERS
A.	Currently enrolled	41%	7%	82%	52%
		(667)	(219)	(2,128)	(818)
B.	Highest grade completed				
	8th or less	15%	30%	6%	14%
	9th	17	34	17	23
	10th	27	22	32	31
	11th	26	11	25	20
	12th	15	3	20	12
		100%	100%	100%	100%
		(636)	(204)	(2,089)	(795)
C.	Plans to return to school	73%	39%	90%	71%
		(645)	(207)	(2,090)	(785)
D.	Education desired				
	Less than high school	5%	9%	2%	8%
	Finish high school	47	57	33	48
	Some college	15	12	17	14
	Finish college	27	16	39	23
	Graduate school	6	6	9	7
		100%	100%	100%	100%
		(656)	(212)	(2,107)	(803)

upper high school grades. Black nonmothers are more likely to be in school and to have completed higher grades than the other groups. From this sample, we conclude that Black mothers are not as educationally handicapped by their parenting status as are whites. Table 8C shows the percentage of youths who are looking forward to returning to school in September. Clearly nonmothers are planning to return to school and 73 percent of the Black mothers are anticipating school in the upcoming fall. However, the majority of white mothers do not plan to return to school.

Virtually all the teenagers plan to finish high school (Crowley and Shapiro, 1982). An important part of the American dream is to complete college. College education assists upward mobility. Forty percent of all the female youths aspire to complete college. Among our typology of youths by race and parenting status, Table 8D indicates that Black non-mothers are most ambitious—approximately half of them desire a college or graduate education. Thirty-three percent of Black mothers desire at least a college education. Only 30 percent of white non-mothers ideally plan to finish college and graduate school and white mothers are least likely to consider college in their life plans. Overall, Black teenagers, regardless of parental status, are more likely to aspire to the middle-class aspiration of college education and advanced training.

In summary, we find that low-income Black youth and Black mothers have a greater school attachment than low-income white youth. A larger percentage of Black mothers are attending school and completing more grades. In addition, we find the educational goals of impoverished Black adolescent girls, regardless of parenting status, are higher than white youth. As other researchers (Crowley and Shapiro, 1982; Dawkins, 1981) report, minority youth realize that they are more dependent on educational institutions to achieve upward mobility. Our research confirms that motherhood is correlated with less ambitious educational goals and school participation, but more so for white girls than for Blacks.

Conclusion

American cultural stereotypes focus on how Blacks more than whites are caught in the devastating "culture of poverty" or "underclass" because of higher incidences of out-of-wedlock children born during their adolescent years. Our data suggest that these generalizations apply more to young white women than to Blacks. For the most part, young Black mothers are not demoralized about their future; in fact, they are more likely to have high educational expectations, greater school attachment, and access to child care (because of the proximity to their supportive families). We find that young white mothers tend to marry earlier and to drop out of school at higher rates than Blacks. White females are most likely to experience accelerated adult role entry by becoming not only mothers but wives. Young Black mothers are willing to postpone marriage and accept the low-income Black community norm that the role of mother is more important than wife, particularly when an unstable marriage is foreseen. The role of adolescence, when time is used to prepare for the future by completing school, does not appear to be terminated for a substantial number of Black mothers. The aspirations of young Black mothers concerning delayed marriage entry and higher education are more compatible with the trends in the larger society than are those of whites.

Although a longitudinal study would better assess whether poor households transfer poverty to successive generations, this research suggests that young white women suffer more immediate educational handicaps from counternormative role transitions than young Black women. In addition, the general problem facing low-income Black and white mothers is the lack of institutional support. To avoid economic disadvantages associated with early childbearing, teenage mothers must be afforded the opportunity to complete their education. In order to do this, many young mothers need low-cost child care services; and family financial assistance is needed for youth who remain at home. Vocational training programs and public service jobs are necessary to assist them to achieve economic independence and adult status, and to minimize the perpetuation of the feminization of poverty.

References

Barclay, Suzanne, et al.
1979 "Schooling and Work among Youth from Low-Income Households: A Baseline Report from the Entitlement Demonstration." New York: Manpower Demonstration Research Corporation.

Chilman, Catherine
1983 *Adolescent Sexuality in a Changing American Society, Second Edition.* New York: Wiley.

Crowley, Joan E., and David Shapiro
1982 "Aspirations and Expectations of Youth in the United States. Part I. Education and Fertility." *Youth and Society* 13 (4):391–422.

Dawkins, Marvin P.
1981 "Mobility Aspirations of Black Adolescents: A Comparison of Males and Females." *Adolescence* 16 (Fall):701–710.

Elder, Glen, and R. Rockwell
1976 "Marital Timing in Women's Life Patterns." *Journal of Family History* 1 (Autumn):34–53.

Furstenberg, Frank
1976 *Unplanned Parenthood: The Social Consequences of Teenage Childbearing.* New York: Free Press.

Hofferth, Sandra, and Kristen Moore
1979 "Early Childbearing and Later Economic Well-Being." *American Sociological Review* 44: 787–815.

Howell, Frank M., and Wolfgang Frese
1982 "Adult Role Transitions, Parental Influence, and Status Aspirations Early in the Life Course." *Journal of Marriage and the Family* 44 (1): 35–49.

Kenkel, William F.
1981 "Black-White Differences in Age at Marriage Expectations of Low Income High School Girls." *The Journal of Negro Education* (Fall):425–438.

Ladner, Joyce A.
1972 *Tomorrow's Tomorrow: The Black Woman.* Garden City, N.Y.: Doubleday.

Presser, Harriet
1975 "Some Consequences of Adolescent Pregnancies." Paper presented at the National Institute of Child Health and Human Development Conference, Bethesda, Md.

Rubin, Lillian
1976 *Worlds of Pain.* New York: Basic Books.

Stack, Carol B.
1974 *All Our Kin: Strategies for Survival in a Black Community.* New York: Harper & Row.

U.S. Commission on Civil Rights
1983 Clearinghouse Publication 78. *Disadvantaged Women and Their Children.* Washington, D.C.: U.S. Government Printing Office.

U.S. Department of Health and Human Services
1981 *Vital Statistics of the United States Annual.* Washington, D.C.: U.S. Government Printing Office.

Waite, L. J., and K. A. Moore
1978 "The Impact of an Early First Birth on Young Women's Educational Attainment." *Social Forces* 56 (March):845–865.

11 / Socioeconomic Characteristics

THE BLACK FAMILY AND SOCIAL CLASS

Charles V. Willie

Nine Black families representing three socio-economic classes (middle class, working class, and lower class) were investigated. Some values common to each class are examined and provide a prototype of each economic group. All three groups, though varied and unique, show a strong sense of survival.

... My interest in understanding the way of life of blacks independent of any reference to the way of life of whites is due to a desire (1) to extricate the social and behavioral sciences from a white ethno-centric perspective, and (2) to increase their contribution to the understanding of social change. Innovations in life-styles, including family life-styles, often develop among minority populations in the society before they are adopted by the majority. Such innovations may not be recognized when the way of life of the majority is looked upon as the "ideal type" and the behavior of others is considered deviant.

Method

During the past few years we have compiled approximately 200 case studies of black families, many southern migrants or descendants of southern migrants who now live in the northeastern region of the United States. The case studies were obtained as an assignment for students enrolled in a course on "The Black Family." The responsibility for locating a black family was that of each student. Many students interviewed families in their home towns scattered throughout the region. They interviewed families who were friends, referred to them by friends, referred by an agency, or selected at random by knocking on the door of a stranger. Students were provided with an interview schedule that requested specific information about economic, social and demographic characteristics, family customs, aspirations of parents for children, and patterns of authority within the family. Interviewers were black and white undergraduate students.

Abridged from the *American Journal of Orthopsychiatry* 44 (January 1974):50–60. © 1974 by the American Orthopsychiatric Association, Inc. Reprinted by permission. Footnotes have been renumbered.

Out of the 200 or more case studies, nine were selected for detailed analysis in this paper as a composite representation of three income groups. Household income was the primary basis for more or less arbitrarily selecting three families each for middle-income, marginal-income, and lower-income groups. Utilized in this study were the student reports that contained the most complete and detailed descriptions. We cannot claim to have randomly selected the families for analysis. But we can say that the bias of the investigator was not the basic factor that determined whether or not a family was included among the nine for intensive study. The income groups studied ranged from $3000 to $6000 (low-income), $6000 to $10,000 (marginal-income), and $10,000 to $20,000 (middle-income). Essentially, this study is an example of inductive analysis. Two variables—race and economic status—were used. Since blacks often are referred to as if they were a homogeneous group, nine families of the same race but of different income groups were studied to determine if, in fact, their way of life, customs, and practices were similar. Probability sampling, of course, would be necessary if the goal had been to make generalizations about the frequency of certain behavior forms within the total black population. This was not our goal. Thus, less rigor in the process of selecting the families for intensive analysis was possible.

Social class refers to style of life as well as economic resources. No operational definition of social class was developed for this study. The middle-class, working-class, and lower-class categories referred to later in this paper were derived from the analysis. The composite picture for the three families in each of the income groups was different from the style of life of black families in other income groups. Only the composite picture of the style of life for a social class is given. Detailed information on each of the nine families is presented elsewhere in a book-length manuscript.[1] The three social classes included in this study represent about 75% of all blacks. Not included are the upper middle class and the upper class, probably few in number, and at the other end of the stratification hierarchy, the under class—20% to 25% of all blacks.

Findings

Middle Class: The Affluent Conformists

Middle-class status for most black families is a function of dual employment of husband and wife. Black men and women have relied heavily on the public sector for employment at livable wages.

The public school has been an employment haven for black working wives. It has provided steady and continuous work and often has been the one occupational role in the family which has enabled it to lay claim to a professional style of life. Because of educational requirements, black female teachers of middle-class families are likely to be more highly educated than their male spouses. The length of employment of professional working wives is likely to be as long as that of their husbands, with only brief interruptions for childbearing. The numbers of children in black middle-class families tend to be small, ranging from one to three, but more often two or less. Thus, the black woman, in a public sector job with prescribed yearly increments and retirement benefits and with only a few interruptions in her labor force status, tends to draw a decent income by the time she reaches middle age.

Continuity in employment also is a characteristic of black men in middle-class families. Public sector jobs, especially in the postal service, have been a source of support and security over the years. Some black men have, however, received financially rewarding professional positions in industry.

The economic foundation for middle-class black families is a product of the cooperation of the husband and wife. Their way of life is a genuine illustration of a team effort. Few, if any, family functions, including cooking, cleaning, and buying, are considered to be the exclusive prerogative of the husband or wife. Probably the best example of the liberated wife in American society is the wife in the black middle-class family. She and her husband have acted as partners out of necessity and thus have carved out an equalitarian pattern of interaction in which neither husband nor wife has ultimate authority. He or she alone could not achieve a comfortable style of life, because of racial discrimination and the resulting income limitations of the kinds of jobs available to most blacks. Together they are able to make it, and this they have done. In the 1970s middle-class black families earned $10,000 to $20,000 a year—the joint income of husband and wife.

Such income is lavishly spent on a home and on the education of children. Unless restricted by racial discrimination, middle-class black families tend to trade in older homes for new structures as their income and savings increase. Thus, families in the income range mentioned above are likely to be found in houses valued from $25,000 to $35,000. The real expense in housing, however, is in the up-to-date furnishings and modern appliances. For most middle-class black families, their home is their castle and it is outfitted as such.

Because work is so consuming for the husband and wife, little time is left for socializing. Most families have nearby relatives—usually the reason for migrating to a particular city. They visit relatives occasionally, may hold membership in a social organization, participate regularly in church activities, and spend the remainder of their free time in household upkeep and maintenance chores.

In most middle-class black families, one member almost always has attended college. Often both have attended college. The husband and wife struggled and made great sacrifices to complete their formal education. Not infrequently, college and graduate school are completed on a part-time basis after adulthood and while the husband or wife, who also may be a parent, is employed full-time. Parents who have experienced these struggles and hardships know that their middle-class status, which usually is not achieved until middle age, is directly correlated with their increased education. New jobs, especially public school teaching, and salary increments can be traced directly to the added schooling. Education has been a major contributor to upward mobility for blacks.

Because education and, consequently, economic affluence are so closely tied together for middle-class black households, parents tend to go all out for their offspring. Particularly do they wish their children to go to college immediately after graduating from high school so that they will not have to struggle as long as did their parents whom middle-class status eluded during young-adult years. An ambition of most parents is to give to their children opportunities they did not have.

As a starter, almost all children in middle-class households are given music lessons. Daughters, in particular, are expected to learn to play a musical instrument, usually the piano. Recreational skills are developed, too. Most children in middle-class black families are expected to work around the house for an allowance. Families try to inculcate in their children positive attitudes toward work and thrift.

Active involvement in community affairs that take on the characteristics of a movement is not the cup of tea for most black middle-class, middle-aged adults. Their adolescent children may be deeply involved in various liberation movements but seldom are the parents.

Middle-class black families in America, probably more so than any other population group in this society, manifest the Puritan orientation toward work and success that is characteristic of our basic values. For them, work is a consuming experience. Little time is left for recreation and other kinds of community participation, except regular involvement in church affairs. The way of life of black middle-class Americans is a scenario patterned after Weber,[2] except that most blacks have little capital other than the house they own, which, of course, is their primary symbol of success.

Working Class: The Innovative Marginals

Family life in the black working class is a struggle for survival that requires the cooperative efforts of all—husband, wife, and children. Income for black working-class families ranged from $6,000 to $10,000 during the 1970s. This is hardly enough for luxury living when the family size is considered. Black working-class families tend to be larger families, consisting of five or more children.

There is some indication that the size of the family is a source of pride for the parents, especially the father and maybe the mother too. The bearing and rearing of children are considered to be an important responsibility, so much so that black working-class parents make great personal sacrifices for their families. They tend to look upon children as their unique contribution to society, a contribution they are unable to make through their work roles, which at best are semi-skilled. The family size of the black working-class also may be a function of age at marriage, usually before twenty-one for the wife and mother and often during the late teens. Husbands tend to assume parenthood responsibilities early too; often they are only one or two years older than their spouses.

The cohesion of the black working-class family results not so much from understanding and tenderness shown by one for the other as from the joint and heroic effort to stave off adversity. Without the income of either parent or the contributions of children from part-time employment, the family would topple back into poverty.

The parents in black working-class families are literate but of limited education. Most have completed elementary school but may be high school drop-outs. Seldom do any have more than a high school education. This is the educational level they wish their children to achieve, although some families hope that one or two of the smarter children in their brood will go on to college. The jobs they wish for their children also are those that require only a high school or junior college education, like work as a secretary, nurse, mechanic, or bank messenger.

Racial discrimination, on the one hand, and insufficient education, on the other, have teamed up to delimit the employment opportunities for black working-class families. Their mobility from rural to urban areas and from the South to the North usually has been in search for a better life. Families tend to be attracted to a particular community because of the presence of other relatives who sometime provided temporary housing.

In general, the moves have opened up new opportunities and modest advancement such as from gas station attendant to truck driver, or from farm laborer to dairy tanker. The northern n igration has resulted in some disappointments, too. On balance, new employment opportunities have resulted from the move from South to North, particularly for wives who have found work in institutional settings such as hospitals more profitable than private household work. Nursing aide and cooking jobs have been outlets for women and have enabled them to supplement the family income.

One sacrifice that the members of black working-class families have made so as to pull out of and stay beyond the clutches of poverty is to give up on doing things together as a family. Long working hours and sometimes two jobs leave little time for the father to interact with family members. In some households, the husband works during the daytime and the wife works during the evening hours. In other families, children work up to twenty hours a week after school and on weekends. These kinds of work schedules mean that the family as a unit is not able to share any meals together, except possibly on Sunday.

Despite the hardships, there is a constancy among the members of black working-class families that tends to pull them through. Some husbands and wives have been married more than two decades; they tend to have been residents of their neighborhoods for ten or more years and to have worked for the same employer over a long period of time. Though their earnings are modest, this continuity in area of residence and in other experiences has stabilized these families and enabled their members to accumulate the makings of a tolerable existence without the losses that come from frequent stops and starts.

Another stabilizing experience is the home that some black working-class families own. Rather than renting, many are paying mortgages. Their homes may range in value from $10,000 to $15,000, may be located in isolated rural or unsightly urban areas, and may be in a poor state of exterior repair but neat and clean on the inside. Home ownership for black working-class families is not so much a symbol of success as an indicator of respectability.

Black working-class parents boast of the fact that their children are good and have not been in trouble with the police. They also have a strong sense of morality, which emphasizes "clean living." The home they own is part of their claim to respectability. The owned home is one blessing that can be counted. It is a haven from the harsh and sometimes unfriendly world.

There is little time for community activities for black working-class families. Most spare time is devoted to associating with household members or with nearby relatives. Religion is important; but participation in church activities is limited to regular or occasional attendance at Sunday worship services. The mother in such families tries to maintain tenuous contacts with at least one community institution, such as the school. She even may be a member of the Parents–Teachers Association but is not deeply involved in organizational maintenance work as a volunteer.

Black working-class parents do well by their children if no special problems are presented. Their comprehension of psychological maladaptation, however, is limited. These problems are dealt with by a series of intended remedial actions that seem to be of little assistance in solving the child's real problem and usually result in frustration both for the parent and for the offspring. Black working-class families have learned to endure; and so they bear with the afflictions of their members—those they do not understand as well as those with obvious sources of causation.

Cooperation for survival is so basic in black working-class families that relationships between the husband and wife take on an equalitarian character. Each knows that his or her destiny is dependent upon the actions of the other. Within the family, however, husbands and wives tend to have assigned roles, although in time of crisis, these roles can change. The husband tends to make decisions about financial expenditures, including the spending of money for furniture. He also has basic responsibility for household upkeep. The father is the chief advisor for the boys. The mother tends to be responsible for the cooking and cleaning, although she may delegate these chores to the children. She is the chief advisor for the girls. She also maintains a liaison relationship with the school and may be the adult link between the family and the church if the father is not inclined to participate.

We tend to think in terms of upward mobility in American society. Indeed, this is what many working-class families are—households moving out of poverty into respectability; households that emphasize mobility, goal, and purpose; households committed to making a contribution to society by raising and maintaining a family of good citizens. This, of course, involves a struggle. But the struggle may be a function of the ending of good times rather than the overcoming of adversity. A black working-class family may be of a lower-income household on its way up or a middle-income household on its way down. A middle-income family beset with illness, for example, could slip into the working-class status due to reduction in income and the requirement for change in style of living. How often this occurs, we do not know. It does occur often enough to keep the working class from becoming a homogeneous lot. For this and other reasons, one should not expect to find a common philosophical orientation within the working-class.

Lower Class: The Struggling Poor

The most important fact about black lower-class families is their low-income status; it forces them to make a number of clever, ingenious, and sometimes foolish arrangements to exist. These range from extended households consisting of several generations under one roof to taking in boarders or foster children for pay. Boyfriend–girlfriend relationships between adults often assume some parental functions when children are involved, while the participants maintain their autonomy unfettered by marital bonds. Because every penny counts, poor households often do whatever they must do to bring money in. Conventional practices of morality may be set aside for expedient arrangements that offer the hope of a livable existence. The struggle among poor families is a struggle for existence. All else is secondary. Family income tends to vary from $3000 to $6000, and more often than not the household does not receive public welfare.

The struggle is severe and there is little margin for error. Black low-income families learn to live with contingency. They hope for little and expect less. Parents love their children but seldom understand them. Men and women become sexually involved but are afraid to entrust their futures to each other. There is much disappointment. The parents in broken families often have broken spirits—too broken to risk a new disappointment. For this reason, black lower-class parents often appear to be uncommitted to anyone or to anything when in actuality they are afraid to trust.

Movement is constant, as if one were afraid to stay put and settle down. Jobs, houses, and cities are changed; so are spouses and boyfriends and girlfriends. Unemployment is a constant specter. The womenfolk in the household usually find employment as maids or private household workers. The males are unskilled factory workers or maintenance men between periods of no work at all.

Marriage may occur at an early age, as early as sixteen years for some girls. The first child is sometimes born before the first marriage. Others tend to come in rapid succession. Some families have as many as eight or more children, while others are smaller. When the burdens of child care, illness, and unemployment strike at the same time, they often are overwhelming. Drinking, gambling, and other escape behavior may increase. A fragile love and capacity for endurance are shattered, and the man in the house moves out, no longer able to take it. One more failure is experienced.

The parents in black lower-class families are grade school or high school drop-outs. Neither spouse has more education than the other. Thus, parents in lower-class families sometimes hold themselves up to their children as failures, as negative images of what not to do. There is only limited ability to give guidance concerning what ought to be done. Thus, children are advised not to marry early, not to drop out of school, and not to do this and not to do that. There is admonition but little concrete effort at prevention.

Scapegoating is a common way of explaining deviant behavior in children. Juvenile delinquency may be attributed to the disreputable parent. The mother on location seldom knows what to do. Although little love may exist between parents, there is fierce loyalty between mothers and offspring, and between grandmothers and children. The children come first. Mothers will extend every effort to take care of their sons and daughters, even into adulthood. Grandparents are excellent babysitters. They are expected to teach their grandchildren good manners and other fundamentals.

A strong custom of brothers and sisters helping each other exists in the lower class. The problem is that siblings are struggling too. About the most one can do for the other is share already overcrowded living quarters when a new member comes to town or when a two-parent family breaks down. The move from one city to another often is for the purpose of being near kinsmen. There is strong loyalty between siblings and a standing obligation to help.

Little participation in any community association is seen. Religion is important for some black lower-class families. But for others, it is no more than a delusion. Those who attend church regularly tend to engulf their lives with religion and especially with affirmations about its saving grace and reward system after death. Some shy away from the church as one more disappointing promise that has copped out on the poor without really helping. Black lower-class people are seldom lukewarm about religion. They are either all for it or all against it, although the latter are reluctant to deny their children religious experience, just in case there is more to it than was realized.

It is hard for a poor black family to overcome poverty; so much is lined up against it. If illness or unemployment do not drain away resources, there is a high probability that old age will.

Conclusion

We turn now to a theoretical discussion of the differences that have been observed. In his classic article "Social Structure and Anomie," Robert Merton[3] identified five kinds of adaptations by individuals to social organizations: conformity, innovation, ritualism, retreatism, rebellion. We shall discuss three of the adaptations to explain the way of life of the three different social classes. The conformist acknowledges the legitimacy of societal values and goals and also accepts the means that are sanctioned and prescribed for achieving them. The innovationist believes in the socially sanctioned goals but must improvise new and different means. The retreatist gives up on the socially sanctioned values and goals as well as the means and, therefore, is declared to be in a state of anomie or normlessness. This theoretical formulation provides a helpful way conceptually for approaching an understanding of the differences between middle-class, working-class, and lower-class black families.

Middle-class black families subscribe to the basic values and goals in American society and utilize appropriately prescribed means for their achievement. Its members are success-oriented, upwardly mobile, materialistic, and equalitarian. They consume themselves in work and leave little time for leisure. Education, hard work, and thrift are accepted as the means for the achievement of success. Property, especially residential property, is a major symbol of success. This is the American way and the prevailing way of life to which the middle-class black family in America conforms. Thus, its members may be called conformists.

Black working-class families also have internalized the basic values and goals of this nation. They too are success-oriented and upwardly mobile. However, their symbol of success differs from that of the black middle-class. The welfare of the total family is the principal measure of effective functioning. A black working-class family is successful if it is respectable. A family is respectable when its members are well-fed, well-clothed, and well-housed, and do not get into trouble with the police.

The location and value of a house is not so important. Home ownership is important but home value is something else. In the latter respect, the black working class differs from the black middle class, in which an expensive home is the symbol of success.

Almost everything that the black working-class parents do to achieve success and respectability is extraordinary, compared with the black middle class. Their education is limited; their occupations are unskilled; their income is modest; and their families are relatively larger. Yet they dream the impossible dreams about doing for their children what they could not do for themselves. By hook or crook, they—the parents—manage to do it when others said it couldn't be done. The members of the working class are the creative innovationists of our times. They strive to achieve the societal values and goals, are deficient in the possession of socially sanctioned means, but somehow overcome.

The black lower class is fatalistic. No note of hope does it sing. Failure and disappointment recur repeatedly, as if they were a refrain. Unable to deal with the difficulties presented, black lower-class families withdraw. The parents appear to be uninvolved with anyone or anything. They have retreated from social organizations but not necessarily from all social relations for we know of their loyalty to their children.

The retreatist behavior of black lower-class families is sometimes described as being in opposition to the basic values and goals of social organization—a rejection of that which is socially sanctioned. This may not be the case, however, but only the way it appears. Presumably, lower-class households, like the working class, wish for family cohesion. The tie between mother and offspring is a residual family relationship indicative of this desire. Presumably, also, lower-class families, like the middle class, wish for material comforts and new experiences. Spending sprees and impulse traveling are indicative of these desires.

Because of inadequate resources, lower-class families dare not hope for the fulfillment of their wishes in a systematic and regularized way. To protect themselves from more disappointment, denial of the wish for improvement is one approach and poking fun at the struggle for social mobility is another.

A fuller explanation of the retreatist behavior of the lower class requires examination of the interaction between objective and subjective dimensions of social structure. Despite the rhetoric about self-reliance and self-sufficiency, the family members of the working class and the middle class did not make it on their own unassisted by the social system. They acknowledged their interdependence, and asked for and received help when they need it. Upward social mobility involves giving and receiving from others. The poor are given precious little in our society and so their capacity to receive is underdeveloped. In the giving of help, we learn to love. In the receiving of assistance, we learn to trust. Because the poor have been given so little in society, the poor have not learned how to receive—which is to say, the poor have not learned how to trust.

We learn to trust before we learn to love. Love involves commitment to persons, social groups, and social organizations. The members of lower-class families can commit themselves to persons, especially the mothers to their offspring and the siblings to each other; but they cannot commit themselves to a society they have never learned to trust. Thus, the retreatist behavior of the lower-class may be a manifestation of the absence of trust rather than a rejection of social organization in favor of social disorganization.

This paper clearly demonstrates that it is inappropriate to say, "a black family is a black family is a black family." Styles of life do vary among blacks by social class. Recognition of this should serve as a corrective against stereotyping black ways of life.

The neat way in which the different black family life-styles by social class fit into the theoretical model developed by Robert Merton for explaining variation in adaptations to the social organization also suggests that all black families, including the middle-class, the working-class, and the lower-class, participate in a common system of values shared by all families, including blacks and whites in the United States.

Finally, there was evidence of limited opportunities available to blacks due largely to racial discrimination. This was a common experience of most black families of all social classes. A frequent manifestation of racial discrimination was the delimitation of economic opportunity. Inadequate financial resources frequently resulted in the joint participation of husband and wife in the labor force—a circumstance more or less pervasive among black families, especially those who were upwardly mobile.

On the basis of this analysis, one may conclude (1) that black and white families in America share a common value system, (2) that they adapt to the society and its values in different ways, largely because of racial discrimination, and (3) that the unique adaptation by blacks is further differentiated by variations in style of life by social class.

Our initial assumption that the way of life of blacks in America can be understood independent of their involvement with whites appears to be unwarranted. Moreover, the life-styles of different social classes cannot be understood apart from the rest of society.

Referring to the interdependence of blacks and whites in America, this paper ends with the statement of a modified version of the wisdom of Eliza Doolittle, created by George Bernard Shaw. She said that she discovered the difference between a flower girl and a lady is not so much how she acts but how she is treated. Our revised version emphasizes *both* personal action *and* social reaction. We assert that the differences among the families of racial groups in the United States and the differences among the families of various social classes within the racial groups are a result of how each family acts *as well as* how each family is treated.

---

[1]Willie, C. 1976. A New Look at Black Families *(Bayside, N.Y.: General Hall Publishers)*.

[2]Weber, M. 1948. The Protestant Ethic and the Spirit of Capitalism *(London: George Allen and Unwin)*.

[3]Merton, R. 1949. Social Structure and Social Theory *(New York: Free Press), p. 133*.

THE "FLIP-SIDE" OF BLACK FAMILIES HEADED BY WOMEN:
The Economic Status of Black Men

The Center for the Study of Social Policy

This paper notes that parallel with the increase in single-parent Black families has been a deterioration in the economic status of Black men. Recent figures show that only 55 percent of Black men are currently in the labor force; the remainder are unemployed, discouraged and not seeking work, in correctional facilities, or unaccounted for.

In both 1960 and 1982, the median income of black families was 55 percent that of white families. One quick conclusion is that black Americans have made little or no relative economic progress in the past two decades. But such gross numbers mask a complex phenomenon: the changing structure of black families. The rising number of black families headed by women has hindered the economic progress of black Americans.

All this is fairly common knowledge. But still the numbers are worth recalling (see Table 1):

1. Since 1960, the number of black families headed by women has more than tripled.
2. 49 percent of all black families with children are headed by women (the comparable figure for whites is 15 percent).
3. The median income of black female-headed families is less than one-third the national median.
4. More than 60 percent of black female-headed families with children live in poverty.

The economic status of black Americans is perhaps best assessed as a dual phenomenon, divided by family type. For example, while the poverty rate among black married-couple families has dropped dramatically from more than 50 percent in 1959 to 20 percent in 1982, the poverty rate among black female-headed families has only dropped from 70 percent to 59 percent. Similarly, since 1968 the median income for black married-couple families has risen 11 percent (in constant dollars), while the median income for black female-headed families has fallen by 14 percent. This dichotomy is manifest in the changing composition of the poverty population. In 1959, less than 30 percent of all blacks in poverty lived in female-headed families; today, more than 67 percent of all poor blacks live in such families (see Figure 1).

The real victims in the erosion of the black family are children. Today, of the 4.6 million black children growing up without a father, 3.3 million live in poverty (see Figure 2). With poverty often comes poor nutrition, poor health, low academic achievement, and high unemployment.

Most commentators stop with the family composition explanation of the black/white income disparity. In doing so, however, they neglect a prior and equally perplexing question: why the boom in black female-headed families? In response to that question, this paper sketches a hypothesis: that the increase in black female-headed families is linked to equally noteworthy and startling trends in the

The Center for the Study of Social Policy, April 1984. Reprinted by permission. Footnotes and tables have been renumbered. This work was supported by the Field Foundation.

TABLE 1   Black Female-Headed Families, 1960–1990

YEAR	BLACK FEMALE-HEADED FAMILIES		CHILDREN IN BLACK FEMALE-HEADED FAMILIES	
	Total (1,000's)	Percent of Black Families	Total (1,000's)	In Poverty (1,000's)
1960	889	20.9	1,808	1,475
1965	1,125	23.7	2,751	2,107
1970	1,382	28.3	3,520	2,383
1975	1,940	35.3	4,127	2,724
1980	2,495	40.3	4,543	2,944
1983	2,734	41.9	4,624	3,269
1990 (projected)	3,531	48.3	5,979	—

Source: U.S. Bureau of the Census. Projections based on percentage trends from 1960–1983 and Census projections of black population. Projections of children based on 1983 average family size.

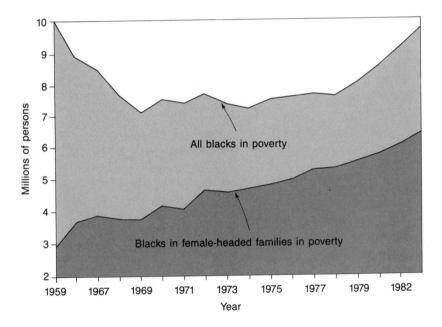

FIGURE 1   Trends in Black Poverty, 1960–1982

economic and social status of black males. The plight of black men is the other, virtually unnoticed, side of the troubling increase in single-parent black families. Simply put, the economic status of many black men is deteriorating.

It is axiomatic that unemployment among blacks is twice the national rate. Moreover, in hard times, employed blacks are laid off earlier and re-hired later. Thus, even in the midst of [the 1983] recovery when national unemployment was 9 percent, unemployment among blacks was 19 percent; 1.4 million black men could not find work.

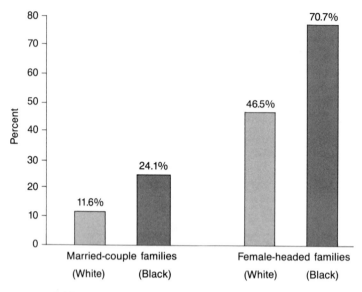

FIGURE 2 Poverty Rates among Children, 1982
(by Race and Family Type)

But unemployment is only part of the story. Unemployment rates reflect only the status of persons "in the labor force." In addition, there are millions of persons who, for various reasons, are not looking for work. Among black men, some are full-time students, some are physically disabled, a few are needed in the home, and some are simply discouraged workers who have stopped looking for work after repeated failures. Twenty percent of all working-age black men—nearly two million persons—were out of the labor force in 1982. For more detailed analysis of those out of the labor force and sources for these data, see Table 2. This dropout is a recent phenomenon: since 1960, the number of black men out of the labor force has more than tripled (see Table 3).

The combination of unemployment and labor force data more accurately reflects the status of black men than either gauge taken alone. In 1960, nearly three-quarters of all black men included in Census data were working; today, only 55 percent are working.

The picture gets even worse. There are an estimated 925,000 working-age black men whose labor force status cannot be determined because they are missed in the Census. This "undercount" in the Census is most severe among black men,

amounting to more than 10 percent among working-age black men, compared to less than one percent for working-age white men. (See Table 2 for a more detailed discussion of the undercount.)

The cumulative impact of these measures—unemployment, labor force participation, and the "missing" black men—is startling. For each black man we count as unemployed, another two are out of the labor force. Figure 3 shows the labor force status of black men age 16–64: 4 million out of the 8.8 million working-age black men, or 46 percent, are without jobs; i.e., they are either unemployed, out of the labor force, in correctional facilities, or unaccounted for. These data are even more noteworthy when juxtaposed with comparable data for white men. In 1982, while 78 percent of all working-age white men were employed, only 54 percent of all working-age black men had jobs.

Looking at this another way, the percent of working-age black men who are unemployed, discouraged workers, or unaccounted for is almost three times that for white men. Thirty percent of all working-age black men are in these categories, compared to only 11 percent of working-age white men.

The importance of these figures lies in the link between the economic alienation of black men and the erosion of the black family. Graphing the

TABLE 2   Where Black and White Men Are (1982) (Sources for Figure 3)

TOTAL WORKING-AGE MALE POPULATION

Statistical Abstract of the United States, 1984, Table 33, page 33. The 1982 figures for males 65–74 and 75 and over were subtracted from the number of males 16 years and over. There were 7,998,000 black men 16–64 in 1982 and 63,774,000 white men. In addition, the publication *Coverage of the National Population in the 1980 Census by Age, Sex, and Race*, U.S. Bureau of the Census, Current Population Reports (CPR), P-23, No. 115, Table 3, shows that there were an estimated 824,000 black men age 15–64 who were not counted in the 1980 Census and an "overcount" of 114,000 white males age 16–64. This brings the universe of black males 16–64 to 8.8 million (7,998,000 plus 824,000) and the universe of white males 16–64 to 63.7 million.

ARMED FORCES

Statistical Abstract of the United States, 1984, Tables 574 and 577, pages 353 and 354. Because 25 percent of all armed service personnel are overseas, the number of military personnel on active duty was reduced by 25 percent to yield the number within the United States. Table 574, after this reduction, shows 273,000 black men and 1,033,000 white men. These figures are not broken down by age, but they, by definition, include few if any men under age 16 or over age 64.

EMPLOYED, UNEMPLOYED, AND NOT IN LABOR FORCE
Employed

Data about the employed, unemployed, and those not in the labor force are annual averages of monthly figures for 1982. *Employment and Earnings, January 1982* (Bureau of Labor Statistics, U.S. Department of Labor) shows 4,515,000 black males age 16–64 and 48,663,000 white males ages 16–64 employed in the civilian labor force.

Unemployed

Employment and Earnings shows 1,155,000 black men age 16–64 and 4,793,000 white men age 16–64 unemployed in 1982.

Not in the Labor Force

Employment and Earnings shows 1,769,000 black men age 16–64 and 8,389,000 white men age 16–64 not in the labor force in 1982.

A further breakdown of the reasons black and white men 16–64 are out of the labor force is found in quarterly Bureau of Labor Statistics (BLS) data. The following detailed data are unpublished BLS data for the quarter January–March 1984:

White Men 16–64 9,216,000		Reason Not in Labor Force TOTAL	Black Men 16–64 1,944,000	
4,066,000	(44%)	In school	(47%)	908,000
1,495,000	(16%)	Ill health	(15%)	291,000
1,559,000	(17%)	Retired	(8%)	155,000
147,000	(2%)	Needed at home	(2%)	42,000
1,949,000	(21%)	Other	(28%)	548,000

It should be noted that the categories "in school" and "ill health" may actually include discouraged workers. In fact, 26 percent of black men and 17 percent of white men who were out of the labor force because they were in school wanted a job but did not have one. Similarly, of those out of the labor force because of ill health, 18 percent of black men and 17 percent of white men wanted a job.

CORRECTIONAL INSTITUTIONS

1980 Census of Population, Detailed Population Characteristics, PC80–1–D1, Table 266 (forthcoming) shows 186,137 black men and 211,652 white men age 15–64 in correctional facilities in 1980.

LABOR FORCE STATUS UNDETERMINED

This estimate is derived by the Census Bureau from the difference between an expected population taken from birth, death, immigration, and emigration records as well as other sources and the actual census counts obtained from the decennial census.

The omission rates were most severe for black men age 20–64. In 1980, the Census Bureau estimates that it undercounted the black male population age 35–54 by more than 15 percent, and those age 20–34 by 9.4 percent. In contrast, they undercounted white males age 35–54 by only 1.5 percent, and they actually overcounted white males age 20–34 by 1.3 percent.

Recognizing its high undercount among minority men between the ages of 20 and 50, the Census Bureau has conducted several special studies to determine some of the characteristics of these "missing" black males.[1]

One study used a "casual interview technique" in bars, restaurants, pool rooms, on street corners, park benches, and similar locations, and was concentrated in urban poverty areas since these were thought to be where the highest undercounts were. Some information was obtained in three central cities, but we still do not know where the unaccounted for men are nationwide.

In addition to the 824,000 black men not counted in the 1980 census, there are approximately another 101,000 black men not counted in the 1982 CPS data. This brings the total number of working-age black men whose labor force status cannot be determined to 925,000, or 10.5 percent of the total working age black male population. In addition to the 114,000 overcount of white men in the 1980 Census, there was an undercount of 684,000 white men in the 1982 CPS data, bringing the total undercount of white men 16–64 to 570,000, or less than one percent of the white male population age 16–64.

---

[1] See, for example, "Status of Men Missed in the Census," Special Labor Force Report 117, U.S. Department of Labor, Bureau of Labor Statistics, 1982.

TABLE 3   Selected Unemployment and Labor Force Data, 1960–1982[1]

	MALE UNEMPLOYMENT		Black Men Unemployed (in Millions)	Black Men Out of Labor Force (in Millions)	Black Men Unemployed Plus Out of Labor Force (in Millions)
Year	White Rate	Black Rate			
1960	4.8%	10.7%	0.45	0.86	1.31
1965	3.6	7.4	0.32	1.13	1.45
1970	4.0	7.3	0.34	1.43	1.77
1975	7.2	13.6	0.74	2.04	2.78
1980	6.1	13.2	0.82	2.33	3.15
1982	8.8	20.1	1.17	2.48	3.65

[1]Data are for all men 16 and older (not only 16–64).
Source: Bureau of Labor Statistics. 1960, 1965, and 1970 data are estimates based on data for black and other races.

percentage of black men out of the labor force or unemployed and the percentage of black families headed by women yields two roughly parallel lines (see Figure 4). [Just from 1977 to 1983,] the number of black families headed by women [rose] by 700,000 and the ranks of black men out of the labor force or unemployed . . . increased by the same number.

The rise in black families headed by women is the result of multiple forces, and these data suggest that the increase is due at least in part to the increasing economic anomie of black men. If 46 percent of all black men are jobless—either unemployed, not looking for work, in correctional facilities, or unaccounted for—it is little wonder that an increasing number of black women are raising families alone.

These data on black men suggest that researchers may be treating the symptoms of poverty rather than the ailment. Current research emphasizes unwed mothers and income programs for female-headed families. At the very least, one can neither fully understand nor slow the growth of female-headed families without first assessing the deteriorating status of black men.

These data support a hypothesis that the erosion of the black family is not necessarily a mystical cultural trend but a palpable economic event. The boom in black families headed by women is not the simple result of the "welfare curse," pervasive and invidious discrimination, or changing sexual mores. Instead, the problem lies in an intricate economic and social dynamic. The anomie of black men is the upshot of subtle social and economic cues which we have barely begun to decipher.

These brief data on the status of black men are far from sufficient to explain the economic differentials between blacks and whites. In fact, they provoke many more questions. The dimensions of the social attrition of black men demand a diagnostic study of their status: Where are these men: homeless? part of an underground economy? How have they dropped out of the mainstream economy? How does their attrition affect black women and children?

One area for more immediate action is employment policies. Detailed labor force data by age illustrate the process of economic alienation. High unemployment among black teenagers leads to decreased labor force participation among black men in their 20's which leads to high Census undercounts among black men in their 30's.

Clearly, new measures must be developed to encourage those out of the labor force to re-enter the economy. More importantly, youth training and employment programs must be strengthened and reshaped with a new urgency that recognizes this process of alienation. Youth employment is not only

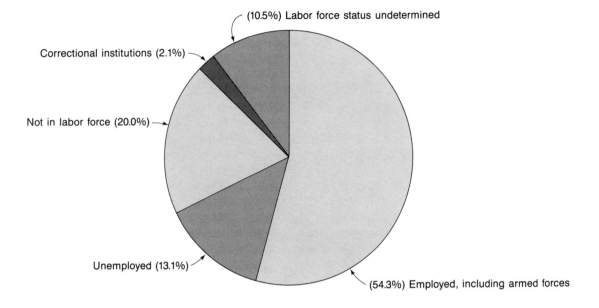

(10.5%) Labor force status undetermined

Correctional institutions (2.1%)

Not in labor force (20.0%)

Unemployed (13.1%)

(54.3%) Employed, including armed forces

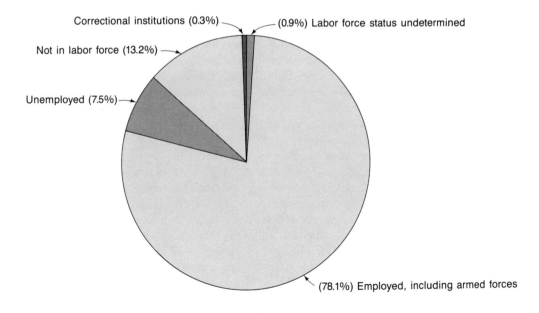

Correctional institutions (0.3%)

(0.9%) Labor force status undetermined

Not in labor force (13.2%)

Unemployed (7.5%)

(78.1%) Employed, including armed forces

FIGURE 3b White Men: Where They Are (1982)
(Age 16–64; Total 63.7 Million)

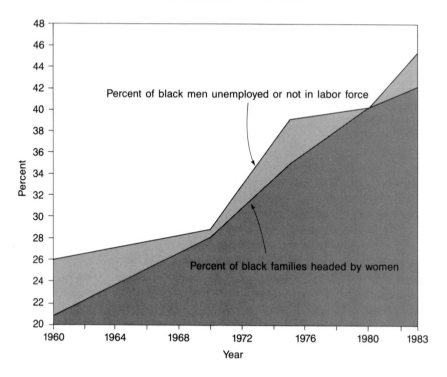

FIGURE 4 Trends in Black Families, 1960–1983
Source: U.S. Bureau of the Census, Bureau of Labor Statistics, 1983.

an end in itself but as well a means to preventing the economic attrition of black men and improving the structure and economic status of black families.

The plight of black men is of critical importance because of the enormous number of black children growing up in poverty today. If we are to stem the tide of female-headed families and the attendant rise of poverty, we must begin to investigate the social attrition of America's black men.

The persistent alienation and attrition of black men constitutes a formidable challenge to both researchers and policymakers, a challenge that is only now beginning to be recognized. How to study, understand, and eventually respond to this phenomenon are fresh and troubling issues. But they are, as well, critical issues, for the human costs of the continued erosion of the black family are socially, politically, and morally unacceptable.

Given the bleak prospects for narrowing the income gap between single-parent and two-parent families, questions surrounding the economic and social status of black men are at the heart of a fundamental social problem. Past efforts to remedy this problem have been entirely inadequate, and we are now witnessing the consequences of our failures. The attrition of black men from the labor force may be the result of institutional discrimination, weak affirmative action policies, ineffective youth employment programs, lack of quality education, changing sexual mores and many other economic and cultural forces.

Clearly, the problem pervades the fabric of our society and economy and requires an attack on all fronts. Neither a single commission nor a discrete piece of legislation will suffice as a response. The continued erosion of the black family should be a national priority that is addressed through decisive action initiated at all levels of government.

POVERTY: NOT FOR WOMEN ONLY—
A Critique of the "Feminization of Poverty"

Alliance Against Women's Oppression

This paper criticizes the feminization of poverty perspective, which—ignoring differences in race and class—suggests that all women are in danger of becoming poor. Rather, the "poor" are members of the lower working class—an unemployed or underemployed reserve of surplus workers segregated more by racism than sexism. The economic status of Black men has actually deteriorated since the sixties, with 50 percent now unemployed.

- **"2 out of 3 American adults living in poverty are women."**
- **"Families headed by women live on 40% of the income of those headed by men."**
- **"The causes of women's poverty are different from men's."**
- **"A man becomes single and a woman becomes a single parent."**
- **Women are only a husband away from poverty."**

These are but a few of the most popular catchphrases of an analysis termed the "feminization of poverty." This perspective has captured the imagination of a diverse array of political forces ranging from the Democratic Party to the Democratic Socialists of America (DSA), from liberal feminists of the National Organization for Women (NOW) to the radical sector of the women's movement, from *Off Our Backs* and the feminist press to the *Guardian* newspaper.

The heart of the "feminization of poverty" perspective is the proposition that women are bearing the brunt of economic hardship in the Reagan era and now make up the "new American underclass." Specifically, it argues that all or almost all of today's poor are women and that all or almost all women are in imminent danger of becoming poor.

Two trends are used to back up this assertion: first, the disintegration of two-parent families which leaves women to bear the responsibility and expense for child-rearing alone; and second, the low-wage status of women and their reliance on ever scarcer social services in order to survive.

"Feminization of poverty" is not only an analysis of women's declining status. Its promoters also see it as the basis for an organizing strategy with the potential to mobilize millions of women and revive the women's movement in the 1980s. This vision is shared by liberals, radicals and socialists alike. According to the May 1983 issue of the DSA's Bay Area newsletter, "A focus on the feminization of poverty is important for the women's movement. . . . It offers a new bond which cuts across class, age, race and sexual preference because women are in fact just a husband away from poverty." Vulnerability to impoverishment is seen as the common condition of all women and, thus, the issue to organize them into united political action.

Although it is riddled with distortions about who indeed has borne the brunt of poverty in this country, the "feminization of poverty" analysis has rapidly gained widespread popularity as an accurate

---

From *AAWO Discussion Paper No. 3* (September, 1983). Reprinted by permission. Footnotes have been renumbered and some art and tables have been deleted.

depiction of women's current condition. That the liberal feminists have advanced such an analysis is no particular surprise. They have never gotten high marks for remembering the widely divergent class realities faced by different strata of women. But the fact that the left, too, has swallowed this analysis hook, line and sinker is highly problematic. It indicates the superficial understanding of the relationship between women's oppression, class exploitation and racism that prevails among left forces, including those within the women's movement. The "feminization of poverty" analysis deserves to be carefully critiqued rather than embraced without question. This discussion paper is written in order to initiate that process.

Class and Racial Blinders

The "feminization of poverty" view does, in fact, point to certain economic realities affecting many women in the U.S. There is also no question that Reaganism includes a ruthless sexist attack on women's rights and living standards. However, the fatal flaw of the "feminization of poverty" analysis is that it treats all women as members of an oppressed class. On the one hand, it minimizes the differences in condition and consciousness among women. On the other hand, it minimizes the commonality in condition and consciousness between women and men of the same class or racial group.

Liberal advocates of the "feminization of poverty" perspective are quite direct about the fact that any class or racial differences that might exist among women are distinctly secondary or even irrelevant to their analysis. Diana Pearce, Director of Research for the Center of National Policy Review at Catholic University in Washington, D.C., and the one who coined the phrase "feminization of poverty," writes that her analysis is concerned with "those women who are poor because they are women. . . . For a woman, race is a relatively unimportant consideration in determining economic status."

The socialist feminist proponents of the "feminization of poverty" have incorporated the same essential vantage point into their analyses. They submerge the class and race differences that exist among women and then focus on the fate of one particular sector. In an article for *Ms.* magazine en-

titled "The Nouveau Poor," Barbara Ehrenreich and Karin Stallard tell the story of "Avis . . . , one of the 'nouveau poor': middle class by birth and marriage, she is now raising her three youngest children on a tenuous combination of welfare, child support, and her native Yankee ingenuity. . . . With her handsome New England features and hearty outgoing manner. . . . Not the kind of person you would expect to catch paying for her groceries with food stamps, she is in some ways typical of the new female poor."

The focus on the "human interest" dimension of this story has a political objective: to bridge the gap between two different sets of women. First and foremost, white middle class women, the actual or potential "new poor," are supposed to identify with Avis' "native Yankee ingenuity" and "New England features." Second, the "old poor," women for whom poverty is a chronic condition, are supposed to empathize with Avis' plight as a newcomer to the welfare rolls.

This attempt to bring women together by minimizing the class and race differences between them leads to distortions on three fronts. First, it paints a false picture of women. Second, it redefines poverty, its causes as well as its historic and current victims. Third, it gives rise to a political strategy that speaks to the problems faced by a certain sector of white middle class women—but which is incapable of representing the interests of those poor women who suffer not only from sex discrimination but also from class and race oppression.

Not All Women Are Poor

· ***"Virtually all women are vulnerable— a divorce or widowhood is all it takes to throw many middle class women into poverty."***[1]

This "feminization of poverty" line is wrong—empirically and theoretically—in its starting assumption that all women are in relatively equal and imminent danger of becoming poor. Women are far from a homogeneous group. Some women are indeed poor and getting poorer, but many others are rich and getting richer.

It is popular among radical sectors of the feminist movement to cast the ruling class as a bunch of greedy white men who oppress every other social group. But this description conveniently drops out the fact that women of the ruling elite enjoy the prerogatives of the rest of their class and stand in an exploitative relation to men and women of the working class. These women own and control much of the wealth of the ruling class and are not about to slip into poverty, regardless of their marital status. The only thing they have in common with working class women is their biology.

While women of the petit bourgeoisie have a long way to go to overcome sex discrimination within their class, most are not "just a husband away from poverty." It is true that, in the case of divorce, they may experience a fairly dramatic drop in income and standard of living. However, many of these women have the independent property, financial resources, education and skills to live comfortably with or without men. Furthermore, the majority of these women remarry. And, when they do, it is generally to men of their class.

In addition, the greatest impact of the affirmative action and special admissions programs won through the civil rights struggles of the 1960s has been to increase the access of women of the petit bourgeoisie and some of the upper strata of the working class to middle management, to a number of the professions and to institutions of higher education. For example, in 1981, women made up 14% of the nation's lawyers and judges, up from 4% in 1971, while Black men had gained only 1.9% and Black women only 0.8% of these positions. In 1981, women were 22%, or one in five, of all doctors, up from 9% in 1971. By contrast, 2.7% of all doctors were Black men, and 0.7% were Black women. From 1972 to 1980, women increased their share of Master's degrees from 40% to 50% and doubled their share of doctoral degrees from one-sixth to one-third.

These women are overwhelmingly white; they are not particularly vulnerable to Reagan's social austerity program; and they do not become welfare mothers upon divorce.

Poverty Is a Class Condition

Before [we rush] to "feminize" poverty, a note on the causes of poverty and its principal victims is in order. Poverty is overwhelmingly the problem of the "old poor." The adage "the poor get poorer" identifies the deepening emiseration of the entire lower strata of the working class.

Many hopes and illusions are fostered about the possibility of ending poverty in the U.S. But poverty is a class condition and is structural to U.S. capitalism. It is the constant companion to members of the least stable strata of the working class and afflicts men, women and children. A more or less permanent reserve of unemployed or underemployed workers is the by-product of a profit oriented economy. This is the sector of the population most devastated by dislocations in the economy and by political attacks on the class.

There are, to be sure, millions of women whose lives are shaped by sex-segregated, low-paying, low-status jobs; unemployment; and cutbacks in vital social services. But these are not women in general—they are women of the working class. The class exploitation suffered by these women guarantees that they experience women's oppression in a way qualitatively different from women of the owning classes.

Yet, even within the working class there are major differences among women. These differences occur between the sector of the class that has enjoyed stable economic conditions and a relatively high standard of living and the sector that has been kept on the lowest rungs of the economic ladder. In the U.S., it has been *racism*, not sexism, that has been the main factor determining who falls on which side of this divide. This division within the working class makes all the difference in a woman's standard of living, income, vulnerability to recessions, unemployment and poverty, the condition of her neighborhood, the schools her children attend, and her access to decent health care.

Women in the lower strata, especially minority women, have long been forced to seek wage work. In the past, minority women's participation in the labor force has been much higher than that of white women. The lower incomes of minority men required that every able-bodied adult in the family, female and male, look for work, since family survival depended on multiple wage earners. It is the lower strata of the working class, with its high concentration of minority workers, that makes up the "working poor."

However, over the years the odds have gone up that the men of this strata may either be permanently unemployed or incarcerated. Many leave their families because they can no longer fulfill the role of male breadwinner. In any case, poverty is the principal source of the enormous social pressure that leads to the disproportionately high rate of divorce among Black families.

In addition, many men and women of this strata continue to be denied the education, training and opportunity to enter the labor market at all. Thus, they are dependent on the "largesse" of the U.S. government to meet their survival needs. Given that the attitude toward the poor ranges from "benign neglect" to outright hostility, this is a precarious existence indeed.

Sexism and Working Class Women

Of course women are affected in a particular way by poverty because of the role they play in childrearing. Since sexism has assigned them principal or sole responsibility for raising children, the meager wages that poor women receive, or the inadequate welfare checks, must stretch to sustain the kids as well. These are the factors that have locked portions of the working class into a cycle of poverty that will not be broken short of a major social transformation. But it is not these women (or men) that the "feminization of poverty" advocates are primarily concerned about. Their main focus is on the "Avises" of the world—the so-called "nouveau poor," the women who had become accustomed to economic stability and for whom not having quite enough to make ends meet comes as a rude shock.

Poverty has, in fact, claimed some new victims. Many women who were part of the more stable and comfortable sector of the working class have been caught in the squeeze between two trends. First, over the past 40 years, white women's participation in the labor force has risen dramatically to 50%, almost catching up with the 53% of minority women who work. Since World War II the deepening exploitation of the working class has made the two-wage family the norm and the only way to maintain a comfortable standard of living.

Entry into the paid labor force has been a double-edged sword. On one hand, it affords women an important measure of economic independence from men. On the other hand, since women's incorporation into the workforce takes place on a discriminatory basis, their substandard wages mean that they face economic hardship if they become the sole support of their families.

Secondly, the increasing instability of the "nuclear family" has meant that more and more women from the stable strata of the working class find themselves in exactly this position. When the men in two-parent families leave, the standard of living of these families drops, both because of the women's low-wage status and because of the vacuum of social supports available for raising children. In the current period of social austerity, the lower strata is growing in size and changing in composition. New social groups are being forced to face the bottom-line realities of U.S. capitalism, creating the "new poor." Among them are the women caught in the nexus of these two social trends—the women for whom poverty has been "feminized."

But, before taking pity of the plight of the "nouveau poor," it might be useful to recall that women who thought that the color line and a working husband would protect them from the worst that capitalism has to offer have shown no particular concern for the permanently impoverished sectors of the U.S. population. The oppressive conditions faced by the poor were acceptable and easily overlooked, as long as they mainly affected those people whose poverty was viewed as almost a genetic deformity—the "coloreds" and "foreigners." Poverty has been rediscovered now that increasing numbers of working class whites are in danger of defaulting on their mortgage to the "American Dream."

Whether this sector will establish political unity with the "old poor" or whether they will struggle to regain their material privileges remains to be seen. But there is nothing yet to indicate that the branch of American womanhood represented by Avis will become the most reliable combatants in the struggle to defend the poor against political and economic attack and to strike at the class roots of poverty in the U.S. The potential for these women

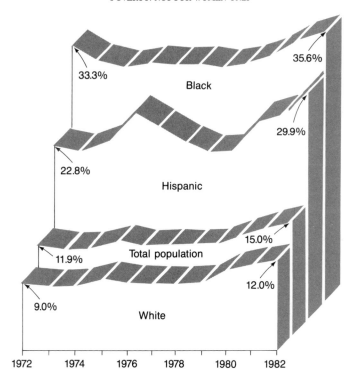

33.3%

35.6%

Black

22.8%

29.9%

Hispanic

15.0%

11.9%

Total population

12.0%

9.0%

White

1972   1974   1976   1978   1980   1982

FIGURE 1 Poverty Rates in the United States,
1972–1982

For each category, percentage of the population living below the poverty level.
Hispanic people may be of either race. Source: U.S. Bureau of the Census.

to identify with and fight against the conditions suffered by the "old poor" depends entirely upon the extent to which sharp and consistent struggle is taken up against racism and class oppression.

Not All Poor People Are Women

• *"By the year 2000, all of the nation's poor will be women and their dependent children."*[2]

This prediction is a favorite in "feminization of poverty" literature. It seems to assume that by the year 2000 all of those men who are presently poor will be either rich or dead. Furthermore, it indicates that the "feminization of poverty" perspective not only provides a distorted view of women but also leaves

men, minority men in particular, entirely out of the analysis.

While poverty is intensified by sexism, women's oppression is not its sole or even fundamental determinant. The profile of the poor is incomplete without putting men back into the picture. Here again the conditions faced by minority men most starkly reveal the life conditions of the lower strata of the class. . . .

While 20 years ago 75% of Black men were employed, today an astounding 45% of all Black men do not have jobs. . . . Men who immigrate from Mexico, Central America and the Caribbean in search of work hardly fare better. The educational and employment opportunities available to Puerto Rican, Native American and Mexican-American men are severely restricted.

Thus, for many minority men, the military

(poverty draft), the streets or prison have become the only remaining "career" options open. Those who do find work are generally at the lower end of the wage scale in the service and agricultural sectors of the economy.

While poor women were forced into dependence on Aid to Families with Dependent Children (AFDC) to raise the kids, it should not be forgotten that general assistance, which provided some support for adult men, was virtually eliminated some time ago. Other programs designed to improve the employment opportunities of minority men have also gotten the axe. It should not need saying, but the men who depended on such programs and services have neither disappeared nor become wealthy. In minority communities, poverty has not been "feminized." Though women face distinct kinds of difficulties and hardships, poverty is the common condition of a large portion of these communities which include men, women and children. The "feminization of poverty" analysis is unlikely to find many adherents among the women who inhabit the inner cities, ghettos, barrios and reservations of America. For these women, reality includes the fact that their male children will have only a fifty-fifty chance of ever finding a job. It includes the fact that many of the adult men of their community have been driven close to desperation by the bitter dynamics of capitalism and racism.

"Feminization of Poverty" or Poverty of Socialist Feminism?

- *"2 out of 3 people in poverty are women. What if we all went to the polls?"*[3]

This slogan now being popularized by feminist organizers aptly sums up the strategic implications of the "feminization of poverty" perspective. Although not everyone attracted to the "feminization of poverty" line has linked it to a definite strategy to rebuild the women's movement, the women who lead liberal feminist organizations such as NOW and the National Women's Political Caucus certainly have. For them, the "feminization of poverty" analysis provides a lever to widen the "gender gap" (the

significantly greater percentage of women than of men supporting Democrats over Republicans). The issue of female poverty is seized upon as an electoral tool to cohere the Democratic Party's base of support among women voters. Of course, it is no small matter that the U.S. government is currently headed up by reactionary, anti-woman Republicans, the likes of Ronald Reagan. Supporting politicians committed to a more liberal social program is certainly in the common interest of the vast majority of women. However, there are serious problems in promoting the illusion that getting more Democrats into office can qualitatively alter, much less reverse, the trends in women's oppression, racism and poverty.

But the liberals of the feminist movement and of the Democratic Party cannot be expected to sort out the complexities of class, race and sex nor to create a program that focuses on the issues that most affect working class women. What is extremely disturbing, however, is that some of the most avid and prolific adherents of the "feminization of poverty" view are those feminists who identify as socialists. In particular, the trend of social democracy, represented primarily by the DSA, has become a highly active advocate of this analysis and strategy. One might expect that socialist feminists and social democrats would be more wary about adopting a perspective that, in its origins, explicitly drops class and race out of consideration. Quite to the contrary, these particular socialists have built a political career wishing that the knotty problems of race and class that divide women would simply do a disappearing act. "Feminization of poverty" as a strategy provides a new magic wand—attractive because of its seeming concern for the poor and oppressed.

The incidence of women's oppression and poverty is a critical question which does shape the survival of peoples of color and significant sectors of the rest of the U.S. working class. However, promoting the "feminization of poverty" as the issue that can "unite women across class, race, age and sexual preference" is a highly dubious enterprise. Feminist strategies that seek to unite women across the class spectrum while remaining oblivious both to the particularities of the conditions faced by minority and poor women and to the oppression suffered by minority and other working class men have always doomed the women's movement to remaining under the hegemony of white women of the middle classes. The "feminization of poverty" analysis and strategy promises to be a repeat performance.

The "feminization of poverty" will certainly be projected, with greater frequency as the 1984 elections approach, as the guide to women's fightback in the 1980s and as the antidote to Reaganism.

But, this analysis should be treated with great suspicion by the left. It draws the class line incorrectly, ejecting minority and other working class men from the fight against poverty while including women who are not threatened by poverty at all. It envisions no independent voice for working class forces in the women's movement. It must be rejected as an analysis of women's condition and a strategy for women's liberation.[4]

---

[1]*From* Poverty in the American Dream/Women and Children First, *by Karin Stallard, Barbara Ehrenreich and Holly Sklar.*
[2]*From the 1980* National Advisory Council on Economic Opportunity *report to then-President Carter and cited in* Ms. *magazine, July/August 1982, and the* Guardian, *June 29, 1983.*
[3]*Slogan of the East Bay Women's Coalition.*
[4]*In preparing this discussion paper we have primarily used the following sources:* A Dream Deferred: The Economic Status

of Black Americans, *The Center for the Study of Social Policy, Washington, D.C., July 1983.* Unemployment and Underemployment among Blacks, Hispanics, & Women, *U.S. Commission on Civil Rights, Nov. 1982.* A Growing Crisis—Disadvantaged Women and Their Children, *U.S. Commission on Civil Rights, May 1983.* Equal Employment Opportunity for Women: U.S. Policies, *U.S. Dept. of Labor, Office of the Secretary, Women's Bureau, 1982.*

CAN THIS LINE BE SAVED?

The "feminization of poverty" analysis has recently been given a dramatic face-lift. In particular, the pamphlet entitled *Poverty in the American Dream—Women and Children First*, by Karin Stallard, Barbara Ehrenreich and Holly Sklar is a significant improvement on the article entitled the "Nouveau Poor" written by the same authors for *Ms.* magazine in August 1982.

The pamphlet more consistently incorporates the conditions faced by minority women and includes many individual stories of women of color struggling to survive the rigors of the welfare system or low-wage jobs. In addition, in recounting the story of Avis (whose fine New England features were a focal point of the *Ms.* article), the most blatant appeal to WASP interests is dropped. The character trait that enables Avis to make ends meet is transformed from "native Yankee ingenuity" to a colorless "thriftiness." Presumably, these kinds of changes come as the result of some criticism directed at the social democratic advocates of the

"feminization of poverty." To the extent that these writers have been forced to take some note of the considerable material differences among women, this is a positive development.

However, the pamphlet does not correct any of the basic flaws in the "feminization of poverty" analysis. Once again, all women are depicted as confronting essentially the same economic prospects. And, once again, minority and poor men are entirely absent from the picture. The pamphlet contains such tell-tale bloopers as the following:

- ***"While individual women moved up the career ladder, women as a class slid backwards, with those who were doubly discriminated against—women of color—taking the heaviest losses."***

Women of color have, indeed, taken the heaviest losses. But it is simply not true that "women as a class slid backwards." Women of a *particular* class did the sliding. But women of the petit bourgeoisie and ruling class (who represent more than just "individual women") have done just fine.

- *". . . there is a fundamental difference between male and female poverty: for men, poverty is often the consequence of unemployment and a job is generally an effective remedy. While female poverty often exists even when a woman works full-time."*

What this has conveniently obscured is that the effective remedy of employment is absolutely unavailable to large numbers of men. True, sexism imposes an additional burden on poor, women-headed households since, in the majority of instances, the children stay with the mother. But this does not negate the *fundamental similarities* between the causes of male and female poverty. Both are caused by unemployment and underemployment in an economic system that regenerates an impoverished layer of the working class made up of women, men and children.

- *"The short-lived 'war on poverty' has become a war on the poor in which women and children are the main*

casualties. . . . Women are the first fired, last hired and lowest paid in the best of times."

In attempting to capitalize on the consciousness developed to target the oppression of minority peoples, the authors have converted "last hired, first fired" into a feminist slogan. Thus, the historic racialization of poverty in the U.S. is effectively downplayed as is the fact that it is minority women whose economic condition is the *main* factor behind the escalation in female poverty.

The "feminization of poverty" analysis distorts reality and cannot be salvaged by the addition of references to women of color. This is because the "feminization of poverty" framework, even the new and improved version, highlights the commonality of all women as a group (*"virtually all women are vulnerable"*), thereby *glossing* over the class and racial privilege enjoyed by white women of the middle and upper classes. At the same time, this analysis argues for the fundamental difference between male and female poverty, thereby driving a wedge between poor and minority women on the one hand and their class brothers on the other. In conclusion, the "feminization of poverty" analysis misleads both the overall struggle against poverty and the struggle to improve the condition of poor women.

PART FOUR

Black Families and the Future

Alternative Life-Styles

Making predictions about the future nature of any group's family life is a risky endeavor. Few, for instance, could have projected what has happened to the American family as a whole since 1970. Certainly there were trends leading us in certain directions, but it was the acceleration of those trends that caught many of us by surprise. In the case of the Black family, the research literature is still so sparse and biased that we have practically no attempts to analyze Black families of the future or alternative family life-styles. Certain barometers of the future can be seen in light of the existing social conditions for Blacks and the trends in sexual behavior, fertility patterns, sex role changes, and marital adjustments.

Some adaptations to alternative life-styles will occur because large numbers of Blacks, especially in the middle class, are taking on the values of the majority culture. Family relations in the majority culture are changing and many Blacks will follow their trends. However, Blacks as a group will continue to face certain problems that may not be unique to them except to the extent of their prevalence. The continuing high unemployment rate among Black men and women will still have serious ramifications for the kind of family life they will have. That will primarily be a problem of the lower-class group, but all classes will have to adapt to the increasing critical problem of a male shortage and the consequences thereof.

Up to this time the problem of the male shortage has been handled by a type of serial polygyny whereby Black men have more than one wife in a lifetime but not at the same time. Some men remain married but are free-floating in their relations with other women. This kind of male-sharing may be necessary for a group with such an imbalanced sex ratio. It, however, gives rise to many conflicts between men and women who are strongly socialized into monogamous values. The instability of many Black marriages can be accounted for by this factor as well as by the general range of forces that cause marital disruption. In the future alternative family life-styles should be well thought out and implemented in ways conducive to individual and group harmony.

The article by Staples, "Change and Adaptation in the Black Family," examines the gamut of changes occurring among Black families. Some of his predictions may need to be altered in light of a different trend within certain segments of the Black community. The sexual revolution has cooled off among many Blacks because of the fear of socially transmitted diseases and the aging of the Black population. Nationalist sentiments are not as strong as they were in the 1970s, and assimilation into mainstream values has gained ascendency among middle class Blacks. During the early part of the 1980s, a period of economic recession, interracial marriages actually declined as the races became more socially isolated from each other. The continuing division of the Black community into a healthy middle class and a growing underclass still exists, as does the shortage of desirable Black men available for monogamous marriage.

Semaj's article "Polygamy Reconsidered" contains a historical analysis of polygyny and finds it to be causally related to a low sex ratio. He attempts to assess the relative evaluations of Black women and men of the possible options for coping with the shortage of available and desirable Black males for marriage. Although recognizing the difficulties of maintaining a polygynous marriage in a culture that socializes individuals into monogamous marriage values, he nonetheless feels it is incumbent on the Black community to reconsider polygamy as a viable option.

Public Policy and Black Families

According to Bell and Vogel (1968), the family contributes its loyalty to the government in exchange for leadership, which will provide direct and indirect benefits for the nuclear family. Although there is little doubt that Black families have been loyal to the political state in the United States, it appears that they have derived few reciprocal benefits in return. Although the political system has the power to affect many of the conditions influencing Black family life, it has failed to intervene in the service of the Black population and, in fact, has been more of a negative force in shaping the conditions under which Black families must live. As Billingsley (1968:177) has stated, "no subsystem has been more oppressive of the Negro people or holds greater promise for their development."

Historically, we find that state, local, and federal governmental bodies have been willing collaborators in the victimization of Black families. Under slavery, marriages between slaves were not legal because the slave could make no contract. The government did nothing to ensure stable marriages among the slave population or to prevent the arbitrary separation of slave couples by their owners. Moreover, the national government was committed to the institution of slavery, a practice that was most inimical to Black family life (Frazier, 1939).

One function of government has been to protect the sexual integrity of the female population. Until recently, the government has not provided legal or physical protection for the Black woman against sexual advances of white males. Many Black women were forced to engage in intercourse with white males because there was no law that prevented their involuntary seduction. Some state governments passed laws that held that no white man could be convicted for fornication with a Black woman. Other states required a white person as witness to any act of rape against a Black woman (Berry, 1971).

However, the government did pass, and strongly enforce, laws against interracial marriage, which were mainly designed to prevent the mating of Black men and white women. These laws ostensibly were passed to prevent racial amalgamation; but, as Heer (1974) noted, antimiscegenation laws served other functions. The requirement of racially homogamous marriages prevented Blacks from inheriting wealth from any white person through marriage into a family of means. The ban on interracial marriages denied Blacks a chance to become familiar with the white world and to obtain jobs requiring such familiarity. Their class mobility was also restricted by the lack of informal social contacts with whites that can facilitate their entrance into certain jobs, which are acquired through pull and connections.

In more recent years, state governments have tried to impose middle-class values on lower-income families, many of whom are Black. Various state legislatures have passed laws designed to reduce or eliminate welfare benefits to women who have given birth to a child out-of-wedlock. A few states have even attempted to pass laws sterilizing women on welfare who have had more than one "illegitimate" child.

For reasons that may be related to the sacrosanct nature of the family in the United States, this country has rarely had any clearly defined plans or policy concerning the family. The closest thing to it has been the welfare system, which actually worked to disrupt more families than it did to keep them together. In light of the continuing decline of the extended family, which once provided valuable backup services to the nuclear family, some sort of family support system seems necessary. Although the Black family has an extended family character, there is some decline in its viability as a support force. At the same time the central problems facing Black families require to a much greater extent some kind of remedy by a well-formulated public policy and action program addressed to their needs.

Scott (1978) delineated what those needs are in relation to Black women in our society. She described them, most accurately, as a lower-income group with high rates of unemployment and densely concentrated in low-level service-related jobs. Even if employment were offered to Black women who are unemployed, they would have problems because quality day care centers are not often available to them. Some critics of day care program expansion argue that taking care of children is a function of the family, not of the government. Such arguments ignore the realities of today's families, which necessitate either low-cost, government-supervised care of children or the relegation of women to a permanent category of second class citizens.

Those same critics are advocates of involuntary birth control and sterilization programs to prevent women from having "too many" children. This is especially imposed on low-income Black women, who are stereotyped as irresponsible breeders of children. Scott (1978) noted that birth control and sterilization programs often have a higher priority than prenatal health services and sex education programs for Black adolescents. She suggested a number of programs that would assist Black women to maintain healthy families. Elevating their pay and status in the work force is a key one, along with the development of quality day care facilities and promotion of research activities on the mental and physical health problems of Black women, the needs of the Black aged woman, the role of women in the media, and other areas.

In an early article on "Public Policy and the Changing Status of Black Families," Staples (1973) reviewed the past relationship of government to the structure of Black family life. In general, the government's efforts, few as they have been, were sporadic, misguided, and ineffective. Because future trends are in the direction of increasing numbers of female-headed households, which are characterized by a below-average income and above-average number of children, Staples suggested the specific contents of a public policy relevant to Black families. It includes a universal family allowance, elimination of sex discrimination in employment, community controlled day care centers, a child development program, and expanded government employment. Only through a combination of these measures will Blacks have a choice of family arrangements.

This section contains two papers that focus on present public policy as it relates to Black men and women. The article "Disadvantaged Women and Their Children," published by the U.S. Commission on Civil Rights, examines how poverty is endemic among fully employed Black women. Their wages are so low, compared to those of fully employed men, that an employed status is not sufficient to remove them from poverty. U.S. society continues to pay women salaries that are often only adequate when they supplement a male breadwinner's income. Because a near majority of Black families with children under the age of 18 are headed by a woman, who is generally the sole wage earner, these families are consigned to poverty and all its ramifications. Because the educational level of Black women is above that of Black men, the method of comparable worth is one mechanism for attaining income parity with their male counterparts.

However, the article by Leashore documents that Black males have a different set of problems. Many of them are unable to secure full-time employment and have a variety of health and educational problems. Although it may be futile to argue whose situation is the worst, it must be noted that the childless Black male is seldom eligible for any welfare benefits in many states. Other than a life of crime or enlistment in the military, most of them are left without any options for survival in this society. Leashore calls for national efforts to provide health insurance, full employment, family allowances, and actions to reduce incarceration.

References

Bell, N. and E. Vogel

1968 *A Modern Introduction to the Family.* New York: The Free Press.

Berry, M.

1971 *Black Resistance–White Law: A History of Constitutional Racism in America.* New York: Appleton-Century-Crofts.

Billingsley, A.

1968 *Black Families in White America.* Englewood Cliffs, N.J.: Prentice-Hall.

Frazier, E. F.

1939 *The Negro Family in the United States.* Chicago: University of Chicago Press.

Heer, D.

1974 "The Prevalence of Black–White Marriage in the United States, 1960 and 1970." *Journal of Marriage and the Family* 36 (May):246–258.

Scott, P. B.

1978 "Black Female Liberation and Family Action Programs: Some Considerations." In *The Black Family: Essays and Studies* (2nd ed.), R. Staples, ed., pp. 260–263. Belmont, Calif.: Wadsworth.

Staples, R.

1973 "Public Policy and the Changing Status of Black Families." *The Family Coordinator* 22:345–353.

12 / Alternative Life-Styles

CHANGE AND ADAPTATION IN THE BLACK FAMILY

Robert Staples

This article gives special attention to social-psychological trends and the adaptability of the Black family to rapid social changes. The author provides a potpourri of changing social attitudes and habits of the different ideological factions in the Black community. The emphasis is on preserving the Black family in positive ways so as to provide a strong backbone for the Black race.

One of the most fluid institutions in American life is the family. Probably in no other sphere of our society have such rapid and profound changes taken place. While the changes are most significant for white Americans, Blacks too are influenced to some degree by the same forces. Among the most visible trends are the increase in sexual permissiveness, challenges to the traditional concept of woman's role, more divorces, and reductions in the fertility rate. Although Blacks are part of these dynamics, their different history and needs preclude any convergence of their family life-style with that of white families.

There is considerable disagreement over whether a revolution in sexual behavior has occurred. Some argue that only the public acknowledgment of past sexual behavior has happened, giving the appearance of change. Yet, it is impossible to deny there is greater sexual permissiveness and a revolution in attitudes. The most significant change has been the sexual liberation of middle-class white women. There are many indications that the double standard of sexual conduct is disappearing or being modified.

This change in male attitudes about female sexuality has had little effect on Black female sexuality, however, since Black women have rarely been subjected to the same sexual restrictions as white women. Previously, the sexual liberation of Black women had been the source of the white American stereotype of Afro-Americans as morally loose. In reality, Black women escaped the fate of

Adapted from *Introduction to Black Sociology* (New York: McGraw-Hill, 1976), pp. 136–141. © 1976 by McGraw-Hill Book Company. Reprinted by permission.

many white women who were condemned to pre-marital chastity and marital frigidity. The healthy attitudes Blacks have toward sex have aided them in avoiding some of the "deviant" sexual actions more common to whites. One finds a much lower incidence of mate swapping, homosexuality, transvestism, pornography, and incest in the Black population. However, Blacks have shared in the general sexual freedom of whites, especially the Black middle class. There is a greater acceptance of sexual cohabitation, of different forms of sexual expression, of out-of-wedlock births, and so on, among today's Black middle class.

A big part of the sexual revolution has been the challenge to the traditional concept of the woman's role in society. White women are demanding equality in employment and in their legal rights; they are seeking to share responsibility for raising children, and to be freed of the liabilities only women face in the United States. Many Black women see the feminist movement as being anti-female, anti-children, anti-sex, and anti-family; therefore, few Black women are involved in the movement because many of its demands do not seem relevant to their needs. For instance, motherhood and marriage are two institutions that have been denied them in the past. Because they had to work, many were deprived of the time to enjoy their children. Many cannot afford the luxury of marriage, or the conditions of their lives do not provide it.

Many of the methods and goals of the women's liberation movement, however, are important to Black women. As a result of women declaring their independence from the domination of men, there will be a greater acceptance of women heading families by themselves. Perhaps society will then make provisions for eliminating some of the problems associated with female-headed households, for example, child care facilities. Although the demand for equal employment opportunities and income equality for women and men in the same jobs is very important to all women, Black women are more victimized by employment and income discrimination against women. The assumption that women are not supporting their families themselves is one reason they are so low-paid. Because

Black women are more likely than white women to be heads of households, they are hurt more by this discriminatory salary structure.

The shortage of Black males available for marriage may force Black women to rethink the idea of the monogamous marriage that lasts forever. There simply are not enough Black males. Perhaps some convergence of white and Black marital patterns is possible. White women, too, face a shortage of 5 million males due to the higher infant mortality rate for white males. Also, the continued failure of marriage to meet the emotional needs of Black women could bring about a willingness to consider more radical life-styles.

There is some indication of a homogenization of Black family life-styles. This mass family pattern will not be based on the white, middle-class nuclear family model. Rather, the increasing nativist sentiments among Black youth may result in a family system based on a combination of African and Afro-American cultural systems, which will transcend the class and regional variations that now exist. While some white Americans are questioning whether the family as an institution can survive, Blacks may decide that it must become stronger and more relevant to their lives. As the Black youth of America—the group most imbued with the spirit of Black nationalism—becomes the majority of the Black population, this process of Africanizing the Black family may be accelerated. This will depend on whether or not the forces of racial integration and movement into the middle class lead Blacks toward assimilation and acculturation or toward the crystallizing of an Afro-American identity.

Internal Adaptations

The changes in the interior of the Black family, while ideologically in the direction of pan-Africanism, are statistically in the direction of assimilation and acculturation. We can see examples of this phenomenon in the diffusion of Blacks into predominantly white suburbs, in the increase in interracial dating and marriage, in the higher incidence of suicide and mental illness, and in a decline in the extended family pattern, all of which reflect the variation in the Black community. What is surprising, given the pace of racial integration in American society, is that more Blacks have not become assimilated into the majority's mode of behavior. The integration of school systems, desegregation of suburbia, and greater access to knowledge of majority cultural norms through the mass media have provided unprecedented opportunities for Black acculturation.

Yet some Blacks demand separate facilities and organizations on white university campuses, and some Blacks who moved to the suburbs continue their social lives in the inner cities. While the extended family may not live in the same household, it still provides emotional solidarity and other kinds of support. Moreover, the concept of the extended family has broadened to include all members of the Black community. These internal adaptations made by the Black community prevent racial integration from diluting their cultural unity.

In contrast to the demands of the women's liberation movement for emancipation from the passive role ascribed to women, some Black women are discussing adopting the subordinate position of African women. Their contention is that the roles of men and women are different, not unequal. In some of the Black nationalist organizations, women are placed in auxiliary groups, while men take the leadership. Much of this is a reaction to the time when Black women had the leadership of the family thrust upon them and Black men were not allowed to fulfill the ascribed male role. Hence, in some circles it is now believed that Black women should step back and let Black men emerge as the leaders of the family and the race.

Another important adaptation under consideration by some Blacks is adopting polygyny as the Black marriage system. Because there are not enough Black males, the idea is that the sharing of husbands could stabilize Black marriages and provide certain legal benefits to women now deprived of them. At least two Black nationalist organizations are on record as advocates of polygyny for the Black population. The actual number of Black polygynous marriages is unknown, but probably quite low. In African society, the practice of polygyny is closely related to the economic system and people are socialized to accept it, but such marriages are illegal in the United States, and the second wife has no legal benefits.

Problems and Prospects

The problems Black people face have been essentially the same for a century. These problems are not related to family stability, but to the socioeconomic conditions that tear families asunder. In general, the problems have been and still are poverty and racism. While the past decade has produced a decline in racial segregation and white stereotypes of Black inferiority. Blacks still receive discriminatory treatment in every sphere of American life. Moreover, while whites agree that there is discrimination against Blacks, any national effort toward further remedy for these racist practices has a low priority among white Americans.

Low socioeconomic status continues to plague many Black families. Whereas some Blacks have achieved a higher standard of living as a result of the civil rights movement, many continue to live below the poverty level. A disproportionate number of these Blacks are female heads of families. They have more responsibilities and less income than any other group in American society, yet child care facilities are few and inadequate. Few effective programs are being proposed to meet the needs of this group—one third of all Black families.

Racism is still a problem with interracial marriages. The increased rate of interracial marriages will continue because more Blacks and whites will meet as peers. One reason some Black men will marry white women is because society's standards of beauty are still white. More Black women will marry white men for greater economic security and because they have become disenchanted with Black men. Whatever the reason, these marriages will face many obstacles. In an era of unabated white racism and Black nationalism, many interracial couples will become outcasts in Black communities as well as white. The problems of marital conflict will be compounded by these external pressures.

It is difficult to project the future of Black families because several parallel trends are occurring at once. Many Blacks are entering the middle class as a result of higher education and increased opportunities. At the same time the future is dim for those Blacks in the lower class. Automation and computer technology are rendering obsolete the labor of unskilled Black men and threatening to render them permanently unemployed. The status of Black women is in a state of flux. Some welcome liberation from male control, while others urge a

regeneration of Black male leadership. Easier access to contraceptives and abortion may mean a considerable decline in the Black fertility rate. Simultaneously, many Blacks express concern with the implications of genocide in Black family limitation. Whatever the future of Black families, it is time to put to rest all the theories about Black family instability and recognize the crucial role of this institution in the Black struggle for survival.

POLYGAMY RECONSIDERED:
Causes and Consequences of Declining Sex Ratio in African-American Society

Leahcim Tufani Semaj

The Black family is under assault from within and without. Among the factors contributing to this situation is the declining sex ratio. It has become necessary to evaluate various family life-styles because it is impossible for every Black woman to enter into a monogamous relationship with a Black man. Various options were examined. The sexes were found to differ in that women ranked monogamy, the option of women choosing a white mate, and the condition that Black men not choose white mates significantly higher than men did. These findings suggest that overt sharing relationships may be a viable option.

In 1974 Robert Staples concluded that due to the absence of available men, it was impossible for every Black woman to be in a monogamous relationship. This fact alone, he believed, would force Black people to adopt alternative family lifestyles (Staples, 1974:6). In 1978, Staples expanded on this idea showing how the situation had worsened for the Black family and especially for the Black

From the *Journal of Black Psychology* 9 (August 1982): 29–43. © 1982 by the Association of Black Psychologists. Reprinted by permission. This study was supported by a postdoctoral fellowship from the Social Learning Laboratory of the Educational Testing Service, Princeton, New Jersey, 1978–1979. This paper was presented at the 12th Annual National Convention of the Association of Black Psychologists, August 8–12, 1979, Atlanta, Georgia. The author is most grateful to Rraine Semaj and Paula Hodge for their assistance in the literature review and data collection.

woman.... He discussed the role that the continuing shortage of Black men played in the existing situation. He also examined possible solutions showing the pitfalls of interracial marriages and homosexuality as options and the problems present in the de facto sharing that now exists. However, he suggested that acknowledged and agreed upon sharing would be hard given our present socialization (Staples, 1978).

The problems of low sex ratio (number of males per 100 females) has been ignored by most social scientists. However, Oliver Cox (1940) showed that marriage rates were directly related to sex ratio, and that this relationship was most visible in the percentage of Black females married. Jacquelyne Jackson (1971, 1973) went further and showed that a significant inverse relationship existed between sex ratio and number of female headed households ($r = -.68$). As sex ratio decreased, number of female headed households increased. However, during this time sociologists and psychologists have been postulating intrapsychic explanations for the existence of female headed households in the Black community.

Jackson shows that since 1850 Blacks have had a low sex ratio, especially the last 50 years (Table 1). This has given African-Americans a headstart on whites in developing alternative forms of marital and family life in the absence of sufficient males. Notice that the white sex ratio has been falling (Table 1), especially since 1960. During this same time we have seen the development of the white women's liberation movement and the shift from the negative "father absent" concept to the "single parent family." It appears that both these developments are associated with the decline in sex ratio among whites, providing a legitimization of alternative lifestyles due to the increasing problems of white women finding mates.

Other Black scholars, notably Joseph Scott (1976) and Haki Madhubuti (1978), have examined the sex ratio problem especially as it relates to Black women. Scott demonstrates that "the sharing of the scarce available desirable Black males has definitely become one recognizable family arrangement" (1976:19). "What today are called broken homes may in fact be polygamous-type families wherein

TABLE 1	Sex Ratio by Race, 1850–1976	
YEAR	BLACK	WHITE
1850	99.1	105.2
1900	98.2	104.9
1950	94.3	99.1
1960	93.4	97.4
1970	90.8	95.3
1976	83.3	92.3

Source: Jackson (1971) and U.S. Department of Commerce, Bureau of the Census (1977).

the men are part-time members of households but nevertheless emotionally, financially, and sexually integrated in them in an organic way." Madhubuti examines the relative merits of a variety of solutions, but we will discuss these later. Even *Ebony* has gotten into the act and in 1978, Sheila Banks explained some of the problems faced by the successful and attractive Black women in finding a mate who is her "social equal" (Banks, 1978).

. . . .

The Options

What are some of the options given this situation?

Monogamy We need not discuss the pros and cons of monogamy, defined as one man and one woman with an "exclusive" commitment to each other, and to any offspring of their union. Even if this is the ideal, the reality is that it is not possible for many Black women to be in such a relationship given the number of men available.

Celibacy and Homosexuality Similarly, we need not spend too much time on celibacy and homosexuality as options because neither of these produce life (even though they may represent personal preferences). Celibacy does not represent a traditional way of life in African society nor in African-American society. Neither does homosexuality whose roots are in Greco/Roman culture. Of late, more Blacks are becoming involved in homosexual relationships as a result of incarceration. More college educated Black women are reported to be experimenting with both homo- and bi-sexuality. Madhubuti (1978:143) suggests that this may represent "a compensatory move towards fulfilling their sexual desires, possibly as a result of not having comfortable and non-frustrating relationships with Black men." Homosexuality does not contribute towards building Black "families." However, we should be aware of the role that the unmarried and often childless "Aunt" has played in the Black society by providing support to her "nieces" and "nephews."

Prostitution Prostitution does not represent a contribution towards building Black families. This reduces both women and sex to commodities.

Interracial Relationships Interracial relationship is suggested as the option that educated and professional Black women are most likely to accept. Madhubuti sees this option as the most dangerous and the one most pushed by the dominant society, and by some Blacks (notably *Jet* and *Ebony* magazines). Some Black people who chose to be a-political and a-historical believe that race and cultural differences make little sense in the direction of their personal lives. But that is not so:

> *The political reality is this: If the country is geared towards the complete destruction of the Black man as we believe it is, what you do in fact is destroy the seed. If white men are pushed on Black women or if white men become the accepted option for Black women and this option results in the formation of families, there is very serious consequence in terms of Black genocide.*
>
> **1.** *Most children from such a union will probably grow up with the father's values and outlook on life (white).*
> **2.** *Even though the Black genes will dominate, the children will probably still be light-skinned and whether we want to admit this or not, there is still a color problem within the Black race between the*

> *light-skinned and dark-skinned even though this is not as serious as it once was.*
>
> **3.** *By having a white father who is generally the dominant figure in the family, the children will not only be inculcated with his values and direction but they will probably live in an all-white or mostly-white community, and for all practical purposes will grow up as confused men and women or confirmed half-white men and women who will try their damndest to be as white as possible. This will result in further mating with whites. What you have here if this continues and becomes epidemic is that over 3 or 4 generations (which is no time in the river of history), the wiping out of the Black strain in the U.S. is an unlaughable possibility.*
>
> **4.** *Of course this is beautiful for the white supremacist because in effect what he has done is subtly control the reproductive processes of Black women, which goes hand in hand with the physical destruction of Black men and Black families. (Madhubuti, 1978:144–145)*

Historical Responses to Declining Sex Ratio

Before we examine polygamy in traditional African society or neo-polygyny in contemporary American society, let us look back at both Europe and Africa and see how the two continents historically responded to declining sex ratios.

In an article by Herbert Moller (1971) the response of European society was examined. Between the tenth and eighteenth centuries many areas of Europe experienced out migration of males who were engaged in the conquest of Africa and the "New World." This resulted in a reduction of the sex ratio and the development of "affect mysticism." This is a state of "religious eroticism" due to an "invasion of sexual imagery into religion" resulting in a "regression to the state of a love-craving child and blissful feelings of union with God" (1971:331). What this means is that for many women (and some men) God became an object of erotic love. This was a peculiar Western development. The other phenomenon that developed in relation to "affect mysticism" was the establishment of large numbers of convents in which much of the surplus female populations lived, giving their life to Christ in a "spiritual marriage." (Is this not a form of symbolic polygyny?)

Cairncross (1974) has also documented the varied "Social History of Christian Polygamy" between the fourteenth and eighteenth centuries. For example, in response to the reduction in the male population in Europe following the Thirty Year War (1618–1648) both the Catholic and Protestant churches made new rules regarding marriage. On February 14, 1650, the Regency Council of Catholic Franconia and the Archbishops of Bamburg and Wurzburg decided to limit the admission of young men into monasteries, to encourage priests to marry (one wife) and allow laymen to marry two wives for the next ten years.

Melvin Ember (1974) believed that the common explanation that polygyny will develop in societies that have a long post-partum sex-taboo was somewhat lacking. Why should a man assume all the responsibility of an additional wife solely for the purpose of sexual outlet, when extramarital affairs would do just fine? For his data base a random sample was drawn from the Human Relations Area Files (HRAF). The results indicated that societies with high male mortality were generally likely to have imbalanced sex ratio, and since permanent spinsterhood was not viable in traditional African societies, polygyny was practiced. When mortality rate was controlled, post-partum differences disappeared.

Further evidence in support of the relationship between sex ratio and polygyny can be found in Jamaican society. Between 1881 and 1970 the sex ratio for mating age population (men 20–54 years/ women 15–59 years) was as follows; 1881—80.8, 1891—73.4, 1911—75.3, 1921–69.6, 1943—81.3, 1960—78.1 and 1970—78.4 (Agyei, 1978). In this society polygynous unions are quite common and distinct from mere "male philandering" (Whitehead,

1978:823). Even though these relations are not legally sanctioned, they receive much community support. Responding to the widespread existence of these consensual relationships, new laws were enacted in 1976 giving all children equal status, irrespective of the legal status of their parents' relationship.

Polygamy in Traditional African Societies

The issue of polygamy usually surprises and titillates people socialized in a culture that only sanctions monogamous and sequential polygamous relationships. The image usually conjured is one of harems and sexual marathons. However, the eroticism associated with polygamy, which is the central issue to westerners, is the least important aspect of this institution. Plural wives usually mean sexual variety for the man but this is only a subsidiary, although agreeable consequence. This sexual variety is probably insignificant in contrast to the frequency of extramarital relationships documented in this society (Balandier and Marquet, 1974).

In Traditional Africa the institution of the harem does not exist. Polygamy does not imply that all the wives and children share a single dwelling. The usual arrangement in the case of plural marriage is the poly-nuclear family. Each wife, her children and the husband comprise a self-supporting nuclear family unit, usually within close proximity of each other. The husband usually shares each household according to strict rotation. Frequent interaction between wives usually occurs if they are good friends—but is not mandatory (Radcliffe–Brown and Forde, 1970).

About 80% of all societies practice polygyny; this includes all (Black) African societies (Balandier and Marquet, 1974). In Africa, polyandry (one woman married to several men) is very rare (Ottenburg and Ottenburg, 1960). Polygamous relationships were and are considered prestigious. Even so most marriages are monogamous and it is rare that unions include more than two or three wives (Hillman, 1975). Within African society the incidence of plural marriage (polygyny) generally depended on the productive value of the female, rules of residence followed by the culture, a stabilized mode of agricultural production, and whether or not the individual males held higher than average positions (Clignet, 1970). The last variable indicates that men of better means were able to afford more than one wife (Balandier, 1970:128). Co-wives were sometimes recruited using the principle of levirate which was an inheritance of widows (Kirwen, 1979), and through sororal polygamy whereby a man married sisters (Clignet, 1970). The latter method was seen as a way to reduce jealousy. Some have tried to use jealousy as a reason why polygyny should be forbidden, but this is a poor argument because monogamy has not overcome jealousy, which is a human condition that can and will exist in any type of relationship (Mbiti, 1970:186). Polygyny, it should be pointed out, does not imply promiscuity or inequality. With the exception of the senior co-wife, all are given equal standing. The senior co-wife was given special privileges and powers. She distributed the workload, divided monetary rewards, and was usually consulted by the husband when he wanted to recruit another spouse. The co-wives' functions (including the senior co-wife) were generally determined by the number of children they had borne, the extent to which they participated in husbands' economic enterprises, and the extent of their participation in the socialization and disciplining of the children. As her function increased so did her power; thus she was more likely to cooperate with the other co-wives.

Contemporary View on Polygyny

There is a paucity of reseach on polygyny in contemporary societies. However Helen Ware (1979) points out that when studied, issues relating to polygyny are usually studied by anthropologists and not sociologists (nor psychologists). Thus, the institution is often seen only as part of a traditional way of life which will "disappear under pressures of urbanization, wage employment, Christianity and general modernization" (1979:185). She contrasts this view with the works of Clignet (1970) and Hill-

man (1975) who see polygyny as a viable part of contemporary African society. However, she raises the concern that only the male viewpoint on polygyny has been publicized (e.g., Kenyatta, 1965, and Mbiti, 1973). To correct this situation she conducted an in-depth study of 250 married women ages 13–78 in Ibadan, Nigeria, where 46% of wives live in polygynous unions. The opinions expressed by these women were often quite revealing. For example, 75% said they prefer that their husband took another wife than have a series of mistresses; 60% said they would be pleased if their husband took another wife. However 85% cited jealousy and related issues as bad things about being the wife of a man who has several wives. With a smaller sample from Lagos and Ifaka, Nigeria, Delores Mack (1978) reported similar findings on the attitudes of Nigerian women to polygynous and extramarital relationships.

Some interesting research relating to polygyny (Blumberg, 1977) has shown that both female headed households as we know them in American society and the mother–child residential unit found in most polygynous societies are determined by similar forces in the political economy of the society. Five conditions for the emergence, prevalence and persistence of mother headed households were hypothesized and supported by evidence. The following are the conditions:

1. *The unit of labor, the unit of compensation, and the unit of property accumulation is the individual, independent of gender.*
2. *Female has independent access to subsistent opportunities.*
3. *Subsistence opportunities open to females can be reconciled with child care responsibilities.*
4. *The woman's subsistence opportunities from all sources in the absence of a male head are not drastically less than those of the men of her class.*
5. *The political economy of the society produces and profits from a surplus labor population, and the female headed household unit reproduces the surplus labor population. (1977:150–151)*

On the other hand, Goody (1973), in his analysis of the relationship among "Polygyny, Economy and the Role of Women," agrees that some economic systems permit a greater degree of polygyny. However, he believes that "the reasons behind polygyny are sexual and reproductive rather than economic and productive" (1973:189). Obviously, further research is required in this area.

The present study attempted to evaluate the various options in male/female relationships, given the low sex ratio in African-American society.

Method

In order to evaluate the options available given the sex-ratio situation, we administered the Male–Female Relationship Survey to a sample of Black men ($N = 48$) and women ($N = 42$). The mean age of the sample was 25.3 years (women 25.2 and men 25.4). Mean level of education was 15.0 years (women 15.1 and men 14.8). These respondents were recruited primarily on the streets and public places in central New Jersey, while a few were recruited through acquaintances of the research apprentice and principal investigator.

Respondents were instructed as follows:

This is a scientific study of male/female relationships. There are no right or wrong answers in this study; the best answer is your own personal opinion.

They were then posed the following question.

Being aware of the shortage of Black men, especially those "educated" and employed, how would you rank order the following options for a Black woman?

A   *She should establish an intimate/familial relationship with a non-Black man of color (e.g., Asians, Indians).*

B   *She should give up seeking intimate/familial relationships with men.*

C   *She should keep waiting and hoping that her "Mr. Right" will come along.*

D   *She should establish an intimate/familial relationship with a white man.*

E   *She should "share" a man with another woman, but not with that woman's knowledge. (Covert sharing)*

F   *She should expect a man to have an intimate/familial relationship exclusively with her. (Monogamy)*

G   *She should establish an intimate relationship with another woman. (Homosexuality)*

H   *She should establish casual intermittent relationships with Black men. (Dating)*

I   *She should "share" a man who is willing and able to meet her needs openly with another woman. (Overt sharing)*

After they had rank ordered the options for women, they were posed another question.

Given the present disproportionate numbers of Black women over men, especially those who are "educated" and employed, how would you rank order the following choices for a Black man?

A   *He should establish intimate/familial relationships with more than one Black woman, but without each woman knowing about the other. (Familial covert sharing)*

B   *He should establish an intimate/familial relationship with only one Black woman. (Monogamy)*

C   *He should establish simultaneous casual intimate relationships with more than one Black woman, but without them knowing about each other. (Casual covert sharing)*

D   *He should establish an intimate/familial relationship with one Black woman while having other casual intimate relationship(s) with other Black women, but without the women knowing about the situation. (Covert familial/casual)*

E   *He should not establish intimate/ familial relationships with non-Black women. (No non-Black women)*

F   *He should establish intimate/familial relationships with more than one Black woman with the women knowing about and sanctioning the situation. (Familial overt sharing)*

G   *He should not establish homosexual relationships. (No homosexuality)*

H   *He should establish simultaneous casual intimate relationships with more than one Black woman, but with each woman being aware of the situation. (Casual overt sharing)*

I   *He should establish an intimate/ familial relationship with one Black woman while having another casual relationship with another Black woman with the women knowing of the situation. (Overt familial/casual)*

Respondents were instructed to:

Study the list(s) carefully. Then place a "1" next to the option you find most desirable, place a "2" next to the option which is second most desirable, etc. The option which is least desirable should be ranked "9."

Results and Discussion

The results indicated that irrespective of sex, marital status, level of education or age, the relative ranking of the available options were very stable. Monogamy was seen as the most desirable option followed by "overt sharing" (Table 2). The least desirable options were women "giving up," "establishing an intimate relationship with another woman" and men establishing relationships with more than one woman without each woman knowing about the

situation. However, women ranked monogamy significantly higher than did men even though the entire sample ranked this option relatively high.

Among men there was much agreement across age, education, and marital status as to what the women should do (monogamy, overt sharing) and should not do (homosexuality, give up). But there was more variation on the question of what men should do. For example, men with four or more years of college saw it as more important that Black men "not establish intimate/familial relationships with non-Black women" than did men with less than four years of college. The composite rank orders were 6 and 9, respectively. There were also similar educational differences among men on the question of Black men "not establishing homosexual relations." The more educated group ranked this option 1 while for the less educated group it was 6. Men 18–23 years old ranked this option 2 and those 24–45 ranked it 7.

The women showed similar agreement across age, education and marital status as to what were the most and least desirable options. However, unmarried women evaluated establishing "casual and intermittent relationships with Black men" (mean rank 2.7) more desirable than married women (mean rank 3.9). The women with more than four years of college were most favorable to "share a man who is willing and able to meet her needs openly with another woman" than those women with less education. Some respondents indicated that the women's options were easier to rank than those for men because the choices for women were more clear cut. Also the sample size makes the results tentative. However, these findings suggest that in light of the declining sex ratio, overt sharing (polygynous) relationships were viewed as a desirable option. This option was less desirable than monogamy but more desirable than all other options.

Neo-Polygyny

At this point it should be pointed out that we do not advocate some utopian return to the past. Any attempt at an exact replication of our past would mean that we would make the same mistakes again,

TABLE 2 Ranking of the Options on the Male–Female Relationship Survey[1]

	BY SEX		BY MARITAL STATUS		BY EDUCATION		BY AGE	
	Women (N = 42)	Men (N = 48)	Married (N = 26)	Unmarried (N = 64)	Less than 4 years college (N = 51)	4 or more years college (N = 39)	18–23 years (N = 43)	24–45 years (N = 47)
Options for Women								
A. Non-Black Man of Color	4.4(4)	4.4(5)	4.5(4)	4.4(5)	4.5(5)	4.4(4)	4.2(3)	4.7(5)
B. Give Up	6.9(8)	6.9(8)	7.3(9)	6.8(8)	6.9(8)	7.0(8)	6.8(8)	7.0(8)
C. Keep Waiting	5.0(6)	4.2(4)*	5.2(6)	4.4(5)	4.3(4)	5.0(6)	4.4(5)	4.9(6)
D. White Man	6.1(7)	6.6(7)*	6.2(7)	6.4(7)	6.6(7)	6.0(7)	6.3(7)	6.4(7)
E. Covert Sharing	5.0(6)	5.0(6)	4.9(5)	5.1(6)	5.1(6)	4.9(5)	5.4(6)	4.7(5)*
F. Monogamy	2.1(1)	3.3(2)*	2.5(1)	3.0(2)	2.7(1)	3.1(1)	2.7(1)	3.0(1)
G. Homosexuality	7.9(9)	7.5(9)	7.3(9)	7.9(9)	7.7(9)	7.7(9)	8.0(9)	7.4(9)
H. Dating	3.0(2)	3.3(2)	3.7(3)	3.0(2)	3.0(2)	3.4(3)	3.0(2)	3.4(2)
I. Overt Sharing	4.3(3)	3.7(3)	3.5(2)	3.0(2)*	4.3(4)	3.4(3)*	4.3(4)	3.6(3)*
Options for Men								
A. Familial Covert Sharing	5.7(8)	6.1(9)	5.8(8)	6.0(9)	5.9(8)	5.9(8)	6.4(9)	5.5(6)*
B. Monogamy	2.1(1)	3.2(1)*	2.9(1)	2.6(1)	2.2(1)	3.3(1)*	2.3(1)	3.0(1)
C. Casual Covert Sharing	5.6(7)	5.3(6)	5.3(6)	5.6(6)	5.5(5)	5.5(7)	5.8(8)	5.2(5)
D. Covert Familial/Casual	5.8(9)	6.0(7)	6.2(9)	5.9(8)	5.7(7)	6.2(9)	5.8(8)	6.0(9)
E. No Non-Black Women	5.2(5)	6.1(9)	5.8(8)	5.7(7)	6.3(9)	4.9(5)**	5.6(6)	5.8(7)
F. Familial Overt Sharing	5.1(4)	4.4(2)	4.5(3)	4.8(4)	4.5(2)	5.0(6)*	5.0(5)	4.4(2)
G. No Homosexuality	5.6(7)	4.8(5)	5.3(6)	5.1(5)	5.7(7)	4.6(2)	4.4(2)	5.9(8)*
H. Casual Overt Sharing	5.1(4)	4.5(3)	4.7(4)	4.8(4)	4.7(4)	4.9(5)	5.0(5)	4.5(3)
I. Overt Familial/Casual	4.7(2)	4.6(4)	4.5(3)	4.7(2)	4.6(3)	4.7(3)	4.6(3)	4.7(4)

[1]Figures shown are mean rankings and, in parentheses, composite
rank orders. *p < .05, nonparametric ANOVA; **p < .01.

thus ending up in the same position we are today (Brown, 1979). We should, therefore, attempt to draw from the past relevant and viable options, not replications.

What is neo-polygyny? The prefix "neo" is used to indicate that the concept is old but some important components are new. However, less formal synonyms have been suggested, namely "sharing" by Madhubuti (1978) and "New Marriage" by Obadele (1975). In contrast to traditional polygyny, neo-polygyny would have the following features:

1. The relationship would exist in opposition to the norms of the dominant racial/culture group and to the norms of those Africans who have internalized alien values.
2. Rules governing the relationship would be derived, reinforced, sanctioned, and when necessary changed at the individual/significant-other/community levels.
3. This relationship would be adaptable to an urban/industrial life style.
4. Women would be able to pursue careers without having to sacrifice children and family.

We can find many examples of neo-polygynous relations, but because the culture only recognizes monogamy, these relationships are misunderstood. Primary example is what is commonly called the "single parent family." Close analysis would show that many of these units are poly-nuclear families. In one situation with which we are familiar the male has three "wives" but he lives by himself and each "wife" lives with her children. He spends time at all the homes and provides some support (financial and otherwise). However, anyone knowing only one of the women and not the full picture would classify her as a single-mother and her situation as a single-parent family. A similar analysis can be presented if we examine the situation in which a man is supporting an ex-wife and her children as well as his present family. One woman is classified as a divorcee, the other as married, but the total family dynamics is often neo-polygynous (and poly-nuclear).

Who Could Deal with Neo-Polygyny?

First, we must realize that the idea is not for the majority of families to be polygynous. This is neither possible, desirable, nor practical. Further, we recognize that many women and men have internalized the values of monogamy and sequential polygamy and so, would rather do the "right" thing for the "wrong" reason than the "wrong" thing for the "right" reason. Many people are restricted by their socialization, so irrespective of a new condition or new information to which they may be exposed will continue to respond in the old familiar manner. Also, many women and men do not understand the magnitude of the problems and the possible long term problems that the Black community will be faced with unless a conscious decision is made to fully investigate possible solutions and methods for implementation. What we are left with is a small minority who can understand and respond to these threats to the race and culture. It is only this small group that is capable of responding to this situation in a responsible manner based on careful study of all relevant variables. Any form of conscious cultural transformation requires hard work and commitment and we can all do our part in our own lives even if not personally interested in polygyny. Black men need to stop exploiting the sex-ratio situation and stop playing games on/with the Sisters. Many Black men need to make the first step and establish even one commitment (with a Black woman); we cannot afford to glorify the "playboy" image. We also need to strengthen existing relations by communicating and growing with our partners.

Finally, if one is not willing to experiment, at least one should respect those who are, in the interest of collective survival. A growing number of polygynous Black families presently exist in the United States and research is presently being conducted (by the author) to document such issues as: (1) motives for becoming involved in polygynous family form; (2) the process by which the family was established; (3) the advantages and disadvantages of the relationships; and (4) household management. This information should be useful to those who chose to reconsider polygamy.

References

Agyei, William K. A.
1978 "Emigration, Sex-Ratio and Fertility in Jamaica." *Journal of Social and Behavioral Sciences* 24 (3):116–124.

Balandier, Georges
1970 *The Sociology of Black Africa.* New York: Praeger.

Balandier, Georges, and Jacques Marquet
1974 *Dictionary of Black African Civilization.* New York: Leon Amiel.

Banks, Sheila
1978 "Success and Beauty: A Blessing or a Curse." *Ebony* September:33–42.

Blumberg, Rae L.
1977 "The Political Economy of the Mother–Child Household." In Robert F. Winch, ed., *Familial Organization: A Quest for Determinants.* New York: Free Press.

Brown, Irvin
1979 "A Cultural Integrity Approach to the Black Experience." Paper presented at the Social Learning Laboratory seminar series, Educational Testing Service, Princeton, N.J.

Cairncross, John
1974 *After Polygamy Was Made a Sin: The Social History of Christian Polygamy.* Routledge & Kegan Paul.

Clignet, Remi
1970 *Many Wives, Many Powers: Authority and Power in Polygamous Families.* Evanston, Ill: Northwestern University Press.

Cox, Oliver C.
1940 "Sex Ratio & Marital Status among Negroes." *American Sociological Review* 5:937–947.

Ember, Melvin
1974 "Warfare, Sex Ratio, and Polygyny." *Ethnology* 8:197–206.

Goody, Jack
1973 "Polygyny, Economy and the Role of Women." In Jack Goody, ed., *The Character of Kinship.* Cambridge, England: Cambridge University Press.

Hillman, Eugene
1975 *Polygamy Reconsidered: African Plural Marriages and the Christian Churches.* New York: Orbis.

Jackson, Jacquelyne
1971 But Where Are the Men? *The Black Scholar* December:30–41.
1973 "Black Women in a Racist Society." In Charles V. Willie, Bernard M. Kramer, and Bertram S. Brown, eds., *Racism and Mental Health.* Pittsburgh: University of Pittsburgh Press.

Kenyatta, Jomo
1965 *Facing Mount Kenya.* New York: Vintage.

Kirwen, Michael C.
1979 *African Widows.* Maryknoll, N.Y.: Orbis.

Mack, Delores E.
1978 "Husbands and Wives in Lagos: The Effects of Socioeconomic Status on the Pattern of Family Living." *Journal of Marriage and Family* 40 (4):807–816.

Madhubuti, Haki R.
1973 *Book of Life.* Chicago: Institute of Positive Education.
1978 *Enemies: The Clash of Races.* Chicago: Third World Press.

Mbiti, John S.
1970 *African Religions and Philosophy.* New York: Anchor.
1973 *Love and Marriage in Africa.* London: Longmans.

Moller, Herbert
1971 "The Social Causation of Affective Mysticism." *Journal of Social History* 4:305–338.

Obadele, Imari Abubakari
1975 *Foundations of the Black Nation.* Detroit: The House of Songhay.

Ottenburg, Simon, and Pheobe Ottenburg, eds.
1960 *Cultures and Societies of Africa.* New York: Random House.

Radcliffe-Brown, A. R., Daryll Forde, eds.
1970 *African Systems of Kinship and Marriage.* New York: Oxford University Press.

Scott, Joseph W.
1976 "Polygamy: A Futuristic Family Arrangement for African Americans." *Black Books Bulletin* Summer:13–19.

Staples, Robert

1974　"The Black Family in Evolutionary Respective." *The Black Scholar* 5 (June):2–10.

1978　"The Myth of Black Sexual Superiority, A Re-Examination." *The Black Scholar* 7 (April): 16–23.

U.S. Department of Commerce, Bureau of the Census

1977　*Statistical Abstract of the United States, 1977.* Washington, D.C.: U.S. Government Printing Office.

Ware, Helen

1979　"Polygyny: Women's Views in a Transitional Society, Nigeria 1975." *Journal of Marriage and the Family* 41:185–195.

Whitehead, Tony L.

1978　"Residence, Kinship and Mating as Survival Strategies: A West Indian Example." *Journal of Marriage and the Family* 40 (4):817–828.

13 / Public Policy and Black Families

DISADVANTAGED WOMEN AND THEIR CHILDREN

United States Commission on Civil Rights

A summary and analysis of the employment problems of women, especially Black women, as they are caused by gender-linked occupations and employer discrimination. Practical solutions to the low wages paid women are explored, such as comparable worth methods and enforcement of equal opportunity laws. Federal welfare programs and their ability to reduce female poverty are examined.

Poor women do participate in the labor force. Their work orientation and life goals are quite similar to those of other Americans.[1] The problem is they are often unable to find work, must work part time, or the jobs do not pay a wage adequate to support a family. The Commission has found that 61 percent of black, 51 percent of Hispanic, and 45 percent of white women in the labor force in 1980 were either unemployed or underemployed, compared to 35 percent of white men.[2] Not all of these women were poor, but in 1979, 3.1 million women sought public assistance because they were unable to support their families.[3] Inadequate earnings, dependence, and poverty over time are associated with loss of

confidence, making efforts to improve their status more difficult.[4]

This chapter discusses the relationship of employment status and poverty, the concentration of women in low-wage jobs, inequalities in wages paid to women, and work disincentives in Federal programs. Labor market data presented are for fully employed[5] women unless otherwise noted because they provide the most realistic means of comparison to men.

Employment and Poverty

Recent studies have shown that millions of working Americans endure economic hardship, and the most disadvantaged of these are women. Bureau of Labor Statistics studies of poverty by employment and marital status in 1979 and 1980 are most revealing.[6] Although no poverty rates are given by both race and sex, the rates are reported for women maintaining families alone and express the severity of their problems.[7]

Many fully employed women heading households are poor in spite of their work efforts. In 1980,

From *Disadvantaged Women and Their Children*, U.S. Commission on Civil Rights (Washington, D.C.: U.S. Government Printing Office, 1983), pp. 13–35. Tables and some footnotes have been renumbered.

23 million women were fully employed, of whom 3.2 million were heads of household. The poverty rate for the women heading their own families was 5.4 percent, almost 2.5 times that for nuclear families, and twice the rate for men maintaining families with no spouse present (see Table 1). Since all cash income is included when calculating poverty rates,[8] the data show that, in spite of full-time work, these women are poor, and after welfare payments (if they are eligible), they are still poor.

Of all persons who have less than full-time employment, women heading families are most likely to be poor. The poverty rates for those who could only find part-time work in 1980 exceeded 56 percent for women maintaining families and 26 percent for husbands (in nuclear families).[9] Almost 56 percent of women maintaining families who were unemployed at any time during 1980 were poor. The corresponding rate for husbands experiencing unemployment was 14 percent. The poverty rates for women who looked for, but could not find work at all during 1980 were extremely high, reaching 85 percent for women maintaining families alone. The rate for husbands was 53 percent.

In general, the poverty figures in Table 1 for women maintaining their own families indicate their lack of personal financial resources to carry them through periods of unemployment or reduced employment. In some cases a dependent child or other relative living in the home may help out, but they are frequently unable to make up the income lost by the primary breadwinner.[10]

The minimum wage provides a benchmark for determining the adequacy of employment. In 1980 full-time work[11] at the minimum wage ($3.10) provided an income of $6,448, just under the $6,570 poverty level for a family of three that year. (The average size of a family headed by a woman receiving aid to families with dependent children is three.)[12]

The 1980 earnings distribution for full-time workers shows disparities at the high as well as the low end of the scale. Over 2.8 million women (13 percent) who were fully employed had earnings of $7,000 or less, compared to 4.4 percent of fully employed men (see Table 2). Eighty-eight percent of the men earned over $10,000, compared to 63 percent of white, 57 percent of black, and 48 percent of

Hispanic women. These figures do not tell the whole story, however. Most of the women were clustered in the $7,000 to $15,000 range, with a total of 9.6 percent earning over $20,000, while most of the men earned over $15,000, with 46.5 percent earning over $20,000. Among the women, 10 percent of whites, 6.4 percent of blacks, and 5.1 percent of Hispanics earned over $20,000.

The poverty level is a severe measure of hardship and does not give a complete indication of how many families are really under stress trying to make ends meet. Table 3 presents another view of fully employed women and how they and their families are concentrated at the low end of the income and earnings distribution. By increasing the hardship standard to 1.25 times the official poverty threshold, the proportion of female-headed families in distress almost doubles. The proportion for men who maintain families alone increases at almost the same rate; however, only half as many men meet this definition of hardship.

Acquiring full-time employment will not necessarily solve the poverty problem for the many women who are unemployed or employed less than full time. This is apparent from the poverty figures for fully employed women given above. Guaranteed employment at the minimum wage may not be enough either. The fact is that a job often is not enough to enable women to leave poverty. The next section discusses aspects of occupations and wages, illuminating further the dilemma of women in the labor market.

Occupations and Wages

A woman's occupation has a major effect on her earnings. However, most women are concentrated in a few occupations that are typically low wage with little room for advancement. This concentration of women in certain occupations may be due to discrimination, which is a process that can be transposed from individual attitudes and actions into social structures and business organizations.[13] Once institutionalized, discriminatory procedures cause: "unequal results along the lines of race, sex, and national origin, which in turn reinforce existing practices and breed damaging stereotypes which

TABLE 1 Women and Men Maintaining Families below the Poverty Level,[1] 1980

	WOMEN WHO MAINTAIN FAMILIES[2]	HUSBANDS IN NUCLEAR FAMILIES	MEN WHO MAINTAIN FAMILIES[2]	TOTAL ALL MEN AND WOMEN
Fully employed[3]	5.4%	2.6%	2.8%	2.5%
Partially employed[4]	39.9	11.0	20.2	11.8
Involuntary part-time[5]				
Could only find part-time work	56.6	26.2	([6])	22.2
Slack work, material shortage	28.3	11.8	22.0	11.9
Unemployed at some time*	55.6	14.3	24.0	17.5
Did not work	53.5	13.7	21.3	20.9
Ill, disabled	49.3	20.8	24.9	33.3
Taking care of home	59.4	([6])	([6])	18.1
Going to school	81.9	37.7	([6])	20.5
Unable to find work	85.1	53.4	([6])	44.7
Retired	11.1	7.9	11.3	13.5

*This item may be read as follows: Of all persons who were unemployed at some time during 1980, 17.5 percent were in poor families. Of women who maintained families alone and experienced unemployment, 53.5 percent were poor, compared to 21.3 percent of men who maintained families alone.

Notes: The employment categories may overlap. Data are not available by race.

[1]After inclusion of cash transfers and excluding in-kind transfers such as food stamps and housing.

[2]Men and women maintaining families have no spouse present.

[3]Persons who worked 50–52 weeks of the year usually at a full-time job. Also referred to as full-time, year-round workers.

[4]Persons who worked less than 50 weeks of the year in either full-time or part-time jobs, and persons who worked part time 50–52 weeks.

[5]Persons who worked less than 35 hours for at least 1 week during the year (a) because they could only find part-time work or (b) because of the slack work or material shortages.

[6]Data not shown where base is less than 75,000.

Source: U.S., Department of Labor, Bureau of Labor Statistics, *Linking Employment Problems to Economic Status: Data for 1980* (1982), tables 4, 10, 13, 17 and 26.

TABLE 2 Earnings of Fully Employed Workers, 1980

	ALL MEN	ALL WOMEN	WOMEN White	WOMEN Black	WOMEN Hispanic
Total	100.0%	100.0%	100.0%	100.0%	100.0%
Under $4,000	1.1	2.2	2.1	3.1	2.6
$4,000–6,999	3.3	10.8	10.1	15.6	21.4
$7,000–9,999*	7.7	24.6	24.6	24.3	28.1
$10,000–14,999	20.1	36.4	36.8	34.3	30.7
$15,000–19,999	21.4	16.5	16.4	16.3	12.0
$20,000–24,999	19.1	6.2	6.5	4.1	3.2
$25,000 & over	27.4	3.4	3.5	2.3	1.9
Median earnings	$18,910	$11,287	$11,413	$10,609	$9,769

*This item may be read as follows: In 1980, 28.1 percent of fully employed Hispanic women earned between $7,000 and $9,999.

Source: U.S., Department of Labor, Bureau of Labor Statistics, unpublished tabulations, 1980.

then promote the existing inequalities that set the process in motion in the first place."[14]

Large disparities in income, occupational, and wage statistics lend credence to the theory of discrimination. The Supreme Court has noted that statistics showing racial or ethnic imbalance are important in legal proceedings:

> [B]ecause such imbalance is often a telltale sign of purposeful discrimination; absent explanation, it is ordinarily to be expected that nondiscriminatory hiring practices will in time result in a work force more or less representative of the racial and ethnic composition of the population in the community from which employees are hired.[15]

Since the passage of Title VII of the Civil Rights Act of 1964 and other equal employment legislation, employers have been required to give women equal consideration in employment, training, promotions, and salaries.[16]

Occupations

Before legislation requiring equal opportunity, and even now, most women worked in occupations traditionally dominated by females. . . . Although the jobs are not always low skill, they do tend to be low wage and to have little promotion potential. The Commission has found that more than 26 percent of black, 23 percent of Hispanic, and 20 percent of white women are overeducated for their jobs.[17] This means they may have a college education, but work in jobs only requiring a high school diploma, or have a high school diploma, but work in jobs requiring an elementary school education. Even in "female" professions such as nursing, teaching, social work, and academic librarianship, men are disproportionately represented in positions that involve supervision, direction, and planning, and they consistently earn higher wages.[18]

Two major explanations for occupational segregation have been investigated by Andrea Beller. The first is that women choose traditionally female occupations, and the second is that employer discrimination leaves them no choice. Research by Beller supports the latter theory.[19] The first theory

is a human capital approach,[20] developed by Solomon Polachek.[21] The theory is based on sex role differentiation and contends that women "find occupations attractive in which skills deteriorate the least with absences from the labor force, and they enter them disproportionately."[22] The second explanation is a discrimination theory of employer choice developed by Barbara Bergmann.[23] It holds that:

> because women face barriers to entry into certain occupations, they tend to become crowded into a small number of occupations without barriers. Increasing the supply of labor reduces earnings in these . . . occupations, and limiting the supply of labor raises earnings in the occupations that become male.[24]

In research concerning these theories, Beller states:

> if women freely choose to enter only a third of all occupations and those occupations pay less, then women's lower earnings may not be a fundamental social problem. The major issue is whether the dramatic differences in the occupational distributions of the sexes result from different choices made by each, given equal opportunities, or from unequal opportunities to make similar choices.[25]

Occupational discrimination diminished somewhat during the 1970s, and enforcement of Title VII of the Civil Rights Act of 1964 and the Federal contract compliance program were found to be associated with an increase in the probability of a woman's being employed in a male-dominated occupation compared to a man's probability, thus supporting Bergmann's theory of employer discrimination.[26]

Women in Traditional Occupations

Women accounted for a disproportionate share (65 percent) of the increase in employment during the period 1972–82, and the occupations experiencing the greatest growth in employment tended to be

TABLE 3   Poverty Status of Families of Fully Employed Workers, 1980

	TOTAL (1,000)	BELOW POVERTY[1]	BELOW 1.25 POVERTY LEVEL	BELOW 1.50 POVERTY LEVEL	BELOW 2.00 POVERTY LEVEL	MEDIAN FAMILY INCOME
Women who maintain families*	3,240	5.4%	10.4%	17.4%	34.1%	$15,843
Median personal earnings		$5,192	$6,130	$6,900	$ 8,347	
Husbands	31,063	2.6%	4.5%	6.9%	13.8%	$27,677
Median personal earnings		$4,489	$6,515	$8,220	$10,446	
Men who maintain families*	1,038	2.8%	5.6%	9.3%	18.3%	$22,788
Median personal earnings		(²)	(²)	(²)	(²)	

*These items may be read as follows: Although median family income for men who maintained families alone in 1980 was $22,788, median income for women maintaining families was $15,834. Of women maintaining families, 17.4 percent had incomes below 1.5 times the poverty level (median earnings were $6,900), and 9.3 percent of men maintaining families had earnings below 1.5 times poverty (median earnings not available).

[1]The 1980 poverty level for a family of three was $6,570. The data presented here take into account the poverty thresholds for families of different sizes.

²Data not shown where base is less than 75,000.

Source: U.S., Department of Labor, Bureau of Labor Statistics, *Linking Employment Problems to Economic Status: Data for 1980,* (1982), table B–1.

those already dominated by women, such as secretaries, cashiers, registered nurses, and bookkeepers.[27] Women accounted for at least half of the increase in each occupational category experiencing growth, with the exception of craft and kindred jobs, where they accounted for 20 percent of the increase.[28]

The concentration of women in a few traditionally female occupations is closely related to low wages. (A discussion of women's low wages follows this section.) A large number of women can be found in jobs characterized as marginal. They "tend to have low wages and fringe benefits, poor working conditions, high labor turnover, little chance of advancement, and often arbitrary and capricious supervision."[29] In a recent report, the Commission found that 21.6 percent of black, 18.5 percent of Hispanic, and 13.9 percent of white women were employed in relatively low-paying jobs requiring less than 3 months of training.[30] Of all majority males, just 5.3 percent were in such occupations.[31] Table 4 gives the occupational distribution and the ratio of female to male salaries of all fully employed men and women in 1980.

Women of all races are concentrated in the clerical and kindred category that, although it provides approximately 18 percent of all full-time jobs, employs 40 percent of white, almost 35 percent of black, and 36 percent of Hispanic women. These jobs include bank tellers, billing clerks, bookkeepers, and cashiers.[32] Median annual earnings for women clerical and kindred workers were $10,909; for men, $18,474.[33]

Another occupational category in which women are overrepresented is service work. Although 8.7 percent of all full-time workers are in this field, more than 24 percent of black, 13 percent of Hispanic, and 10 percent of white women work in such service jobs as cooks, dishwashers, food counter and fountain workers, cleaning service workers, waiters, nurse's aides, child care workers, and dental assistants.[34] Less than 7 percent of men are service workers. Median annual earnings for service workers were $8,043 for women and $13,140 for men.[35]

Hispanic women are particularly underrepresented among professional, technical, and kindred workers (11 percent compared to 18 percent for both sexes and 19.5 percent for white women). The professions they have penetrated are probably those typically associated with women, such as librarians, teachers, nurses, and health technologists.

In 1980 women in professional and technical occupations earned $11,140, compared to $18,750 for men.[36]

Hispanic women are especially overrepresented among operatives. Although 10 percent of all fully employed workers are operatives, 22 percent of Hispanic women are in these jobs. This rate compares with 9.7 percent of white and 11.3 percent of black women. The operative jobs in which women are predominantly employed include laundry and dry cleaning operatives, packers and wrappers, sewers and stitchers, shoemaking machine operatives, and textile operatives, such as spinners, twisters, and winders.[37] Median annual earnings of operatives were $9,476 for women and $15,743 for men.[38]

Most of the women earning low wages are in typically female occupations. Among the 2 million fully employed women who earned less than $6,000 in 1980 (less than the minimum wage), 31 percent were service workers, 23 percent were clerical and kindred workers, and 11 percent were operatives.[39] These low earners constituted 8.8 percent of all fully employed women. The proportion of men earning low wages was 4.8 percent.[40]

Women in Nontraditional Occupations

Women in nontraditional employment tend to have children, have usually tried other jobs, and have realized that they could never earn an adequate living at them.[41] In fact, the probability that a working woman is employed in a nontraditional occupation increases as the number of her children increases.[42] However, just 2 percent of all female workers are craft and kindred workers (traditionally male occupations). Nevertheless, recent Bureau of Labor Statistics data show that, as a proportion of all craft workers, they increased from 3.6 percent in 1972 to 6 percent in 1980.[43] This translates into an increase of 365,000 during the period.[44]

Table 5 reflects some of the gains women have made in these occupations. In spite of large percentage gains, the absolute numbers are small (generally less than 0.05 percent in each occupation) relative to total women in the work force, and

women have much to achieve to gain access to apprenticeships and vocational training in these better paying, nontraditional occupations.

Assuming no barriers to women's entering traditionally male occupations, 60 percent of currently employed women would have to change occupations for women to have the same occupational profile as men, and this figure has changed little since 1900.[45] However, it takes a strenuous, conscious effort for change to take place.

A recent study of sex segregation concluded that, "Neither demographic trends, technological change, nor bureaucratic imperatives are 'natural' forces that lead to balanced sex ratios within jobs or firms," and that, "policy intervention is unlikely to make matters worse—most establishments are about as segregated as they can possibly be."[46]

Severe external pressure and, where possible, a large percentage of women already employed in an organization facilitate desegregation of the work force.[47] Desegregation occurs most easily in large firms that have government contracts and are subject to Federal regulations.[48] However, the outlook is not bright for women employed in smaller and less visible firms that may do nothing or make only token changes, since they are less likely to be subject to enforcement activities.[49]

Changing jobs is not a practical solution to the low-wage problems of many currently employed women. Women already in traditionally female occupations would lose seniority and vested benefits in their current jobs, would have to pay for retraining, and would have no guarantee that they would be hired by employers in their new field. It is important, however, that young women receive adequate counseling on the benefits or possible drawbacks of nontraditional employment. It is also important that equal employment opportunity laws be strictly enforced so that investment in nontraditional training will pay off. The following section reviews other explanations for women's low wages relative to men's.

Wages

Women earn less than men: 59 percent as much in 1981, a decrease from 64 percent in 1955.[50] Table 6

TABLE 4   Occupations of Fully Employed Workers, 1980

	ALL MEN	BOTH SEXES	WHITE WOMEN	BLACK WOMEN	HISPANIC WOMEN	RATIO OF MEDIAN EARNINGS OF WOMEN AND MEN
Total	100%	100%	100%	100%	100%	59.4%
Professional, technical, and kindred	17.6	18.2	19.5	17.6	10.9	65.6
Managers and administrators, except farm	18.2	15.3	11.0	4.3	7.1	55.3
Sales workers	6.1	5.5	4.7	2.6	4.0	48.9
Clerical and kindred workers*	6.2	17.9	40.2	34.8	36.2	59.1
Craftworkers, foremen, and kindred	21.5	14.6	2.2	1.4	3.2	61.5
Operatives, except transport	10.1	10.1	9.7	11.3	22.0	60.4
Transport equipment operatives	5.2	3.5	0.4	0.3	0.1	61.5
Laborers, except farm and mine	4.5	3.3	1.0	1.4	1.4	59.0
Private household workers	(¹)	0.3	0.6	2.0	2.3	75.1
Service workers	6.9	8.7	10.1	24.4	13.0	(¹)
Farmers and farm managers	2.5	1.7	0.3	(¹)	(¹)	61.2
Farm laborers and foremen	1.1	0.9	0.4	(¹)	0.1	(¹)

*This item may be read as follows: In 1980, 17.9 percent of all fully employed workers were in clerical and kindred jobs; however, 6.2 percent of all men, compared to 40.2 percent of white women, were in these occupations. The median earnings of all women in these jobs were 59.1 percent of the earnings of men in these jobs.

¹Data not shown where base is less than 75,000.
Source: U.S., Department of Labor, Bureau of Labor Statistics, calculated from unpublished data, 1980.

TABLE 5   Female Craft and Kindred Workers

	1972	1980	PERCENT GAIN
Carpenters	5,000	18,000	260
Other construction craftworkers	11,000	50,000	354
Machinists	2,000	18,000	800
Heavy equipment mechanics*	5,000	15,000	200
Telephone installers and repairers	6,000	27,000	350

*This item may be read as follows: Between 1972 and 1980, the number of women employed as heavy equipment mechanics increased from 5,000 to 15,000, a 200 percent increase.

Source: Carol Boyd Leon, "Occupational Winners and Losers: Who They Were during 1972–80," *Monthly Labor Review*, June 1982, p. 28.

shows how earnings are distributed by sex, race, and ethnicity for fully employed workers.

All women are at an earnings disadvantage when compared to men, but black and Hispanic women are the most disadvantaged. Hispanic women earn one-half the median income of white men, while black and white women earn 54 and 58 percent, respectively.

Some of the explanations that have been offered on women's occupational distribution and wages include both direct and indirect discrimination. Following are possible reasons for the unex-

TABLE 6   Median Earnings of Fully Employed Persons, 1980

	WOMEN	MEN	RATIO OF FEMALE TO MALE EARNINGS	RATIO OF FEMALE TO WHITE MALE EARNINGS
White	$11,413	$19,570	58.3%	58.3%
Black*	10,609	13,737	77.2	54.2
Hispanic	9,769	13,717	71.2	49.9

*This item may be read as follows: In 1980 fully employed black women earned 77.2 percent as much as fully employed black men and 54.2 percent as much as fully employed white men.

Source: U.S., Department of Labor, Bureau of Labor Statistics, unpublished tabulations.

plained disparities in wages between men and women.[51] Not all researchers agree on the importance of different factors, and although no single one will suggest a solution to all of the economic problems of women, an investigation of each highlights issues that concern both female employees and their employers.

Personal Choice or Sex Role Stereotyping Many women continue in jobs in spite of their low rates of pay. A study done for the Equal Employment Opportunity Council concluded that, "It is difficult to assess the relative importance of the choices women make in the labor market and of the factors affecting their choices."[52]

The first factor is the effect of socialization, in which some women come to believe that only certain jobs are appropriate for women, and they may never even consider other types of jobs.[53] Second, women may have chosen or have been directed into courses of study or training that did not provide qualifications for other jobs.[54] The third explanation says that women lack information about other jobs, their salaries, working conditions, and how to obtain access to them.[55]

A fourth explanation is that women know they have other options, but choose to limit their training and labor force participation because of actual or expected family obligations. If they do work, they take jobs requiring limited overtime and travel or jobs they would not mind leaving if their husbands' career advancement requires transfer.[56]

Fifth, discrimination may cause women to believe that they cannot gain access to certain jobs or

that the jobs themselves would be made unpleasant. This belief guides their education and training decisions.[57]

Once employed in a low-wage, low-skill job, a woman may find her employer reluctant to invest in on-the-job training for her because he may not believe she is interested in advancement, or because he thinks that she may soon leave her job.[58] All women suffer as a result of these experiences and decisions, for it is likely that they will spend more years in the labor force than expected at the time they made choices regarding education and training.[59]

Discrimination Discrimination against women in the form of low pay is well documented. While men tend to obtain good jobs with rapid advancement, women receive unequal pay for equal work and are assigned to low-level jobs without promotion potential.[60]

Minority women have had to deal with the effects of both racial and sex discrimination. In 1920 black women were largely restricted to agricultural labor, domestic service, and laundry work, which accounted for 75 percent of jobs held by black women in the labor force.[61] During this period black women were able to replace immigrant women in unskilled jobs in candy factories and to replace men in some heavy jobs,[62] but:

To do so, they had to accept less pay than a white person doing an equivalent job would have received. One observer commented that as soon as Washington, D.C., laundries real-

ized they might have to pay a minimum wage, they "began to ask the employment bureaus about the possibility of obtaining white girls" to replace the Negro women. Married women could be hired to do the heavy unskilled work of men for up to one-third less than employers had to pay the latter. Yet these jobs were attractive to women who had few options.[63]

In 1940 more than half of the 2 million women who earned wages working in someone else's home were black and Hispanic.[64] They were among the poorest paid and hardest working, but were not protected by the Fair Labor Standards Act or other protective legislation.[65] In Lynchburg, Virginia, $6.00 for a 72-hour week was a typical wage for a domestic.[66]

The facts that the median earnings of black women are now 94 percent of those of white women and that the occupational distribution of young black women has improved dramatically in the last 20 years have created concern that policy-makers will conclude that black women are no longer disadvantaged (on the basis of race) in the labor market.[67] To compare black and white women is to compare one disadvantaged group to another. And because black men continue to be discriminated against, one author concludes: "Although the elimination of sex discrimination would, by definition, produce economic equality between white men and women, black women would fare no better than black men and continue to earn less than white men (and white women)."[68]

Research on Wage Disparities Factors such as education, age, and work experience generally explain less than half of the difference in wages between men and women.[69] Statistical studies have tested whether enforcement of equal opportunity provisions has had an effect on reducing discrimination and, thus, wage disparities between men and women. One study found that variables related to work experience, such as years of training and on-the-job training, accounted for 29 percent of the gap. However, formal education (usually defined as years of school) explained just 2 percent of the difference between white men and white women.[70]

Education explained 11 percent of the difference between white men and black women.[71] Although poverty rates for both men and women decline as educational levels increase, proportionally more women are poor because they earn less than men at all educational levels. . . .

The effectiveness of equal employment laws varies depending on the following factors:

(1) the completeness of the law in specifying every manifestation of discrimination as illegal behavior; (2) the percentage of employment covered by the law; (3) the enforcement of the law; and (4) the extent of the penalties imposed. If the law makes certain forms of discrimination illegal but leaves others unmentioned, then employers are free to adjust their behavior so that discrimination persists and is reflected in new and unanticipated forms of disadvantage. But even illegal forms of discrimination will persist if the benefits of continued discrimination are seen to exceed the costs, in terms of the chances of being caught and the penalty if and when that occurs.[72]

Andrea Beller has found that enforcement of equal employment opportunity laws increased female earnings by 4.7 percent between 1967 and 1974.[73] Enforcement for race discrimination had a net effect on the earnings of black women of 1.2 percent during the same period.[74] Executive Order 11246, issued in 1965, which requires Federal contractors to establish goals and timetables for achieving reasonable representation of minorities and women in their labor force, and Title VII of the Civil Rights Act of 1964, which established sex as one of several bases for protection against discrimination in employment, were studied. Using Current Population Survey and Equal Employment Opportunity Commission data for the 1968 to 1974 period, Beller reached the following conclusions:

1. Enforcement of Title VII increases female earnings within industries and occupations, while the Federal contract compliance program increases earnings by lessening entry restrictions across industries and occupations.[75]

2. When enforcement activities are visible, they provide a deterrent effect that extends beyond the scope of the original charge.[76]

3. Although black women have benefited from Title VII enforcement against racial discrimination, they seem to have benefited more from enforcement against sex discrimination.[77]

4. The most powerful tool for increasing the earnings of women is probably enforcement against sex discrimination.[78]

5. Worsening economic conditions, as measured by unemployment rates, curtailed, but did not eliminate, the effectiveness of Title VII, for the sex differential in earnings might have increased.[79]

Although an overall effect on wages at the national level may be difficult to measure, there is no doubt that many women are better off as a direct result of litigation on their behalf, and countless others benefit from the deterrent effects of visible enforcement. Had equal employment opportunity legislation not been passed, the gap between men and women in wages earned could have increased more than it did during the last decade.[80]

Comparable Worth An explanation for wage disparities that has gained considerable momentum in recent years is referred to as "comparable worth." This theory is based on the concept that, "within a given organization, jobs that are equal in their value to the organization ought to be equally compensated, whether or not the work content of these jobs is similar."[81] The literature located for this report on comparable worth was based on sex differentials, not both race and sex. However, a major study conducted for the Equal Employment Opportunity Commission states:

> *despite the apparently greater immediate relevance of the comparable worth issue to women than to minorities, our analysis is applicable whenever substantial job segregation between different groups exists and whenever particular jobs are dominated by particular groups.*[82]

Proponents of this theory believe that many jobs in which women predominate are compensated at a lower rate because they are held by women, constituting discrimination.[83] Furthermore, employers may separate similar jobs, providing lower wages and less upward mobility for those held by women.

The Congress clearly indicated that it rejected the comparable worth theory and favored a strict equal work requirement when it passed the Equal Pay Act of 1963.[84] To claim equal wages, the burden of proof falls on the plaintiffs suing under the Equal Pay Act of 1963, which is restricted to equal pay for equal work. Equal work is that "which requires equal skill, effort, and responsibility... performed under similar working conditions...."[85]

Title VII of the Civil Rights Act of 1964 has thus become central to the comparable worth issue because it affects the full range of employment practices and specifically forbids discrimination in compensation.[86] Title VII affords protection against employment practices that, although fair in form and administration, have disparate impact.[87] When neutral policies and practices affect a protected group more harshly than others, there may be a basis for a Title VII complaint.

Although some employers have established job evaluation systems to provide objective standards of job worth to be used in setting wages,[88] studies indicate that they have violated their own standards, "either to implement an explicit decision to pay women or minority workers less than men or whites or to conform to an external standard for establishing pay rates."[89] Many employers survey the local labor market and use the "prevailing rate" as a basis for establishing their own wage schedule. In doing so they may assume they are being nondiscriminatory, but in fact they may be continuing disparities and discriminatory personnel practices of the other firms or those that were established because of discrimination in the past.[90]

Wage disparities for jobs of comparable worth have been found in several cities and States that have performed job evaluations to determine if they underpay predominantly female jobs. For example, in Minnesota, the predominantly female position of typing pool supervisor was rated higher than the predominantly male position of painter, yet the women were paid $334 a month less than the men (see Table 7). In Washington State, licensed practi-

TABLE 7   Comparable Jobs Inequitably Paid

JOB TITLE		MONTHLY SALARY	NUMBER OF POINTS
Minnesota	Registered nurse (F)*	$1,723	275
	Vocational ed. teacher (M)	2,260	275
	Typing pool supervisor (F)	1,373	199
	Painter (M)	1,707	185
San Jose, California	Senior legal secretary (F)	665	226
	Senior carpenter (M)	1,040	226
	Senior librarian (F)	898	493
	Senior chemist (M)	1,119	493
Washington State	Licensed practical nurse (F)	1,030	173
	Correctional officer (M)	1,436	173
	Secretary (F)	1,122	197
	Maintenance carpenter (M)	1,707	197

*This item may be read as follows: In Minnesota, the traditionally female job of registered nurse was rated equal to the traditionally male job of vocational education teacher according to standards of training and responsibility established by the State; even so, the nurses were paid $537 a month less.

Source: Nancy D. Perlman, chair, National Committee on Pay Equity, testimony before the U.S. House of Representatives, Subcommittees on Civil Service, Human Resources, and Compensation and Employee Benefits, Sept. 16, 1982.

cal nurses received more than $400 a month less than correctional officers even though their jobs were rated as being equal according to standards established by the State.

The Equal Employment Opportunity Commission asked the National Research Council of the National Academy of Sciences to make a judgment as to whether low-paying jobs are low paying because of the sex, race, or ethnicity of the people who tend to hold them or because the jobs themselves are not worth higher pay. The study concluded:

> several types of evidence support our judgment that . . . in many instances jobs held mainly by women and minorities pay less at least in part because they are held mainly by women and minorities. First, the differentials in average pay for jobs held mainly by women and those held mainly by men persist when the characteristics of jobs thought to affect their value and the characteristics of workers thought to affect their productivity are held constant. Second, prior to the legis-

> lation of the last two decades, differentials in pay for men and women and for minorities and nonminorities were often acceptable and were, in fact, prevalent. The tradition embodied in such practices was built into wage structures, and its effects continue to influence these structures. Finally, at the level of the specific firm, several studies show that women's jobs are paid less on the average than men's jobs with the same scores derived from job evaluation plans. The evidence is not complete or conclusive, but the consistency of the results in many different job categories and in several different types of studies, the size of the pay differentials (even after worker and job characteristics have been taken into account), and the lack of evidence for alternative explanations strongly suggest that wage discrimination is widespread.[91]

Many women are not made aware of the effect of the undervaluation of traditionally female jobs or of the economics of self-support when they are young enough to make crucial training and employment decisions. The result has meant poverty for a large number.

One alternative to economic independence is public assistance. The next section reviews Federal programs assisting the poor to see how they affect the efforts of poor women trying to become self-sufficient.

Federal Welfare Programs and Work

As a result of the factors discussed above, it is not surprising that many women who rely on earnings to support themselves and their children are poor. Women do have other resources; however, the biggest factor in reducing their poverty rate is welfare programs. One study found that 51 percent of un-married household heads with children[92] were poor in terms of their earnings in 1975. Private pension plans and annuities reduced the rate to 50.8 percent. Social security payments, unemployment benefits, and worker's compensation payments reduced the rate to 45.2 percent. The women still in poverty were dependent upon outside (and sometimes unreliable) sources of income such as alimony, child support, money from friends and relatives, and welfare payments. These sources reduced the rate by 9.3 percent. After all of these payments, 28.7 percent were still poor.[93]

The effect of welfare payments on reducing poverty for the working poor was very low; it reduced by 0.4 percent the 4.6 percent who were in poverty.[94] . . .

Aid to Families with Dependent Children

The aid to families with dependent children program is administered by State and local governments under Federal guidelines. . . . 80 percent of AFDC recipient families in 1979 were headed by women. Forty-three percent of AFDC families were black, 40 percent white, and 14 percent Hispanic.[95] In 1979, 3.4 million families, with 7.2 million chil-dren, received AFDC.[96] Forty-nine percent of the children were white and 46 percent were black. Five percent were of other races or ethnicities.[97] Fifty-five percent of AFDC families had a child under 6 years of age, a factor affecting the employability of the mother. Mothers of children under 6 were not required to register for work or training in 1979; however, they could volunteer and be given preference in the provision of services. (The Omnibus Budget Reconciliation Act of 1981 requires mothers of children 3 years of age or older to register for community work experience programs (CWEP) in States that have them.)[98] Based on data for 1979, 64 percent of AFDC families would be required to meet job search or work requirements under CWEP unless exempt because of age, disability, or remoteness of residence.[99]

Many recipients of aid to families with dependent children have a commitment to work in spite of personal handicaps such as lack of schooling and the presence of young children. Of 3.1 million mothers receiving AFDC in 1979, the latest year for which data are available, almost 9 percent were employed full time, over 5 percent were employed part time, and 10.5 percent were seeking work or awaiting recall. Among those not employed, 6.6 percent were incapacitated, 2.8 percent were in school, and 39.8 percent were homemakers.[100]

As noted at the beginning of this chapter, 5.4 percent of fully employed women maintaining their own families had incomes below the Federal poverty threshold in 1980, even after including cash welfare payments. The poverty rates for those women who worked part time involuntarily or who were unemployed exceeded 55 percent. Recent changes in AFDC eligibility may have the effect of making their work efforts seem even more futile. The Federal Government establishes general eligibility criteria for AFDC, but individual States determine their own "standards of need" (poverty thresholds) for eligibility purposes and the amount of their welfare payments. States are not required to provide welfare benefits equal to their own standard of need or the Federal poverty threshold.

Federal AFDC eligibility criteria and benefit levels changed considerably with the passage of the Omnibus Budget Reconciliation Act in 1981. Previously, AFDC recipients who worked knew they could increase their disposable income. AFDC regulations permitted administrators to disregard the first $30 of monthly earnings plus one-third of the remaining earnings when recalculating eligibility for AFDC. Reasonable work-related expenses were also disregarded.[101]

A major study by Tom Joe of the Center for the Study of Social Policy reported the effects on the working poor of the changes that became effective in fiscal year 1982 and also projected the effects of the proposed changes for 1983.[102] One of the primary measures used by Joe was the reduction in allowance for work-related expenses, which has the effect of reducing net income available to the working recipient.... Joe's study was not designed to prove whether working welfare recipients would actually decrease their work efforts. His primary concern was to show that welfare benefits were being decreased extensively and that the working poor were especially hard hit—to the point where it might seem rational to give up trying to hold a job.[103] ...

Summary

Employment is generally considered the key to economic independence in our society, but it does not unlock the door for many women. A combination of socialization and apparent discrimination has created a situation in which women do not obtain labor market benefits comparable to those earned by men with similar education and training. Although equal employment laws have affected the occupational distribution and wages of some women, a large gap remains between men and women in these two areas that will require major efforts to overcome if women are to achieve economic security comparable to that enjoyed by most men.

As a proportion of white males' income, fully employed white, black, and Hispanic women earned 58.3, 54.2, and 49.9 percent, respectively. Such large disparities are a reflection of both past and present discrimination by race and sex. Studies indicate that women are concentrated in occupations already dominated by women and that these jobs are undervalued relative to men's jobs.

Although many women are poor in spite of their work efforts, other poor women are not able to obtain work because they lack training, experience, or important supportive services, such as child care and transportation. It is not clear whether workfare programs for welfare recipients will provide the type of experience or training necessary for these women to obtain private sector jobs and become economically independent. In addition, changes in eligibility requirements for aid to families with dependent children have created incentives in some States for welfare recipients to quit work because benefits are higher for nonworkers.

Executive orders and laws requiring equal employment opportunity have been most effective in businesses that already employ large numbers of women and are subject to government regulations. Considerable effort is required to reach smaller firms, which have little incentive to provide equal opportunity to women.

Federal support for employment and training programs has decreased dramatically, and therefore, special efforts will be needed to provide alternative sources of skill training for poor women unable to gain access to currently available resources. If not, they may find themselves trapped in poverty in spite of their best efforts to avoid or overcome their dependency.

[1]U.S., Department of Labor, Employment and Training Administration, The Work Incentive (WIN) Program and Related Experiences, by Leonard Goodwin, R&D monograph 49 (1977), pp. 10–11.
[2]U.S., Commission on Civil Rights, Unemployment and Underemployment among Blacks, Hispanics, and Women (1982), p. 5 (hereafter cited as Unemployment and Underemployment).
[3]Henrietta J. Duvall, Karen W. Goudreau, and Robert E. Marsh, "Aid to Families with Dependent Children: Characteristics of Recipients in 1979," Social Security Bulletin, vol. 45, no. 4 (April 1982), p. 6 (hereafter cited as "AFDC: Characteristics").
[4]U.S., Department of Labor, The Work Incentive (WIN) Program and Related Experiences, p. 11.

[5]*A fully employed woman is defined as one who has worked at least 35 hours a week, at least 50 weeks during the year.*

[6]*U.S., Department of Labor, Bureau of Labor Statistics, Linking Employment Problems to Economic Status, Bulletin 2123 (January 1982), and Linking Employment Problems to Economic Status: Data for 1980 (1982).*

[7]*To produce most of its general labor force studies, the Bureau of Labor Statistics uses data from the Current Population Survey, conducted monthly by the Bureau of the Census. Because of the sample size, the data are not considered reliable for minority groups such as Asian and Pacific Island Americans, American Indians, and Alaskan Natives. Reliable data for these groups are obtained only during the decennial census, and special reports from the 1980 census are not yet available. Although tabulations for blacks and Hispanics would have been reliable, they were not produced for these reports. (The report using 1981 data is expected to provide data for these two groups.)*

[8]*Poverty data used by the Bureau of Labor Statistics are provided by the Bureau of the Census and include all cash transfer payments (such as social security, AFDC, pensions, interest income) as income before determining whether the family is in poverty. In-kind benefits such as food stamps and housing are not counted.*

[9]*The "husband" rate includes all married men whether or not their wives are in the labor force. All poverty rates are based on total family income.*

[10]*U.S., Department of Labor, Bureau of Labor Statistics, calculated from unpublished data for 1981.*

[11]*Full-time work in this example is defined as working 40 hours a week, 52 weeks a year.*

[12]*Duvall and others, "AFDC: Characteristics," table 3, p. 7.*

[13]*U.S., Commission on Civil Rights, Affirmative Action in the 1980s: Dismantling the Process of Discrimination (1981), p. 5.*

[14]*Ibid.*

[15]*International Brotherhood of Teamsters v. United States, 431 U.S. 324, 339 n. 20 (1977).*

[16]*The Civil Rights Act of 1964, 42 U.S.C. §2000e-2(a) (1976 & Supp. IV 1980), makes unlawful the following employer practices:*

> *(1) to fail or refuse to hire or to discharge any individual, or otherwise to discriminate against any individual with respect to his compensation, terms, conditions, or privileges of employment, because of such individual's race, color, religion, sex, or national origin; or*
> *(2) to limit, segregate, or classify his employees or applicants for employment in any way which would deprive or tend to deprive any individual of employment opportunities or otherwise adversely affect his status as an employee, because of such individual's race, color, religion, sex, or national origin.*

The Equal Pay Act of 1963, 29 U.S.C. §206(d)(1) (1976 & Supp. IV 1980), states that an employer may not discriminate between:

> *[E]mployees on the basis of sex by paying wages to employees in such establishment at a rate less than the rate at which he pays wages to employees of the opposite sex in such establishment for equal work on jobs the performance of which requires equal skill, effort, and responsibility, and which are performed under similar working conditions, except where such payment is made pursuant to (i) a seniority system; (ii) a merit system; (iii) a system which measures earnings by quantity or quality of production; or (iv) a differential based on any other factor other than sex[.]*

Title IX of the Education Amendments of 1972, 20 U.S.C. §1681(a) (1976), provides:

> *No person in the United States shall, on the basis of sex, be excluded from participation in, be denied the benefits of, or be subjected to discrimination under any education program or activity receiving Federal financial assistance.*

Executive Order No. 11246, 3 C.F.R. 339 (1965), amended by Executive Order No. 11375, 3 C.F.R. 493 (1967), reprinted in 42 U.S.C. §2000e app. at 1233 (1976), requires that employers holding Federal contracts and federally assisted contracts:

> *[W]ill not discriminate against any employee or applicant for employment because of race, color, religion, sex, or national origin. The contractor will take affirmative action to ensure that applicants are employed, and that employees are treated during employment, without regard to their race, color, religion, sex, or national origin. Such action shall include, but not be limited to the following: employment, upgrading, demotion, or transfer; recruitment or recruitment advertising; layoff or termination; rates of pay or other forms of compensation; and selection for training, including apprenticeship.*

[17]Unemployment and Underemployment, pp. 9–10.

[18]*Wendy Wolf and Neil Fligstein, "Sex and Authority in the Workplace: Causes of Sexual Inequality," American Sociological Review, vol. 44, no. 2 (April 1979), p. 236; and James W. Grim and Robert N. Stern, "Sex Roles and Internal Labor Market Structures: The 'Female' Semi-Professions," Social Problems, vol. 21 (1974), pp. 690–705.*

[19]*Andrea H. Beller, "Occupational Segregation by Sex: Determinants and Changes," The Journal of Human Resources, vol. 17, no. 3 (Summer 1982).*

[20]*Human capital theory uses characteristics of individuals, such as education, training, ability, experience, and personal choice, to explain differences between men and women in occupational distribution, occupational status, and wages.*

[21]*Solomon W. Polachek, "Occupational Segregation Among Women: Theory, Evidence, and a Prognosis," in Women in the Labor Market, ed. Cynthia B. Lloyd (New York: Columbia University Press, 1979).*

[22]*Beller, "Occupational Segregation by Sex," p. 372. See Polachek, "Occupational Segregation Among Women."*

[23]*Barbara Bergmann, "Occupational Segregation, Wages and Profits When Employers Discriminate by Race or Sex," Eastern Economic Journal, vol. 1 (April 1974), pp. 103–10.*

[24]*Beller, "Occupational Segregation by Sex," p. 372. See Polachek, "Occupational Segregation Among Women," and Bergmann, "Occupational Segregation, Wages and Profits," pp. 103–10.*

[25]*Beller, "Occupational Segregation by Sex," p. 372.*

[26]Ibid., p. 391.

[27]*Carol Boyd Leon, "Occupational Winners and Losers: Who They Were During 1972–80," Monthly Labor Review, June 1982, pp. 18–19.*

[28]Ibid.

[29]*Peter Doeringer and Michael Piore, Internal Labor Markets and Manpower Analysis (Lexington, Mass.: Heath Lexington Books, 1971), p. 165, cited in Unemployment and Underemployment, pp. 7–8.*

[30]Unemployment and Underemployment, pp. 7–8.

[31]Ibid., p. 8.

[32]*Nancy F. Rytina, "Earnings of Men and Women: A Look at Specific Occupations," in U.S., Department of Labor, Bureau of Labor Statistics, Analyzing 1981 Earnings Data from the Current Population Survey, Bulletin 2149 (September 1982), p. 27.*

[33]*U.S., Department of Labor, Bureau of Labor Statistics, Linking Employment Problems to Economic Status: Data for 1980, table 2.*

[34]*Rytina, "Earnings of Men and Women," p. 29.*

[35]*U.S., Department of Labor, Bureau of Labor Statistics, Linking Employment Problems to Economic Status: Data for 1980, table 2.*

[36]Ibid.

[37]*Rytina, "Earnings of Men and Women," p. 29.*

[38]*U.S., Department of Labor, Bureau of Labor Statistics, Linking Employment Problems to Economic Status: Data for 1980, table 2.*

[39]Ibid.

[40]Ibid.

[41]*U.S., Department of Labor, Employment and Training Administration,* Enhanced Work Projects—The Interim Findings from the Ventures in Community Improvement Demonstration, *Youth Knowledge Development Report 7.5, by the Corporation for Public/Private Ventures (May 1980), p. 11.*

[42]*Beller, "Occupational Segregation by Sex," p. 383.*

[43]*Leon, "Occupational Winners and Losers," p. 24.*

[44]Ibid.

[45]*William T. Bielby and James N. Baron, "A Woman's Place is with Other Women: Sex Segregation in the Workplace" (paper prepared for the National Research Council's Workshop on Job Segregation by Sex, May 24–25, 1982, Washington, D.C.), p. 2.*

[46]*Ibid., pp. 39–40.*

[47]*Ibid., pp. 40–41.*

[48]*Ibid., p. 40.*

[49]Ibid.

[50]*See Cynthia B. Lloyd and Beth T. Niemi,* The Economics of Sex Differentials *(New York: Columbia University Press, 1979), p. 152.*

[51]*Donald J. Trieman and Heidi I. Hartmann, eds.,* Women, Work, and Wages: Equal Pay for Jobs of Equal Value *(Washington, D.C.: National Academy Press, 1981), pp. 52–66.*

[52]Ibid.

[53]*Ibid., p. 53.*

[54]Ibid.

[55]Ibid.

[56]Ibid. *See Polachek, "Occupational Segregation among Women."*

[57]Ibid.

[58]*Steven H. Sandell and David Shapiro, "Work Expectations, Human Capital Accumulation, and the Wages of Young Women,"* The Journal of Human Resources, *vol. 15, no. 3 (Summer 1980), p. 337.*

[59]Ibid.

[60]*Winn Newman, "Pay Equity Emerges as a Top Labor Issue in the 1980's,"* Monthly Labor Review, *April 1982, pp. 49–50.*

[61]*Alice Kessler-Harris,* Out to Work: A History of Wage Earning Women in the United States *(New York: Oxford University Press, 1982), p. 237.*

[62]*Ibid., p. 238.*

[63]Ibid.

[64]Ibid.

[65]*Ibid., p. 270.*

[66]*Ibid., p. 271.*

[67]*Allan G. King, "Labor Market Racial Discrimination against Black Women,"* The Review of Black Political Economy, *vol. 8, no. 4 (Summer 1978).*

[68]*Ibid., p. 334.*

[69]*See Lloyd and Niemi,* The Economics of Sex Differentials, *pp. 232–39 for a list of over 20 such studies.*

[70]*Mary Corcoran and Greg J. Duncan, "Do Women Deserve to Earn Less than Men?" Institute for Social Research, Univ. of Michigan (undated), p. 8.*

[71]Ibid.

[72]*Lloyd and Niemi,* The Economics of Sex Differentials, *pp. 301–02.*

[73]*Andrea H. Beller, "EEO Laws and the Earnings of Women" (paper presented at a joint session of the Industrial Relations Research Association and the American Economics Association, Sept. 16–18, 1976), p. 8.*

[74]*Ibid., p. 9.*

[75]*Ibid., p. 11.*

[76]Ibid.

[77]Ibid.

[78]Ibid.

[79]*Andrea Beller, "The Effect of Economic Conditions on the Success of Equal Employment Opportunity Laws,"* The Review of Economics and Statistics, *vol. 62 (August 1980), p. 387.*

[80]*Lloyd and Niemi,* The Economics of Sex Differentials, *p. 306.*

[81]*Trieman and Hartmann,* Women, Work, and Wages, *p. i.*

[82]*Ibid., p. 16.*

[83]*Ibid., p. 9.*

[84]*See the Supreme Court's discussion of the legislative history of comparable worth in Corning Glass Works v. Brennan, 417 U.S. 188, 198–205 (1974).*

[85]*29 U.S.C. §206(d)(1) (1976).*

[86]*42 U.S.C. §§2000e–2000e (17).*

[87]*Griggs v. Duke Power Co., 4011 U.S. 424 (1971) cited in John R. Schnebly, "Comparable Worth: A Legal Overview,"* Personnel Administrator, *April 1982.*

[88]*In general, standards of job worth are based on job evaluation plans that try to rate numerically the basic features of jobs, such as skills, effort, responsibility, and working conditions. These features may have different weights, depending on the nature of the job. The ratings are totaled to provide an overall measure of job worth. The process can be quite complicated; it can be biased, but it has been done successfully. For a further discussion, see Trieman and Hartmann,* Women, Work, and Wages, *pp. 71–80, and 115–30. Also see table 7 in this chapter.*

[89]*Trieman and Hartmann,* Women, Work, and Wages, *pp. 56–57.*

[90]*Ibid., p. 61.*

[91]*Ibid., p. 93.*

[92]*Richard D. Coe, "Dependency and Poverty in the Short and Long Run," in* Five Thousand American Families, *ed. Greg J. Duncan and James N. Morgan (Ann Arbor: The Institute for Social Research, Univ. of Michigan, 1978), vol. VI, p. 277. The data do not distinguish between male and female unmarried household heads with children; the great majority, however, are female.*

[93]Ibid.

[94]Ibid.

[95]*U.S., Department of Health and Human Services, Social Security Administration,* 1979 Recipient Characteristics Study *(1982), part 1, p. 1.*

[96]*Ibid., p. 37.*

[97]Ibid.

[98]*42 U.S.C.A. §609(b)(2) (West Supp. 1975–1981).*

[99]*U.S., Department of Health and Human Services,* 1979 Recipient Characteristics Study, *part 1, p. 17.*

[100]*Duvall and others, "AFDC: Characteristics," p. 3.*

[101]*U.S., Department of Labor,* WIN Handbook *(3rd ed.), p. XIV–3.*

[102]*Tom Joe,* Profiles of Families in Poverty: Effects of the FY 1983 Budget Proposals on the Poor *(Washington, D.C.: Center for the Study of Social Policy, February 1982).*

[103]*Tom Joe, director, Center for the Study of Social Policy, Washington, D.C., interview by telephone, Nov. 17, 1982.*

SOCIAL POLICIES, BLACK MALES, AND BLACK FAMILIES

Bogart R. Leashore

This chapter illustrates how social policies operate to maintain racial inequality, especially with respect to Black males. It is shown how domestic policies related to taxes and budget cuts have differentially affected Black families and how racism and ideologies have influenced the development of social policies in the United States. Health care, employment and income support, and crime and justice are three areas delineated for alternative social policies.

The convergence of some socioeconomic indicators between Blacks and whites over the last few decades has prompted some social scientists and others to conclude that the significance of race has declined in the United States.[1] Statistically significant differences between Blacks and whites on several socioeconomic measures have declined.[2] However, it is erroneous to conclude therefore that racial inequality no longer exists in the United States. For example, in April 1985 the net seasonally adjusted unemployment rate for Blacks age 16 to 19 years was 37 percent, compared to 14.4 percent for whites in the same age group.[3] Similarly, significant differences exist between Blacks and whites on family income, infant mortality, life expectancy, incarceration, the number of children living in poverty, and in other areas.[4] As was recently observed by a white U.S. journalist:

It was only yesterday that racial discrimination was legal in vast parts of the country. . . .

Racism remains a fact of life in this country—it may be abating, it may be weakening, but it is certainly not ready to be mounted for the Smithsonian.[5]

In short, race remains a critical factor in the quality of life in the United States.

This chapter draws attention to the roles played by social policies in maintaining racial inequality, particularly with respect to Black males; why and how this has occurred; and how social policies might be altered to enhance the well-being of Black males, Black families, and other Americans as well. Black males are of special interest because of the high risk status they face compared to white males, and the significant roles they continue to assume in Black family life despite the "feminization of poverty."[6] . . .

Tax Increases and Budget Cuts

A comprehensive analysis of U.S. domestic policies observed that between 1980 and 1984 Black families, regardless of the presence or absence of a male head, were helped less than or hurt more than were white families.[7] Analysis of the current U.S. tax system indicated that the federal government is taxing the poor at levels "without equal in history."[8] A disproportionate number of blacks—males and females—are low wage workers, or working poor and near poor. This group has experienced the sharpest increases in taxes over the past few years,

Unpublished paper, 1985. Printed by permission. Footnotes have been renumbered.

TABLE 1   Budget Cuts in Programs with High Black Participation

PROGRAM	DEGREE OF BLACK PARTICIPATION	BUDGET CUT
Public Service Employment (CETA)	30%	− 100%
Employment and Training	37	− 39
Work Incentive Program	34	− 35
Child Nutrition	17	− 28
Legal Services	24	− 28
Compensatory Education (Title I)	32	− 28
Pell Grants and other Financial Aid for Needy Students	34	− 16
Food Stamps	37	− 14
Aid to Families with Dependent Children	46	− 11
Subsidized Housing	45	− 11

Source: Center on Budget and Policy Priorities, *Falling Behind: A Report on How Blacks Have Fared under the Reagan Policies* (Washington, D.C.: Author, October 1984), p. 12.

as well as the sharpest cutbacks in social programs. Further, prior to the 1981 tax act, most families in poverty were exempt from federal income tax. In 1978, a family of four at the poverty line paid only $269 in federal taxes, which increased to $460 in 1980. By 1984, a family of four at the poverty line paid $1,076 in taxes.[9]

Since 1980, budget cuts in social programs designed for those with low and moderate incomes have been greater than cuts in programs not designed for this group. Programs designed for low and moderate income persons represented less than one-tenth of the federal budget, yet these programs accounted for close to one-third of the total number of cuts in all federal programs. Black Americans comprise 30 percent to 40 percent of the beneficiaries of most of the low income programs that received the greatest cuts. It has been shown that the 1981 budget cuts cost the average Black family three times as much in lost income and benefits as they cost the average white family. This has been attributed to cuts in programs with high participation by Blacks. For example, as shown in Table 1, employment and job training programs received the greatest cuts in 1985—and more than 30 percent of the participants in these programs were Black.[10]

Racism, Social Darwinism, and Laissez-Faire Ideology

The social welfare policies of the United States lag significantly behind those of many countries of the world.[11] For some, the existence of this lag is deliberate and is not coincidental. Claiming that race impacts on the development as well as the implementation of social welfare policies can be a highly controversial position. Nevertheless, it seems clear that Blacks disproportionately have to turn to social programs for assistance in providing for their daily needs. Drawing on the premises of social Darwinism and laissez-faire ideology, some social and behavioral scientists, policymakers, and others attribute this disproportionate reliance to the failure of individuals and tend to absolve government from sharing any responsibility.[12] The paradox of these circumstances becomes more apparent when recognition is given to the role the U.S. government has historically played in promoting and maintaining racial inequality. For example, little more than a decade ago, federal, state, and local governments knowingly participated in and supported a racist medical experiment on uninformed Black males.

The experiment was conducted from 1932 to 1972 and is documented in the work *Bad Blood: The Tuskegee Syphilis Experiment*.[13] More recently, national efforts have turned to child support enforcement in response to the increasing numbers of families headed by women.[14] Rooted in coercive and punitive social policy, Black males are more likely to be the victims of child support enforcement programs because they experience a higher rate of unemployment, receive lower wages, and are therefore less likely able to pay than white males. . . .

With specific reference to Blacks, conservatives and some liberals raise their voices against affirmative action and other federal interventions to promote racial equality. There is an insistence that adequate opportunities are available for those who are motivated toward individual achievement. Pathological views of Blacks and the poor suggest that the problems of poverty are rooted in individual deficits, such as indolence. Futile and endless rhetoric continues about the deserving and nondeserving poor. It is assumed that people are poor because they don't try, that governmental assistance is more of a hindrance than help, and that little can be done to improve "the lot of the less fortunate." Little regard is given to the demographics of poverty, which include the following facts: close to one-half of the adult non-aged poor work part time or full time but do not earn enough to escape poverty; others, for health or child care reasons, cannot enter the labor force; and most poor families do not remain in poverty for prolonged periods nor do they perpetuate a "culture of poverty" from one generation to the next. It has been stated that conservative attacks on government-sponsored social programs are "replete with erroneous conclusions flowing from doubtful assumptions" and that these conservatives "offer no alternative means of bolstering opportunity and advancement for the nation's disadvantaged and working poor."[15]

Mobilizing for Alternative Social Policies

Although the United States is hailed as the land of opportunity, and indeed is so for some, too many Black Americans continue to face structural barriers that block their entry into the socioeconomic mainstream of the society. Joblessness, low wages, poverty, inadequate medical care, substandard housing, poor education, and incarceration are conditions of life that need to be addressed if the defeminization of poverty is to occur. Too often, these conditions of living have reduced the family availability of many Black males. . . .

The probability of being able to function as family provider is related to opportunities for working and receiving adequate financial compensation. Given these highly probable relations, it seems that serious attention should be given to the life circumstances of Black males. In the context of social policies, efforts should be directed toward the elimination of social welfare assaults on Black males and others. Special emphasis should be given to the following areas: health care, employment, wages and income support, and crime and justice.

Health Care Policy

The overall health status of U.S. Blacks continues to lag behind that of whites on several measures. These include higher rates of infant and maternal mortality and shorter life expectancy. Research has shown that Black women are more likely than white women to die because of childbirth complications; that low birth weight is more prevalent among Black than white infants; that Blacks in general and Black males in particular live shorter lives than whites; and that whites receive considerably more preventive and routine medical care than Blacks.[16] These results ring clear the need for an effective program of national health insurance.

Historically, health care policy has focused on three issues: access to care, quality of care, and cost of care. However, preoccupation with cost has resulted in less interest in access and quality of care. For example, profit-oriented hospitals have been shown to be more expensive than nonprofit or public institutions. Those most likely to be without health insurance including Medicaid are women, people of color, and older people. If they cannot pay, health services are not accessible. If they have little to pay with, the quality of care is likely to be what has been characterized as "junk medicine"—

for example, unnecessary tests and procedural duplications.[17]

Politicians, labor, religious, service, and charitable organizations, and consumer groups should reassert the need for a program of national health insurance with wide coverage and a larger federal financial role. These forces must seize control of the health care industry from the hands of physicians, private hospitals, and private health insurance companies.[18] A universal program of quality health care that is attractive to the nonpoor, as well as the poor, is needed. Broad benefits, public financing, and administration by the federal government should be key features of social policy for national health insurance.[19] Various industrialized nations of the world have implemented a range of programs that guarantee equal access to medical care as a citizen right.[20] That the United States remains without such a health care policy not only defies reason, but also continues to be a source of international embarrassment.

Employment and Income Support Policies

Poverty statistics, economic, and employment differences between Blacks and whites have been established. What seems needed are social policies that will reduce and eliminate economic inequality, which is deeply embedded in the structure of U.S. society. Programs increasing the taxes of those with low and moderate incomes while reducing the tax burden of the affluent and big business have done little to improve the U.S. economy. The failure to ensure equal job opportunities for Blacks have placed them at the bottom of the U.S. socioeconomic structure. Weakened commitments of government to civil rights and affirmative action have only worsened the situation. Federal policies to create jobs can reduce unemployment and ensure minimal adequate incomes. Moreover, tax credits and wage subsidies designed for low income and low skill workers can be as economically efficient as public employment policies.[21]

Classical economic theory accuses trade unions of pushing wages up, which prices workers out of jobs and thereby keeps unemployment high.

On the contrary, other evidence indicates that productivity can be improved by giving workers a formal voice in the workplace. If unions coalesced, broadened their interests, and shifted pressure for wage increases, they could become a greater positive force for full employment. In lieu of short-run wage increases, an organized and cohesive labor movement could bargain for full employment, egalitarian wage distributions, opportunities for retraining, workplace enrichment, and welfare objectives.[22]

Aid to Families with Dependent Children (AFDC) has long been stigmatized as a program for those who do not want to work. As a means-tested program, it separates "them" from "us" and has a history of contributing to father absence and family breakup. Family allowance and cash housing allowances based on family size and family income exist in much of Europe. They are available to all moderate income families as well as to the poor. The combined allowances have been considered an income support system that guarantees a higher standard of living, especially for those families with special needs (e.g., female-headed families).[23]

As an expression of important U.S. values, the development of AFDC policy has been consistently directed toward punishing poor parents, especially single mothers, while moving away from promoting the well-being of dependent children. Specifically, values related to capitalism, liberalism, and positivism have been influential in the development of AFDC. The work ethic, individualism, personal freedom, the free market, and the worthiness of individuals have greatly influenced AFDC policy. Racial discrimination against Black families in the early days of AFDC further contributed to the humiliating welfare system of today.[24]

A recent historical study of the Social Security system in the United States vividly depicts the process of institutionalizing antipoor biases in the system. Among other things, it is shown why and how the phrase *social security* has come to mean social insurance even though the legislation of 1935 included public assistance. It is concluded that policy developments relative to public assistance were so constrained that many of the needy went without adequate support.[25] Critical assessments of the Social Security Act of 1935 have posited several relations between the state and the economy, or how political power gets translated into economic power. A recent assessment concludes that

> *in a hierarchical state structure, capitalist groups with varying economic interests exerted their influence at different levels in the hierarchy. . . . Economic power then gets translated into political power through the direct intervention of corporate liberals and through the hierarchical structure of the state, which allows competing factions to petition state managers for direct agendas in social policy.*[26]

Actions for Social Security reform should include a comprehensive analysis of the age requirement for receipt of benefits. Particular attention should be given to any disparities between males of color and white males relative to life expectancy and the age at which benefits can be received. Should Black and other males of color be eligible for Social Security benefits at an earlier age than white males because the latter have a longer life expectancy?[27] Relative to AFDC all states should be prohibited from using the absence of father in families as an eligibility requirement. In the case of child welfare, federal and state legislation and policies should be modified to include subsidized and legal guardianship as another plan of care for abused and neglected children, in addition to foster care and adoption. Far too many Black children, as well as others, linger in foster care.[28] More importantly, efforts need to be directed toward eliminating circumstances that necessitate taking children from their biological families, especially inadequate income and housing. Entitlement programs of the federal government for children, specifically AFDC, continue to lag behind those for other groups (e.g., veterans, the aged, the disabled, and those who are retired). Equal treatment for children through some form of federalized payments is not beyond the capacity of our government.[29]

Cutbacks in federal funds for child day care and nutrition should not only be restored, but increased. Similarly, federal aid for low and moderate income college students and food stamps should be restored and/or increased.

Crime and Justice

One of the most glaring differences between Blacks and whites in the United States is the disturbingly higher involvement of Blacks as compared with whites in the criminal justice system. . . .

Conditions of prison overcrowding, environmental conditions, idleness, violence, limited staffing, and inadequate medical care characterize many state prisons. Resulting court actions have included orders to reduce prison populations, to provide meaningful work, to provide meaningful opportunities for educational and vocational training, to expand prerelease transition programs, to provide medical care and staffing that meet certain standards, and to prevent violence.[30] With specific reference to Black homicide, the highest rates have been found among unemployed and underemployed Black youth and young adults. Thus, it can be argued that, like reduction of poverty and other social problems, homicide reduction can be achieved through major political and social changes.[31]

Given the high incarceration rate for Black males, new policy initiatives need to be established. These should include sentencing reform, plea bargaining, and employment opportunities for ex-offenders. Regarding the latter, any significant reduction in crime will require better employment opportunities for ex-offenders as well as for delinquents. New policy initiatives for the employment of ex-offenders can be specifically designed for ex-offenders, or created in conjunction with new programs for the employment of disadvantaged workers in general.[32] Suggested areas for prevention and intervention concerning homicide include gun control, community organization and education, and more effective responses to prehomicide behavior.[33]

Summary and Conclusions

This chapter has focused on social policies and how they have had an impact on Black males in particular and Black families in general. It is shown how domestic policies related to taxes and budget cuts have differentially affected Black families and how racism and ideologies have influenced the development and implementation of social policies in the United States. Attention is called to three areas in which there is a need for alternative social policies: (1) health care, (2) employment and income support, and (3) crime and justice. National and local efforts are needed to provide an effective program of national health insurance, full employment, family allowances, and actions to reduce incarceration.

The achievement of the social policy initiatives presented in this chapter will require deliberate efforts on the part of many parties, including Blacks and other people of color and supportive whites. In so doing, system-challenging political strategies should be used both within and outside of social institutions. Mass actions and collective efforts by multiethnic liberal challenging coalitions can result in social change for female-headed families and others who do not have basic power resources. Strategies that can be used include demonstrations, congressional lobbying, and voting. Black leaders and organizations can function in a national leadership capacity to achieve desired social change.[34] In the meantime, fraternal, business, and religious organizations should implement broad-based supportive and educational programs targeted for Black males including those who are institutionalized (e.g., those in prison).

Several conscious strategies should be developed within the Black community. These should include an internal Black agenda with a recommitment to Black community development or institution building. Further, Blacks can generate an internal economy with a capacity to absorb the marginally unemployed. Resources can be pooled into economic development institutions that go beyond providing technical assistance to small businesses but can also provide capital for large-scale enterprises that contribute to meaningful employment. An economic development institution could plan the organization and distribution of financial resources in order to promote economic stability and security within Black communities. Political activities should include mobilizing the voting power of the Black community so that officials are elected who are sensitive to and understand their needs. Black institutions such as churches can establish

priorities of social needs and can commit resources toward designated ends—as has been the case with a national network of Black churches that was organized to provide financial assistance to needy Black college students. This requires the involvement of organizations cutting across special interests, social classes, and resources so that a sense of community is restored. Special uses of mass media can be applied in order to bring leadership together to plan and promote goals and strategies. Local needs should be clearly linked to national issues; similarly, national activities should involve local programming.[35]

The mobilization of people of color and others for meaningful social change requires removal of blocks or barriers to power including internal and external political and economic forces that serve to maintain powerlessness among oppressed groups. Through the process of empowerment, Blacks and others can exert influence and overcome obstacles to meeting their needs. Basic to the process of empowerment, Blacks and others must understand the consequences of powerlessness. Moreover, there should be an understanding of and an appreciation for the capacity to bring about change.[36] With particular reference to Black males, it has been suggested that myths have been perpetuated in response to "an unmitigated fear of black male power."[37] Intertwined with racism and other factors, this fear has resulted in a range of social and economic assaults, which have been operationalized through punitive and coercive social policies and social services.

Black social and behavioral scientists, as well as others, should draw attention to research that supports the need for new social policy initiatives. Black scholars and researchers can ill afford the luxury of academic isolation, lest their contributions be minimized. Fresh perspectives and progressive thinking are needed for examining social issues related to the well-being of Black people and that of all Americans. This should include a more balanced view of racism that analyzes not only the consequences for the victim, but also the motivations of the perpetrator. Knowledge and understanding is needed regarding why and how racism is nurtured and sustained in the United States, and what mechanisms can be used to eliminate it. In addition, white Americans should be educated about the social benefits which they stand to gain through the enactment of constructive social policies.

---

[1]*William Julius Wilson*, The Declining Significance of Race: Blacks and Changing American Institutions *(Chicago: The University of Chicago Press, 1980); Michael Hout, "Occupational Mobility of Black Men: 1962 to 1973,"* American Sociological Review, *49 (June 1984), pp. 308–322.*

[2]*Reynolds Farley*, Catching Up: Recent Changes in the Social and Economic Status of Blacks *(Cambridge: Harvard University Press, 1983); Richard B. Freeman,* The Black Elite *(New York: McGraw-Hill, 1976).*

[3]*U.S. Department of Labor, Bureau of Labor Statistics, USDL85-184, Washington, D.C. (May 1985), Table A-3.*

[4]*Theodore Cross,* The Black Power Imperative: Racial Inequality and the Politics of Nonviolence *(New York: Faulkner Books, 1984); Children's Defense Fund,* Portrait of Inequality: Black and White Children in America *(Washington, D.C.: Children's Defense Fund, 1980); National Urban League, Inc.,* The State of Black America, 1984 *(New York: National Urban League, 1984).*

[5]*Richard Cohen, "Racism Recollected,"* Washington Post, *August 10, 1985, p. A19.*

[6]*Lawrence E. Gary and Bogart R. Leashore, "High-Risk Status of Black Men,"* Social Work, *27 (January 1982), pp. 54–58; Gary and Leashore, "Black Men in White America: Critical Issues,"* in Color in a White Society, Barbara White (ed.) (Silver Spring, Md.: National Association of Social Workers, 1984), pp. 115–125.*

[7]*John L. Palmer and Isabel V. Sawhill,* The Reagan Record: An Assessment of America's Changing Domestic Priorities *(Cambridge, Mass.: Ballinger, 1984).*

[8]*Daniel Patrick Moynihan, "Family and Nation," Cambridge, Mass.: Harvard University, the Godkin Lectures, 1985).*

[9]*Center on Budget and Policy Priorities,* Falling Behind: A Report on How Blacks Have Fared under the Reagan Policies *(Washington, D.C.: Author, October 1984).*

[10]Ibid.

[11]*Robert Kuttner,* The Economic Illusion *(Boston: Houghton Mifflin, 1984).*

[12]Ibid.; *Sar A. Levitan and Clifford M. Johnson,* Beyond the Safety Net: Reviving the Promise of Opportunity in America *(Cambridge, Mass.: Ballinger, 1985), pp. 6–18.*

[13]*James Jones,* Bad Blood: The Tuskegee Syphilis Experiment *(New York: Free Press, 1981).*

[14]*Joyce E. Everett, "An Examination of Child Support Enforcement Issues," in Harriette McAdoo and T. M. Jim Parham (eds.),* Services to Young Families Program Review and Policy Recommendations *(Washington, D.C.: American Public Welfare Association, 1985), pp. 75–112.*

[15]*Levitan and Johnson,* Beyond the Safety Net, *pp. 6–18.*

[16]A Dream Deferred: The Economic Status of Black Americans, *a*

working paper *(Washington, D.C.: The Center for the Study of Social Policy, 1983).*

[17]*Michael Clark, "What Hath Reagan Wrought,"* Health PAC Bulletin, *15 (July–August 1984), pp. 3–4.*

[18]*Kuttner,* The Economic Illusion, *pp. 249–250.*

[19]*Theodore R. Marmor, Judith Feder, and John Holahan,* National Health Insurance: Conflicting Goals and Policy Choices *(Washington, D.C.: The Urban Institute, 1980).*

[20]*Kuttner,* The Economic Illusion.

[21]*Irwin Garfinkel and John L. Palmer, "Issues, Evidence, and Implications," in* Creating Jobs: Public Employment Programs and Wage Subsidies *(Washington, D.C.: The Brookings Institution, 1978).*

[22]*Kuttner,* The Economic Illusion, *pp. 136–186.*

[23]*Kuttner,* The Economic Illusion, *pp. 243–247.*

[24]*Jan Mason, John S. Wodarski, and T. M. Jim Parham, "Work and Welfare. A Reevaluation of AFDC,"* Social Work, *30 (May–June 1985), pp. 197–203.*

[25]*Jerry R. Cates,* Insuring Inequality: Administrative Leadership in Social Security, 1935–54 *(Ann Arbor: The University of Michigan Press, 1983).*

[26]*Jill S. Quadagno, "Welfare Capitalism and the Social Security Act of 1935,"* American Sociological Review, *49 (October 1984), p. 645.*

[27]*Gary and Leashore,* Social Work, *27 (January 1982), p. 57.*

[28]*Bogart R. Leashore, "Demystifying Legal Guardianship: An Unexplored Option for Dependent Children,"* Journal of Family Law, *23 (1984), pp. 391–400.*

[29]*Moynihan, "Family and Nation," pp. 43–44.*

[30]*Alvin J. Bronstein, "Prisoners and Their Endangered Rights,"* The Prison Journal, *LXV (Spring–Summer 1985), pp. 4–5.*

[31]*Darnell F. Hawkins, "Black Homicide: The Adequacy of Existing Research for Devising Prevention Strategies,"* Crime and Delinquency, *31 (January 1985), p. 94–97.*

[32]*James B. Jacobs, Richard McGahey, and Robert Minion, "Ex-Offender Employment, Recidivism, and Manpower Policy: CETA, TJIC, and Future Initiatives,"* Crime and Delinquency, *30 (October 1984), pp. 486–503.*

[33]*Hawkins, "Black Homicide," p. 96.*

[34]*Ronald Walters, "Imperatives of Black Leadership: Policy Mobilization and Community Development,"* The Urban League Review, *9 (Summer 1985), pp. 20–41.*

[35]Ibid.

[36]*Barbara Bryant Solomon,* Black Empowerment: Social Work in Oppressed Communities *(New York: Columbia University Press, 1976).*

[37]*Robert Staples, "The Myth of the Impotent Black Male," in* The Black Family: Essays and Studies *(2nd ed.) (Belmont, Calif.: Wadsworth, 1978), p. 99.*